Making History

Richard Flacks

MAKING HISTORY
The Radical Tradition in American Life

Columbia University Press
NEW YORK 1988

Columbia University Press
New York   Guildford, Surrey
Copyright © 1988 Columbia University Press
All rights reserved
Printed in the United States of America

Library of Congress Cataloging-in-Publication Data

Flacks, Richard.
Making history: the radical tradition in American life/Richard Flacks.
p.   cm.
Bibliography: p.
Includes index.
ISBN 0-231-04832-7
1. Political participation—United States.
2. Radicalism—States.   I. Title.
JK1764.F57 1988
323′.042′0973—dc19   87-33851
                                              CIP

Hardback editions of Columbia University Press books are Symth-sewn
and are printed on permanent and durable acid-free paper.

Book design by Jennifer Dossin

Contents

An Introduction

THIS BOOK is an exploration of the potentialities for popular participation and social responsibility in present-day U.S. society. It is animated by two fundamental moral concerns: first, to promote an increase in the ability and willingness of people to take responsibility for the direction of the society and its institutions; second, to promote the restructuring of society in such a way that the people are increasingly empowered to make history in and through their daily lives.

My writing is motivated, and prejudiced, by my personal history of political identification with the left in the United States. I was born and raised in Brooklyn, in that peculiar New York Jewish milieu that has been disproportionately influential in American culture during the last half-century. It was a milieu in which one took for granted a concern for politics, a commitment to social justice, a disdain for conventional success. My grandparents were socialists; my parents, both school teachers, were activists in the left-wing teachers union and in the ghetto school districts where they taught. Their idealism seemed to them to lead naturally to an allegiance to the American Communist Party, and, eventually, they were publicly purged from the New York school system because they refused to answer questions about their political beliefs during the McCarthy era. At Brooklyn College, which I attended in the fifties, there were maybe two dozen students who did any kind of politics at all—tiny handfuls of Young Democrats, Student ADAers, Labor Youth Leaguers, Young Socialists—all of us more or less huddled together in a sea of fifteen thousand willfully apolitical fellow students. In the fifties one could not escape the feeling that politics at the grass roots were over in this country; C. Wright Mills' image of mass apathy, of millions of "Cheerful Robots" being herded through history by a small elite, seemed depressingly accurate. Yet with apparent suddenness, events in the sixties transformed the scene. Almost overnight it seemed possible for small groups of principled youth to change the course of history, as the student sit-inners in the South so rapidly did. In the early sixties, as a graduate student at the University of Michigan, I became involved with the group of people who founded the Students for a Democratic Society and played an active role in SDS in the several years before it emerged as the leading national organization of mass student protest. Getting a Ph.D. and a faculty job meant, for me, "graduation" from SDS as well, but I continued, through the rest of the decade, to participate actively in organizing opposition to the Vietnam War and in helping to articulate and develop the political perspective of the New Left. In the seventies, along with many others of my generation of activists, I increasingly devoted my political energy to community level politics.

Meanwhile, as a professional sociologist, I have, during this same period, tried, from a number of different angles, to study the conditions that affect human capacities to take political initiative, to rebel against authority, to operate democratically. These intellectual and research interests are stimulated and nourished by my political identity—the continuing cycles of exhileration and frustration that the political activist experiences in trying to catalyze participation by the less active, to mobilize support for his or her projects. In my own direct experience I have seen massive "apathy" quite quickly give way to massive upsurges of protest—and then witnessed the rapid going out of the political tide. As a leftist, I have experienced both a strong sense of communion with large numbers of fellow Americans, and a terrible sense of cold isolation. At times, I have been enormously proud of the courage, insight, and popular resonance of individual radicals and left organizations; at other times; I have been disgusted by the rigidity, the moral blindness, the self-destructiveness of many on the left. The startling contradictoriness of political experience provides much of the energy for my work as a social scientist. There is a need to find a coherent way of interpreting this experience and, if possible, to break out of the endless and ultimately frustrating cycle of hope and despair that the political activist experiences. But what is at stake is more than just achieving a subjective sense of the order of things. My most important hope, in this book, is to help reshape the practice of democratic activists in order to improve the chances of democratic restructuring.

A primary source of "data" for this book rests on my efforts to codify my own personal political experience over the last quarter of a century. A second primary source consists of a series of interviews coworkers and I have been collecting over the last several years. In 1973 and '74, Beulah Engelsberg, under my supervision, interviewed 29 residents in Santa Barbara, selected in such a way as to minimize the likelihood that those interviewed would be politically active. Since we wanted to do interviews that would take at least six hours, it did not seem practical to try to develop a random sample; instead, using a variety of channels of publicity and acquaintance, especially the auspices of adult education programs in the community, we managed to get a number of volunteers and tried to ensure that the set of interviews would include a good mix of age groups, men and women, levels of income, education, and occupational status. Many of the interview questions were drawn from similar studies of the political perspectives of "average citizens" that had been done in the 1950s—particularly Robert Lane's *Political Ideology* and David Reisman's *Faces in the Crowd*.

During the last several years Jack Whalen and I have undertaken two studies of political activists. Both entailed extensive depth interviewing of small numbers of persons. The first involved contacting a group of people who, a decade earlier, had been students at the University of California, Santa Barbara. About half of those interviewed were former student activists—people who had been indicted on major felony charges connected with student protest, including the famous "bank-burning" in Isla Vista; the other half were a roughly matched sample of students who had been members of fraternities and sororities or who had otherwise been identifiably resistant to the student movement of the sixties.

A second study on which Whalen and I collaborated involved repeated detailed interviewing (and related methods such as diary-keeping) of 20 persons in the Santa Barbara area who were, at the time of initial contact, active in various forms of grass-roots community organization.

The goal of both of these studies was to understand forces in personal life that foster and constrain long-term commitment to social action. In the study of former student activists, we wanted to see how commitments to engage in historical action formed in youth influence, and are changed by, the growing involvement of the person in everyday adult life. In the study of present-day activists, all of whom are already adult, we were trying to see, over a three-year period, how public commitment is made possible and interfered with by everyday arrangements and demands.

A final source of primary data for this book has been the work of my student Craig Reinarman, who undertook similar depth interviewing in the early eighties with small matched samples of two groups of workers, one a group of public employees, the other a group of workers in a private firm. Reinarman's interviews were similar to those collected in the earlier studies, but included systematic attention to attitudes toward "Reaganomics" and related topics. The results of his work are reported in *American States of Mind* (Reinarman 1987).

These primary materials are supplemented by two broad streams of literature: social science research literature on public opinion, political participation, and the experienced quality of life; and academic and polemical analysis of the history of protest and radicalism in the United States.

This book is written as a reflective essay on these materials. The interviews we have collected and listened to serve have two functions: first, they have been heuristic devices that spark hypotheses; second, they provide quotations and case studies that help illustrate various analytic points. More technical treatment of our studies appear in separate publications (see Whalen and Flacks 1980, 1983; Whalen and Flacks, forthcoming; Reinarman 1984, Reinarman, 1987). This book does not claim to present "findings"; it is rather an essay in interpretation that, it is hoped, suggests a framework for understanding some of the dynamics of American political consciousness. That framework I feel to be empirically well-grounded—in observation, in the interviews, and in the established research literature. But it is not here tested in any rigorous sense.

ACKNOWLEDGMENTS

MY INTELLECTUAL debts are many. Although this book criticizes many of the fundamental suppositions of the organized left, it is rooted in the work of certain left activist intellectuals. My most obvious debt is to C. Wright Mills, whose stance inspired many of us, in the early sixties when we were students, to try to re-create an American left, and whose theoretical categories strongly influenced the writing of this book.

A. J. Muste, in the 1950s, began to search for ways to break down the boundaries that divided leftwing activists; his vision of how radical activists could engage in history while retaining their moral vitality is something I have tried to incorporate here.

In 1962, Tom Hayden made me believe that an authentically American left was possible. He did this, in part, through his personal presence as a key organizer of the Students for a Democratic Society—for Tom came out of the American heartland, and had no personal roots in what we early new leftists saw as the "old" and moribund left. More than that, however, Tom envisioned a left that spoke an American language—and he helped write that language in the *Port Huron Statement*. And, more profoundly, Tom grasped that an American left had to ground its vision and its program in American experience—rather than "theory." This book reflects the pragmatism he helped me learn—even as it argues implicitly with some of the directions he has taken.

Michael Harrington was one of the few heirs of the "old left" able to serve as a bridge to the new. But early in the development of SDS, he came to oppose it, dismayed by its refusal to adopt his generation's anti-communist formulas. Mike Harrington later confessed that he had been wrong about this—but new leftists have learned that he had been right about many other things. In particular, Mike Harrington has taught that in the U.S., the "left" is far broader than the tiny band that calls itself "so-cialist," and that reforms may advance, as well as limit, potentials for so-cialist transformation. Mike Harrington has helped left activists understand the need for coalition and for involvement in the electoral process while he has tried to keep the distinct vision of socialism a living reality. I am a rather inactive member of the organization he helped create, the Demo-cratic Socialists of America. I don't discuss DSA directly in this book, but its problems, as I understand them, have helped me define the issues fac-ing contemporary left activists.

I have borrowed much from a number of other people, most especially Jeremy Brecher, James O'Connor, Stanley Aronowitz, Frances Piven and Richard Cloward, David Wellman, Julia Reichert and Jim Klein, Ed Kirschner. My understanding of the American left has been greatly enriched by in-terchange with Dave Dellinger, Dorothy Healey, Harold Cruse, Hank and Sylvia Aron, Harold and May Hartman, David and Mildred Flacks, Sid Lens, Stan Weir, and many other veterans of the thirties and forties I've gotten to know over the years.

This book is an expression of a political identity formed in the early sixties in that band of friends and comrades that I had the great good luck to be a part of—the "founders" of Students for a Democratic Society. That group remains, I suppose, one of my primary political and personal ref-erence points; among the ones from whom I have gained lasting insights are: Bob Ross, Robb Burlage, Paul Booth, Maria Verela, Steve Max, Al Haber, Barbara Haber, Sharon Jeffrey, Lee Webb, and the late Paul Potter.

I've had the good fortune to work with several students whose own research provided important resources for this book. These include Rob Rosenthal, Craig Reinarman, Jack Whalen, and Joyce Rothschild. Some of the material in chapter 2 is based on interviews conducted by Beulah En-gelsberg with "ordinary" Santa Barbarans. Many of the ideas I've devel-oped here were first tested in my graduate seminars on political conscious-ness in the Sociology Department at UCSB; I am certain that I, rather than the students, derived the main benefits from these discussions.

I am deeply grateful for the encouragement I've received from Richard Rothstein, Leni Wildflower, Harvey Molotch, Harry Boyte, Sara Evans, Barbara Laslett, Hannah Pitkin, Michael Kazin, Joey Kasof, Jeff Mattison —and to the editors of *Working Papers for a New Society,* and *Socialist Review* for publishing early versions of pieces of this work. Derek Shearer's enthusiasm for this project, his counsel, and his pioneering work on economic democracy all have been essential resources for me.

Peter Dreier, Jane Mansbridge, Todd Gitlin, and Beth Schneider read and commented extensively on the manuscript at various stages. Given its length and redundancies, these efforts were truly heroic, and enormously helpful. I am supremely grateful to William Domhoff, who gave unstinting editorial help, and who has been a constant source of encouragement, advice and ideas.

Thanks to people at Columbia University Press—to John Moore, for his good-natured patience, to Louise Waller, for important encouragement and praise, and to Leslie Bialler, for help with important details.

Charles Wright Flacks provided valuable feedback on the manuscript, and helped do the index. Marc Ajay Flacks surprised me by being able to quote from the manuscript without having read it—suggesting osmotic processes previously unknown to science.

I have been married to Mickey Flacks for almost 30 years. We have collaborated in making our lives and our politics—and this book is one result. Over these years we have talked endlessly about the roots we both have in the left tradition and our responsibility to those roots. Mickey has taught me much about the contradictions between making history and living life, and we have struggled together to find ways to fuse and balance these realms of action. This book implicitly records what we have learned about that. Mickey read and criticized the manuscript, providing me with encouragement when most badly needed. Much to my surprise she was willing to help with proofreading and with indexing. I could not have had a life—or a book—without her.

Richard Flacks
—*Santa Barbara, California*
February 11, 1988

Making History

1

History and the Everyday

History takes no note when a woman feeds her family.

—George Konrad

*Every revolutionary protest is also a protest against people being
reduced to the particles of history . . . Revolutionary situations
are rare. Feelings of opposition to history, however are constant,
even if unarticulated. They often find their expression in what is
called private life.*

—John Berger

*Peace is stronger than war because the weight of everyday life is
on its side.*

—George Konrad

LET US begin by distinguishing two arenas of human action. On the one
hand, there is action directed at the sustaining of everyday life; on the
other, there is action directed at the making of history.

In everyday life, we are concerned with the survival and the maintenance
of our own selves and of definite others who are dependent on us or to
whom we feel obligated. Such activity is, first of all, biological: the first
priority of everyday activity is to provide for physical preservation of oneself and one's dependents. Essential to the meaning of civilization is that
sheer survival is replaced by more differentiated purposes. People seek
various degrees and forms of physical well-being. Their needs are elaborated far beyond those given by essential biological constitution. Role requirements themselves create chains of necessary activity that are enforced by elaborated patterns of expectation, rule, and motive rather than
by immediate pressures of physical need. For most of us most of the time

survival and maintenance of the self and one's dependents therefore means doing a round of activity required for and by our livelihood and the maintenance of our household and its members. Most such activity is experienced as necessary; the majority of our daily time is taken up with fulfilling the need for sleep, the doing of work and household tasks, eating and other consummatory activity felt to be needed for life and physical health.

In addition to all those activities that are ultimately grounded in physical survival, everyday life is constituted by activity and experience designed to sustain one's self as a human being—to validate or fulfill the meaning of one's life, reinforce or enhance one's sense of self-worth, achieve satisfaction and pleasure or, negatively, to overcome distress, resolve problems, restore continuity, do duties so that the life one believes or expects one to have or be entitled to can be lived. In our culture, one can summarize this dimension of daily life by saying that much of our time is devoted to sustaining our *identities*—that is, the sense of our selves as individuals, having a unique biography, a particular character, our own configuration of interests, needs, and traits.

A portion of our daily time is thus expected to be "free"—that is, unconstrained by the demands of necessity, available for uses that are discretionary, self-chosen, expressive of individuality. People in all societies must spend much of their day in livelihood, household, and physically necessary consummatory activity, but it is not universally true that time left over is left to individual discretion (Bensman and Lilienfelt 1979). On the contrary, cultures are likely to elaborate a variety of spiritual and communal obligations, rituals and observances that members are expected to participate in, either in assemblages or private spaces. In our culture, uses of free time are also patterned, but the individual is thought to be free to select from a great range of patterns, to vary his or her choices at will, to invent new uses, to do nothing.

If we define everyday life as constituted by activity relevant to the survival, maintenance, and development of self and of one's dependents, we can identify another dimension of human activity—action relevant to the survival, maintenance, and development of society. Let us call such action "history making." History is being made when rules are promulgated and laws are passed; when investment decisions create or destroy opportunities to work; when it is decided that land should be used to grow sugar or resort condominiums; when it is decided to market a given product at a given price; when a song is sung, a book written, a slogan shouted that provides a dispersed and cowed populace with a sense of unity and strength; when a directive is written that orders the landing of a contingent of marines on a foreign shore; when a court sanctions the right of a chief executive to tap the telephones of those deemed problematic for the national security; when interest rates are raised a point. Historical action is not necessarily noted or recorded, nor is it always embodied in the kinds of public happenings that are taught as history in schools. A historical act may appear as exceedingly mundane behavior. A telephone call, a scribble on a memo pad, a push of a button can initiate a chain of actions and events that fundamentally reshape the lives of millions. What we mean by history making are activities that have the effect of changing one or more features of the patterned everyday ways of life characteristic of a community or a society. Such features include the modes and opportunities for making a living, the norms and rules that are understood to govern behavior, the goods that constitute consumption, the time and space available for various daily activities, the values and identities that define virtue and purpose, the rituals, symbols, and styles that express and reinforce collective identification, the opportunities available for personal choice and self-expression. *History is constituted by activity that inflences the conditions and terms of everyday life of a collectivity.*

In one sense, history making is inherently carried on in and through everyday life. To pursue one's personal livelihood is to simultaneously participate in production of goods and services that enable society as a whole to exist and function. The everyday activity of families and households *reproduces* socially needed human beings and the capacities that society needs its members to have. But a fundamental feature of daily experience is that many of the conditions and terms of everyday life are beyond our control—that history is being made and we are at its mercy. Moreover, most people most of the time perceive their productive and reproductive activity not primarily as means for participating in history, but as done in defense or behalf of self or family. Indeed, from the point of view of society, the individual *que* worker and parent is a more or less interchangeable unit; accordingly it is essential to one's sense of individuality that one sees work and family life as necessary for self-maintenance rather than as a means to maintain the social order. Such subjective understanding is not only crucial to identity, it is also inherent in the logic of practical daily life. However much one's work, childrearing, and consumption contribute to societal maintenance, one can protect one's life chances only by shaping such activity in terms of personal, rather than social, interest. "If I am not for myself, who will be?" is a primary rule of daily existence.

Organized human activity is thus self-serving and socially serving simultaneously; to make one's own personal life is also to be taking part in the making of history. Yet, simultaneously, the self- and social-orientations of daily action are in conflict with each other; orientation to the collectivity contains inherent dangers to essential personal interests and to identity itself; egocentrism inherently endangers cooperation, coordination, harmony. This dialectic constitutes daily life. It is intrinsic to each human act.

POWER AND HISTORY

THERE IS, however, another source of tension between everyday life and history—one that is not universally present nor intrinsic to human social life in general. That is the tension that derives from the fact of power.

C. Wright Mills began his seminal work *The Power Elite* as follows:

> The powers of ordinary men are circumscribed by the everyday world in which they live, yet even in these rounds of job, family, and neighborhood they often seem driven by forces they can neither understand nor govern. "Great changes" are beyond their control, but affect their conduct and outlook none the less. The very framework of modern society confines them to projects not their own, but from every side, such changes press upon the men and women of the mass society, who accordingly feel that they are without purpose in an epoch in which they are without power.
>
> But not all men are in this sense ordinary. As the means of information and of power are centralized, some men come to occupy positions in American society from which they can look down upon, so to speak, and by their decisions mightily affect, the everyday worlds of ordinary men and women. They are not made by their jobs; they set up and break down jobs for thousands of others; they are not confined by simple family responsibilities; they can escape. . . . They need not merely "meet the demands of the day and the hour"; in some part, they create these demands, and cause others to meet them. (Mills 1956:31)

Insofar as society is organized so that the conditions and terms of daily life can be shaped by conscious human decision, and insofar as such decisions can be made by a relative few and implemented effectively, then the distribution of power becomes a central reality in social life.

One can imagine social arrangements in which power differentials are largely absent. For example, there is the situation of small and scattered human settlements, whose daily lifeways are shaped by a high degree of local self-sufficiency and governed by tradition. In such circumstances history is determined by the forces of nature and the efforts by settlements to accommodate to these; indeed, in such circumstances "history" is less salient than are the cycles of the seasons and of human lives. Alternatively, one can envision social arrangements in which the conditions and terms of daily life are under the direct and conscious control of those living within them—where, in the ideal case, no modifications of the frameworks of daily life can be decided or decisively influenced by those not directly subject to these conditions. Where history is dominated by forces beyond conscious control, or where it is constituted directly by members of a community as a conscious and integral feature of their daily activity, then inequalities in power are not fundamental to social organization and human experience. If we define power as *the capacity to make history—to influence the conditions and terms of everyday life in a collectivity*—then, to the extent that power differentials exist, there will be a generalized experience of separation between everyday life and history. To the extent that history making is centralized, then people not at the center are likely to feel that daily life and history occur in two different realms, that they themselves are objects of historical forces alien to themselves, that they themselves are without power.

The experience that daily life and history are two distinct realms is grounded then in the structural separation of the many from the centers of institutional decision making that significantly affect their lives. Insofar as daily livelihood depends on employment provided by large, hierarchical organizations, insofar as the goods and services consumed in households are provided by such organizations, insofar as daily life is structured and constrained by laws and regulations set and enforced by state officials, insofar as centralized decisions can have ramifying effects on prices, employment, available services, insofar as people are compelled to serve in armies and to organize their lives in behalf of war efforts planned by central authorities, insofar as the future of life itself can be terminated by small groups authorized to press a few buttons—these are contemporary circumstances that exhibit the structural fact that the terms and conditions of everyday life can be fundamentally affected by decisions taken at the "top" or the "center." That we have a national political economy dominated by national corporations and a national state means that, inescapably, everyday life and history will be experienced as two separated realms.

As Mills suggested, that experience is reinforced by the observation that those at the top exercise their historical power as a routine feature of their daily lives. Their mundane acts—conversing, telephoning, writing on a pad—are behaviorally identical to the routines of any white-collar worker, yet are freighted with historical meaning. It is not only that "they" are situated to make historical decisions, but that these are done as a feature of daily routine (meanwhile, they are very likely to be exempt from many of the onerous routines of self-maintenance that burden the rest of us). Ordinary experience is qualitatively different. Not only are "we" situated far from the centers of historical power, but efforts we may want to make to intervene in the historical process require a break with our own daily routines. Thus even if we were assured that our interventions could have effect (and of course we are never so assured), our effort to intervene entails the costs of interrupting the activities we normally pursue as role requirements. The "power elite" is in the unique position of being able to influence history while simultaneously maintaining and enhancing their own personal lives. For the rest of us, historical intervention is experienced as entailing some degree of self-sacrifice and risk.

POWERS OF THE PEOPLE

NECESSITIES of survival and existence are the grounds for commitment to everyday life. Hierarchical organization of institutions, centralization of economic and political decision making and of the media of mass communication constitute the structural basis for the experience that history is made in a realm apart from daily life. Such structures facilitate the power of elite groups to formulate projects, plans, and decisions that fundamentally affect the conditions and terms of everyday life for the society as a whole.

The ability to supply what is needed is a resource for power, but so also is the ability to interrupt that supply or disrupt ongoing processes of daily life. Accordingly, although a group may be subordinated and unable to make decisions that will initiate plans and projects that shape or reshape daily life, that same group may be in a position to frustrate such plans and projects or to disrupt the ongoing flow of everyday life in the collectivity. The powerless mass, by definition, depends on elites in authority to provide the livelihoods and frameworks that make daily life possible, and this dependence is the source of elite power. But those same elites depend on the cooperation of the mass to implement their projects and plans; to the degree that such cooperation is required, then to that same degree there is a potential source of popular power.

In contemporary society there are at least three discernible capabilities for historical intervention available to people in the mass.

First, there are opportunities to frustrate or veto the historical plans and projects of elites or to lend support to one elite faction against another when such factions are competing for position. In formal democracies, some of these opportunities are legitimated in the electoral process and related avenues of formal mass participation. In addition, there are opportunities for blocking elites available outside of the electoral system, and many of these are not formalized or legitimated. These non-institutionalized opportunities may frequently be more effective as resources for popular power than those that are formally provided.

Second, there are opportunities to directly disrupt established, ongoing processes of daily life. Such disruptive effects of collective action range from localized, relatively marginal or transitory impacts to impacts that are national, far-reaching, and longer range.

Third, there are opportunities to directly reconstruct the terms and conditions of collective everyday life. Some of the features of daily life are only partially dependent on centralized decisions and structures and are shaped more by patterns of daily interaction. Such normative structures can be reconstructed directly, and such direct reconstruction is a form of history making when carried out collectively and articulated as an expression of collective intention. The capacity to collectively innovate culturally is a primary resource of popular power.

Thus, although elites are structurally in positions that routinely enable them to make decisions, plans, and projects that reshape the terms and conditions of everyday life, their power is circumscribed by their dependence on the cooperation of the subordinated and is limited by the fact that some of the conditions and terms of everyday life are determined through ongoing processes of negotiation among people as they make their day. These circumstances have provided the opportunities for the long tradition of human quest for an alternative to elite domination of history. This is the tradition of *democracy*—the idea that the people themselves can and should rule. The democratic ideal has been carried by a variety of ideological streams during the last two centuries. Radical democracy, populism, socialism, communism, syndicalism, anarcho-communism, pacifism—all of these are labels for ideologies and organized political forces that, despite their manifold differences and mutual hostilities, have espoused a common idea. This idea is that the people are capable of and ought to be making their own history, that the making of history ought to be integrated with everyday life, that all social arrangements that perpetuate separation of history making from daily life can and must be replaced by frameworks that permit routine access and participation by all in the decisions that affect their lives. Because I want to stress the commonalities of such ideological and political streams, and because I want to distinguish their shared tradition from the dominant ideological framework in the United States, which also has often called itself democratic, I think it useful to label all forces in our society that have sought to democratize politics, institutions, or culture and have sought to encourage relatively powerless groups to intervene in history as the "tradition of the left."

A fundamental theme of this book is that those committed to democratization must face the fact that in general people are committed to the making of their lives rather than history. I have already suggested that such commitment is inherent in the logic of personal survival. But such commitment is not explicable simply by reference to universal human nature or the human condition. Historical circumstances and cultural frameworks provide particular configurations of contingency. The reason that democracy persists as an ideal at all is that people at times have transcended their everyday lives in order to make history. Moreover, in our culture, the idea of democracy is not simply the property of the left; it is an ideal embodied in the official rationales of our society, fundamental in the founding of the American nation-state, espoused as the essence of civic virtue. Thus, throughout human history people seemingly locked into the constraints of daily life have sometimes made history; in the United States not only has such democratic upsurge been a recurrent feature of our history, but also the ideal of democratic organization and of individual, citizenly participation has been taken for granted as an essential feature of our national identity.

The left finds its validation in the history of popular struggle and in the prevalence of principles of self-government and popular sovereignty as bases for legitimation. Thus the left often constitutes that force that demands that the society practice what it preaches. But the left understands itself not only as the conscience of the status quo, but also as a leadership for fundamental change. The left's critique typically does not rest on the simple assertion that society's institutions do not live up to their democratic promise, but on the premise that institutional structure, established belief systems and the frameworks of daily life are inherently undemocratic. Lefts therefore seek to go beyond officially prescribed notions of democracy to transform institutional structures and to change the ways people orient to their daily lives.

The tradition of the left then comes up against a fundamental and profound dilemma. It calls on people to make their history, but finds people making their own lives. One of my central motives in writing this book is to explore why it is that people persist in preoccupation with everyday life even though our culture values public participation and social responsibility, and the left offers them a vision of a world in which they can shape their own future.

DEMOCRACY AND LIBERTY

OUR CULTURE values self-sacrifice in the public interest and celebrates those who have placed social responsibility ahead of self-seeking. The left opposition seeks to extend the sense of social responsibility and expand the opportunities for collective participation; it has tried to teach that the pursuit of private self-interest is, in many ways, self-defeating, that true human fulfillment derives from commitment to the social good. These themes, emanating from both the conventional cultural institutions and from radical centers of dissent, have been important ones in American cultural and social development. Yet such teachings have not been sufficient to overcome the propensity of most people to devote primary commitment to their everyday lives and to eschew all but the most minimal involvement in public matters. In chapter 2, I will explore in some detail how Americans tend to think about and act out their "commitment to everyday life." But here I want to suggest that alongside cultural traditions that call upon members to be socially responsible citizens, there are others, at least equally influential and legitimate, that stress the moral primacy of everyday life.

If the American revolution was fought in the name of democracy, it was also, and perhaps even more, a struggle for *liberty*. If the ideal of democracy is that of citizens actively engaged in the making of their collective history, the ideal of liberty in contrast is that of free individual men making their own lives. Liberty idealizes self-sufficiency rather than interdependence. It regards the individual household (rather than the community) as the center of human happiness. It views the good society as one in which each household has substantial economic independence, has some capacity for self-defense, has sufficient freedom from intervention and regulation, and enough privacy so that members can make lives as they see fit. Government and other large collective structures are seen as primarily threatening to liberty; their functions ought to be held to the minimum necessary to ensure the security and safety of individual free space. In the terms I am using, the libertarian perspective solves the tension between history and everyday life by seeking, as much as possible, to abolish history. What is real and valuable for the authentic libertarian is the individual and his interests,[1] not the society and its potential.

Primitive or pure libertarianism seems to require an agrarian setting, since only a household living off the land seems capable of approaching the possibility of maximum self-sufficiency. Yet liberty as a core moral aspi-

---

1. Only recently—if at all—have libertarians in the American grain been likely to include an independent "her" in their vision.

ration for Americans has not died out with the onrush of urbanization, industrialization, and the creation of a national society of enormously complex
interdependence. On the contrary—the ideal of liberty has constituted a
renewable resource for morally evaluating and justifying Americans' individual life situations. Liberty modernized as an ideal has come to mean the
right to have personal control over one's space and time—some definite,
if demarcated, opportunity in everyday life to be oneself.

There are at least three ways that the idea of liberty has evolved to
take account of modern conditions. First, people have come to feel entitled
to varying degrees of liberty contingent on certain qualifications and the
willingness to make certain tradeoffs. Second, the idea of liberty has come
to be an important basis for defining people's intentions and interests as
consumers and workers. Third, the ideal of the self-sufficient household,
impossible in modern society, has been replaced by demands and expectations for free time and space.

I will argue that insofar as Americans experience themselves as free to
make their own lives, they find both moral and practical reasons for committing themselves to their daily lives rather than to larger public, historical
responsibilities. The potentials for experiencing liberty thus limit the potentials of democracy. Still, I will try to show throughout this book that
the experience of liberty is itself a democratic achievement, and the experience of threats to liberty constitutes a basis for possible democratic
renewal.

Aspirations for, and experiences of, liberty are not the only or necessarily even the primary features of consciousness that bind commitment
to everyday life. We will explore other features as well—these range from
fear of the risks of public utterance to withdrawal from the complexity of
political action, to manifold ideological formulations that foster the "personal" rather than the "political." Political moralists and activists, faced
with "apathy," have called attention to many such mechanisms; the politically committed frequently search for grounds to account for or preach
against apathy. What such accounts and critiques typically fail to come to
grips with is the moral basis for commitment to everyday life and the ways
in which that commitment can represent a positive quest for freedom rather
than simply an escape from it. Democratic activists appeal to Americans
to take control of their history and fulfill their social responsibilities. My
purpose here is to understand why Americans tend to resist such appeals
and to interpret such resistance not simply as a sign of "narcissism," "false
consciousness," or "repression" but as a form of political expression that
is itself freighted with history.

LIBERALISM

AT FIRST glance, in the debate between democracy and liberty the latter has the psychological advantage. The ideal of liberty speaks to the natural disposition of people to give primacy to their individual lives and argues that the best route to the good society is to free people to make their own lives and pursue their personal interests. From the angle of individual selves, democracy seems to entail sacrifice of time and energy to a social interest that may in turn oppressively infringe individual liberty. Except for a fringe of individualist anarchists and radical libertarians, however, most advocates of liberty have recognized that some government authority must exist to enforce rules that protect individual free space, provide for certain common goods, defend national boundaries. "Liberalism" is the name for various ideological solutions to the tension between liberty and democracy. Liberalism is grounded in the primacy of individual freedom to make one's own life, but argues for the necessity of certain societal frameworks requisite for such freedom. To protect personal liberty government must be organized according to principles of representative democracy—i.e., the governing groups must be made systematically accountable to the populace and able to be replaced by them. A representative democracy permits people to lead their own lives while appointing specialists to do the governing, subject to periodic recall.

Second, liberty requires an economy organized by market principles— i.e., people make their lives by being left free to participate in a variety of reciprocal relationships with others, regulated by the capacities of all persons to rationally pursue and protect their individual self-interest. For the liberal, then, democracy ought to exist in a restricted sphere, residing in the process of choosing government representatives whose scope of operations is limited. In order to be responsible citizens, members must pay some attention to political events occurring outside their everyday worlds and must be able and willing to communicate about public matters. But such collective action should not extend to activity that can be performed through markets. When acting in the market, members should not be thinking of their social responsibility and the public welfare, but of their self interests. The liberal, recognizing the inescapable interdependence of human beings in the modern world, finds that the way to protect the ability of people to make their own lives is in the institution of private property and the free flourishing of markets as systems of allocation. For the liberal, history occurs not primarily as the result of conscious decisions by elites or collective action by masses, but as the byproduct of a multiplicity of individual initiatives designed to enhance individual well-being rather than social development. Such initiatives—for example, introduction of new technology or opening up of new markets—may have major social effects that will be experienced as disruptive. But over time, says the liberal faith, market processes create new equilibria that can be seen, at least in retrospect, as socially progressive.

There is, however, a fundamental flaw in the social psychology of liberalism. While liberalism encourages the avid pursuit of individual self-interest, it nevertheless argues that individuals ought to accept the fate they suffer at the "invisible" hand of the market. Those threatened by destruction in the competitive struggle, those thrown out of work by technological advance, those unemployed in a periodic business slump, those uprooted from traditional communities by the advent of market agriculture—all are expected (in libertarian and free market perspectives) to accept the diseconomies of their everyday lives, seek out new ones, and patiently wait the restoration of equilibrium.

People facing circumstances such as these have, however, typically not accepted them—no doubt in part because of liberalism's stress on the right of each individual to live his own life. In other words, what liberalism in its classic form seems not to see is that capitalism and its "gales of creative destruction" (in Schumpeter's phrase) has manifold unwanted impacts on the daily lives of millions, and that, in the face of historical threats to daily life, these millions have sought to make history themselves.

MARX

KARL MARX made certain decisive contributions to resolving the tension between liberty and democracy. One of them was to emphasize that despite the definite creativity and progress that derived from capitalist market economies, such economies inherently and profoundly destabilized and destroyed everyday lives of most people living under their sway. Unlike classic liberals, Marx did not treat such creative destruction as a transitory byproduct of capitalist development, but as a necessary central feature of it. He tried to show that capitalism was inherently destructive at every stage of its development. In its beginnings, traditional classes and their ways were undermined and obliterated, and areas of the globe accustomed to local self-sufficiency were swamped by commodities, with populations forced off the land to become wage-earning proletarians. Once well-established, the "anarchy" of capitalist production would result in periodic booms and busts that would perpetuate massive insecurity and periodic misery.

Capitalist competition would progressively destroy the ability of weaker capitalists to survive, and thus progressively increase the concentration of wealth, while perpetuating large-scale impoverishment. International competitive pressures would increase the likelihood of global warfare, with all the attendant destruction of life and living arrangements. Finally, capitalism as it matured would enter a period of crisis—of economic stagnation and decline—resulting inevitably from the disparity between the system's productive capacity and the ability of capitalists to realize profits from actually using that capacity.

In short, Marx argued that capitalism could never deliver the liberty it promised to most of those who lived within its framework. For the system required that most people be dependent on capitalist firms for livelihood and for the goods and services needed for daily life. Only a few could achieve or maintain the degree of liberty associated with property and entrepreneurship. Moreover, every gain, in the form of improved wages or local economic independence, that workers might achieve under capitalism was incentive to capitalists to undermine that situation. High wages motivate employers to find substitute labor at lower costs, for example. Periods of high employment and relative well-being would surely be followed by periods of depression. Marx could not deny—indeed he sometimes paid tribute to—capitalism's ability to create opportunities for self-realization and self-fulfillment for large numbers. But one of the fundamental themes of his life's work was to show that such opportunities remained systematically unavailable to the millions and were likely to be ephemeral even for many of those who thought they had it made.

Marx was, of course, not satisfied simply to criticize liberalism's illusory promise. As his early writings show, Marx shared the belief that human beings ought to be free to make their lives and to realize their potential. What the liberal fails to see, he argued, is that such freedom is not possible so long as the means to make history are controlled by a few.

What are the means of making history? If history is constituted by action that affects the conditions of daily life of a community or a society, then the most fundamental way of influencing history is to exercise control over the things people need in order to live. One of the defining features of capitalism is that the necessaries of material existence are increasingly available primarily as commodities—as goods produced for and acquired through markets—instead of being produced by the users themselves for their own immediate need. Thus the power to make history in capitalist society rests fundamentally with those who control the production of commodities—a power that increases as people become increasingly dependent on commodities for daily living and on the system of commodity production as the place to earn a livelihood.

We have already seen that capitalists, in their activity as capitalists, make history as a byproduct of their economic pursuits, although the effect their individual and cumulative actions have on the everyday lives of millions may well not be expected or wanted by the capitalist actors. Marx argued that this power to influence daily life conditions is further multiplied by the fact that capitalists have both opportunity and motive to band together as a conscious group to influence the state. The latter institution, although formally independent from the processes that supply the necessities of daily life, greatly influences the conditions and terms of everyday existence by the implementation of laws and rules and the conduct of all sorts of policies, including, most far-reachingly, those policies that lead toward war. But insofar as the material conditions of life are controlled by a defined group, that group, when it acts concertedly, can dominate the state in numerous direct and indirect ways. Thus capitalism undermines its promise of democracy as well as liberty; instead of guaranteeing these, over time its development as a system increases the concentration of historical power in the hands of the capitalist class.

Conditions of daily life flow from economic and political decisions; in additon there is a third form of historical influence—the ability to influence the meanings people give to their daily lives, the materials by which they construct their identities, articulate their motives, define their goals, decide their loyalties. As with economics and politics, this symbolic intervention is dominated by specialists: priests, intellectuals, artists, prophets, teachers, journalists. For Marx, the apparent autonomy of symbolic specialists also declines as capitalism develops. Insofar as power rests in the capitalist class, then intellectuals who want to have historical effect need to ally themselves with that class, and they may be well-rewarded materially if they do so.

Thus Marx showed that the economic power of individual capitalists and their capacity for political power and ideological influence when they organized themselves as a class would continuously exacerbate the gap between everyday life and history, thereby undermining the bases for both liberty and democracy. But, unlike others who criticized the elitist and destructive propensities of capitalism, Marx noticed that the development of the system created potentialities for counter-tendencies as well. The historical power of capitalists is grounded in their control over the processes necessary to sustain everyday life. But capitalists as such do not literally have their hands on the production process. They do not physically produce the goods necessary for everyday life, but instead control through the exercise of property rights. Production itself cannot occur unless workers—who themselves have no property rights—actually do it. This means that the workers—those self-same millions whose daily lives have been uprooted, impoverished, and otherwise threatened or disrupted by capitalism's advent, and who have become progressively more dependent for livelihood and life's necessities on capitalist firms—have enormous potential historical power of their own. They run—and can stop—the machines on which the everyday life of society is increasingly dependent.

In this sense, the historical power of workers is even more direct than that of the capitalist, since the latter's control over processes necessary for life is exercised through chains of command. Indeed, in principle the workers as a group have the greater power. They could activate or stall the production process without the capitalists, whereas the latter must always have workers. Here is the great irony of historical development, as Marx saw it. That class most dependent for daily survival, most lacking in its own resources for making daily life—the proletariat—is uniquely situated to bring into being a situation in which the people themselves can, at last, make history. For the system of commodity production creates an interdependent world, obliterates the ability of local groups to sustain autonomous histories, and yet at the same time puts the entire production of the material basis of daily life in the hands of the people themselves.

Capitalism is a system that forces each person's daily life to be increasingly shaped by interdependence—and therefore subject to historical decision. The capitalists' capacity to make history is itself dependent on the cooperation of wage workers and other employees, and therefore the historical powerlessness experienced by subordinates is illusory, for the historical projects of elites cannot be accomplished without their participation, their labor power. Yet in everyday life there is a fundamental difference between the power exercised by the capitalist and that of the worker. The capitalist, by acting in his everyday roles, makes history according to his intentions. The worker, acting in his everyday roles, provides the means of history making for the capitalist. The power of subordinated groups to make history in their own interest rests precisely on their willingness to stop their everyday lives, to break with routine, to disrupt the accustomed processes of daily production and reproduction. Thus the power potentially available to workers cannot be routinely or even readily exercised, since the attempt to exercise that power contradicts the activity needed for life. The worker lives by selling his labor power to the capitalist; he can exercise historical power by not selling labor power, but then living itself becomes problematic.

Equally problematic is the fact that the individual worker has no power as an individual—his personal refusal to work by itself has no disruptive effect on the production process. The historical power of workers comes into being only as a collective act, and only insofar as it really does disrupt production. If a group of workers is not strategically significant to a production process or if they can be readily replaced with others, then even determined collective action is likely to appear fruitless. Moreover, for workers to have significant historical effect they must act concertedly not just in a given workplace or locale, but on a national—and even global— scale. Workers have enormous historical power—but only if they disrupt processes that provide the basis for daily survival, and only if they subordinate their own immediate, individual, practical opportunities to large-scale collective action.

Thus Marx thought that democracy and liberty could be realized not by criticizing the failure of capitalist society to fulfill its promises, but as a result of the efforts by the proletarians themselves to form a class and intervene in history. Their capacity to win historical power rested on their direct access to the processes of production of commodities (and the extensiveness of the commodification of daily life). It was further grounded on the inevitable growth in the numbers of workers, a growing source of strength in efforts to influence the state. Workers' capacity to form a class was enormously facilitated by the fact that the factory and other workplaces aggregated large numbers, thereby aiding communication; ability to communicate was further amplified by modern means of communication and transportation. Thus, unlike oppressed classes in earlier epochs, the modern industrial workers had both the power and opportunity to make history. Marx, however, seemed to recognize that the *will* to use this power was problematic. For, as I have already pointed out, the resources available to workers were effective only if they risked livelihood, stepped outside of their daily lives, and did so *collectively*. The possibility of working-class action required workers to transcend immediately perceived self-interest and the immediate reality of everyday life. Despite this, Marx did not attempt to formulate a detailed analysis of the social and psychological conditions under which such transcendence might take place. The reason he did not was that he believed that everyday life for workers under capitalism would never provide sufficient security, well-being, or moral force to enforce commitment to it. Economic conditions would always be so unstable, wage and working conditions so abysmal or insecure, massive dislocation, war, and depression so often impending, and traditional moral constraints so eradicated by the cold rationalities of market society that workers would, he thought, readily see the necessity for collective action and the promise of their class power.

Moreover, Marx foresaw that it would not be long before workers would develop organization, in the form of trade unions and political parties, so that they would to no longer rely simply on their spontaneous readiness to strike in order to engage in historical struggle. Organizational development would provide some framework of representation and resources for material support and spiritual sustenance, so that workers would come to feel their power rather than their vulnerability and find their best chance for everyday security within the frameworks created by their class rather than in the institutional frameworks of capitalism per se.

Marx, however, saw two problems arising from the effective organization of the working class. First, there was the possibility that workers would satisfy themselves with short-run reform of working and living conditions within capitalism, not seeing that in the longer run improvements in living standards under capitalism would always be temporary. Second, it seemed likely to him that workers would fight to defend themselves within the boundaries of particular national or ethnic cultures, since it was only within these boundaries that human beings have had a common language and a common bond. But such provincialism, he perceived, was fatal to the working class' ability to make history, because in the long run it would permit capital to escape the control of workers, it would result in intensified internal division among workers and allow the growth of global inequality and international warfare. The workers' possibility of taking control of history—that is, of taking control of the means of production of daily life—was realizable only as a global process in which workers had their class as their primary collective loyalty and identification, not their nationality, race, or religion.

Marx' faith in the workers' capacity ultimately to achieve this kind of internationalist class consciousness rested on his assumption that the experience of living under capitalism would demonstrate to them the impermanence of reformism and the illusory security of nationalism and ethnocentrism (i.e., that there would be "nothing to lose but your chains)." But, as the *Communist Manifesto* shows, he was unwilling to leave the emergence of such consciousness simply to processes of natural evolution. He saw a definite role for *communists*—that is, intellectuals and political activists drawn from the ranks of workers or drawn to those ranks from other classes who had the capacity for long-range and global theorizing. This role, as he and Engels defined it in the *Manifesto,* was not to dominate the working class or compete with other leadership elements, but to teach the necessity for the abolition of private property and for internationalizing the class struggle. Presumably, without the influence of communist tutelage, workers who achieved some immediate gain from organization and collective action would settle for the opportunities available within capitalism and the nation-state to return to everyday commitments.

Marx therefore implicitly recognized that everyday life, rather than the making of history, would typically remain a priority for workers. Out of the disruption and impoverishment of daily life, workers would move to historical struggle—but once having waged struggle effective enough to win back the chance of daily living, they would seize this chance and thereby lose the opportunity they had as a class to fundamentally remake history. Marx' solution to this was to highlight the importance of specialists in history making—those willing to give history, rather than everyday life, priority. These people—self-declared communists—were to serve as the social conscience of their class, pointing, always, beyond the immediate realities of daily life to the larger historical mission and the fact of global interdependence. Marx knew that people disposed to make history—as politicians or intellectuals—would have an easier chance of personal success if they allied with the bourgeoisie or other classes positioned to rule. But he was saying to people who had such personal options (including himself) something like the following: Not only is it more moral to ally with the oppressed, but by giving yourself to the working class you will be allying with the only force capable or actually bringing into being a fully human and rational society. If you want your ideals of liberty, democracy, and social rationality to be realized, if you want your words and thoughts to actually make a historical difference, you cannot stand aloof from the class struggle, and you should not ally with established elites. If your point is not simply to criticize the world but to change it, then you must join with the workers to help realize their historical mission.

Thus Marx shares with the liberal the understanding that individual human beings seek to make their own lives as their first priority, rather then committing themselves to the development of society. But, of course, he was most unlike liberals in seeing that a system based on the private appropriation of the means of life provided the chance of individual self-fulfillment only to the few with private property, while making the ability of the vast majority to lead their own lives continuously problematic. Although groups of workers may win the chance to lead decent, secure everyday lives for periods of time, liberty for all can never be secured so long as the ability to control the production needed for daily life is possessed by a few, and so long as that production is guided by criteria of profitability rather than human need. If the workers of the world want to secure their liberty, they will have to secure control over that production process. But their willingness to engage that deeply in prolonged historical transformation is offset by the partial and temporary opportunities relatively advantaged groups of workers will have to depart from the historical stage and make their own lives. It is the existence of a minority of persons who prefer to live for history that can hold the historical mission together under these circumstances. Unlike elite history makers who seek personal power, "communist" activists and intellectuals find their capacity to make history in their ability to teach and inspire and enable workers to act for themselves.

The history of the last hundred years amply demonstrates that Marx was right to expect workers to undertake collective action to protect and advance their interests. His prediction that they would organize themselves in a continuing and expanding effort to exercise their power in the production process was effectively confirmed by the growth of the trade union movements under capitalism. He assumed that workers would also seek political representation through working-class political parties; such parties have become powerful political forces in every capitalist country— with the crucial exception of the United States. Moreover, there is no question that the workers' struggles, organization, and political expression have fundamentally determined the history of all capitalist societies over the last several decades. Transformations of the state, the political economy, and the content of daily life all can be understood only by seeing these as outcomes of class conflict.

Yet one of the fundamental ironies of our era is that although the very class struggle predicted by Marx has taken place, its result, at least so far, has been to modernize capitalism, not overthrow it. The rise of the welfare state, of administered economies, of the global corporation, of mass production technologies and mass media of communication—all these processes would not have happened or would have happened at a far slower rate had industrial workers merely accepted their fate within the rules of the market and the disciplines of the factory. The demands of the working class for the right to security and well-being in daily life, expressed through militant protest and political organization, compelled measures that would raise wages, provide for social wages, smooth the business cycle, and enable workers to participate as consumers. Such developments are understandable in terms of Marx's model even if he did not predict them. Marx undoubtedly underestimated the capacity of the capitalist state to incorporate mass working-class parties into government. He could not have anticipated some of the technological potentialities that would restore economic growth and provide a material basis for everyday feelings of freedom and well-being.

He certainly did not give sufficient weight to nationalism as a more ready basis of collective mobilization than proletarian consciousness. Marx did not anticipate the degree to which effective efforts at historical intervention by the working class would bring about sufficient improvements in conditions of daily life to persuade workers that living their own lives was more rational and practical than making history. The logic of class conflict does not lead in a straight line to revolution; instead (and Marx certainly recognized this) it leads toward efforts to exhaust every opportunity to find acceptable accommodations within the possibilities of the existing system. Marx saw far fewer possibilities for such accomodation—expected far more rapid exhaustion of the potentialities for coherent everyday life—within capitalism than were actually found by workers when they sought to claim them through practical action.

If there is no linear relationship between capitalist development and class consciousness, then Marxism provides little help in understanding the conditions under which popular political participation occurs, the forms that such participation takes, or the potentialities for social change that might result. Indeed, as I have already suggested, the first warnings that Marxism was a limited framework for such analysis appear in the *Communist Manifesto,* when Marx seems to recognize that left to "natural evolution" the workers themselves might never really comprehend their mission to create a global revolution to overthrow capitalism. It was the role of communists, he implies, to define a historical mission for the working class that workers, evaluating their direct experience, would not discover readily (or at all) for themselves.

This was a theme picked up forcibly by Lenin, to whom it was clear that a professional revolutionary leadership was needed to transform the "trade union mentality" of average workers into a readiness for revolution. Lenin's great intellectual antagonist, Rosa Luxembourg, could see the flashes of revolutionary awareness arising spontaneously in the midst of mass protest and regarded such flashes as far more meaningful than the maneuvers of a disciplined cadre, but her own hopes for a revolutionary movement among German workers were never fulfilled. Even more traumatic to orthodox Marxism's belief in the natural evolution of revolutionary class consciousness was the rise of fascism as a mass movement in Italy and Germany—a development that forced the recognition that something more than "objective conditions" and "correct leadership" had to be taken into account in understanding what Wilhelm Reich called "mass psychology." Meanwhile, in the United States, the failure of various left political parties to win mass adherence, the lack of support among workers for socialism (contrary to the experience in most other capitalist countries, where the word "socialism" is a label that any politician needs to wear if he hopes to win substantial working-class following), and their failure to form an independent labor party provided further impetus to abandon or go beyond Marx in trying to understand the dynamics of political consciousness and action.

In abandoning Marx as a guide to this terrain, however, I, for one, do not think we can abandon the goal he sought. Our exploration has the same end—to locate and strengthen human capacities to take control of history, to enable the people themselves to make their history, to end the experienced chasm between everyday life and history, to promote the full democratization of society and its institutions.

THE NECESSITY FOR DEMOCRACY

OBVIOUSLY, in seeking to promote such ends, I assume that democracy is preferable to various forms of domination, hierarchy, and elite rule, even when these appear to provide a considerable space for personal liberty. I assume the necessity for democracy on a number of grounds.

First, I believe that Marx was essentially right in arguing that the private control of a centralized, interdependent economic system perpetuates conditions of everyday unfreedom for millions because of inherent threats to basic material security, inherent conditions of material deprivation, and inherent conditions of subordination in the workplace. The attainment and preservation of even the promised liberty of capitalism requires that workers and other "propertyless" groups continuously undertake collective action to protect their security, improve living standards, and achieve greater voice in conditions of their work. Moreover, in the end, Marxists and other socialists may be proven right—the only way to secure everyday freedom is to achieve full-scale democratic control over the economy and internal democracy in the operation of economic organizations.

Second, in addition to these traditional socialist arguments about the ways in which capitalism denies everyday freedom to the majority, there are traditional and contemporary arguments about the dangers of concentrated power in the national state. The growth of a centralized state bureaucracy results in innumerable planning decisions that reshape daily life in communities without reference to concrete local needs. The growth of bureaucracies of social control develops potentialities for surveillance and intimidation that profoundly threaten privacy and liberty. State services and subsidies are organized in ways that frustrate creativity, increase dependency, promote conformity, fail to meet needs they were designed to serve. Above all, a giant military establishment distorts and blocks possibilities for humanly relevant economic development, conscripts youth to highly authoritarian and destructive servitude, increases risks of war and intensifies a climate of international hostility that poses a constant threat to daily wellbeing and creates the realistic possibility of global holocaust. Only organized and semi-organized forms of popular political expression provide hope of offsetting drift toward technocratic domination, garrison statism, "friendly fascism," imperial adventure, nuclear annihilation. Such forms of expression include the revitalization of dissent, the fostering of formats of public debate, the elaboration of multiple channels of public information, the organization of grass-roots pressure groups, neighborhood organization, consumer and client organization, public interest lobbying, new electoral organizations and campaigns, protest and civil disobedience. These increase the possibilities of realizing the liberal promise of political pluralism and republican control over elites. But anarchists and other radicals may well be right that the only way to end the threat of war and state tyranny is to achieve a fundamental decentralization of power, the abolition of the national state in favor of a world organized by self-determining, interdependent communities.

Third, there is a need to increase individual readiness to assume social responsibility. It is simply magical thinking to imagine that the pursuit of self-interest is the best way to ensure a good society. For example, it is now clear that Americans, at the level of daily life, must learn to take account of the effects of their "life-styles" on the world's supply of food and natural resources. Whether one is talking about conservation or child-rearing, about taxes or health, the seemingly private choices of individuals are actually linked to social development as a whole. Many would argue that it is not really possible to "socialize" human beings to take responsibility for more than themselves and their immediate families. Such views deny the possibility that personal growth can reach "higher" levels of social concern than are now understood to be "normal." But it seems to me precisely the task of systematic social inquiry to comprehend not only the limits but also the potentialities of human development, and to attempt to specify the conditions under which such potentialities may be realizable. Democratization may be thought of as an effort to socialize persons so that they learn to take account of social welfare and the social future in their everyday activity. Ultimately such socialization may be neither possible nor liberating unless, in addition to a sense of responsibility, people also have the reality of empowerment in their daily lives. Still, the social restructuring that can provide such empowerment cannot be brought about unless there are also changes in the priorities and practices of individuals in their daily lives. Accordingly, it seems necessary to understand more deeply than we now do the conditions in present-day society that facilitate people's willingness to forego immediate self-interest in favor of collective goals, or to merge their own fates with those of others, or to consider the long-run consequences of short-run advantages. Liberty is not an adequate basis for self-realization; it must somehow be fused with awareness of the social basis of selfhood.

In short, I consider democratization to be essential to the achievement of rational social and economic development, necessitated by the drift toward tyranny and war, and integral to the development of the individual person. These considerations form the central biases of this book.

THE "ACTIVIST" AND THE "AVERAGE PERSON"

THE CENTRAL theme of this book is the experienced disjunction between making history and making one's own life. One way in which this disjunction operates is manifested in the divergence between the orientation of the activist vs. the orientations of the "average citizen." The activist organizes his or her everyday life to facilitate participation in historical processes, is likely to give lower priority or even no priority to ordinary concerns of livelihood, family, and household, or arranges the day so that such concerns do not drain time and energy from activity directed at political/historical influence. The average citizen is trying to live his or her life, is preoccupied with activities directed at self-maintenance, finds time and energy bound by such activity, and, as we shall see, is likely to engage in political action in order to protect the possibility of everyday life—not as an end in itself. In other words, the activist and the average person may be thought of as living in two divergent realms—the realm of history vs. the realm of everyday living. This circumstance makes communication between activist and private person problematic; the goals, experiences, language, and information used by each are likely to be discrepant. This failure of political communication is the starting point of my inquiry and what I hope to help overcome through it. The logic of democratic action requires that those who specialize in historical awareness and leadership be in deep communication with those for whom they claim to speak and whom they hope to lead; the logic of democratization requires that the privatized become increasingly conscious of their citizenship—that is, increasingly aware of the relationships between their personal lives and history.

A first step in establishing such communication is to deepen understanding of how average people actually experience the relationship between their lives and the larger society and polity, how commitment to everyday life is enforced structurally, reinforced ideologically, understood cognitively, welcomed emotionally, evaluated morally. This is the topic of chapter 2. What I want to show, however, is not simply that people, on the average, are "privatized" or politically uninvolved. Political orientations are a feature of everyday life; political activity, most obviously voting, is engaged in. History, and our own time, is filled with instances of active, forceful interventions by masses of people in the history-making realm. I want to try to show that "commitment to everyday life" can serve as a framework for understanding both political apathy *and* mass political action and provides important clues for understanding the seeming contradictoriness of popular participation. So chapter 3 sketches an interpretive framework for the analysis of popular participation in politics and protest.

A small minority of Americans are political activists, committed to "history" rather than "everyday life." Much political activism is directed toward the exercise of power within the established institutional frameworks of society. But throughout our history some activists have claimed to be after something other than personal power or position, seeking instead to democratize history making itself. The democratic current in political activism I call the "tradition of the left." In chapter 4, I undertake a critical review of that tradition. In this chapter, I take the view that, despite the left's repeated tendency to divorce itself from the everyday experiences of mainstream America, there have been some significant—and instructive—moments in which such isolation has been overcome. What can we learn from such moments? More broadly, what are the actual ways that left activists have had historical effect? Why have left organizations in this country repeatedly failed to sustain growth and survive? Why, on the other hand, might it be justifiable to say that the left has been a crucial force in the cultural and social development of the United States?

I assume that the future of democracy requires the revitalization of the left tradition. In chapters 5 and 6, I try to formulate how democratic activists can rethink their history-making potentials in light of what we have learned about the left's past interrelationship with mainstream consciousness. In these chapters I rather presumptuously try to sketch some of the forms of action, program, strategy, and organization that might revitalize the left tradition. For, despite the left's record of obtuseness, futility, and irrelevance, I take it as a given that the chances for a realization of democracy depend on the left's renewal.

2

Making Life, Not History

Some Generalizations About How Americans Treat Politics

I do not mean to exclude altogether the Idea of Patriotism. I know it exists, and I know it has done much in the present Contest. But I venture to assert, that a great and lasting War can never be supported on this principle alone. It must be aided by a prospect of Interest or some reward. For a time, it may of itself push Men to Action; to bear much, to encounter difficulties, but it will not endure unassisted by Interest.

—George Washington

The great object of terror and suspicion to the people of the thirteen provinces was power; not merely power in the hands of a president or a prince, of one assembly or several, or many citizens or of few, but of power in the abstract, wherever it existed and under whatever name it was known.

—Henry Adams

What is called politics is comparatively something so superficial and inhuman, that practically I have never recognized that it concerns me at all.

—Henry David Thoreau

AMERICANS participate very little in the formal processes that constitute democratic government. Voting is the most prevalent way that Americans consciously get involved with the political process. Yet voting rates in this country are notoriously lower than those of other industrial democracies. A high turnout in the United States would be 70 percent of eligible voters and recent national elections have featured turnouts of little more than 50 percent—while participation in local contests is usually much lower.

Far fewer participate in other forms of political activity. Only about 8 percent of Americans belong to a political organization; about 10 percent make contributions to political campaigns or organizations; only about 10–15 percent say they have ever tried to contact a public official about a political issue.

A larger proportion of the population—but still a minority—pays some regular and interested attention to political happenings. For example, about 25–30 percent say that they often try to proselytize in behalf of a candidate. About 40 percent report engaging with some frequency in political discussion. Although participation in local elections is usually low, more citizens (about 30 percent) report some history of involvement in organized activity to solve community problems than report involvement in political parties or election campaigns.

About 10–15 percent of the electorate may be counted as political activists—that is, people who are informed and active participants in organizations, parties, or campaigns—people who take some ongoing political responsibility as a feature of their lives. At the opposite pole are about one-fifth of the citizens who do not vote, who do not attend to the news, do not devote any part of their lives to politics.

In this country such differences in political participation are very much related to differences in the amount of formal education people have acquired. In general, those who are politically active are likely to have gone to college. Going to college provides a number of experiences that foster motivations and capacities to participate in political processes. There is, first of all, a likelihood that one will gain some knowledge, skill, and a sense of one's competence relevant to such participation. The college experience, moreover, tends to instill or reinforce the notion that one has a duty to participate. College is the primary entry point to occupations that may provide skills, social contacts, time, and opportunity to engage in organizational activity and to exercise influence.

If having gone to college makes it more likely that one will feel competent and responsible politically and have more opportunity to be politically effective, the extent of political participation is additionally influenced by one's "political socialization"—that is, the degree to which one's family made political participation a salient and significant dimension of experience, inculcated a sense of civic duty, provided some exemplary models of political responsibility, suggested that one was capable of effectively acting in the political sphere. In the United States, relatively few families are strongly oriented to politics in these ways; those that are are likely to be found in the stratum of the college educated.

In short, it is not an exaggeration to say that active political involvement in this country tends to be an elitist orientation. It is a propensity reserved primarily for those who have been raised or trained to feel that they can and should exercise authority and show civic responsibility. Such rearing and training occurs primarily among those of relatively high status and education.

At first glance it may appear natural that political responsibility should be exercised by those most educated, and that those with less schooling should be reticent about injecting themselves into the governing process. But this situation is not universal—even in our country. There are some instructive exceptions to these generalizations. In particular, independent of education political participation is associated with a strong sense of identification with an ethnic group or political party. For example, since the civil rights struggle of the sixties there has been an emerging tendency for blacks, who as a group were far less likely to participate in politics than whites in the past, to now be more politically active than whites of equivalent socioeconomic position. This development was dramatized and intensified by the black response to the Jesse Jackson campaign in 1984—black voting rates in the Democratic primaries exceeded those of non-blacks in many localities. But the Jackson campaign also capitalized on the fact that in a number of communities black voters had already begun to mobilize in surprisingly large proportions.

A fair generalization from research findings about voter participation would be that whereas upper status persons tend to participate out of a felt interest and a sense of "duty," strong political involvement can be found among those lower status people who are involved in subcultures that are linked in some way to politics. That working-class members can be highly motivated to political responsibility and activism is more evident in European countries where parties and traditions of working-class politics have developed over more than a century. In other words, there may be cultural bases for political participation quite distinct from those that depend on formal schooling. In the United States, compared with any other industrial capitalist country, these alternative frameworks of political socialization are relatively weak and scattered. This seems paradoxical, since, more than any other country, our national culture originated in a republican vision and is grounded in the idealization of popular sovereignty and democratic citizenship. It is, therefore, a major irony that the exercise of such citizenship is so strongly skewed toward advantaged groups, so little fostered by the concrete socialization processes experienced by disadvantaged and working class people.

THE ORGANIZATION OF EVERYDAY TIME

IN RECENT years, there has been some research measuring how Americans use their time on an everyday basis. One major study, done in 1965, found that, on the average, adults (between 18–65) spend about 10 1/2 hours taking care of basic bodily needs (sleeping, eating, "personal care"), about 7 1/2 hours in paid work and housework, and about 1/2 hour in "child care." Thus, about 18 hours of the average American day is occupied by more or less obligatory activity—activity required for physical maintenance of oneself and other family members. The remaining 5–6 hours is "discretionary time." About two hours of this remaining time, on the average, is spent watching television. Another hour and a half is spent in casual social interaction; another half hour in "resting" and miscellaneous leisure, and about 50 minutes is spent in travel not connected to going to and from work. Little more than an hour of the average day is left for more active or goal-directed discretionary activity: the average American day involves 12 minutes for study, 10 minutes for religion, 8 minutes for active sports, 6 minutes for going out for entertainment or cultural events, and 6 minutes for participating in voluntary organizations.

A somewhat earlier study of how Americans use their leisure time found that in a typical week most people watched television, about a third visited with friends or relatives, about a third did yard work, and smaller percentages did hobbies, read magazines or books, took pleasure drives, listened to records. The smallest percentage (11 percent) went to a meeting or some other organizational activity.

These sorts of data rather dramatically document that participation in voluntary organizations of any kind is a relatively rare feature of the average American day. Most of the everyday time of most people is obligated by what is regarded as activity necessary for basic survival. Thus, for most, political activity would have to be undertaken during the remaining discretionary time; but the average American is likely to spend most of his or her discretionary hours watching TV and doing other relatively undirected things. Voluntary organizational participation ranks at the bottom of the list of identifiable "leisure" activity—and political participation is probably a small fraction of the organizational activity represented in that category.

Still, about a fourth of the average day is unconstrained—it is likely that our society provides more discretionary time for its average members than has been true in any other time and place. Our era may be the first in which having a substantial block of time "of one's own" is not seen as a right reserved for a privileged few, but a taken-for-granted feature of everybody's every day. If the amount of discretionary time available to average members is a plausible measure of the degree of personal freedom provided by a society—as I think it is—then Americans have a considerable amount of it (although, as we shall see, there are very significant inequalities in the distribution of self-controlled time in our society).

Perhaps the most striking fact about the use of discretionary time is the amount of it spent watching television. The time budget studies I have cited indicate that the average day includes two hours of involvement with the mass media (mostly TV, some radio); other studies suggest that this may for various reasons be an underestimate. For example, studies of the amount of time TV sets are *on* suggest that the figure is closer to five hours a day. Such figures may underestimate television watching among significant groups—for example, the time budget studies do not measure the time use of retired people or of the unemployed. As Comstock et al. summarize the data, "It is clear that television viewing takes up more time than any activity other than work and sleep, and that it . . . dominates leisure time in America" (Comstock et al., 1978:149).

The reasons for this dominance have not been fully plumbed by empirical research; indeed, each of us may be somewhat mystified about the sources of our own addictions to the tube. We can, obviously, rule out the attraction of TV programming itself: there seems to be little correlation between the dissatisfaction people express with the quality of programming and the amount of their viewing. In fact, in the main people are likely to feel that they turn on the set to watch television rather than to see something in particular.

One clue to the nature of the viewing experience is that, to a large extent, watching TV is combined with other activity. It would be a mistake to interpret TV viewing as expressing nothing more than passivity and social withdrawal. Much of the time spent in front of the set occurs in the company of other family members and friends and include a good deal of conversation; in addition, people may be doing a variety of household activities and a range of other things—from reading to making love—with the television as background.

Television's power and social impact are embedded in a bundle of contradictory meanings and effects. TV is a medium of sociability—and also an escape from the strains of interpersonal encounter. It allows family members to be together but reduces the need for them to deal with each other. It has made available, cheaply, a tremendous range of professional entertainment and culture, and thus reduces the boredom and emptiness faced by people with few material resources (TV watching is highest among low-income people). It is at the same time incontrovertibly a "vast wasteland" of trivia and vulgarity whose emotional impact is similar to that of other forms of cheap self-indulgence. Television provides an opportunity for choice and control over one's experience, while it represents a form of controlled leisure and consumption that, more than any other packaged mode of entertainment, erases initiative and undermines imagination. It provides information about, and generates interest in, topics, issues, and experiences that might otherwise be completely unknown to the millions —while drawing patronage away from previously flourishing forms of community-based mass entertainment and recreation.

In short, no simple or straightforward critique of the medium has much value unless it can also explain its attractive power. A pertinent critique ought to have as its first premise the recognition that TV is the cheapest and most convenient means yet devised to provide relief from the contraints and strains of everyday life. Through it can be found a certain kind of freedom otherwise missing in daily life and a way to restore frayed strands of interpersonal and societal connectedness. Probably every culture provides some regularized avenues of escape from mundane anxiety and some ritualized reinforcements of community. Television's great technical advantage in providing these is its cheapness and convenience. In this sense it is the most democratic means of expression. But from the perspective of democracy, television's dominance of leisure time is quite threatening. For, along with its accessibility, it has carried two structural consequences: more than any previous expressive medium, TV has been a one-way process of communication, fostering spectatorship rather than participation; unlike other media of spectacle, TV reduces rather than enhances the physical mingling of people for expressive purposes. As a political force, it seems plausible to say that TV has greatly enhanced the average member's awareness of national and global "history in the making," while structuring a situation in which most experience themselves as isolated spectators.

Television's easy accessibility as a source of gratification accounts in large part for its domination of the average day, but its limitations as a tool for self-expression and ecstasy make it unlikely to be a major source of meaning for most people. Thus, besides TV watching, the average day include a substantial amount of informal sociability with family and friends, and smaller amounts of time spent on hobbies, studying, outdoor recreation, entertainment, and religion. The small amount of average daily time spent in such activity is not a good measure of their significance for the individual; time budget figures represent daily averages of the diverse activities of numerous individuals who may engage in something with great commitment and intensity on a weekly or monthly basis. It would therefore be misleading to believe that Americans, in their free time, can simply be understood as a mass of passive spectators sitting before the tube—the manipulated victims of a system of controlled consumption. Still, among the wide range of self-initiated activities that Americans do undertake in their free time, participation in organized activity directed at societal or community responsibility is one of the least likely ways that people in this country, on the average, use their time.

In 1973 and '74, hoping to gain some insight into "political apathy," I collected interviews with about 30 people living in the Santa Barbara area in an effort to explore the ways in which a more or less representative range of persons understood and accounted for their relationship with the political system and public events. These interviews lasted in each case a total of about six hours, taking place over several sessions. In undertaking this exploration, I was conscious of following in the footsteps of earlier investigators of political consciousness—especially David Reisman and Robert Lane, who had such depth interviews with representative "average Americans" in the 1950s. Indeed, many of the questions we used to organize our interviews were drawn from these earlier studies.

Such techniques do not, in themselves, permit generalizations to be made about the American people as a whole. But they do provide some suggestive leads about how people frame the problems of citizenship, relate themselves to politics and historical events, and think about specific issues and broad ideological themes. Notions derived from absorption in these interview texts can be placed against the results of survey research and voting studies—forms of research that do permit generalization. A trouble with survey research is that it standardizes the interpretive processes of individuals so that political thinking—in all its ambiguity—is turned into discrete "attitudes" and "responses" that can be tabulated. Survey research can be a means of enlightening us about the sources of political consciousness, but only if an effort is made by the analyst to go beyond the data, to attempt creative—and necessarily speculative—interpretation. Thus, one value of "qualitative" depth interviewing is that it generates textual material that can supply frameworks for interpreting the responses measured by survey and election results. The quantitative material derived from these, in turn, constrains and reinforces the sorts of things we can plausibly say after interviewing people in depth.

What I want to do here is some systematic reflection, grounded in my effort to listen in depth to what a fairly diverse set of individuals have tried to say about politics and personal life, and also consistent with what I understand to be the relevant findings of survey research.

MOTIVATED DISENGAGEMENT

THERE ARE two motivational grounds for active political participation. On the one hand, political participation may be *attractive* as a source of self-fulfillment and self-expression, as activity chosen out of the range of possible uses of free time. On the other hand, participation may be *reactive* or instrumental—viewed as a necessary or useful way of defending one's interests, expressing discontent, resolving troubles. For most Americans in our time, political participation is felt neither to be intrinsically attractive as an activity nor is it readily resorted to as a means to advance or protect one's interests.

Why is it that Americans tend to be so weakly motivated with respect to political involvement? The interview texts we have collected provide rich material for reflection on this question.

Depth interviewing uncovers a large reservoir of ambivalent or negative feeling among respondents about active political participation. It is not unusual to find people who are tuned into—or even fascinated by—current events, the news, the political world—but who shy away from direct involvement with political organizations or causes. For some, the experience of participation produces considerable trepidation—a sense that one would be entering unknown terrain where one is likely to encounter strangers, and that in such settings any effort to assert oneself is likely to risk embarrassment. One is not good at speaking before groups, one is unsure of one's knowledge, uncertain of one's convictions. Coupled with such stage-fright is likely to be a sense that the effort to overcome inhibitions would not be worth the cost—a pervasive feeling that political activity accomplished little anyway, so why spend one's time and energy and risk embarrassment for it. Thus, for many, political involvement calls up all of the pain and nervousness that pervade any fact-to-face encounters among strangers. One will be judged and found wanting, ignorant, inarticulate. One will risk disapproval or reprisal for deviation from standard opinion. One will expose oneself to the tensions of social conflict. One will be exposed in public. Obviously the more one feels one has the "background" —the knowledge and skills that come with schooling or family experiences and discussion about politics—the less likely it is that such inhibitions will prevail.

The sense that political activity accomplished little is, of course, grounded in the political structure. Most of my respondents have strongly held images of a pyramid of power, in which the real political influence rests with a few groups at the top. By definition, those at the base (and most respondents see themselves there) are unlikely to find their political efforts paying off. Moreover, even if power were not so vertically organized, its mass character means that, of necessity, the possible contribution of a single person is not likely to be particularly meaningful, nor is one likely to have much control over the collective activity to which one might lend a hand. Some mention that much of what one has to do in political organizations is intrinsically of little or no interest—meetings are likely to be boring or pointless, canvassing neighbors can be embarrassing, trying to get people to do things they otherwise would not is frustrating, stuffing envelopes—who needs it?

Thus, large numbers of citizens may find the political process salient enough to pay attention to, but are very unlikely to choose political activity as a way to spend their free time. For, compared with other leisure-time options, political activity is less free, less self-expressive, less pleasurable, and in various ways, more risky.

Further out on the continuum of nonparticipation are large numbers who pay little or no attention to politics even as news. These people are likely to express a deeper sense of personal inadequacy, feeling that issues and happenings are beyond their understanding, combined with a deeper sense of political alienation, feeling that political processes are pointless and unreal. Such people tend to believe that the effort to be better informed would itself disrupt their lives—not only because they do not have the time or energy to spend, but because such involvement would divert them from their chosen and meaningful modes of getting satisfaction out of life. Thus a significant minority of people appear to believe that it is not their place to take part in the political process. Seeing themselves as lacking the competence to be informed, they feel unqualified as citizens.

Only one of the thirty people we interviewed in 1973 confessed to being a habitual abstainer from voting. He was a 29-year-old mechanic who had attended junior college, but who declared, "I never learned to read, so I don't read the newspaper—I just look at the comic strips." He has never voted. "I don't know how that works. When it comes to electing people there's a lot of issues, and more than one person to vote for. Going in and taking a stand and voting for this one or that one is a hard thing to do . . . For me to take a stand on an issue or a man or two men . . . I would want to be sure in my own mind that I was voting for a person who could handle the job. An unknowledgeable vote isn't worth anything. That's why I haven't voted—I haven't taken the time to become knowledgeable on the issues or people . . . I have left that to the people who wanted to get involved in it and let them do it. It's a laziness thing on my part."

This man was self-deprecating, believing that he lacked the skill to become sufficiently knowledgeable—and that "unknowledgeable" voting is not worth anything. But there is a more prideful element in his self-understanding, a vague sense that he has chosen a way of life that involves a deliberate choice not to vote, that somehow his own independence would be jeopardized if he tried to be a good citizen: "I guess I'll never be a good citizen . . . I haven't any idea what an ideal citizen should do—but if I had my boy scout book I'd bet I'd be able to tell you."

The vast majority of people—whether or not they regularly vote—are likely to firmly declare that voting and paying attention to the news are duties of the good citizen; accordingly, the majority of nonvoters are likely to explain their abstention largely in terms of personal inadequacy—blaming themselves for ignorance and laziness. But the mix of feelings and attitudes expressed by this auto mechanic may well be characteristic of many of the numerous people who came of voting age in the seventies but failed to go to the polls. Along with feelings of political incompetence and futility, nonvoting may, for some, represent a form of political expression—a refusal to affirm one's "duty" as a citizen because to do so would be a sign that one was caving in to a morality one feels to be hollow and self-denying. Such latent, gut-level anarchism has yet to be expressed in any coherent collective way; it can, however, be read between the lines in the private talk of people like this auto mechanic, and in some of the songs and styles that have been popular in his generation.

Many people will say that they participate far less than they ought to— that the ideal citizen would take more time to be well-informed and to express him- or herself than they do. Still, most people who feel that they are not quite doing their duty as citizens are not likely to feel any particular guilt with respect to this. When pressed, people, as a rule, are likely to have some additional *moral* justification for the absence of political participation in the organization of their daily lives. Many are likely to say that commitment to fulfillment of one's everyday role responsibilities—as a parent, worker, taxpayer—in a law-abiding, decent, honest, and effective way, is what they really owe to society. To do what one is supposed to do in holding one's life together, in caring for others, in respecting the norms and laws of society—this is a more fundamental and perfectly honorable way of being a good citizen.

People with this perspective are likely to add that, of course, one should also vote. For many, voting (except perhaps in times of crisis) is little more than a symbolic gesture—a ritual expression of support for the polity and an affirmation of one's citizenship. The act of voting thus rounds out and reinforces one's conception of oneself as a good person, as does going to church on Sunday. In these terms, voting is not a minimal way of being political but a culminating one. Whereas the politically active are likely to see voting as the least one can do, the most mundane way to be involved, those who are committed to their everyday lives are more likely to see it as an unusual and special ritual.

The notion that fulfillment of daily obligation and private roles takes moral priority over public participation is strongly reinforced in our culture by the ideology of liberty. From this perspective, the purpose of the polity is to guarantee one's ability to live one's chosen life; therefore, if one is able to be free, one ought to live out one's freedom. If I am self-reliant, self-governing, coping effectively with personal problems, achieving personal goals, then I am fulfilling the ideal of individual liberty. This is just as honorable—even more so, perhaps—then spending my time worrying about, or trying to influence, what politicians do. "You don't always have to have an organized group to do something about what's going on," a middle-aged housewife told us. "I think sometimes things are better done on an individual basis and not in an organized thing. Controlling your own family, your own children, your own life more responsibly—that's the most important."

Thus, many Americans do not find it hard to justify political inactivity. They find their justifications in the morality of everyday commitment. On the one hand, one can be a good person in daily life and, by being good, help to produce and reproduce the things, relationships, and values that keep society going. Alternatively, one can strive for *excellence*—achieving one's potential, living meaningfully, overcoming troubles self-reliantly. By so doing, one is not only helping to keep society going, but fulfilling its central virtues—proving that in America one actually has "life, liberty, and the pursuit of happiness."

The materials we have been discussing tell us something about individual action and belief; they also indicate a crucial feature of our collective life. The United States lacks a strong democratic culture. Such a culture would socialize all its young to feel competent for public participation by providing both the specific skills necessary for public awareness and discourse and a subjective sense of individual self-worth and effectiveness. In the United States, despite the centrality of the democratic ideal, it is clear that socialization for active participation in politics is very differentially available, essentially allocated to those able to acquire a higher education. Moreover, and more subtly, our culture provides very weak motivational bases for political participation; on the contrary, the strongest motivational structures developed in our culture are those that energize people toward private life and personal fulfillment. Whatever it is that enables some people to get positive gratification out of influencing public events remains poorly developed in most Americans. A major paradox of American social and cultural development is this: more than any society we have the idea of democracy in our origin and legitimation; yet to a very large degree this society has failed to sustain institutional or cultural means to foster ready individual interest in democratic participation.

I have so far been discussing political involvement as a source of positive interest and attraction, wondering why the majority of people find so little intrinsic satisfaction in political activity and are so rarely motivated to active involvment by a sense of civic duty. But there are other motives than duty and intrinsic gratification for political action. Although democratic theorists have often hoped that citizenly activity would be a source of "public happiness" and personal growth, a less romantic view of politics sees political action as necessarily instrumental. In this view, it is understandable that those who are satisfied with their private lives are likely to be politically uninvolved; instead, politics ought to be germane when people have the need to defend their interests, express discontent, resolve their troubles. It is plausible that politics will be pursued more often as a means than as an end, and many of our respondents declared that they would be more active if something were happening on the public level that affected their interests. Still it seems that individual Americans do not readily choose political means to defend their interests, solve their problems, or redress their grievances. I do not mean that average Americans never do this; on the contrary, in chapter 3 I will explore the manifold ways in which political expression has in fact been an outcome of everyday experience in this society. But on the average, and in the abstract, people do not "naturally" seek political avenues for protecting and advancing their personal interests. Instead, the "natural" propensity is to define personal life as a distinct sphere and to seek solutions to experienced troubles within it.

An interesting finding that shows up in occasional surveys is the degree to which Americans tend to separate their dissatisfaction with the state of the country from their experience of personal happiness or satisfaction. For example, a major study of the sources and extent of satisfaction in American life found that dissatisfaction with the government was one of the poorest predictors of overall well-being among a variety of "domains" (Campbell et al. 1976:85). Studies by Cantril and others indicate that, during the seventies, Americans tended to express a sense of national decline and a pessimism about the national future, while simultaneously feeling that their own lives would improve and their own personal futures would be brighter still. Cantril's data suggest that Americans are more likely to perceive their personal well-being as independent from the perceived state of society than are people in other societies (Cantrill and Roll 1971).

The tendency to separate one's personal fate from societal conditions appear to be deeply rooted culturally. There are, of course, conditions, including mass unemployment, inflation, and the threat of war, that can have a deep impact on the everyday feelings of well-being of average Americans. Moreover, the tendency to make this separation varies among different sectors of the American population. Those experiencing economic strain are likely to feel personally pessimistic and to see their private troubles as having some connection with societal conditions. Still, several generations of commentators on American culture have noted the degree to which Americans tend to see difficulties—including unemployment—as the result of personal rather than societal failure. In the seventies, Americans across the ideological spectrum and in all classes became increasingly dissatisfied with government and other public institutions, with the quality of public life, the state of the economy, and the international situation. Yet, on the average, such dissatisfactions were not, in themselves, spurs to political involvement since they were typically defined as remote in their effects on personal welfare.

Moreover, even when people are dissatisfied with features of their own lives that they link to larger societal or institutional conditions, such dissatisfactions are not very good predictors of "happiness." Campbell et al. remark that "dissatisfaction with one aspect of life can apparently be made up for in straightforward fashion with other satisfactions" (p. 79). Indeed, these researchers find that the domains of life most relevant to overall well-being are marriage and family and the quality and availability of leisure. Dissatisfaction at the workplace may be compensated by achieving well-being at home rather than by efforts to change working conditions. Dissatisfaction with conditions in one's community can be solved by various ways of "getting away from it all" (ranging from vacations to moving out) rather than by efforts to improve the neighborhood.

Here then is a broad generalization that seems to summarize a good deal of systematic and impressionistic data: When Americans are dissatisfied, insofar as they believe that they are free to find solutions or solace in personal life, they will try to do so. The evidence is that beliefs in the availability of such freedom are widespread.

ALIENATION VS. FREEDOM IN EVERYDAY EXPERIENCE

IN GENERAL, individual Americans seek satisfaction and meaning within the framework of their daily lives. They tend to interpret threats to their well-being as either within their individual control or beyond any control. When such threats are perceived, the typical American responds by seeking personal relief, individual solutions, or private escape.

A long tradition of cultural criticism argues that industrial capitalism inherently destroys the capacity of individuals to find such meaning and fulfillment in everyday life. I have already referred to Marx's demonstration that the workings of capitalist political economy generate structures of dependency and conditions of insecurity that prevent capitalist society from providing the material basis for the personal liberty it promises. In addition, of course, Marx emphasized that intrinsic to capitalist social relations was *alienation*—the structured inability of individuals to control the conditions and consequences of their labor; the inability of individuals, so long as they acted within the terms of capitalist society, to achieve community. Alienating conditions required by the division of labor, by class domination, by competition, are further exacerbated by the massive destruction of traditional sources of meaning and by the massive dislocations wrought by industrialization. The result of these structural and dynamic forces for the individual in everyday life was not only economic insecurity and impoverishment, but also an impoverishment of the spirit—the frustration of potentials for creativity, for sensuality, for love.

Similar criticisms of the psychic costs and cultural degradations of capitalism and industrialism have of course come from non-Marxian traditions as well. The Romantic critique, expressed in art, literature, and sociology, is one such critical stress; psychoanalysis, understood as a critique of the social constraints on individual expression, is another.

In recent years, a steady flow of books, generally synthesizing these intellectual traditions, have tended to argue that everyday life of contemporary Americans is fraught with anxiety, isolation, and emptiness, and that, in an effort to escape this emotional wasteland, people engage in a desperate scramble for commodities, status, false gods, and narcotizing pleasure. All available modes of relief, it is argued, tend to be controlled and packaged by corporate or state bureaucracies. Thus, all available personal means for resolving troubles are bound to be inauthentic and unfulfilling, since activity and symbols that have genuine personal meaning cannot by definition come in standardized packages. Furthermore, the very quest for individual satisfaction ends up increasing personal dependency on centralized bureaucracies and reinforcing their control over society. The steady increase in symptoms of personal disorder—crime, divorce, mental illness, drug use—indicates the disintegration of everyday life and the unfulfilling character of bureaucratically controlled consumption. The titles of well-known works in this genre summarize the thesis: *Escape from Free-*

dom, The Lonely Crowd, The Pursuit of Loneliness, One-Dimensional Man, The Culture of Narcissism.

Such social criticism has been deservedly influential. It has led many Americans to reflect on the society and its institutions and on their own lives. There can be little doubt that the main developmental trends in contemporary society—industrialization, urbanization, the competitive drive for profits, technocratic planning, bureaucratization and professionalization of "human services"—all embody logics whose converging impact on everyday life have many of the effects diagnosed by these critical traditions. But the assumption that these logics are the only forces setting the terms and conditions of everyday life tends to make the activity of the mass of Americans appear profoundly irrational. For, despite the assumed "emptiness" of everyday life, Americans persist in trying to live their lives as private persons rather than hoping and acting for a new world. Indeed, some cultural critics conclude that the continuing commitment of Americans to their everyday lives, rather than to historical transformation, is proof that democracy is an illusory project. If people will not refuse to live in the alienating and unfulfilling circumstances they "obviously" inhabit, than the prospects for self-government have come to an end.

It is possible, however, to draw quite different conclusions from the American experience. If we begin with the assumption that individual commitment to everyday life may be rationally grounded and that the struggle to make such life has historical ramifications, we may find ourselves compelled to question the appropriateness of the prevailing critique of everyday existence. Such a reexamination requires, however, a more intimate appreciation of everyday experience than has been typical of the cultural critics.

There can be little doubt that "alienating work" is a fundamental feature of the lives of vast numbers of Americans. Much work is so routine and boring that it cannot provide even minimal opportunities for self-expression. Millions labor at jobs that are physiclly deleterious or that require major risk to health. Millions work in situations in which they are treated like children, degraded by bosses, exploited without much chance to express grievance. Millions have jobs that are decidely insecure. Many white-collar, professional, and managerial workers, whose salaries and physical working conditions are comfortable, are highly stressed by pressures from competition, supervisors, burdens of responsibility. Since work occupies the major part of one's working day, and since our culture links self-worth to the status of one's occupation, people are certainly preoccupied with their jobs and the troubles they encounter there. Only a relative few find their work a source of primary meaning and identity. Professionals and craftsmen, executives and entrepreneurs who have a large measure of control over the nature, timing, and circumstances of their work are likely to find it intrinsically rewarding and self-realizing. Those large masses of workers who lack opportunities for self-expression and pleasure on the job are very unlikely to experience their work in these terms.

Still, about 80 percent of workers tell survey researchers that they would continue their present work even if they did not need to work for wages; the vast number of studies of worker morale generally find that workers have something positive to say about their jobs (Veroff et al. 1984:242–329). In short, accommodation rather than rebellion is the most typical orientation of people to their work situation. How is such accommodation accomplished?

First, workers make use of any available space, time, and opportunity on the job to exercise control over conditions so that the work can be more pleasant, so that time can be freed, so that physical pressures can be re-lived, so that moments of pleasure or relaxation can be seized. Wherever possible individuals, and more usually informal work-groups, undertake nonauthorized rearrangement of their jobs. Such activity constitutes a fundamental everyday means to offset alienation and therefore to live within it.

Second, of course, workers organize more formally in unions to protect interests and rights. The average union member may rarely participate actively in the organization, but the existence of a union contract and griev-ance machinery provides some buffers between the worker and the au-thoritarian and exploitative employer, thereby permitting accommodation.

Third, job mobility is a form of accommodation—insofar as workers be-lieve that they have some opportunity to move and view their current work situation as only temporary, they can more easily make a psychological accommondation to it than if they were convinced that they were perma-nently locked in. Such beliefs are widespread among workers, especially those most objectively "alienated."

The unfreedoms and degradations of the workplace are thus to some degree offset by forms of everyday self-assertion, resistance, and escape that enable workers to be simultaneously freer in and more accommodating to the work situation than they might otherwise be expected to be. But a more fundamental way of adapting to alienating work is to view it as part of a necessary tradeoff: workers in the United States have been willing to exchange lack of meaning and control in the job for the wherewithal to expand their freedom in the nonworking side of life.

The evidence for this tradeoff comes from many sources. One such source is systematic research on worker attitudes. A particularly suggestive study is Sennett and Cobb's *Hidden Injuries of Class*. Their basic argument is that blue-collar workers are able to defend themselves against the potentially destructive psychic effects of having low status jobs and working in degrading circumstances by internalizing the view that their hard work has definite payoffs. Some workers understand their hard work as a form of honorable self-sacrifice, undertaken so that their children will be free of the very burdens that they have had to bear. Earnings from the sweat of one's brow enable one's children to have the education that will qualify them for work that will be freer, more meaningful, more respected. For others, particularly younger workers, the tradeoff is more immediate: the job enables one to buy the means of a life of personal freedom, to obtain the package of goods that enables oneself and one's family to have some space and opportunity for self-chosen pleasure and expression.

The same conclusion can be drawn from understanding the behavior of industrial unions, especially during the thirty years after World War II. In that period unions focused their demands not on conditions in the workplace but on ensuring that wages rose with the cost of living, and that members were entitled to expanding fringe benefits. Long-term contracts were signed that were designed to enable union members to participate as consumers with some security of income. These same contracts restricted workers' capacity to protest workplace conditions by banning "wildcat" strikes and job actions, and by establishing a bureaucratic grievance machinery in place of spontaneous on-the-job protest.

The tradeoff institutionalized in the collective bargaining strategies of industrial unions reflected and reinforced the situation of workers in general in the postwar era. Insofar as the job is a means to an end—the end being a personal life of some security and freedom—then unfreedom on the job is not a primary issue. Under these terms, "alienation from work" becomes both a literal reality and a form of liberty: I don't have to give myself to the job, because I find myself in the time and space I have away from it.

But, argue the critics of American culture, workers ought to find their nonwork time as alienating and empty as their work time. Leisure is dominated by centrally controlled and stultifying mass media. Opportunities for authentic sociability and community are lost in the impersonality of urban life and poisoned by obsessive status anxiety, while suburban blandness breeds boredom and conformity. Bureaucratization of services and commodification of culture rob families of meaningful social functions, but family relations are overloaded with emotional burdens derived from the frustrations and anxieties that are experienced by members as they face the larger world. Confusion and contradiction plague the culture, coherent value systems disintegrate, and the result is that individuals cannot find adequate purpose for their obligations and routines. Thus, the critics declare, daily life is experienced as stultifying, and even the ordinary joys of love, sex, child-rearing, and friendship become problematic.

There is truth in these diagnoses, but they are dangerously one-sided. Dangerous because they leave us with no way to explain why working and middle-class Americans remain committed to their everyday lives. How can so many commit themselves to an existence so pervaded by boredom, anxiety, absurdity, stultification? Cultural criticism of the sort I cite leads us to think that Americans can only be understood as suffering from some form of mass pathology—e.g., authoritarianism, "other-directedness," "one-dimensionality," "narcissism." Yet if the "American character" is defined by such themes then the prospect for democracy are dim indeed.

What the critics of everyday life do not sufficiently appreciate is the enormously broad range of opportunities Americans have elaborated for sustaining individual identity and for achieving emotional repair, relaxation, pleasure, and escape. Postwar American history cannot be understood without grasping the degree to which the pain and boredom of daily work and the strains and suffocations of family intimacy have been made bearable by an expanding array of opportunity for personal expression and choice. If people do not experience themselves as unfree, it is not because they are sheep or robots, but because they believe that they have some time, space, and resources free from necessity and constraint to make lives for themselves. Liberty in one's labor may be lost, but liberty can be found again by using the resources gained from working.

The critics of consumer society argue that much of the freedom of choice people think they have is merely the freedom to buy commodities of dubious value to satisfy needs that have been artificially created by giant corporations. In consumer society, needs and the means to their fulfillment are packaged and sold. But, these critics say, authentic needs for self-expression and community cannot be fulfilled by gadgets, nor can people experience their authentic needs when advertising and marketing efforts continuously exacerbate feelings of unfulfillment. Such criticism, however, usually misses the ways in which the consumer package serves as the material basis for a pervasive sense of personal liberty. The suburban home and its built-in technology, the car and the recreation vehicle, the TV and stereo all share a common attribute—they are instruments of individual independence and choice.

House and yard provide a strong sense of private free space within which household members can lead their lives without being scrutinized by outsiders. In the Southern California suburban tract where I live, this sense of privacy is extreme. Houses lack a front porch, but do have a big backyard and patio screened by fences and foliage from any possibility of visual intrusion. Families can engage in recreation out of doors without unwanted observation from the street, feeling free to control when and with whom to have sociable contact. Home laundry facilities make it unnecessary to adapt one's schedule to a commercial establishment; kitchens contain storage and refrigeration space to accommodate an enormous choice of food. In the living room or "family room" a home entertainment center contains all manner of equipment permitting a considerable range of choice for entertainment, escape and esthetic appreciation. The advent of video tapes, compact discs, and cable programming greatly expands the opportunity to select virtually any item of popular or serious culture, including the simulation of experiences that until now required going out to the movie house, theater, stadium, museum, or concert hall. Thus the fully equipped suburban home provides a framework for living that fundamentally threatens the possibility of public life, sheltering its inhabitants from much raw experience and broad human contact. But it is crucial to understand it also as a space whose attractions include a sense of safety and security and also a sense of control and choice. As the range of cultural experiences available at home broadens, so increasingly does home consumption serve as a primary mode of self-expression—exercised through the tastes one cultivates in books, records, and video, in home decoration and food. Such cultivation not only defines and expresses identity but also provides some deep pleasure, relaxation, and relief.

For every tract home there is at least one car and often other vehicles—an RV, a camper or van, a motorcyle, a boat. These permit a feeling of physical freedom and mobility unprecedented in history. Motor vehicles give one the chance to go wherever one wishes at any time— and the camper permits travel with a high degree of self-sufficiency. To go at high speed at one's will, traveling with the necessary means of survival, is certainly a way to fulfill the idea of liberty—and to acquire the means to do this is certainly an incentive to submit to some measure of alienating routine.

The seductive power of the consumer package lies in the fact that house, car, and related equipment are both symbolic and real means to realize the cultural promise of personal freedom, independence, privacy, and choice. But standardized consumption provides only limited materials for the formation and maintenance of identity and only momentary escape from inevitable troubles, pain, and grief.

For more than a century, cultural critics have emphasized the ways in which the conditions of the modern world erode traditional frameworks for defining individual meanings. Traditional reliance on sacred grounds and transcendental purposes is undermined by prevailing principles of scientific, bureaucratic, and economic rationality as guides to action and evaluation. The decline of the traditional and the sacred results in a yawning vacuum of meaning. This vacuum cannot be filled by the promise of individual liberty—freedom to be oneself is vacuous if one lacks a coherent conception of who one is or what one is living for.

Some cultural critics have thought that secular ideologies of social commitment—ideologies that enable people to define themselves as active contributors to a larger collectivity—would provide the way for "modern man" to fill the void of meaning. Yet Americans in the main have not tended to organize their identities in terms of collective participation or ideological commitment. That neither traditional belief nor secular commitment animate the lives of average Americans provides further reinforcement for the view that everyday life in the United States is "empty."

Such criticism unquestionably dramatizes the dark and problematic side of American culture—warning that, in this culture, individuals can find liberty but not purpose, and that, accordingly, life is experienced as disorder and drift. Cultural emphasis on personal liberty as an ideal and on possessive and competitive individualism as principles of social organization help set the stage for what Durkheim called "anomie"—the disintegration of social norms and standards. Rapid social change, continuous mobility, persistent value conflicts, the relativization of moral beliefs, the structured isolation of personal life—these are the sorts of social conditions that promote anomie. Generations of sociologists since Durkheim have used this insight to interpret and predict increasing rates of social and personal disorder (crime, suicide, and alcoholism, mental illness, rebellious youth, divorce, political extremism, religious fanaticism) as traceable to "anomie."

The American preoccupation with liberty certainly does foster isolation, aimlessness, the breakdown of controls. But the ideal of liberty implies another possibility—namely that individuals can create out of the enormous confusion their own identities. "Identity" is the individualist answer to "anomie." It may be defined as the achievement of a sense of one's own uniqueness, coherently integrated with a sense of connectedness to a tradition or a collectivity. Cultural critics tend to underestimate the extent to which the very conditions for anomie they have identified impel people to seize opportunities to find identity and, by so doing, renew their commitment to their personal lives.

Erik Erikson was the first to systematically explore identity formation as a critical moment in the life course. He argued that "identity crisis"—the sense of disorder, drift, and confusion about who and why one is—is a normal developmental experience, occurring in late adolescence. The crisis provides the person with the opportunity to find a unique social place responsive to his or her needs, suitable for his or her energies and talents. Not to have such a crisis is to lose the chance for personal growth and self-realization. Identity crisis may be painful in the extreme, but its successful resolution is the source of social creativity and coherent personal meaning. Erikson thought that the primary basis for identity lay in vocational choice; to the extent that youths are provided with time, space, and opportunity to choose a life's work that most suits them, social conditions for identity crisis are created—as well as the social basis for individuation and adult self-realization.

The expansion of mass higher education in our society has extended the privilege of role experimentation (once possible only for a narrow upper-class elite) to a large proportion of youth. One result has been that a far wider stratum of the population seeks, and expects to find, "meaningful" identity-relevant work. Thus, despite the "degradation of labor," millions aspire to, and to some degree obtain, careers around which identity is formed and sustained and through which life is given purpose and coherence. Moreover, in addition to the career-oriented college-educated sector, there remain at least a residue of workers who find central purpose in their craft or work situation experienced as authentic expressions of self.

But job and home are, for most, unlikely to be adequate bases for crystallization and maintenance of identity. A repeated, and surprising, theme in my interviews was the extent to which people are engaged in one or more "leisure time" activities that provide, for them, that sense of uniqueness combined with social connectedness that constitutes identity.

One such framework was religious involvement. Among those we interviewed there were several who found central meaning in religion—particularly in such nonconventional sects and cults as the Divine Light Mission and various Christian sects; there happened to be no respondents for whom membership in an established church served as a primary locus for identity. We found, in our interviews, a reflection of the enormous proliferation of "new" religious forms in the late sixties and seventies.

These "new" religious forms have few beliefs in common. What all do provide is the opportunity to choose one's own path to salvation and to make intimate connection with a group of caring others. Of course, one is more likely to convert to a religious form that in some way resonates with the cultural traditions in which one has been reared or that appears relevant to one's immediate troubles and dilemmas. For a great many, the experience of conversion may be only temporary; there are a large number of more or less perpetual seekers, who move among a variety of groups, doctrines, and disciplines. The proliferation of new religious forms thus restores and reinforces a sense of personal freedom while providing opportunities for social connectedness unavailable in the course of daily routine. Involvement in unconventional religious expression may thus be viewed as a critique of established institutions and a kind of protest against conditions of everyday life embodied in jobs, household, and material consumption. But the new religious freedom helps recommit people to their everyday lives. It demonstrates to troubled people that "personal solutions" are available, that they have the option to remake themselves.

Religious innovation is one example of a more general phenomenon of our time: the enormous expansion in the range and vitality of options for personal expression and identity. This elaboration is energized by pervasive restlessness with the routines and constraints of daily life, by the emptiness and loneliness that looms within established institutional arrangements and conventional life-styles. The quest for alternatives is made possible by the free time and disposable income available to individuals. The options that are created derive in part from conscious collective action and "bottom up" initiative and in part from efforts of cultural entrepreneurs inventive enough to capitalize on popular intiative to form new organizations, develop new products, create new symbols.

Athletics provide another set of arenas for the revitalization of everyday life. The last decade witnessed an explosion of sports participation well beyond the established, relatively passive spectator involvement with big-time professional games. Traditional participation sports such as tennis, golf, and sandlot baseball all increased in popularity—but to them have been added a variety of newer one—racketball, volleyball, and skiing being examples. Enthusiasm for physical fitness grew to seemingly obsessive levels of intensity—thousands in any given community were likely to have taken up regular jogging, swimming, bicycling, working out. To these may be added the growing involvement in outdoor activities like camping, hiking, and backpacking; recreational adventuring with motorcycles, sailboats, hang-gliders, and the like. Finally, in any given community, thousands of youngsters are involved in highly organized baseball, football, basketball, soccer, and wrestling leagues, in gymnastic and swim teams—activities that intensively engage parents and other adults as well as children. In all of these cases, the activity as such is the core of what is typically a very elaborate pattern of related activity, including participation in social support groups, subscribing to special interest magazines, the purchasing of relevant equipment and clothing. Even an activity like jogging, which at first glance appears simple, self-oriented, unadorned, has proliferated an enormous array of special clothing, magazines, books, and collective rituals.

Thus, seemingly peripheral leisure activities become the center of what amount to subcultures, as initiatives and innovations undertaken by individuals or small groups become structured or commercialized by organizational and business entrepreneurs. These avocational subcultures in turn become significant foci of involvement and identity for many. They provide activities that give shape to everyday life and opportunities for social con-

nectedness, friendship, and intimacy. In our interviews, many kinds of av-
ocations in addition to religion and sports were mentioned by respondents
as providing similar kinds of focus and direction; for example, gardening,
Esperanto, volunteer social service, cooking, adult education, bird watching.

Alongside the proliferation of life-centering religious and avocational groups
and activities, there has been a parallel diversification of options for finding
release, relaxation, and pleasure in ways that take people out of their daily
routine while renewing their commitment to the private sphere. These
range from forms of home entertainment and sociability to expensive and
elaborately planned sorts of consumption, entertainment, and travel. Re-
finements of taste and pleasure once reserved for aristocratic or bohemian
elites are now readily accessible to the millions. Handbooks and magazines
instruct in precise detail on how to achieve gourmet tastes in food, wine,
and sex; exotic experience in remote places; aesthetic decoration of home
and body. Further help on such matters can be obtained from myriads of
specialists in instruction and facilitation.

Elaboration of options for pleasure and refinement is paralleled by proliferation of technical methods for overcoming distress, pain, physical and
psychic inadequacy. Until recently, there were only limited means available
to most for curing or coping with physical or psychological distress; these
were embodied in the professional domains of physician, priest, or psy-
chiatrist, and those who did not take their curable troubles to a professional
were thought to be backward. In the past decade or so the diversification
and accessibility of therapeutic options have grown enormously. This growth
undoubtedly reflects considerable grassroots dissatisfaction with institutionalized therapeutic means—but it also has come about through the in-
ventiveness of therapeutic entrepreneurs capitalizing on this dissatisfaction.

The quest for therapy reflects the psychic distress of daily life. The
therapy seeker refuses to be resigned to that distress and searches for
techniques for daily coping. An essential message of the new therapies is
that one need not be captive to the physical pain or psychic inadequacy
one routinely experiences, nor need one define these troubles as illnesses
requiring the ministrations of remote and costly professionals. Instead, these
therapies say that the solutions to chronic feelings of inadequacy are available directly to the person through techniques of self-regeneration or
awareness that can be incorporated into the routines of daily life—for example, meditation, dietary changes, physical regimes, counselling, mas-
sage, sexual regimens. Like the other cultural innovations I have mentioned, the therapeutic elaboration resonates with the libertarian ideal,
fostering the sense that opportunities for freedom and self-determinantion

are expanding, while simultaneously instructing that both the sources and solutions to daily trouble are located in the problems of and potentials for making one's own life.

During the three decades after the end of World War II, then, the great majority of Americans found it practical and possible to find fulfillment and to cope effectively with troubles within the terms and conditions of their private lives. Economic growth, coupled with the supports of the welfare state and the union contract, enabled those in the great middle to feel that they could reliably provide for the necessities of family maintenance over the long term. Job security and rising real wages, in addition, enabled workers to acquire those consumer goods that served as tools for the expansion of personal freedom and the construction of personal space that felt self-determined. Moreover, rather than settle for the already packaged identity kits provided by mass media and established cultural institutions, millions of Americans explored the steadily expanding variety of alternatives for self-expression that proliferated in the sixties and seventies. The political apathy and conservatism of the fifties resulted, in large part, from the mass discovery of everyday possibility. But rather than presaging the age of mass conformity expected by critical intellectuals, this mass quest for personal fulfillment led to a surprising cultural pluralism. And, despite efforts by mass media to channel and commercialize this quest, many were able to find "authentic" modes of self-expression by pursuing avocational alternatives. Until the postwar period, it had not been possible for the great majority of Americans to believe that they could fulfill those cultural prescriptions that defined the good life in terms of the exercise of personal liberty and individual responsibility. Now, for the first time, there was a material basis for wholehearted acceptance of such prescriptions and Americans were accordingly, more likely than ever to commit themselves to the making of their lives, rather than to the making or remaking of the society.

The strength of such commitment began to be tested by the middle of the seventies. Inflation was undermining the returns from working at alienating jobs, thus eroding the promise of fulfillment through material consumption. Declining investment in the public sector severely restricted the previously expanding market for college graduates interested in education, social service, and intellectually oriented kinds of work—thereby reducing access to what many young people had assumed were the most intrinsically meaningful and self-expressive career paths. The "energy crisis" reduced the utility of the private car as a means to liberating physical mobility. It was becoming progressively harder for many to afford the very goods, entertainment, and services that had been regarded as major means for obtaining freedom, identity, pleasure, and relief in daily life.

Americans' reactions to the economic crises of the last several years testify to the ingenuity embedded in our culture for restoring the habitability of the everyday world. Although, as we shall see, deterioration in the opportunities for everyday fulfillment stimulated new levels of political mobilization, true to form the typical ways people coped with economic pressures in the seventies involved further innovation in everyday life patterns rather than resort to political action. To illustrate:

■ There was an expansion of the secondhand economy. In flea markets, swap mets, secondhand stores, and bartering were found means to acquire, affordably, what might otherwise have been inaccessible. Moreover, many came to regard the second hand as more stylish than the new.

■ Recycling, home insulation, bicycle riding, and other energy conservation efforts may have been necessary adaptations to skyrocketing energy costs; it was, however, remarkable how frequently such activities were said be more fulfilling, more happiness creating than the wasteful and indulgent lifestyles that had previously prevailed.

■ As the dangers of rape and mugging became increasingly terrifying, many learned the arts of self-defense, both in hope of coping with the menace of the streets, and also to improve their self-esteem and their bodies in the process.

■ As human service jobs for young adults with college degrees became scarce many took odd and menial work, hoping to enjoy freedom from the rat race. Alternatively, many decided to join the rat race, finding that they enjoyed the competitive "game." "Maturity," it was said, must replace youthful "idealism."

■ As housing prices threatened the newly married couple's ability to afford a place to live, many found ways to share housing and enjoy the benefits of collective living.

Thus, one of the remarkable features of the seventies was the extent to which middle-class people were able to find personal gratification both in spite and because of inflation, energy crisis, and unemployment. That many could make a virtue out of the necessary reductions in living standards they faced was in large part traceable to the ways that the counterculture of the sixties had made simplicity, non-striving, and sharing high ideals—a frame of mind that became more functional for the society in the seventies than it had been during the apparent affluence of the previous decade.

Such values were of course far more likely to be attractive to people who had already come to feel that conventional middle-class lifestyles were

For example, a central assumption of American culture is represented by the ideal of liberty—that people ought to be free to make their own lives. Average Americans assume this right as they go about their day, assert this right in the way they use time and interpret responsibility for their problems. Liberty is a taken-for-granted dimension of private existence—but it is also a political demand. Each individual, acting on the assumption that liberty exists, is asserting that the state must protect, and not infringe upon, personal freedom. In the United States, political guarantees of liberty are explicitly chartered in the Bill of Rights, restricting the state's authority to invade the sphere of personal life and expression, and in the whole structure of laws and provisions by which the state undertakes to protect the life, property, and space of individual citizens from the transgressions of others. Moreover, the state claims to provide for the national defense against foreign efforts to invade or injure Americans' liberty. Thus daily life in this society assumes a political structure protecting liberty. Each individual inhabits some free space in the present that was won in the past by citizens struggling against authority, demanding rights, exercising political initiative—in the name of winning and securing liberty.

Liberty is not the only residue of past political conflict embodied in everyday life. American history is a rich record of widespread and often militant popular demands for the state to go beyond protection of liberty by intervening in civil society so that unpropertied and disadvantaged millions would have increased chances to live stable everyday lives. The demand that state power be used to advance equality as well as liberty has been expressed in struggles to limit the power of economic dominants to enslave or exploit workers (e.g., abolitionism, struggle for the eight-hour day, for child and female labor laws); to seek limits on economic power that threaten the well-being of farmers, small businessmen, and consumers; to establish state protection of the rights of workers to organize; to extend the franchise to politically deprived groups such as women and Southern blacks; to achieve state provision of social insurance and social wages to protect groups unable to obtain adequate income in the labor market and to support the survival of people harmed by large-scale economic change; and, finally, to pressure the state to shape the market itself to ensure economic growth, prevent unemployment, reduce inflation, promote prosperity. In all of these campaigns for reform, large numbers of people, usually immersed in individual struggles for personal survival, put aside their everyday routines —and indeed often risked their well-being and their lives—to participate in a variety of collective historical struggles. It is a characteristic of everyday life that we take for granted its context, inescapably forgetting all the while that others have risked and sacrificed their lives so that history would be turned in a direction that enables us, now, to live.

It is useful to imagine that the cumulative effect of past political struggles has been to create a (largely implicit) "sociocultural charter"—a set of rights (including ones less explicitly guaranteed than those in the Bill of Rights) that belong to each of us in exchange for our conformity with certain rules and social obligations. Insofar as this charter is operating as it should, and entitlements are appropriately balanced with individual responsibility, then the established structure of authority is accorded a high degree of legitimacy, and the mood of the people appears to be conservative and acquiescent. The majority, under these conditions, tend to take for granted the possibility of a reasonable daily life, immerse themselves in private space, experience history as a realm apart. A fundamental irony then of American history, therefore, is that the popular conservatism and privatism of the present is made possible by the popular radicalism and collective protest of the past.

This time-honored notion of the social contract (or "cultural charter") helps summarize the melange of promises and demands that form the content of political rhetoric. Since the charter is not written down, and since little systematic social research has been done to map its contents, an effort to define what it may contain at any given time necessarily involves speculative interpretation. We can attempt to "read" surveys, election results, and the totality of political activity in such a way as to find plausible answers to questions like the following: What, on the average, do people believe the boundaries of their liberty ought to be? What conditions of their existence ought to be subject to their choice or voice? What do they believe they are entitled to with respect to economic opportunity and security? What do they believe can legitimately be expected of the government and other institutions with respect to the protection of liberty and security? What do they believe they can legitimately be expected to do in return for such protections? How do these beliefs and expectations vary in different sectors of the population?

THE POSTWAR CHARTER

I HAVE suggested that since World War II everyday life for the majority of Americans has been organized around several possible kinds of tradeoffs. Certain kinds of constraints and unfreedoms are accepted because they are expected to provide definite opportunities for personal freedom and security. The tradeoffs undertaken by traditional blue- and white-collar wage workers are different from those sought by the college educated:

■ Members of the industrial and white-collar working class are willing to accept onerous, unfree working conditions in return for incomes that provide resources adequate for a sense of freedom in leisure time and the means to provide opportunity for upward mobility (i.e., more freedom) for one's offspring.

■ The college educated on the other hand expect careers that provide work that is intrinsically meaningful and self-expressive. In return for such career opportunity there is acceptance of responsibility (increasing over the course of the career) for the functioning of the institutions within which the career is embedded, and a willingness to submit to meritocratic competition for position and status.

These personal tradeoffs are at the core of contemporary political and institutional stability in the United States. Seeing everyday life and personal aspiration in terms of these sorts of tradeoffs is, for me, the most plausible way of explaining the apparent role conformity and political acquiescence pervasive in the middle and working classes. It is not that people are trying to "escape from freedom," or have become "robotized," but that they accept a degree of subordination as practically necessary if they are to have the means to maintain some space and opportunity in their lives for freedom and meaning. That this, on the whole, has seemed to work is, of course, what drives home the practicality of such choices.

It is crucial to see, however, that these tradeoffs embody a set of political expectations. In order for the tradeoffs to work for individuals, the system as a whole has to provide the material basis for their expectations to be realized. What are these political expectations?

If workers submit to alienating jobs in order to be able to participate effectively as consumers, then they expect as a necessary condition of their political acquiescence that there will be job security, growth in real wages, or in social benefits that maintain and improve income, and educational opportunity that permits upward mobility for their offspring.

If college-educated workers expect career opportunities and the chance to compete for meaningful work, then they expect that the political economy will provide an adequate number of jobs commensurate with their training.

In short, the terms by which the majority of workers in postward America organize their daily lives depend on the system's capacity to sustain economic growth that supports full employment, an adequately funded structure of social benefits, and an expanding investment in activities that provide career opportunities for those with technical and professional training.

These expectations derive from the political struggles of the past that sought state protection of daily life. Most immediately, they derive from

the political experience of the thirties. The Great Depression destroyed
the belief that the private economy would automatically ensure progress
in improving the conditions of daily life. Massive and militant protest by
industrial workers forced a recognition among political and corporate elites
that fundamental reforms in state policy and a fundamentally different governing ideology were needed to prevent rending social upheaval. As a result, a new political synthesis—the New Deal—was achieved that legitimated the expectation that the state would actively organize the economy
to provide protection for everyday life.

But it was really the postwar economic boom that permitted delivery on
the promises of the New Deal. Economic growth after World War II, fueled
by postwar recovery, by the unchallenged global position of U.S. corporations, by the permanent war economy, generated relatively full employment, steady increase in real wages, a fiscal dividend for increased social
benefits, and massive state investments in higher education, scientific research, and other activity that greatly expanded career opportunities for
technically and professionally educated people. New Deal ideology con-
verged with the economic power of the giant corporations and the growth
of the defense establishment so that, culturally and structurally, the expectations of full employment, an expanded welfare state, and expanding
career opportunities were made practical possibilities.

The postwar political economy provided not only a degree of security
never before available to average Americans, but also forms of personal
freedom that most had not imagined to be within their grasp. Three major
social developments helped expand the material base for personal freedom:
the development of affordable private homes in the suburbs, the availability
of the private car as the primary mode of personal travel, and the expansion of mass higher education. These developments permitted individual
workers and their families to experience a sense of private space and personal choice in daily life. Each of these developments was made possible
by major innovations in state policy: government credit programs for home
ownership, federal investment in a massive interstate highway system, and
large state and federal investment in higher education.

For millions of working- and middle-class people, the contrast between
the fifties and the thirties was nothing short of miraculous. Having experienced in the depression a situation in which personal security and freedom seemed permanently out of reach, they found available after the war
a set of opportunities for safe and decent daily life previously unimagined.
For many, this contrast justified the pain and sacrifice of the depression
and war years, and the boredom and alienation they found in their postwar
work.

Such feelings help account for the surprising decline in labor militancy in the years after the war. In most of the major industries once volatile labor forces agreed to long-term contracts with the major corporations that established a new era of relative industrial stability. These contracts provided substantial guarantees of union members' ability to participate in the burgeoning consumer society. Cost-of-living escalator clauses enabled wages to rise with inflation. Health, pension, vacation, and unemployment benefits added significantly to workers' security and freedom off the job. It was characteristic of these contracts that they traded away many of the forms of shop floor control that workers had developed to protect themselves against harsh supervision, excessive work pressures, and unsafe conditions. Also characteristic of these contracts was that unions agreed to support increased worker productivity by preventing wildcat strikes and slow-downs, enforcing contract specifications about work rates, and, most important, by accepting technological developments that increased worker ouput (thereby reducing employment opportunities in the industry). In effect, the postwar labor contract represented an arrangement in which workers gave up much of their ability and interest in controlling daily working conditions and accepted job subordination in return for the means to greater freedom and security off the job.

Thus, industrial workers' ability to live for themselves in the fifties was made possible by their earlier willingness to act collectively in order to affect the course of history. This victory, however, had major costs. The improved living standards of industrial workers were financed by their improved productivity and by the ability of the large corporations to pass on the cost of wage increases in the form of higher prices (an ability made possible by the monopolistic position these corporations had on the world market). Productivity gains in many industries resulted in shrinkage in the number of available industrial jobs. As a result, millions of new workers had much less chance to work in unionized factories and were forced to accept lower wage, less secure jobs in more marginal sectors of the economy. The gains made by unionized workers led to their individual privatization. These gains were implemented not at the expense of the dominant class, but by passing on their costs to weaker strata and to future generations. In this way, individual privatization was mirrored in and reinforced by the policies and politics of the industrial unions—by their decline as agencies of general social reform, by their transformation into instruments of narrow group interest.

The effort to stabilize social relations and legitimate authority by recognizing certain rights to everyday freedom and security means that when the system delivers the expected goods to strategically located groups, it appears enormously durable and unassailable, "one-dimensional" and conservative. But that same set of promises, when unfulfilled, sets the stage for potentially far-reaching erosion in legitimacy. Legitimation grounded on the *performance* of those in authority, and particularly on the way that performance affects the experience of people in their everyday lives, is therefore highly contingent. When that performance is effective, the majority will go about the making of their lives, trading role conformity and political acquiescence for the going definition of personal well-being. Such majorities, organized in this way, are likely to be economically productive and tend to grant elites rather wide leeway to pursue predatory goals. In such times, social critics are appalled at the moral callousness, the lack of democratic initiative, the selfishness, prevailing in the citizenry. Such critics try to awaken popular consciousness to the dangers inherent in leaving history making to elites and to the specific depredations and depravities of those wielding power. But the imperviousness of the many to such prophesying can seem terribly monolithic.

This situation is not new; in one form or another we can find it recurring in social life throughout history; the Bible itself is a rich source of documentation of the interplay between a self-centered people and their impotent prophets. The postwar era in the United States was a particularly dramatic case, since the kind of historical power delegated to elites by the people included the capacity to terminate history itself, while the kind of everyday life being made by the people seemed particularly self-centered.

But a full understanding of this situation requires a dialectical perspective. Those self-centered "masses," by opting out of history, are sending a mixed message to history-making elites. The message is that we will let you alone if you leave us alone. For commitment to everyday life in our time rests on the assumption that history will be made so that our daily lives can be lived. Accordingly, it is not only the preachments of prophets that are ignored but also the shouting of patrioteers. Moreover (and this is the main point I have been driving at so far in this chapter) the people have learned to demand *more* than the right to be left alone to live; they have come to expect explicit performance, by the master social institutions, that facilitates the opportunity and provides the resources for everyday freedom and security. To read commitment to everyday life as simple subservience, as blind obedience, as political indifference is, therefore, to misread it. If people are committed to their accustomed lives, they are prepared to act to protect those lives. The protection of everyday life or the desire to see the promises made in the prevailing social charter concerning everyday life fulfilled can serve as the basis for opting out of history and, under certain circumstances, as the motivating force for trying to make it.

THE EROSION OF THE POSTWAR CHARTER

THE POST WAR politico-cultural charter contained some fundamental flaws, but it was not until the 1960s that these became expressed in forms of social unrest. Its most glaring deficiency was its failure to provide equal guarantees of security and freedom or an adequate basis for reasonable daily lives for blacks and other minorities and for millions of poor whites as well. For workers employed in sectors marginal to the industrial center of the economy, daily life was dependent on work that was low-wage, seasonal, highly insecure. Such jobs, provided mainly by small, localized firms in competitive, rather than oligopolized markets, were extremely difficult to unionize and provided a terrain that was most inhospitable to the kinds of union contracts possible in large industry. The competitive positions of such firms made it difficult for them to pass along costs of increased wages; the labor-intensive character of their operations made it unlikely that substantial productivity gains could be achieved. Thus, the postwar labor contracts and the broader structure of the political economy that made them possible fostered a dual-labor market; one tier of workers had the leverage and organizational power to secure their daily lives; at a lower tier were millions of unorganized workers, excluded by technological change from access to jobs in advanced industry, whose lives were characterized by very insecure employment and wages close to the subsistence level. These workers tended to be black, or whites from locales such as Appalachia that had suffered marked economic decline. Alongside the employed poor were additional millions of similar social background who could not work—single mothers and their children and the aged poor.

The black population suffered not only these sorts of economic disadvantage, but also the distinctive systematic oppression that resulted from the established structures of white supremacy and segregation. In the Southern states, the black populace was denied even the basic rights explicit in the Constitution: the right to vote, to speak, or organize politically. In the deep South, repression was enforced by a well-established structure of terror, linking police forces and private vigilante groups. Throughout the United States, blacks were subject to routine discrimination in employment and housing; in the South such discrimination was implemented by the informal practices customary in the rest of the country as well as an elaborate framework of legalized segregation in education and all forms of public accommodation—indeed in every area of daily life. Blacks in the United States after World War II were, therefore, not only excluded from the new rights to participation in the consumer society, but also from the basic constitutional rights established when the nation began. Many observers in the immediate postwar period predicted that progress in overcoming these exclusions would inevitably come, but government efforts in these directions were fitful and largely symbolic. It was difficult, until the sixties, to even hear lip-service being paid by Presidents and other top officials to the idea that barriers to black inclusion should be abolished.

That blacks were excluded from the postwar charter is obvious; women were also excluded, but in more subtle ways. At the center of the charter was the idea that freedom and fulfillment were to be found in nonwork time and space, in consumption and leisure and intimate relationships. Such assumptions obviously renewed the importance of the family and household as the center of real commitment in life. Betty Friedan's classic, *The Feminine Mystique* (Friedan 1963), documented the degree to which, in the postwar world, media, advertising, and other sources of ideology systematically encouraged the notion that women's primary role was to make the household, child-raising, and the family the center of their daily activity. Friedan argued persuasively that this ideology was not simply a continuation of traditional patriarchal perspectives. Instead, it represented a move away from feminist progress that had been occurring in earlier decades; in the twenties and thirties there had been a growing emphasis on the possibilities of career and independence for women—and in World War II millions of women took over men's work in production as husbands, brothers, and fathers went off to war. It is certainly true that many women yearned for security and stability that had been denied during the war years; the ideological promotion of the feminine mystique resonated with the feeling that the restoration of a secure and happy home was the best sign that peace had come. Moreover, the new world of consumer goods laid open by the postwar economy was undoubtedly more attractive for many women than the kinds of drudgery implied by either factory work or "old-fashioned" housework. But there can be no doubt that the postwar social arrangements provided a much more restricted range of options for working- or middle-class women that it did for men. To spend one's full time at home, largely in the company of preschool children, preoccupied by the minutiae of household maintenance, is to be denied many of the obvious forms of freedom that men could take for granted. Moreover, traditional patriarchal norms continued to prevail; thus, even in the home, the wife and mother was expected to make service to husband and children a higher priority than her own needs. To a considerable extent, the politico-cultural charter of the postwar years had as a crucial ingredient the willingness of wives to serve the everyday needs for freedom and self-expression of husbands, rather than considering their own, autonomous, interests.

The inequities built into the postwar compact became evident by the 1960s when blacks and other disadvantaged groups replaced political acquiescence and subordination with massive and militant protests. These were soon followed by the many-faceted woman's liberation movement. Both the black liberation movement and the women's movement were, in part, constituted by demands for full equality on the same terms previously achieved by white working-class and middle-class men (although both movements also embodied ideological elements that transcended the established cultural framework).

The sixties was also, of course, the decade of widespread militant protest by students and other youth. The youth revolt and the parallel emergence of a widely diffused "counterculture" among young people were signs that the postwar charter was flawed in ways other than its failure to provide equality of coverage to disadvantaged groups. Many of the youth most disposed to protest were those most positioned to take advantage of the freedom and security offered by the postwar political economy. Moreover, the content of youth protest involved a rejection of prevailing values and roles, rather than a demand for equal access to them.

Interpretations of the causes of the youth revolt are legion. But the most plausible are those that interpret generational protest as an outcome of "cultural contradiction." Such contradictions include incompatibilities between the kinds of motives and aspirations fostered in young people by socializing institutions and the opportunities for fulfillment actually available, as well as incongruities among the values promulgated by these institutions. Youth are particularly sensitive to such contradictions because they are, by definition, engaged in processes of identity formation and role selection. Gaps between cultural promise and social reality, between what one aspires to be and to feel and what one is permitted to be and feel are the source of individual crises of identity. Fundamental discrepancies between what is inculcated in the home, indoctrinated in the schools, preached in the churches, and touted in the mass media create a cultural climate of incoherence. This climate is experienced not only in the public life of society, but also in one's relations with parents, who themselves are likely to be confused and ambivalent when cultural contradictions are manifest. A culturally contradictory environment provides the catalyst for, and shapes the content of, youth protest.

The postwar charter exacerbated cultural contradictions already growing in American society.

What Max Weber called the "Protestant Ethic" is a shorthand expression for a cultural framework that emphasizes individual self-reliance, the strict regulation of personal desire and feeling, working for the future as morally necessary and as a practical means to the good life. The stress on striving through productive work, on saving and self-denial in the interest of future gain, was, as Weber pointed out, fundamental to the development of American culture. But, sociologists have believed, such values have been on the decline in the United States since the turn of the century. Intellectuals and artists protested the enormous psychic costs of puritan self-denial and the rampant hypocrisies associated with puritan morality. The development of ethnic and class-based organizations among workers provided a practical collective alternative to the cultural emphasis on individualistic self-reliance. The rise of the giant corporation made individual entrepreneurship socially marginal, thereby reducing the cultural relevance of the character types encouraged by the "Protestant Ethic." Mass emigration from small towns and rural areas to big cities brough millions of those reared in puritanism into a physical and social environment in which traditional modes of self-reliance were simply irrelevant. All of these developments, as they unfolded over the decades, eroded established frameworks of child-rearing, family socialization, indoctrination, and preachment. They created the need for a new cultural synthesis able to encompass the increasing diversity of social experience, the kinds of roles that new patterns of social organization required, and the sorts of aspirations and identities being formed. Yet, by the 1960s no such synthesis had come into being.

The post war "charter" legitimated, more fully than had previously been the case, a search for meaning and fulfillment in consumption and leisure rather than in productive work. It stressed self-expression, consuming, and spending—not self-denial, thrift, and postponement of gratification. Children raised in the postwar climate were likely to be confronted with quite contradictory messages. From the TV tube came a continuous stream of appeals to live for now, have fun, spend and indulge; in school they experienced a much more traditional set of demands for self-discipline and adherence to strait-laced morality—while parents were typically unable to be clear about how one should live. Thus, one major contradiction in the postwar "charter" was its promise of wide opportunity for free time and space for personal expression, in a cultural context in which such freedom was still treated as morally dubious and in which few materials for such expression were readily accessible.

Many young people were likely to experience other contradictions as well. For college-educated youth, there was considerable question about whether opportunities for "meaningful" careers, providing autonomy, self-expression, and responsibility, were to be as widely available as promised. By the early sixties, the quest for an authentic career had become central for young intellectuals; anti-careerism was founded on the perception that professional and intellectual work had become locked into bureaucratic organizations and tied to pecuniary rather than altruistic goals. Thus, while job opportunities for the educated were viewed as plentiful, many young people were nevertheless restless with the nature of the work offered in conventional career programs. By the late sixties it was becoming clear that the job opportunities in such fields as education, social service, scientific research, and other "knowledge industry" areas would not keep pace with the numbers trained to fill them. Meanwhile, millions of students in junior colleges and other "lower track" post-secondary educational institutions were to discover that vistas of personal choice beyond the working class were not as broad as they had been led to believe.

The most obvious threat to the everyday freedom and security of young men was, of course, the draft. For a number of years, this threat was substantially mitigated by an elaborate system of deferments and exemptions designed to "channel" career and educational choices of youth by providing preferential treatment to those who made personal choices deemed in the national interest. This state intervention into fundamental areas of private decision was largely unnoticed and unprotested until draftees began being sent to Vietnam and student deferments were threatened with elimination. Under these conditions, the contradiction between promised opportunity for freedom and fulfillment and the military priorities of the state became part of the concrete experience of millions of youth.

Thus the postwar social arrangements and the "charter" that legitimated them produced a sense of possibility in and commitment to everyday life among the majority. But those same arrangements produced a deepening sense of exclusion, constraint, and disillusionment among significant minorities. Therefore, by the sixties structural and cultural frameworks designed to establish social stability instead set the stage for new forms of upheaval, protest, and conflict.

Lyndon Johnson's "Great Society" was an attempt to maintain the established charter by expanding opportunities for excluded groups to participate in consumer society. Welfare state benefit programs were instituted to increase the social wage available to those who could not obtain adequate incomes from the labor market. Public investment in urban development was envisioned as a means to increase employment, alleviate poor living conditions, and revitalize declining sectors of the economy. Expansion of the public sector provided job opportunities both for low-income people and for large numbers of the college educated interested in education and public service. Moreover, public employees, whose incomes had, by and large, not kept pace with workers in the industrial sector, were now able to organize unions and negotiate improved incomes and benefits.

The Great Society initiatives were thought of as a culmination of the logic of the New Deal; social peace was to be reestablished by enabling members of protesting groups to acquire the material means to establish adequate conditions for everyday life. If such means could not be provided in the private sector, then the public sector could compensate through social wage entitlements and through investment in growth and employment generating activity.

The tragedy of the Great Society was that its vision could not be financed, especially while the Johnson administration was also committed to escalating the Vietnam War. Johnson's reckless effort to fund both domestic revitalization and imperial adventure contributed to the undoing of both. By the time of the 1968 election, it became evident that domestic protest could not be assuaged by relying on the framework of the established charter. The war on poverty was far too limited to quiet the discontent of the mobilized poor; the war on Vietnam far too intense to be left to the management of the national security elites. At the same time, conservative resistance to domestic reform was evidently growing. Nixon and Wallace successfully began to mobilize the anxieties of those who felt threatened by protest, by black gains, by expanding Federal programs, by countercultural challenge to traditional morality.

Some of this "backlash" had its roots in the postwar charter itself. The New Deal and the corporate-labor deal had, from the beginning, threatened the economic position of those who benefited most from low taxes and from a low-wage, high-unemployment economy. Thousands of small and medium-sized businesses were undoubtedly disadvantaged by the postwar arrangements. Millions of Americans whose outlooks were shaped by the small town, traditional religion, and the Protestant Ethic were undoubtedly uneasy in the postwar world. The sixties experience further exacerbated these anxieties, to which were added various forms of hostility to black liberation and to rebellious youth. George Wallace market-tested a revitalized right-wing rhetoric that proved surprisingly effective in mobilizing an electoral base—and Richard Nixon was the first presidential beneficiary of Wallace's initiatives.

Some conservative warnings about the social effects of "liberalism" were not only rhetorically effective in mobilizing a mass base, but were also soon validated by experience. The expanding warfare/welfare Federal budget helped spark an inflationary surge. Budgetary increases at all levels of government noticeably increased the tax burden on the middle classes. By the beginning of the seventies, disillusionment with the "government" was rampant on both the "left" and the "right." The postwar consensus was evidently coming unglued.

THE TERMINATION OF THE POSTWAR CONTRACT

IN THE seventies the workability of the postwar model began to be questioned even by groups that had constituted parts of the majority consensus during the previous quarter century. For example, even the previously unchallenged assumption that economic growth was the foundation of a decent everyday life was coming under attack. People in many social locations became increasingly discommoded in their daily lives by such negative impacts of growth as air pollution, traffic congestion, oil spills, and other episodes of dangerous or environmentally degrading pollution, destruction of traditional urban neighborhoods and rural areas by imposed land developments, proliferation of poisonous materials in food and other commodities and in workplaces. Everyday degradation of the environment has been a characteristic of life since the beginning of the industrial era and has always been a basis for criticism of industrial society. What was new was the pervasiveness of concern and anxiety. The rapid rise of "environmentalism" as a feature of *mass* consciousness resulted from the sense that such degradation not only was unpleasant, but now also violated the promised rights of the people to everyday fulfillment.

Meanwhile, the capacity of the political economy to generate continuous economic growth became demonstrably more problematic as the decade wore on. For the first time since the war, the unlimited domination of the world market by U.S.-based corporations was fundamentally challenged by the rising strength of Japanese and German competitors; meanwhile, the increasingly transnational character of American financial and industrial corporations permitted major shifts of capital away from the domestic United States economy. The postwar labor-management deal that had stabilized the major industrial sectors of the American economy was premised on the global dominance of the American economy; accordingly, that deal was not holding in the seventies. The postwar charter assumed that workers' real wages would steadily rise, but that assumption depended on continuing corporate investment to improve productivity and monopolistic corporate power to pass along the costs of wage increases. By the seventies the major corporations were less willing or able to sustain these arrangements; on the contrary, considerable disinvestment—attended by unemployment and economic decline in the older industrial regions of the United States —characterized the decade. The postwar charter was also premised on the capacity of the defense budget to support economic growth and employment; by the seventies defense expenditures had become far less potent as a source of jobs and productive investment.

The declining effectiveness of these established economic control mechanisms was inherent in the logic of their development; it was obvious, in retrospect, that the domestic American economy could not forever maintain its uniquely advantaged position in the world system. Thus the economic foundations of the postwar charter were inevitably temporary.

An economy that had relatively steadily grown for twenty-five years, that had provided a generation of industrial workers with steadily rising real wages, that had enabled the provision of an increasing social wage now was characterized by stagnation, high levels of unemployment, and, most disturbing to everyday life-ways, an accelerating rate of inflation. By the late seventies real wage increases were stalled, public budgets were severely strained, and insecurity about the economic foundations of daily life had become pervasive.

There can be little question, then, that the post-World War II era, organized by its distinctive "politico-cultural" charter," ended in the seventies. During that decade major gains were made in the definition of rights recognized as necessary for everyday security and freedom. Blacks and other minorities achieved voice and guarantees of rights previously unavailable. The concept of affirmative action broadened educational and career opportunities for minorities and women. Blacks and other minorities developed considerable capacities for political organization and made substantial gains in political representation—and the same can be said for women.

Meanwhile, there was a dramatic expansion during this period of the scope for freedom of expression and personal conduct provided by legislation and court decision and expressed in the mass media. Such reforms as the freedom of information act, protection of privacy legislation, the expansion of public television and radio, the development of alternative media, homosexual rights, abortion rights substantially improved the legal and material basis for personal liberty. Such publicly ratified social and cultural changes were matched, in the private sphere, by the efforts we have sketched by millions to find fulfillment and meaning through experiment with forms of cultural innovation that expanded the range of avenues for identity, release, and relief—an effort aided by the political reforms achieved in the aftermath of the sixties and Watergate.

The disintegration of the established charter was therefore reflected in both increasing levels of political participation on behalf of reform and intensifying privatization. But the last decade witnessed also a third response to the erosion of established frameworks of legitimacy, namely, an expanded base for a new politics of rearguard conservatism. Reagan's ascension and popularity, I think, resulted in part from his seeming to promise—unlike any other national politician—that a new socio-cultural charter could actually be devised and implemented, and that, therefore, the years of turmoil, drift, stalemate, and decline could be permanently left behind.

The Reagan charter seemed to share with the postwar one the assumption that economic growth is an absolutely necessary basis for providing the material basis for adequate daily life. But it is assumed that the only reliable basis for such growth is the revitalization of opportunity for profit-maximization. Its thrust was not to guarantee all citizens the right to participate in consumer society in return for certain sacrifices and obligations, but to promise some sort of *future* prosperity for all, if workers accept *reduced* living standards in the present. Meanwhile, the Reagan charter offered the relatively advantaged even more advantages—in the form of reduced inflation, lower taxes, public deregulation, and symbolic reassurances about their right to be self-interested. To those who are materially disadvantaged in the present, Reagan also offered certain kinds of symbolic reassurances—namely, a sense of pride in the revitalization of American power and comfort from the notion that the party of order (rather than disorderly change) is in charge.

The appeal of such a charter to those who already have substantial economic security is evident. For the first time since the New Deal, the well-off in this country could feel that the national government was only protecting their advantages through practical policy (this has almost always been true) but also was speaking their language and thereby providing them a kind of moral protection. The number of those who felt thus protected was not small. What seems unlikely, however, is that the Reagan charter has achieved the long-term acquiescence of the great majority. For its explicit terms required many to scale down their expectations about the material basis for everyday life. Among the many being so asked were the very groups who won the most in the postwar period and in the sixties—industrial workers, public employees, racial minorities, senior citizens, and women. Moreover, the Reagan charter required all to accept levels of environmental degradation that the great majority had come to find unacceptable during the last decade. Finally, the reassertion of national power it embodied demonstrably heightened popular anxieties about international instability and war. Thus, despite Reagan's personal popularity, and despite the appeal of his program to some sizable constituencies, it failed to be implemented as a national consensus.

In fact, Reaganism's political strength and its impact on popular consciousness had to do less with its intrinsic appeal than with the fact that no coherent alternative has been articulated in national politics. If the great majority of people are powerfully and continuously motivated by a commitment to everyday life, then any strongly articulated political framework that offers a promise of relegitimating elite rule will get an attentive popular hearing—since commitment to everyday life is fundamentally grounded on the assumption of an intact social fabric. Reagan got such a hearing and the result was not simply a popular upwelling of consent but an upsurge of opposition as well. Meanwhile, in between rearguard and protest, there is a great middle, attempting to cope with the manifold uncertainties of history by burrowing as deeply as possible into the space available for daily life.

3

Making History to Make Life
Everyday Life as the Seedbed
of Political Action

*With the psychology of a trade unionist who will not stay off his
work on May Day unless he is assured in advance of a definite
amount of support in the event of his being victimized, neither
revolution nor mass strike can be made. But in the storm of the
revolutionary period even the proletarian is transformed from a
proper pater familias demanding support, into a "revolutionary
romanticist," for whom even the highest good—life itself—to say
nothing of material well-being, possesses but little in comparison
with the ideals of the struggle.*

—*Rosa Luxemburg*

THE MOBILIZATION
OF EVERYDAY COMMITMENT

LIBERAL democracy is a model of government that permits a degree of
routinized popular intervention in history—namely, periodic opportunities
to choose between competing elites and to vote established leaders out.
Although such popular intervention is formally restricted to occasional election days, the electoral process opens up a wider range of less formal ways
that average citizens can have historical effect. Numbers of people can,
more or less routinely, signal to elites that a continuation of a particular
plan or project or the making of a particular decision may jeopardize them
in a future election. Such popular signalling, in the form of petitions, communications to officials, expressions of opinions in surveys, attendance at
demonstrations and assemblies, and verbalizations in everyday conversation represent forms of popular intervention that are tied directly to the

voting process and may be effective in modifying or blocking elite-initiated courses of action—if they are read as potential electoral threats.

Voting is a form of participation that can be undertaken without significant alteration of the patterns of daily life. Still, as we saw in chapter 2, many find even this level of activity too costly in terms of time and energy; for large numbers, voting and other minimal forms of participation are not routine but are engaged in only under special circumstances. Furthermore, many who do vote as a matter of course do not see voting as a way of influencing history so much as a way of fulfilling their duty as citizens and thereby ratifying, rather than checking, elite projects.

Indeed, voting is inherently a limited method of historical intervention. Its mass character inescapably leads each individual to doubt the significance of his or her vote—and, more significantly, makes it difficult for minority interests to be expressed or defended. Second, extremely important elites—particularly those in charge of economic activity—are not subject to election and therefore cannot be threatened fundamentally by the forms of expression embodied in the electoral system.

Third, the structure of the electoral process contains inherent limitations on its effectiveness. Because elections occur only at widely spaced intervals, crucial decisions can be made without direct electoral accountability; such decisions can have far-reaching historical effects that render future electoral reactions irrelevant. Election campaigns are notoriously misleading about the true character of contending elites or their future intentions. Elections inherently involve attention to symbol; an endemic characteristic of liberal democracies is the gap between the policies advocated by contending politicians and the concrete ways in which benefits are allocated and policies are enforced in practice.

These circumstances illustrate the numerous ways that elections as such fail to provide adequate means for popular intervention—even if the electoral process were operated according to liberal ideals. Such ideals are rarely operative, of course, and so the electoral process is further limited by the ways in which politicians systematically seek to deceive voters about their intentions, by the fact that a large proportion of the decisions and projects on the public agenda are not worked up for meaningful electoral choice, and by the relative nonparticipation of significant constituencies.

SOCIAL MOVEMENTS

THE LIMITATIONS of voting and other routinized means of supporting, vetoing, or choosing between elites create grounds for more direct forms of popular historical intervention. The term "social movements" is a summary expression for a variety of collective efforts by the relatively powerless to exercise historical power. Participation in movement activity may include the use of the ballot and related forms of expression, but a defining characteristic of movement participation is that it entails a significant disruption or alteration of the participants' everyday routines.

The logic of hierarchically organized role relations is this: Those positioned to participate in elite transactions can influence the terms and conditions of a collectivity's daily life as an inherent part of their own daily routine. Those without such position can influence history to the degree that they have the ability to disrupt elite plans or the processes of daily life. In order to take such disruptive actions they must be ready to break with, step out of, stop complying with, the terms and conditions of their accustomed daily lives. When we say that a group is "powerless," then, we do not mean that they do not have any capacity to influence their life circumstances, but that efforts to exercise the capacity they do have involve personal risks and costs. At a minimum, such costs include the interruption of daily activity felt to be required for self-maintenance.

Thus the most obvious issue in trying to understand the historical potentials of social movements is: Under what circumstances do people, involved with their individual lives, become ready to leave off or reorganize the daily round of roles and responsibilities in order to enter history?

A second key problem in the analysis of social movements is to understand the means by which powerless people who have mobilized can influence history. What resources for disrupting elite projects and social processes are available? What problems arise in the effort to use such resources? Since movements are by definition forms of collective action, what are the problems of collective mobilization and organization that movements face? How can movement strategies—i.e., efforts to solve problems of resource deployment and organization—be defined?

The final key question about social movements is the question of historical impact, of outcome. What can count as successful historical action by powerless masses? What can be said about the circumstances that facilitate success? What are the likely fates of social movements? What impact does movement participation have on individual participants?

Such questions define the field, in academic sociology, of "social movements." A rather rapidly growing literature, including a number of fairly weighty textbooks, is attempting to deal with these issues. I am not, here, going to try to deal with these issues in any detail. Instead, I want to sketch a perspective that derives from the overall argument I have been making. This perspective is that popular historical intervention is grounded in, and shaped by, the logic of commitment to everyday life.

Resistance

This logic entails an effort to resolve troubles within the framework of the personal. By this logic, we expect that *the most likely circumstance in which collective mobilization occurs is a situation of perceived threat to accustomed patterns of everday life*. Such threats lead to collective, historical action when they are perceived to come from decisions, plans, or projects of others— as distinguished from the sorts of threats that are seen as arising from natural causes or from forces beyond human control or intention.

In the history of popular protest, certain kinds of threat situations have been classic ones for fostering collective resistance. These include:

■ Enclosures, foreclosures, and other efforts to move peasants or farmers off their lands.

■ Wage cuts, layoffs, disciplinary firings, plant closings, industrial accidents—these illustrate the kinds of disruption of ongoing life that are endemic to industrial work.

■ Precipitous price rises, commodity shortages, mass eviction of tenants—and other threats to accustomed consumption patterns.

■ Imposition of conscription, police crackdowns, increased school discipline, imposition of censorship, deprivation of customary privileges or amenities are classic examples of threats experienced by students and youth.

■ Toxic chemical spills, neighborhood dislocation by urban development, school closings, increased airport noise, neighborhood "incursions" by new ethnic groups illustrate classic threats that mobilize urban neighborhoods.

Such threats are necessary but not sufficient conditions for collective resistance. Threats must be perceived, and action against them must be felt to be possible if collective mobilization is to occur. Such shared perception depends on communication with others sharing the life situation and the threat. The more accessible such others are, and the more interaction about the situation takes place, then the more a sense of common definition and of possibilities for collective action can be achieved. Moreover, since collective action entails emphasis on collective goals and some degree of sacrifice of immediate personal interests, the likelihood of collective action is enhanced to the degree that those facing the threat share a sense of mutual identification.

Accordingly, the probability of collective action is increased if those threatened are in day-to-day physical contact; if they inhabit a space in which face-to-face communication with each other can go on—relatively uncontrolled by those in authority and relatively insulated from counter-acting influences. Communication is made possible by the sharing of a lan-guage; indeed, the more manifold the forms of cultural understanding, the more readily communication leading to collective action can take place.

Because such communication is a crucial condition for collective action, we suppose that the ideal locale for its emergence is a relatively self-con-tained and homogeneous community that is experiencing threat. Some clas-sic examples of such communities include factory and mining towns, res-idential universities, urban ghettoes, and ethnic neighborhoods. Mobilization by such communities is made more likely to the degree that members have available definite public spaces—for example, cafes, bars, churches, meet-ing halls, town squares, and street corners—within which they are rela-tively free to communicate among themselves.

If popular protest moves beyond such enclaves, it is because locales are linked to some networks of association capable of extending channels of communication beyond the daily face-to-face opportunities that occur in self-contained communities. The local and trans-local frameworks of interaction that constitute the social fabric of everyday life and identity are, classically, the circuits along which mobilization for historical action are able to pass.

In addition to perceived threat and opportunities for communication and shared perception, a third necessary condition for collective resistance is the emergence of a *line of action* that appears to members to have a cred-ible chance of working to remove the threat. *Insofar as people are acting out of commitment to protect and maintain their everyday lives, the logic of their action requires a perceptible chance of success in restoring the possibility for everyday life when it is being attacked.*

Because effective action depends on a capacity to check elite projects or to disrupt established patterns of daily life, it requires that numbers of people risk the reprisals and dislocations that such action is likely to entail. For such risk-taking to be undertaken, members must have confidence that, in the end, their participation has a chance to succeed.

The most persuasive lines of action are often those presented in ex-emplary demonstration or that seem to flow naturally out of the logic of a particular situation. Thus, many collective mobilizations seem to arise from a particular "triggering" or "precipitating" event, typically one in which a small number of people make a move that serves as a model of a line of action that appears credible to many others. Some random illustrations:

■ Sit-downs by small groups of workers precipitated the mass sit-down strikes in the auto industry in the 1930s.

■ Mass protest on college campuses in the sixties were precipitated by an event in Berkeley in October 1964 when a handful of students initiated a blockade of a police car that eventuated in an all-night assembly by several thousand.

■ Urban "riots" in the late sixties were often precipitated by a particular act of police brutality viewed by large numbers, already gathered in the street on a hot summer evening; these crowds would immediately intervene and successfully overwhelm police authority in response. Such crowd action would then be followed by several days of looting and property destruction.

Credible advice, as well as exemplary action, may persuade people to act. Organizers with experience in other collective mobilizations may play an important role in suggesting lines of action that have worked in other times and places. Such larger awareness may be brought to the community by an outsider with such wider experience or by indigenous community members with access to such information.

But specialized tactical knowledge may not be necessary. People may arrive at an acceptable and credible line of action out of their own discussion and local experience. By now, there is probably no community that does not contain members with memories of past protest, no community so insulated that members are unaware of some of the repertory of popular action. Indeed, the more members are conscious of the historical development of their collectivities, the more practical knowledge of possibilities for effective collective action there will be.

What we have been talking about so far is a particular form of action that embodies a particular kind of political consciousness. A name for this action and this orientation is *resistance*. Collective actions may be called "resistant" when they are responses to threats to an accustomed, shared pattern of everyday life, responses designed to defend or restore that pattern. When such actions are carried on over time and begin to be articulated in the form of demands and shared objectives, we can speak of a *resistance movement.*

When resistance is dominant in collective political consciousness, then members think and talk in terms of external threats, of ways of life in danger, of territory and rights needing defense, of cherished values being assaulted. Resistance, psychologically, begins in reactions against certain kinds of social changes—out of *conservative* impulses to preserve ways of life that are felt to be endangered. These reactions may be articulated as demands for social reform, for what is being sought are new laws, structures, or social relationships that will prevent or mitigate the threats that sparked the movement in the first place. Thus, resistance movements often seek radical change in authority relations, but their goals are conservative with respect to the terms and meanings of daily life.

When people without power engage in resistance, they undertake lines of action that typically require the *stopping* of their daily lives. This stoppage expresses their collective power, as it entails a refusal to carry on the work or play the roles required by elite projects. The prototypical resistance action is the *strike;* actions comparable in form to strikes include consumer boycotts, draft refusal, rent strikes. Mass occupations of threatened territory, physical refusal to be evicted, direct seizure of commodities, physical interference with officially authorized movements of goods or persons—all illustrate lines of action characteristic of mass resistance.

If we understand how mass resistance is rooted in everyday life, we can make some hypotheses about conditions that affect its likelihood. For example, the readiness of people to stop their daily lives and to take the risks of defiance varies with the scope and severity of the threat they are responding to. Severe threats to livelihood or to the very existence of a settled community not only create a sense of great urgency but, by disrupting the normal flow of daily life, can actually free people's time and energy for collective action. On the other hand, relatively mild threats may be highly mobilizing to the extent that those affected feel they can effectively defend against them with comparatively little cost. Communities rich in internal communication and a sense of common identification that includes a history of resistance are more "volatile" than those that are relatively fragmented and pluralistic. Communities made up of people whose daily lives are relatively unobligated and not settled (for instance, students, unemployed youth, and migratory workers) may be more ready for risky action than those composed of settled families—but the latter may be more disposed to practical, "rational" lines of action and are therefore more successful when they do act.

Thus, there is a considerable degree of predictability about resistance consciousness and action. If we understand the features of a collectivity's daily life patterns that its members regard as practically and morally necessary or that are strongly valued by them, and if we can also foresee the historical circumstances under which such patterns may be disrupted, then it seems possible to predict moments of collective resistance—especially if we are also able to take into account the availability of, and barriers to, opportunities for communication within the collectivity.

Harder to predict are the occurrences of triggering events. Such events are likely to be crucial for the emergence of mass resistance, since, as we have suggested, they provide the occasion for discovering appropriate lines of effective collective action, often a major problem for threatened communities. Many precipitating events are genuinely spontaneous, resulting from an unplanned encounter between group members and agents of social control. The most dramatically precipitant of such encounters are those that take place in the plain view of a crowd. The fact that a crowd is already gathered greatly accelerates processes of communication under conditions in which control agents may be off guard—conditions that lead participants to believe that their collective action may be highly effective. It is relatively rare that an oppressive encounter converges with a popular assembly. Such spontaneous dramas are often necessary triggers for collective mobilization precisely because participants are committed to their everyday lives and not to collective action. Because they are so committed, members avoid facing the implications of external threat, are cautious in undertaking the risks of collective action, and quite pragmatic in their assessment of the costs and benefits of collective identification. Dramas that make the threat unavoidable, that suggest the potential power of the group and the possible weakness of authorities, can transform the cognitive structures that undergird everyday commitment. Such dramas catalyze mobilization even when people seem resigned to the daily experience of accustomed deprivation and deaf to the exhortation of "agitators."

Resistance movements have power to the extent that they sustain a line of action that significantly blocks those in authority from implementing their purposes or significantly disrupts the normal processes of daily life in the wider society. A labor strike is a prototypic form of resistance because it can accomplish both of these strategic objectives simultaneously. Indeed, Marx argued that the industrial proletariat had the greatest potential historical power of any oppressed group, because of its unique capacity—by stopping production—to materially disrupt *both* the plans of the immediate capitalist masters *and* the patterns of daily life in the society at large.

The problem with carrying out such actions is, of course, that the means of daily life of the resisters are also disrupted. Thus the effectiveness of resistance movements often depends on the ability of participants to develop alternative means for supplying basic needs during the course of the struggle. Furthermore, since resistance actions threaten the power of elites and the order of established institutions, participants risk repression and punishment. In order to sustain their lines of action, resistance movements must deal with problems of both supply and defense. The means of such defense have often been military. But nonviolent efforts to disarm the opposition psychologically and win sympathy and support from bystander elements in the larger society are at least as important, since subordinate groups can rarely amass the material resources that would enable them to offset the firepower available to elites.

A movement's efforts at supply and defense constrain and channel the internal organization and patterns of activity that characterize its development. Further, movement development cannot be understood without careful analysis of its interaction with its adversaries, with the state, and with other social groupings. Much of the technical literature in the sociology of social movements is taken up with the analysis of such matters.

Resistance movements eventually ebb. Their demobilization—like their emergence—can be understood in terms of the logic of everyday commitment. If the purpose of a resistance movement is to restore the possibility of living an accustomed life, then such movements achieve success when they have won the removal or reduction of the threats that precipitated them and some explicit guarantee from authorities that such threats will not recur—or that the threatened group will have more institutionalized power in the future to mitigate or prevent it. Often, resistance movements' success can be measured by the granting of formal representation in bargaining or decision making. The movement itself creates an institutional structure that permits such representation, and the state, or other authority structure, creates a legal or formal framework permitting access. These developments permit movement participants to return to daily life, delegating to representatives the capacity to define, voice, and act in their collective interests. In the United States, such institutionalization is best illustrated by the achievement of legalized collective bargaining by the labor movement.

Resistance movements may ebb before they achieve such structural change. Repression combined with concession can make it practical for members to give up, or the movement may be terminated by a successful "divide and conquer" strategy implemented by its adversaries. But when an organized resistance movement seems to disintegrate under pressure, resistance consciousness may persist, ready to eventuate in new actions when new precipitating events and practical lines of action reappear. The U.S. labor movement rose and declined several times in the fifty years prior to the achievement of legalized collective bargaining—the intensity of its mobilization varying with economic conditions and with the felt capacities of groups of workers to wage effective struggles.

Resistance movements may be the crucibles for forms of consciousness that go beyond the cognitive framework of resistance. The experience of collective power, the questioning of conventional values and established authority, the historical awareness that participation fosters can create the basis for the emergence of awareness that the accustomed daily lives that form the ground of resistance are themselves unnecessarily limited or constraining. Aspirations for *liberation* can arise in the process of resistance.

Liberation

Collective action may arise not from the need to defend a threatened way of life but out of a desire to establish a new way. Instead of seeking political guarantees aimed at securing an accustomed way of life, people may seek new rights and entitlements or to rewrite the rules and norms that had previously been regarded as binding. In other words, subordinated groups may orient toward *liberation* rather than resistance.

If the core of popular political consciousness is "commitment to everyday life" then liberation consciousness involves a significant break with the kinds of cognitive structures that arise from both universal human conditions and specific cultural conditioning. When themes of liberation are expressed, people see their accustomed lives as painful, restrictive, backward, undignified, unworthy. They lose the sense that the maintenance of their daily lives is the most practical reality or the most basic moral priority; instead the hope of a better world for oneself and one's children becomes paramount and determinative. Liberation consciousness expresses the sense that the identity provided by the conditions of one's life must be overcome, that self-worth and personal meaning can come only from claiming and achieving rights not now provided.

If people are locked into their daily lives, and, as we argued in chapter 2, if they strive to resolve troubles and relieve pain through means available to them in their private worlds, then how is it possible for liberation to arise and take hold in popular consciousness?

There are, first of all, certain historically specific conditions that have created fundamental cultural grounds for liberation consciousness. These conditions begin with the diffusion of the ideals of the American and French revolutions—that "all men are created equal," that human beings are universally entitled to liberty, that there are universally applicable human rights. These principles have, for two centuries, undermined the legitimacy of all social arrangements entailing enslavement, exploitation, and repression. Such social arrangements have been most readily contested when they exist within societies, such as the United States, whose own legitimating principles rest on notions of equality and natural rights. The diffusion of liberal ideals beyond the boundaries of such societies accompanied the colonization and enslavement of non-Western peoples. Historically, impulses toward liberation have been strongly stimulated by the fact that liberal ideology has been systematically violated by the internal and external practices of liberal societies. These societies, during these centuries, have tended to extend promises of universal emancipation while simultaneously and systematically excluding large masses from opportunities to exercise citizenship. In practice, there was no way that most members of racial and ethnic minorities, or most women, or most members of colonized cultures could achieve the emancipatory promises of liberal civilization by trying to adapt to the rules and roles that liberalism declared to be requisite for liberty. Assimilation and acculturation on terms of equality have been systematically denied such groups by both formal and informal means of exclusion and subordination.

We may state as a principle that liberation movements are most likely to arise in a cultural climate that fosters and promises equality of treatment and opportunity, when this culture is coupled to a social structure that blocks identifiable groups from fulfilling these promises. Discrimination and subordination imposed on a social category lay the basis for mutual identification among its members. The development of group solidarity is, of course, facilitated to the degree that communication among members of the category is possible—by dint of common cultural and linguistic heritage, geographical proximity, the presence of physical and social space within which such perspectives can be communicated freely. Such banding together may originate in defensive efforts to adapt to hardship, to find means of survival within a framework of adjustment to subordination. Over time group identifications formed in these ways are likely to deepen and broaden. The subordinated group may develop an increasingly elaborated cultural heritage—religion, song, story, and lore—that establishes ever more firmly the nature of the group and the identity of its members. Cultural development of oppressed groups may be interpreted as a kind of resistance to oppression—for such cultural expression embodies a refusal to accept the world views of the masters and a search for alternative meanings and self-definitions. But such cultural expression also helps members to make everyday accommodation to their subordination, since much of its content consists of forms of release, relief, and survival lore.

Oppressed groups obviously vary in the degree to which members identify with each other and develop a shared cultural framework. In the case of sexual inequality, although gender is a fundamental basis for identity, women cannot, with exceptions, form a separate, distinctive cultural alternative to the one in which they live and raise their children. Thus the development of women's consciousness has been more gradual and fitful than, say, the development of a distinct cultural framework and group consciousness among oppressed national or racial groups.

Even more fitful and fragmented in the United States has been the development of distinct cultural frameworks and group consciousness on the basis of class differentiation. Although the propertyless in the United States have experienced a variety of forms of inequality and powerlessness, they have never been completely excluded from the political process—as they were in Europe. American social development has been characterized, instead, by a continually shifting differentiation of treatment and experience within the proletariat, due in part to the unmatched ethnic and racial diversity of the working class in this country and the ever-changing reverberations of technological change and geographic mobility on the life situations of its various sectors. As a result, it is not possible to speak of an American working-class culture in the way that one can, say, with respect to England.

When members of a disadvantaged social category share a common culture, identifying themselves with a common fate, then the basis has been laid for the eventual emergence of liberation perspectives among them. But such group identity is not sufficient for such an emergence; a shared culture of oppression may function instead to permit members to sustain a degree of everyday dignity and security within a framework of subordination.

An implication of our definition of resistance movements is that collective resistance often arises when accustomed patterns of group accommodation to subordination are interfered with. Resistance movements often seek, not equality, but the right to continue to live within a traditionally established mode of accommodation. A large proportion of the labor struggles in this country were sparked by the *worsening* of already oppressive condition (for example, wage cuts, price hikes, layoffs, speedups) rather than by impulses to achieve some vision of full emancipation. Such movements may terminate if concessions are made that permit members to resume their customary lives within a structure of inequality.

It is when members of a subordinated group begin to question the moral rightness of their accustomed subordination that we see the emergence of a qualitative development in political consciousness. As such questions begin to be articulated as claims for new rights or demands for the removal of traditional constraints—when a language of egalitarian assertion is being voiced—we can interpret them as signs of a movement of consciousness beyond resistance to liberation.

Such questioning and assertion can arise in the process of collective resistance. Insofar as resistance is met with elite unresponsiveness and repression, and insofar as accustomed patterns continue to be infringed on, participants may become increasingly disillusioned with established structures of authority. They may come to see that further efforts merely to defend their established arrangements will be futile. They may find new sources of potential power and capacities for self-government in the experience of collective struggle. Workers occupying a factory as a technique for resisting a threatened layoff may, in the midst of this situation, discover collective capacities for permanent, rather than tactical, control. A community food riot can create consciousness of the possibilities for community self-government. These examples illustrate that one condition for the emergence of liberation consciousness may be a shared history of collective resistance—a history that serves to delegitimate established authority and to create awareness of the potentials for collective self-organization. The experience of collective resistance can socialize participants to the value and possibility of transcending the established terms of their accustomed everyday life and the value and possibility of questioning established order.

A second condition for the emergence of liberation consciousness may be the erosion of the material basis of traditional beliefs about the moral organization of daily life. Although collective resistance may be mobilized in response to visible, sudden threats to accustomed values and ways of living, there may be, underneath such shocks, a longer term, less observable, more gradual erosion of the foundations of daily life. Economic and technological transformations undermine rural-based cultures, pushing people off the land, pulling them to the cities. Technological and organizational developments make traditional skills and crafts obsolete. Women socialized to domestic roles nevertheless find themselves pressed into the labor force. Economic depression undermines already meager material bases for security and survival.

Such changes—more impersonal and less credibly resistible than those that foster resistance movements—create crises for those affected by them. Under such conditions, traditional subcultures dissipate as emigration and social mobility disperse members, undermine traditional identifications, and destroy traditional meanings. But if discrimination and other barriers to adaptation prevent group members from assimilating into the frameworks of the larger society, the stage is set for revitalization of group identity in terms of demands for liberation. The erosion of traditional bases for everyday life makes the creation of new meanings necessary and frees minds for new ideas. At the same time, newly mobile group members become increasingly aware of the egalitarian promises embedded in the politics and culture of the larger society—promises from which they had, in the past, been relatively insulated.

Liberation movements, far more than resistance movements, elaborate ideologies. Liberative perspectives are internalized to the degree that members come to see that new life-ways, new social arrangements, and new identities are morally, as well as practically, superior to their accustomed ways. Liberation movements commit members to struggle for rights not recognized in the traditional culture of accommodation. Because liberation consciousness requires significant cognitive reorganization, it is not enough that group members experience disadvantage, undergo the loss of traditional bases for daily life, or hear the egalitarian promises of the wider culture. Such experiences need to be interpreted and organized so that established habits of subservience, past beliefs about the practical wisdom of acquiescence, and residues of guilt about abandoning traditional morality can be overcome. Rationales for new claims must be developed, elaborated, and articulated. Such ideological work inescapably is the province of specialists—intellectuals, artists, preachers. These are people, drawn somehow from the oppressed group, who are in a position to translate the egalitarian promises of the wider culture into terms appropriate to the situation of the oppressed. Typically, they are people who have had educational opportunities within the dominant culture but are denied commensurate status opportunities by virtue of their membership in the subordinated group. Their educational (and often economic) advantage distances them from the everyday life situation of their oppressed fellows. "Marginality" (as sociologists have classically labeled this situation) creates a personal tension for individuals so located—a tension that historically has often enabled them to be ideologically creative. Individuals so caught are likely to find that in the production and dissemination of philosophy, poetry, song, or theater that expresses the liberative potentials of their excluded brothers and sisters lie both the resolution of their own identity crises and a historically significant way of being.

When such new cultural expression is produced it is both an indication of, and a spur to, the emergence of a liberation movement. Such expression puts into words the building grievances of the group, intensifies and focuses the communication of such discontent, and provides the basis for legitimating new aspirations and new claims.

Liberation movements employ many of the tactical forms used by resistance movements—demonstrations, strikes, boycotts. But there are likely to be some fundamental differences in the lines of action liberation movements develop—differences understandable in terms of the logic embodied in liberation perspectives:

First, in liberation movements popular mobilization is more likely to be the result of planned initiative than the outcome of reactions to external threat. For example, a key precipitating event in the black liberation movement of the sixties was the sit-in at a Woolworth lunch counter by four black students in Greensboro, North Carolina, in February 1960. These students were not reacting to the introduction of a *new* infringement on their rights; instead, they had *made a decision to violate* a long-standing, customary restriction on their freedom. Their initiative sparked a wave of similar actions across the South. Since liberation movements, by definition, challenge established rules and condition, it is logical that they are often sparked by such conscious initiatives rather than by the sorts of spontaneous reactions to threat that often trigger resistance movements. More-over, given the dependence of liberation consciousness on ideological de-velopment, cognitive reorganization, and the gradual transformation of the conditions of life, it is understandable that triggering events are often not significant features of their development. For example, the women's lib-eration movement of the late sixties did not seem to have had a definite moment of origin; instead it evolved out of a multiplicity of small group responses to a changing ideological climate—a climate fostered in part by the apperance of certain key books (*The Feminine Mystique, The Second Sex*) and by discussions among women already active in New Left circles.

But the most important behavioral difference between resistance and liberation movements lies in their different relations to everyday life. We have said that resistance movements depend for their effectiveness on the mobilization of action that requires participants to *stop* everyday routines and *step outside* of their daily lives. Although liberation movements may make use of strikes and similar forms of mobilization, they exercise their power more fundamentally by fostering historical action *within the frame-work of everyday roles and relationships*. When a liberation movement has really penetrated the imagination of a disadvantaged group, what we can observe is a pattern of *daily assertiveness*. Participants throw off accus-tomed styles of everyday subservience. They change their physical ap-pearance, adopting forms of clothing, hair style, and demeanor that sym-bolize self-assertion and prideful group identification. They are likely to express personal claims of independence, equality, and dignity in face-to-face interaction. Symbolic representations of liberation claims are widely diffused—in songs, signs of greeting, wall-posters, buttons. Alternative institutions emerge, expressing group aspirations for self-determination and socializing group members for liberation consciousness. Such institutions —schools, clinics, cooperatives, theaters, restaurants, sports teams— provide means to fulfill everyday needs within a movement framework.

Along with such everyday means of symbolizing and reinforcing com-mitment, movement participation may involve intensive efforts by numer-ous individuals to renegotiate the terms and conditions of their everyday lives. Thus, for example, with the emergence of women's liberation, the age-old "war between the sexes" is transformed from an endless pattern of privatized conflict into a form of historical activity, in which social change is the conscious goal of personal struggle. Within the framework of liber-ation movements, personal encounters become linked to historical devel-opment. Apparently private, individual decisions take on public, historical meaning—decisions such as the kind of jobs to be applied for, the kinds of recreation to be pursued, the forms of address one uses or responds to, and ultimately the kind of person one aspires to be.

The women's liberation movement exemplifies the ways in which the power to affect history can be found within the framework of everyday life, but similar processes are evident within the terms of black liberation and other minority liberation movements, and in liberation efforts by gays and other stigmatized groups.

We have said that the historical power of the powerless lies in their capacities to refuse cooperation with the projects of elites and to disrupt processes of collective everyday life. Mass action—demonstrating, picketing, striking, blockading, disobedient trespass, boycotting—are examples of such power being exercised in obviously collective, historical, public arenas. Less obvious, because less public, is the way in which historically relevant disobedience and assertion can be undertaken within the spaces that define personal life. Mass action may reinforce, and be reinforced by, such personal initiatives. Mass action and public mobilization may be necessary to achieve the legal reforms and large-scale structural change that liberation movements demand. Yet a liberation movement's social effects cannot be measured simply by observing its capacity to mobilize troops for mass action. For among the most significant and direct historical effects of liberation movements are their impact on the identities and everyday activities of participants. So, for example, whether or not the organized women's movement succeeds in passing the Equal Rights Amendment, the social impact of the movement is carried in the countless acts of self-assertion by women that change the conditions and terms of the daily life they directly inhabit.

Liberation movements decline as participants find new opportunities for freedom and security in their everyday lives. Such re-privatization may begin to happen well before the group as a whole achieves fulfillment of its liberatory visions. Previously marginal intellectuals and activists in liberation movements may find a host of careers opening up to them for self-fulfillment and expression as a result of group demands for equal opportunity. As a result, elements of movement leadership may disengage well before the less advantaged mass constituency has experienced much material improvement. Still, even when such classic "cooptation" occurs, many in the mass of movement supporters are also likely to feel that the movement has succeeded to the degree that past experiences of daily insult no longer occur and experiences of selfhood are less colored by past processes of stereotyping, labeling, and objectification.

Indeed, embedded in the logic of liberation movements is a proposition that can be stated as follows: Insofar as members of a disadvantaged group come to experience their problems in terms of *class position* rather than in terms of a particular ascribed social category, then the liberation movement has, to that degree, been successful. Liberal, capitalist societies do not promise equality of liberty and security for all; instead, liberalism fosters the delegitimation of social conditions that create inequality based on ascription—on qualities over which individuals are thought to have no control. Insofar as liberation movements represent demands that liberalism fulfill its own ideological premises, then such movements may achieve legal and cultural changes that enable group members to participate in, rather than be excluded from, the prevailing sociocultural charter. Because liberation movements derive from and speak to the experience of disadvantaged *minority* sectors, they lack the power, within the terms of their own organization, to fundamentally restructure the economic order. Insofar as a movement arises out of a group that has experienced material impoverishment as well as cultural and political exclusion, the former may be beyond the resources of the movement to fundamentally change.

In the United States, such movements have had the capacity to win major reforms that enable the protesting group to achieve rights established in the Constitution or derived from liberal ideology. These include: the enfranchisement of women and Southern blacks; legal guarantees of equal employment and educational opportunities for women and minorities; the illegalization of segregation in housing, education, and public accommodations; a host of measures providing legal remedies for women, ethnic minorities, gays, and other stigmatized groups to oppose and redress evidence of discrimination. Of course, despite the evident justice of these reforms and their obvious basis in fundamental tenets of official ideology, their achievement required intense struggle that met with fierce resistance. Moreover, the achievement of laws protecting such rights has not meant that they are assured in practice.

Liberation movements have typically tried to push beyond the boundaries of formal equality of opportunity, striving to win political and economic resources that would bring greater equality in living conditions as well as opportunity. Notions of affirmative action, income redistribution, compensatory treatment, and the like have had partial realization in law and social policy—but these have been highly controversial within the terms of liberal doctrine.

Beyond serving as vehicles for structural reform, liberation movements are frameworks for transformation of identity and everyday social interaction. In the last fifteen years, millions of women have experienced liberation in terms of the widening of personal horizons, awareness of personal potentials, and growth in capacities for self-expression and assertion. Relations between the sexes—in the day-to-day realm of families and love affairs, in workplaces and on sports fields—have been fundamentally altered. Obviously, many men—and women—resist the decay of "patriarchy" and male dominance that has resulted; none of the changes have occurred smoothly or linearly. Still they have occurred, exemplifying how "history" can be made in and through "everyday life."

Relations between the sexes constitute the most pervasive power relation experienced in everyday life, but there are many others. Liberation movements demonstrate that the subjective impression that "history" and "daily life" are two separate realms is a kind of false consciousness. Power is not only exercised in remote centers and at the top of national pyramids. It is also an in-built feature of close-up, face-to-face interaction. Insofar as this is the case, then history is being made in daily life to the degree that people who share a common subordination consciously engage in daily strategies and tactics of assertion, nonconformity, and renegotiation. Such activity in itself cannot bring the big historical changes required to achieve an egalitarian social structure. But such activity does enable daily life to be more livable—more free and self-fulfilling—for those traditionally subordinated within it.

Liberation movements begin to lose their intensity as members of the movement find daily space more livable and as the movement achieves some legislative and policy gains in the public arena.

Liberation activists are often likely to experience a sense of loss as former movement participants begin to be able to live in ways more or less like those characteristic of the dominant culture. Such "assimilation" is a double tragedy. First, it means the erosion and dilution of distinctive group cultures and values born in oppression and struggle. Second, it means that movement solidarity and mutual support that once provided hope to the poorest and most disadvantaged members may be largely lost. The severest problems faced by partially successful liberation movements are those related to preserving the vitality of cultural emancipation and the commitment of the more successful members.

Democratic Consciousness

Resistance and liberation are the two modes of political consciousness that have formed the basis of most popular movements of historical intervention in the United States. They do not, however, exhaust the possible permutations of popular consciousness. For, in addition to resistance (defining collective action as a means to protect established everyday life) and liberation (defining collective action as a means to achieve the full measure of everyday rights and opportunities promised in the social charter), there is a third perspective. This we can call "democratic." A democratic perspective is one that envisions the full participation of the people as a whole in decisions that affect them.

Resistance and liberation perspectives are democratic in that they call upon powerless groups to intervene in history. But such interventions are envisaged as temporary or limited in scope. Resistance movements enter history as an effort to defend against it, in behalf of the right to maintain a degree of everyday autonomy and a localized way of life. Liberation movements enter history for relatively particularistic ends—to achieve, on behalf of a specific oppressed group, conditions, terms, and rights in everyday life already promised or achieved by members of the dominant culture. Accordingly, the political mobilization fostered by resistance and liberation modes of consciousness tends to recede as movement participants restore or win the possibility of daily life. Resistance and liberation are, like political noninvolvement, grounded in what we have called "commitment to everyday life." All share the belief that history and daily life are inherently separate realms.

There are, of course, profound qualitative differences, as well as similarities, between resistance and liberation consciousness on the one hand, and the privatized pursuit of personal liberty on the other. Participation in collective action socializes many members to awareness that the gap between history making and the everyday can be closed. Moreover, in liberation movements, members may come to see ways in which personal initiative and self-assertion can have historical as well as private significance.

But what people learn about their potential historical power from participation in collective action is likely to be contradictory. They discover that elites are more vulnerable—and history more permeable—then they had thought. They are likely to learn that there are potentialities for self-fulfillment and self-determination through collective action. These potentialities may suggest that a way of living that is superior to privatized conceptions of liberty is possible. However, collective action is also disillusioning. When strikes, protests, and mobilizations fail to achieve their goals, participants' feelings of powerlessness are reinforced. Collective action may be decidedly unexhilarating if members see that burdens and risks are unevenly distributed and that some of their fellows are quite willing to be free riders. Movements inevitably embody a chronic tension. They inescapably put strains on everyday roles, obligations, and pleasures as family and household needs are sacrificed and private satisfactions forgone in the heat of struggle. This tension between the collective and the personal is most acute when movements call on members to use their most effective resource, namely, their capacity to disrupt the fabric of daily life.

Thus movements inescapably exacerbate the very tensions they seek ultimately to resolve. They inherently highlight the polarization between history and the everyday. They require members to risk their lives in order to make it possible to live. It therefore should not be surprising that movement mobilizations have a periodicity—an ebb and flow—as individual participants oscillate between participation and privatization as means to fulfill their commitments to their lives.

Despite such contradictoriness of the socializing effects of movements, they do create frameworks within which some members discover that there is, in principle, a way to break out of the endless oscillation between daily life and history. That way is *democracy*, by which I want to mean a social arrangement in which the gap between history and everyday life is permanently closed because society's members achieve the ability to make history (i.e., to influence and decide the terms and conditions of their lives) in and through their everyday lives.

Democratic political consciousness is defined by commitment to fundamental restructuring of social institutions and culture so that history making can be a routine feature of everyone's daily life. Democratic movements are those that reach beyond localized and particularized definitions of rights toward a universally relevant vision of self-determination.

Democratic consciousness entails a sharp break with the modes of political belief that prevail in the established culture. Democratic movements argue for direct voice by subordinates in the policies of institutions, for control or replacement of market-based means of reallocating resources by democratic planning mechanisms, for community or neighborhood control over aspects of government that are conventionally controlled more centrally, for giving ordinary citizens forms of information, access, and voice in areas of decision making that established ideology defines as the province of experts, elites, and "private" firms and organizations. To envision such alternatives, to see them as preferable and possible, requires a leap of the imagination.

We do not know very much about the conditions under which such a leap can occur to individuals or within a collectivity. It seems clear that people involved in the rounds of daily life are unlikely to experience such altered states of political consciousness. Light bulbs do not flash on in the brain, nor do bolts from the blue strike individuals—even when they encounter frustrations in their dealings with those above them whose decisions intrude on their lives. Such decisions are typically framed by the legitimations of official ideology, while people in subordinate positions typically doubt that they have the competence to govern. Perhaps the most fundamental constraint on imagining that the structure of authority might be overturned is that such imaginings can undermine the stability of one's practical, felt-to-be-necessary understanding of the everyday world. As a rule, the management of one's personal routine requires the assumption that those at the top know what they are doing and are reasonably benign.

Without such assumptions there could be no sense of everyday security and personal freedom.

Nevertheless, while everyday practical living creates powerful constraints on political imagination, regular dealing with authority structures and officials also generates recognitions that official stupidity and malevolence are commonplace. The daily practice of workers, consumers, students, children, and all other subordinated groups includes efforts to exercise whatever degree of autonomous control over their own activity that they can. Such forms of informal, and often unarticulated, struggle for self-determination are, in large part, motivated by the self-interest of the subordinated—by desires to reduce onerous and costly demands, escape negative sanctions, gain some relief from burdensome imposed routine. But often the evasions, nonconformities, and unauthorized activities of workers and other subordinates are also understood by them to be necessary for the attainment of organizational goals (the improvement of productivity, efficiency, learning, morale) that would largely be unattainable if people actually followed the directives of superiors. Thus daily life inherently involves a kind of double vision. People are constrained to take for granted the established structures of authority, but typically find it necessary to reorganize that structure, to evade or transcend it, in order to make life possible and institutions workable.

There is, I think, a practical political wisdom derivable from such everyday experience. It runs something like this: The authority set-up is more or less stupid and predatory. The best way to deal with it is to try to make your own way, taking what you can, giving back what you must—while always being on the lookout for space and opportunity to enhance your freedom. Don't let yourself be pushed around. Try to do a good job, especially if others you care about depend on it. Don't take risks that you know will get you nothing but trouble. When those in charge act like bastards, if we stand together we ought to be able to get them to back down or strike a deal. By standing together we can gain respect, gain a hearing, protect our rights. We should use the strength that we have to gain what we need to live. If those in charge can accommodate to that, then it's only practical to let them run the show. After all, what choice do we have? If we push them too hard, they've got the fire power. If we push them over, then won't there just be chaos?

Everyday practical wisdom says that to seek a far-reaching transcendence of the terms of the world we know is to court severe repression or social disintegration. It says that it is better to take what you can get from the "real world" than to sacrifice everything for unknown and maybe impossible futures. Such practical wisdom is intrinsic to the belief that the present has something to offer, that the everyday life we now inhabit is valid and valuable.

Populist, democratic imagery and rhetoric nevertheless can have deep appeal when they resonate with the daily experience that those in power are in many ways unqualified, and that we ourselves do not deserve to be as deferential, unconsulted, or as passive as we are. Mass struggle heightens this appeal because, in the midst of movement, people make numerous discoveries about the competence of their fellows and themselves in public affairs. Collective action creates public roles and responsibilities for "ordinary people." It greatly stimulates group discussion about the way things are and how they might be. And it involves confrontation with those in authority that exposes their hypocrisy, callousness, stupidity, and weakness. In the popular assemblies created by resistance and liberation movements, democratic consciousness is likely to flourish.

Yet, I am arguing, such consciousness is simultaneously limited by the practical constraints of everyday exigency. We can imagine that in the midst of mass action each participant hears an inner dialogue between the voice of democratic possibility and the voice of everyday practicality. In the end, it becomes obvious that most will choose to act in terms of practicality rather than vision.

As I suggested in chapter 1, it is useful to use the term "tradition of the left" to refer to the totality of ideological and activist efforts to achieve the democratization of society. The United States, alone among the industrial capitalist societies, has been singularly bereft of a left tradition capable of winning the conscious allegiance of large numbers.

Despite the lack of popular support for left ideology and organizations in this country, there have been several instances in which popularly based movements have gone beyond the frameworks of resistance and liberation to articulate more universal, democratic demands and visions.

These include: the populist movement among Western and Southern farmers in the 1880s and 90s; the Wobbly movement among miners, lumbermen, and immigrant workers before and during World War I; the "popular front" that provided a grassroots basis for New Deal reform during the period 1936–39; and the movement of black and white students, youth and intellectuals in the sixties. In each of these movements, considerable numbers of people were mobilized on behalf of their particular group interests, as well as in terms of a broader social vision of full-scale democratization that transcended the frameworks of official or conventional ideology.

In both their explicit demands and their prevailing rhetorics, these movements aimed at the fundamental restructuring of institutional life along democratic lines. Like all mass movements, they mobilized large numbers who were intially motivated by a "commitment to everyday life." But these movements fostered a cultural climate in which many participants experienced changes in commitment, beginning to see themselves as historical actors dedicated to social transformation.

The presence of such democratic moments (as Lawrence Goodwyn has termed them) in American history suggests that, despite the overwhelming odds favoring commitment to everyday life in the United States, there are conditions under which that commitment can be transcended as a result of participation in grassroots movements.

POPULAR POLITICAL CONSCIOUSNESS: CONCLUSIONS

IN THIS chapter, I have tried to formulate a framework for understanding popular political consciousness in the United States. The core of the argument is that the individual is best understood as acting politically out of a commitment to his or her everyday life. That commitment accounts for privatism—for efforts to resolve personal troubles and achieve identity within the personal sphere. Such efforts, to the extent that they are perceived by actors as possible, reinforce tendencies to evaluate social developments, political processes, and public happenings in terms of their effects on one's ability to lead one's own life.

Thus, "commitment to everyday life" is the basis not only of political withdrawal but of mass political participation as well. At first glance, it may appear to lead to decidedly conservative orientations: individuals committed to their accustomed lives resist change. I have suggested, however, that the willingness of people to inhabit their lives is based on shared assumptions about rights and entitlements that make lives possible and on expectations about the capacity of the state to provide and protect those rights. The political consciousness prevalent in a given period may be understood as structured by such an implicit contract between rulers and ruled; the contractual basis of a given period may be understood as the outcome of preceding popular unrest and mass intervention in history. Such mass interventions come about because of elite failures to fulfill preexisting expectations or because of failings in the charter itself. Groups and communities experiencing threats to their accustomed patterns of life mobilize for resistance. Groups and communities excluded from equal treatment under the established charter may mobilize for "liberation." The conditions that promote the emergence of such movements—and the logic by which they develop and decline—can be understood as deriving from the everyday commitments of their members. Resistance and liberation struggles eventuate in revisions of the structure of rights and entitlements; an era of relative social peace may follow such turmoil if elites succeed in gaining consent to a new contract.

The framework I have sketched is intended to be an alternative to the sort of analysis that tries to interpret popular consciousness by making use of established ideological categories: "liberalism," "conservatism," "left, right, and center," assigning proportions of the population to such categories on the basis of opinion polls, election statistics, or the intuitions of the observer.

Many years ago, the "scientific" analysis of political behavior began to demonstrate that most Americans could not validly be classified as adherents of particular established ideological positions. The average survey respondent was expressing a bundle of inconsistent and often conflicting attitudes and opinions; those whose views could be classified as coherently "liberal" or "conservative" represented very small percentages of the population. Accordingly, social scientists largely abandoned the effort to interpret and predict mass political behavior in terms of ideological commitment. Instead, the individual was understood in terms of his or her group memberships and allegiances; these social ties were the determinative influence on individual political participation and orientation; individuals themselves were interpreted as largely passive receptors of such influence, largely uninterested in making coherent sense, cognitively, of the beliefs and attitudes they held. Politicians, ideologues, and other political mobilizers could influence political behavior of masses, according to this approach, not by appealing to broad ideological themes but by plugging into the web of interest groups and cultural affiliations of target constituencies. Occasionally, political mobilization might effectively override such associations by manipulation of symbolic materials with strong emotional resonance or by emphasizing a particular issue that happened to have broad popular appeal.

There is little doubt that popular political consciousness cannot be understood by attempting to discern the degree to which large masses accept or articulate ideologies of the left or right. Social science emphasis on the ways in which attitudes and action are shaped by socialization, group life, and personal experience was an important intellectual breakthrough in the understanding of mass politics. But that emphasis has fostered the assumption that the "common man" lacks political rationality, that people can be understood as passively reacting to political processes, that they lack the capacity to frame political happenings in terms of a coherent understanding of how such happenings affect their interests.

The framework developed here is designed to show that people do tend to have coherent perspectives on political processes even though they are

not guided by established, "named" political ideologies. Rather than ideologies, Americans are overwhelmingly committed to their lives—by which
I mean, if course, not simply survival as such, but the roles, relationships,
and purposes that constitute daily round and personal identity. That commitment is the bedrock of popular ideology in American society—the
framework people are most likely to use in reacting to political leaders,
events, and issues. Apparent inconsistencies in individual belief and attitude tend to become more "logical" once their connections to the maintenance and development of the individual's everyday life are grasped. Put
another way, it is methodologically more fruitful to regard each individual
as actively striving for political rationality—defined in terms of commitment
to everyday life—than to assume early in the interpretive process that he
or she is merely "inconsistent." Such an interpretive stance requires us
to understand the ways individuals fill their daily time and space and how
they themselves evaluate these ways—as well as the beliefs, perceptions,
and attitudes they have toward "historical" objects and happenings—and
then to interconnect these two sets of evaluations.

If, as we have argued, most Americans are typically disengaged politically, then it follows that a great many attitudes and many votes are merely
efforts to sustain, express, affirm, or reinforce one's accustomed roles and
relationships. Thus, most of the time people vote the party they identify
with, and such identifications are the ones they were brought up to have
and that they share with most of the people they relate to on a daily basis.
The expression of attitudes is often a token of sociability and mutuality, a
way to affirm one's membership in the taken-for-granted consensus of peer
group and subculture.

Furthermore, of course, if one believes that one's life is being well-sup-
ported by a given political leadership, or that one's values and interests
are being voiced by a candidate or leader who "speaks one's language,"
such feelings of affinity (often more "cultural" than "ideological") and material well-being will shape specific votes and opinions.

I have used the terms "resistance" and "liberation" to describe "modes"
of consciousness that underlie social movements. Such movements represent occasions when people, otherwise involved in everyday life, break
out of their accustomed rounds to make history. But these terms—resistance and liberation—may also be helpful in understanding more routine,
more "everyday" political behavior such as voting or expressing oneself in
ordinary conversation or in an opinion poll.

Political attitudes and actions are oriented toward resistance when one
seeks to ward off a threat to one's accustomed ways that is perceived as
coming from the polity (or that can be defended against by recourse to
political action). Heightened political awareness and emotion among aver-

age citizens is, accordingly, most likely when such threats are experienced. To a very great extent, significant shifts in popular attitude and emergent appeals of opposition candidates and leadership elements can be accounted for in terms of resistance.

Commitment to everyday life predisposes people to perceive the state and other centers of power as sources of potential threat, as intruders on, rather than protectors of, one's accustomed life. War is the greatest single threat to everyday life that history presents—and war is, of course, the special province of the state. Lesser state-derived threats abound—taxes, development schemes, laws restricting personal freedom are examples. The establishment of a social charter creates expectations about government protections of rights. These expectations can, when violated, lead people to blame the state for its failure to act effectively in terms of the contract. Thus, in our time the state is blamed for high unemployment and economic recession, for inflation, for corporate malfeasance that the state is supposed to regulate, for crime in the streets and other failures in public services that result in the deterioration of the quality of everyday life.

Threats are also experienced as coming from other groups in the society—and political means are sought to veto or meliorate these. Whites are threatened by racial integration of schools and neighborhoods. Religious traditionalists are repelled by sexual equality, by the secularization of education, by "pluralism" of expression in the mass media, by the legitimization of abortion. Workers are threatened by plant closings, by competition from foreign products or immigrant labor. Communities are threatened by chemical waste dumps, by industrial polluters, by urban developers. Consumers are threatened by utility rate increases, by dangerous products, by exorbitant rent hikes and high bank interest rates.

All of these threats, whether perceived as the result of government intrusion or ineffectiveness or as deriving from the actions of other groups, can, as they become public issues, become the basis for electoral choice. A key working hypothesis in interpreting "trends" in public opinion and electoral politics would be that people in large measure use the routine channels of political expression primarily to veto or resist public policies and social changes that appear to threaten assumed rights and accustomed ways. Opposition politicians—whether of the "left" or the "right"—become popular because they have been able to capitalize on particular feelings of resistance emerging in particular constituencies.

In recent years resistance has been the prevailing mode of political consciousness among those sectors of the population that have sought to express discontent at the ballot box. Media pundits have typically interpreted such expressions as if they represented a "trend to the right" in ideology and politics. Such readings are quite selective, however. They emphasize

evidence for support of right-wing politicians who have capitalized on resistance to high taxes, to "forced" integration, to feminism—while ignoring
political mobilization in behalf of environmental controls, the nuclear freeze,
opposition to nuclear power plants, amelioration of plant closings—all issues, similarly rooted in "resistance," that have won votes for politicians
on the left. A large proportion of the electorate is neither "left" nor
"right"—yet cannot be fruitfully regarded as "centrist" because it is likely
to support relatively "extreme" positions on issues relevant to the maintenance of everyday life. Thus large numbers may vote for a candidate
who strongly opposes school busing and for a nuclear freeze initiative ap-
pearing on the same ballot.

Liberation consciousness is also an important dimension of public opinion
and electoral behavior, but it is less likely to characterize the perspectives
of electoral majorities. "Liberation" entails claims by minorities or subordinated groups for rights promised but denied. Such claims are hard to
advance through an electoral strategy, especially when they are resisted
by sizable mass constituencies who can be mobilized in opposition. Moreover, in the period since the sixties, disadvantaged groups have tended to
share with the dominant majority strong doubts about the willingness and
the ability of politicians to implement effective reforms that will actually
improve everyday life.

Still, aspirations for liberation are strongly voiced by minority sectors in
opinion surveys and are not infrequently decisive in elections when minorities are strategically situated. A recent instance of this is the emergence of the so-called "gender gap"; for the first time in history polls and
elections indicate a sizable difference between men and women in attitude
and behavior—a difference attributable to the spread of women's liberation
as a core dimension of women's political consciousness. During this period
blacks have become increasingly self-conscious as a voting bloc, as have
Mexican-Americans and, in certain communities, homosexuals and other
stigmatized minorities—each mobilized electorally by rhetorical appeals
grounded in "liberation" perspectives.

By focusing, then, on "commitment to everyday life" as the core organizing principle of popular political consciousness we are able to see the
interconnectedness of seemingly diverse and contradictory political orientations and to make some predictions about the dynamics of both "routine"
politics and deroutinized political and cultural movements. From this perspective, political nonparticipation is not necessarily passivity; it is better
understood as an active decision to pursue opportunities for liberty and
identity within the private realm. But because the freedom available in that
realm is politically guaranteed, its infringement can lead to political mobilization expressed as resistance.

Thus political and cultural promises of personal freedom generate privatism while they set the stage for restlessness and political action among groups excluded from the going contract. When its mechanisms of allocation are functioning, a social order that inculcates in its members a universal sense of entitlement to personal freedom may appear highly stable; these same promises, when they are not delivered, are the impetus for delegitimation and instability. In other words, to the extent that Americans evaluate the political system in terms of its capacity to guarantee their daily lives, they are implicitly constraining elites from undertaking projects and policies that put these lives at risk.

The postwar charter was "liberal" in the sense that it granted legitimacy to many of the claims to liberty and equality expressed by the major social movements of the disadvantaged and offered to the labor movement—and later to the black and women's movements—a degree of institutionalized voice in policymaking. Such recognition was based on the assumption that steady economic growth could provide the resources for improving the life chances of the disadvantaged, while expanding opportunities for personal fulfillment for those more advantaged and privileged. The Vietnam experience suggested, however, that domestic peace and popular privatism could not be sustained during a war—that even a "limited" war threatened to undermine the established modus vivendi between elites and masses.

Economic decline in the seventies further called into question the postwar social arrangement. In the climate of "stagflation," some in the policy elite called for a scaling down of U.S. imperial ambition and for a new social contract that recognized a new "era of limits" with respect to economic growth as well as American global power. But these sorts of proposals were eventually overwhelmed by new "conservative" contract proposals aimed at restoring the power and authority of national and corporate elites. The Reagan experiment in social restoration included a concerted effort to delegitimate the major social movements by resisting their claims and excluding their institutionalized leaders from effective representation—and by strongly embracing the claims and leaderships of movements and constituencies who are resistant to the social changes these movements have fostered. It sought a scaling down of the expectations working and middle-class people have about everyday rights and entitlements—including, especially, expectations about job security and the "social wage." It promoted the resurgence of nationalism and "anti-Communism"—in an effort to penetrate the prevailing privatism that is the ground for much popular resistance to remilitarization and war preparation. The Reagan contract thus implicitly recognized that steady economic growth can no longer be counted on to underwrite social peace; instead, it hoped to maintain that peace by achieving fundamental changes in popular beliefs about rights and entitlements coupled to increased mass readiness to accept sacrifice in the name of national power.

The reading of popular consciousness that I have sketched suggests that this contract proposal will have a difficult time achieving the long-term consensus its proponents claim to want. Reagan's popularity, on my reading, was not based on such a consensus. There are to be sure millions who favor it—but they are predominantly white males with some substantial income or property. Reagan's support or acceptance in other sectors was based instead on his skill in providing various forms of reassurance that permitted many to continue to believe that their daily lives were viable. Some of that reassurance was material—Reagan's policies reduced inflation and taxation pressures that in the seventies were experienced as everyday threats by many middle-class Americans. A mild economic recovery, coinciding with the period before and after the 1984 elections, helped mitigate the political damage to the administration of the severe recession that preceded it. But much of Reagan's capacity to reassure was symbolic, projecting simultaneously a sense of "strength" and a sense that the more threatening potentialities of his rhetoric (war, for example) were not really "meant." Moreover, unlike any President since the 1920s, Reagan's rhetoric and style encouraged people to believe that they had the moral right to egocentric fulfillment—a particularly welcome form of reassurance for those in the higher income brackets. But beneath the apparent coherence of Reaganism as an ideological framework lurked rather deep contradictions—nationalistic drum-beating was counterbalanced by considerable practical caution, personal enrichment was encouraged even though dutiful self-sacrifice is what conservative elites hope millions will accept.

The greatest success of the Reagan administration was to differentially distribute the pain of its policies, thereby greatly fragmenting potentialities for resistance. While millions felt relieved from inflation and tax burdens, other millions suffer from the unemployment and dislocation resulting from massive deindustrialization or from reductions in benefits that had once offered them some hope for making an adequate daily life. Those who had felt threatened by the liberation movements of the sixties and seventies were relieved and even elated at finally having a President who spoke *their* language and at the restoration of traditional symbols of national power and "family" virtue—while many others felt despair that hard-won gains in dignity and freedom were fundamentally endangered. Some regions and communities benefited from pumped-up defense contracts, while flag-waving and muscle-flexing felt good to those who had been threatened by the erosion of national or male power—meanwhile, anxiety about war, including nuclear holocaust, was widely, if fitfully, evident.

Thus, despite Reagan's success in consolidating a popular base and his talents at assuaging popular anxieties, many of the conditions for re-emergence of mass resistance were developing during his years. If these have been slow in eventuating in mass mobilization, it is because those who are threatened have found few credible means for effective collective action—especially since the established social contract (that had legitimated their claims) has been terminated by the national elite.

The Reagan years demonstrated some of the strengths and most of the limitations of mass privatism as a framework of popular consciousness. Popular commitment to everyday life prevented the consolidation of the conservative agenda—for if it really were implemented millions know that their everyday security and liberty would be in immediate jeopardy. On the other hand, popular privatism fostered a mass will to believe that the President and his advisors knew what they were doing. By definition, commitment to everyday life encourages people to avert their eyes from present suffering and the future consequences of elite projects—especially if they do not feel immediately threatened. Meanwhile, as elites adhere to strategies of authoritarian control, disadvantaged groups seem locked in oscillating expressions of resistance and frustration.

When even collective resistance seems futile, the chances for democratic breakthrough appear remote indeed. But if pessimism is now fashionable, it may not be all that is warranted. For the collapse of the liberal sociocultural charter may open new possibilities for change in consciousness and new opportunities for democratic action.

To explore such possibilities, we need to go beyond the examination of relations between elite and "mass" consciousness. For alongside those relations there has always been an additional element—segments of society that have sought the democratization of history. These segments—that together constitute what we have called the tradition of the left—have been a determining factor in the development of American culture and the shape of past social contracts. Whether there is a chance for an alternative future to the one proposed by Reaganism depends greatly on the fate of democratic activism in America. I want now to turn to a consideration of that issue.

4

Struggling for the Better Day

The Left Tradition in American History

The little that I am, the little that I am hoping to be, I owe to the socialist movement. It has given me my ideas and ideals; my principles and convictions, and I would not exchange one of them for all of Rockefeller's blood-stained dollars. It has taught me how to serve—a lesson to me of priceless value. It has taught me the ecstasy in the handclasp of a comrade. It has enabled me to hold high communion with you, and made it possible for me to take my place side by side with you in the great struggle for the better day . . . to thrill with fresh-born manhood; to feel life truly worthwhile . . . to realize that, regardless of nationality, race, creed, color or sex, every man, every woman who toils, who renders useful service, every member of the working class without an exception, is my comrade, my brother and sister—and to serve them and their cause is the highest duty of my life.

—Eugene Victor Debs, speaking at Canton, Ohio

HOW CAN we understand the political participation and consciousness of Americans? Only, I have argued, by recognizing that Americans are committed to the making of their lives, entering the political arena, and entertaining political beliefs insofar as these are seen as necessary for the protection or enhancement of one's rightful life.

As we have seen, one implication of this prevailing American political stance is that Americans tend to resist ideological labels. The terms "left," "right," and "center"—whatever utility they may have in defining the political spectrum in European countries—seem to have little use in interpreting the structure of American public opinion.

The decline of ideology in the "West" has not only been frequently noticed, but often celebrated as a sign of political health. There are good reasons for feeling that the abandonment of ideology is a positive sign. The twentieth century is largely a record of the terrible human costs that result from efforts to shape history according to ideology and from the uses of ideology to blind masses of people to their interests. No ideological position is exempt from being charged with such costs and uses. Our time also reveals the degree to which supposedly universalistic ideological bonds disintegrate when placed under pressure by national, ethnic, or racial conflict. We witness on a daily basis the, by now, taken-for-granted chasm between the practices of societal and institutional elites and the ideological principles they claim to represent. Finally, it is certainly clear that none of the classical ideological perspectives that emerged in the nineteenth century speak effectively to the social realities of the late twentieth.

In short, we have all seen too much to believe that history can be totally comprehended or comprehensively directed by a coherent set of principles. Americans are fortunate, it is said, because they are historically relatively immune from such a belief.

American resistance to ideology is usually traced to two features of our polity and culture. First, there is the "genius" of our electoral system. The two-party structure is thought to force coalition and compromise among ideologically divergent groups and to set limits on the degree to which policies based on narrow ideological foundations can be effectuated.

A more fundamental observation is that the United States was the first nation founded on principles, organized in terms of a vision of a new society, rather than on the basis of preestablished cultural and linguistic bonds. Thus American national identity is constituted by a system of universal beliefs. These beliefs are drawn from only a part of the European ideological spectrum. There is, in this view, no "right wing" in the United States, because there is no history of conflict between adherents of the feudal, monarchical past and the classes derived from that past and the adherents and classes rooted in industrial, capitalist modernity. Insofar as principles of liberty, equality, and democracy are integral to American nationhood, they do not become the basis for ideological differentiation and polarization. "Left," "right," and "center" have weak meanings for Americans because they do not exist as distinct frameworks of thought as they do in Europe. In the American context they are all variants of "liberalism." Thus Americans in the late twentieth century are not so much disillusioned with ideological commitment as reinforced in an already strong resistance to it by the multiple traps and tragedies that have characterized twentieth-century history.

Still, I want to suggest that American political consciousness cannot be adequately interpreted without seeing the ideological strands within it and the ideological conflicts that have helped shape it. Americans appear to be unideological because they are committed to their lives rather than to abstractions even when they are engaged in political action. Yet, as I tried to suggest in the first part of this book, the conceptions we have of what we are entitled to in life and of the reciprocal obligations that exist between society and individual members have developed over time as a result of historical struggles. These conceptions are embedded in popular consciousness as largely unarticulated, taken-for-granted premises. They are revealed more in people's everyday activities than in their words.

But these conceptions are likely to have been derived from the visions, programs, and rhetoric of political activists. These activists have themselves been consciously ideological. That is, they have tended to evaluate the existing order in terms of some general set of standards, rather than primarily in terms of their own personal interests or well-being. They have tended to feel impelled to take responsibility for the social order rather than simply their own immediate sphere and have tried to move that order closer to some ideal. And they have been likely to strive to get others to see historical meaning in their personal troubles and discontents.

Thus, the unideological appearance of everyday consciousness conceals the fact that it has been influenced by the ideological expression and the ideologically motivated actions of political activists. It also conceals the fact that the culture within which mundane consciousness is embedded is infused with political principles, including the notions that individual persons ought to be free to make their own lives and that governments ought to exist to support such liberty. That Americans resist commitment to received ideological positions does not mean that the political consciousness of average Americans is purely instrumental or incoherent. That there is a stark contrast between activist and everyday consciousness does not mean that ideologically oriented activists have been without influence.

LEFT, RIGHT, AND CENTER

WHAT DO I mean by the "left"? Earlier, I defined the left as that body of thought and action that favors the democratization of history making, that seeks to expand the capacity of the people themselves to make the decisions that affect the conditions and terms of everyday life. Such a definition, if applied to the actual history of the left, is, however, misleading. Through much of that history, a variety of socialists and reformers advocated models of "planning" and centralized control that were far more technocratic than democratic. For many, "socialism" had appeal as a vision of a "rational," orderly, and harmonious society, as a framework in which people would be *taught* how to be healthy and decent. Moreover, the left has always included some who assumed that they were more capable of directing history than the "masses" themselves.

Such perspectives cannot be excluded from the tradition of the left by defining them away. Even though those of us who were influenced by the New Left have been highly critical of technocratic models of planning and of "vanguard" theories of political leadership, such criticisms were not prevalent within the left in earlier periods. What those who can be classified as standing within the tradition of the left have shared is a vision of a community that determines its future through processes of public discourse—by which I mean deliberate efforts to assess the social benefits and costs of publicly relevant decisions (rather than leaving such decisions to authoritarian elites or markets). Even if authoritarian leftists were antidemocratic in their practice or elitist in their "means," they too claimed to envision a future in which all of society's members would share in the responsibilities and benefits of social development, paying at least lip service to full democracy as a goal. The tradition of the left, then, includes all those who have said that they wanted to replace decision making controlled by private profit and elite domination with processes based on popular voice.

Second, the left tradition encompasses those political or cultural tendencies that have sought to foster in individuals a sense of responsibility for the future of society. By "sense of responsibility" I mean a readiness to take account of the social impact of one's everyday activity, to weigh the degree to which one is contributing to human welfare as well as one's own, to be willing to sacrifice short-run personal gain in the interest of some collective good. I intend to include in the left tradition a variety of efforts, religious as well as secular, cultural as well as political, to expand the boundaries of personal morality beyond narrow conformity, obedience to rules and concern for one's immediate circle of relations, to concern for the communal meaning of one's life.

The tradition of the left, then, is constituted by two kinds of efforts to change the relationship between history and daily life: to change social structures so that, ultimately, historical decisions will be made by those affected by them in the course of their daily lives; to encourage and enable individuals to participate in history before—as well as after—democratic social restructuring has been achieved.

The meaning of the left can be clarified by comparing its perspective with those emanating from the "right" and the "center" as traditions of thought and action.

Right-wing ideological perspectives in the American context emphasize individual "liberty" as the highest goal of the polity, and tend to regard the protection of economic liberty—i.e., the right to amass, deploy, and benefit from private property as one sees fit—as the most important way of preserving liberty in general. Economic liberty is defended on moral grounds—and on the grounds that it is the best arrangement for maximizing general prosperity.

Conservatives recognize that economic liberty results in inequality. Such results are seen as the natural outcome of natural inequalities—in a free market society, each member gets what he or she deserves, according to conservative ideology. But the trouble with inequality is that those who end up losing in competitive struggle try to use political power to gain benefits they cannot get through "free" competition. The American conservative thus views the state as an adversary of liberty and sees democracy as at least as dangerous as autocracy because it gives power to the weak, at the expense of the liberty of those who have been successful.

American conservatism in its pure version is a descendant of classical liberalism—emphasizing the limited state and the free market as the best frameworks for the good society. But to some extent conservatism in the United States has been influenced by European right-wing ideologies that favor elite rule and the preservation of order. Such notions are attractive to professedly libertarian American rightists to the extent that they regard democracy as antithetical to the preservation of property rights.

Right-wing ideology is inherently incongruent with political activism. To the degree that one favors keeping social initiative away from the political process then it seems contradictory to commit oneself to politics, except when necessary to resist state encroachment. For the right, historical "progress," if it is possible at all, is largely made by entrepreneurs, and historical development is stalemated and retarded by those politicians and intellectuals who try to restrict the ability or block the initiative of the entrepreneurial elements. Political activism, in this reading, is thus inherently suspect.

Moreover, to a great extent right-wing ideologies are modes of thought designed not to spur action or to enhance collective responsibility, but to provide a moral justification for egocentricity. The entrepreneur needs no elaborated ideology to energize his efforts—he may need it primarily to demoralize potential political opponents. Insofar as political commitment requires qualities of self-sacrifice or a capacity to find personal fulfillment through social participation, such personal qualities do not resonate well with right-wing ideological perspectives.

Ideologies of the "center" may be thought of as efforts to reconcile "liberty" and "democracy." Liberty remains the central value, but "liberty for all" is regarded by centrists as morally and practically necessary—as compared with the conservative preference for "liberty for those who have made it." For centrists democracy provides a necessary balance wheel for the economic power vested in property—but it need not endanger economic liberty if a certain degree of redistribution and amelioration of inequality is accomplished. Thus American "progressive" or "liberal" thought has put emphasis on the need to provide "equality of opportunity"; economic liberty should not extend to letting the economically successful become a privileged class, aggrandizing control, for their children, of the routes to future success. The state therefore has positive functions—in ensuring a basic decency of living conditions, in providing some of the framework for equal opportunity, in making the nation a community rather than just a market place.

The centrist-liberal tradition is therefore far more resonant with the personal qualities that constitute activism than is the tradition of the right. Although centrist ideologies remain committed to individualism and to privatized conceptions of everyday life, although they stress the basic primacy of the market and private property, they also put positive value on public service, political vocation, and non-pecuniary reward.

But centrist ideologies are rather weak reeds for supporting activist commitment. By definition, they project a politics of melioration and compromise—tending to accept the institutional structures of society as given, proposing to reform these insofar as they glaringly depart from the promise of equal opportunity for private liberty. Democracy is conceived not in terms of popular control of history making, but as a method for providing popular participation in the selection of history makers. Thus the activist who takes a strictly centrist perspective is likely to define problems as technical and administrative, to prefer to operate in terms of the procedures and practices of routine politics, and, sooner or later, to be motivated as much by career considerations as by ideologically grounded principle. Thus centrist ideology, as such, is not likely to be a powerful spur to activism on the part of those who are not political or administrative professionals.

One can be activist in the service of one's self—seeing politics as a way of gaining or protecting one's interest, of warding off an external threat to one's private world, or as a route for achieving status or power. But if political activism is experienced as a central feature of identity, as an intrinsically motivating activity or a moral imperative, then the ideological tradition of the left is most resonant with it. This tradition provides a relatively coherent framework for the socialization of activist orientations. It provides the vision and moral foundations for inspiration and support when facing the daily risks and frustrations of political activity. And it provides the justifications that enable activists to feel that they are more than self-serving when they attempt to intervene in history.

THE TRADITION OF THE LEFT

IN DISCUSSING the tradition of the left I refer to a number of quite diverse and, at least at first glance, quite incompatible ideological strands. Some of these strands have the appearance of considerable coherence and clear definition. Of these, "socialism" is the most significant. For more than a century a fraction of activists have organized themselves as socialists, actively criticizing the established order and other ideologies from what they took to be a clearly defined alternative perspective. "Anarchism" is another apparently coherent ideological thread with a long history, though a less-organized presence in American political life than socialism has had. A third strand has been "populism," usually regarded as a more indigenous, and less coherent, ideological force in American history than the socialist and anarchist traditions.

For a century and a half, however, our politics and culture have featured a variety of radical critics and reformers not easily categorized in terms of the classic streams of left ideology: abolitionists, feminists, radical democrats, laborists, libertarians, left-liberals, anti-imperialists, progressive reformers, New Dealers, one-worlders, peaceniks, environmentalists, and so on. Each of these labels defines a particular style or focus of activism —but, beneath the profusion of causes and labels, and despite the many schisms amongst them, there is a certain commonality of perspective and belief. Moreover, the apparent coherence of the more ideological strands of the left—socialism, anarchism, populism—tends to disintegrate when the history of each of these is looked at even cursorily. Each of these subtraditions was constituted by a host of incongruities and warring factions often sharing little else but a common label. It seems to me inescapable, then, that an understanding of the role and fate of the left in the United States requires us to go beyond examination of the efforts of particular organizations or the influence of particular ideologies. Such organizations and ideologies were expressions of a broad, diffuse current with more eddies and lines of flow than one usually finds in the literature.

The burden of that literature is that the history of the left in the United States is a history of failure. That failure is obvious and relatively easy to describe: (1) During a century of efforts to persuade them, there has never been a time when a substantial proportion—let alone a majority—of American workers have expressed support for socialism; and (2) despite a number of experiments and decades of discussion of its desirability, a political party based in and claiming to speak for the labor movement or the working class in the United States has not emerged.

These two failures have, of course, been profoundly challenging to all those interested in determining the relevance of Marxism to the interpretation of modern society. The logic of Marxian theory depends for its validation on the increasing disaffection of workers with capitalism and their attraction to both a socialist vision and to a political party that can unite and represent them. For decades, students and critics of Marx have been fascinated by the fact that the United States appears to be unique among industrial capitalist societies in not following the developmental logic defined by Marx.

The United States is the only industrial society whose working class has not been influenced by socialist perspectives; the only such society without an explicitly working-class-based political party playing a central role in the state. The contrast can be dramatized further by pointing out that virtually everywhere in the world—in the industrially undeveloped countries as well as in the industrialized ones—wherever a political force has sought a base among workers and other disadvantaged groups, it has tended to call itself socialist. Moreover, identification with socialism has survived and grown even under conditions where such identification could lead to incarceration or death. The socialist movement survived in Mussolini's Italy, in Franco's Spain; it returned to Germany immediately after the defeat of Nazism. Even in Canada, whose living standards and popular culture seem so close to the situation in the States, socialism, while not supported by a majority, nevertheless has solid bases of regional strength, and a viable labor party competes effectively in local and national politics.

The "American exception" is an evident reality—a reality that undoubtedly accounts for the large literature on the seemingly perennial question: "Why no socialism in the United States?" For the unique absence of socialism as a significant force is a fascinating puzzle—and not only to Marxists. For the unlocking of the puzzle seems to require keys to the character of American society itself.

There is a third meaning to the "failure of the American left," having to do with its adherents' inability to sustain any durable organization. Each generation of leftists has tended to start from scratch, finding any existing organizational structures moribund or discredited. If one measures the success of a political enterprise by the sustained growth of its organizational resources, then the American left by this measure has had a dismal record.

The issue of organizational continuity is distinct from the problem of mass acceptance of left ideologies or of successful political organization of the working class. Left ideologies could remain unpopular and political projects unfulfilled without, in principle, preventing left-wing activists from maintaining an ongoing organization. Indeed, this is another sense in which the left experience in the United States appears to be exceptional in comparison with other societies where unpopular or severely repressed lefts continued to sustain the viability of long-established organizations. I am thinking for example of South Africa, where the long-banned African National Congress has continued to function through seventy years of struggle, or of Latin American countries where communist parties continue to have vitality in the face of both considerable isolation and repression. Lefts everywhere experience terrible schism, infighting, and internal competition, but I think the U.S. left is unparalleled in the degree to which organizations came into being, experienced relatively brief periods of rising strength and impact, only to rapidly decline.

The scholarly literature on American exceptionalism has concentrated most on the failure of socialism to win mass acceptance in the United States, and on the related (but distinct) problem of working-class consciousness and the absence of independent political organization by American labor. Less attention in this literature is given to the peculiar organizational fickleness of American leftists. Organizational continuity and growth are typically regarded as unambiguously valid indicators of political success. Scholars and left activists alike assume that political failure naturally leads to organizational disintegration (and vice versa). Presumably, if the objective conditions that have blocked left politics were to change, or the left could overcome its self-defeating ideological handicaps or solve its organizational dilemmas, then left political organization would strengthen its power and resources and that strengthening would mean success. In the course of what follows I want to call all of these assumptions into question.

AMERICA AS EXCEPTIONAL: AN OVERVIEW

THE ARGUMENT of this book provides, I think, a useful basis for analyzing "American exceptionalism." We start with the assumption that human beings are of necessity bound to be preoccupied with the making of their individual lives. The left seeks a world in which such necessity is overcome and people are free in their lives to make history. But people are not free in this sense; moreover, they may not initially want to be nor believe that they can be nor assume that they ought to be. Since Marx, however, the prevailing view on the left has been that the emancipation of humanity's capacity to make history can be achieved only by the collective effort of the people themselves. If, at any given time, only a few believe in the rightness and possibility of such emancipation, if only a few are situated to freely commit themselves to historical projects, these few are both morally and practically unable to bring the new world into being. Lefts everywhere confront the fundamental problem that they are calling on human beings to realize a potentiality which people, as a result of their everyday experience, do not readily perceive in themselves.

This dilemma is solved in theory by assuming that the opportunity of making one's life will be experienced by larger and larger numbers of people as fundamentally frustrated by social conditions. People whose lives have been undermined or destroyed by historical processes will come to feel the necessity of entering history in order to protect or restore their ability to live. Moreover, repeated and cumulative experience in such attempts will work changes on consciousness so that those who enter history out of defensive necessity will increasingly come to see both the need and the possibility of permanently transforming the structures that have kept them powerless. In this way, the human necessity to make one's individual life becomes a necessity to participate in remaking the collective life; the working through of these necessities generates the collective, popular will to emancipation.

Lefts everywhere have assumed that objective conditions of society would create the necessity for collective self-organization among subordinated masses, so that the ranks of those committed to changing history would thus continuously expand and that the interaction between those so committed with relatively privatized, but increasingly discontented, masses would greatly accelerate the processes of emancipation. In their self-conception, left activists everywhere know that they are a specialized history-oriented elite. But they believe that their ranks will increasingly be made up of people drawn from the everyday life of the subordinated groups in society and that they will increasingly be able to connect with the experienced needs and aspirations of those groups.

The tradition of the left, which crystallized in the nineteenth century, was spawned by the great democratic revolutions of the eighteenth. The American and French revolutions promised to bring into being a society which the people would make themselves. These would be societies in which each man would be free to make his own life and all would be equally free to do so. They would be societies in which governments would exist to preserve and protect personal liberty; the guarantee that governments would be so constituted was that the people themselves would choose those who served in government. But these revolutions did not fulfill their promise—particularly the promise of equality of liberty and of voice. And most of the world, including most of Europe, remained, even a half century after these revolutions, locked in the structures of the old regime.

The tradition of the left grew out of these twin incompletions of the eighteenth-century revolutionary spirit. In many countries there were groupings of people whose situations permitted them relative freedom from the conventional constraints of daily life and who were moved by ambition to influence history in terms of the values of the enlightenment and the democratic revolutions. Let us call such groupings "intellectuals," using that word to refer to those in society who are preoccupied with the reconstruction of values, meanings, and beliefs, who are concerned with social development rather than the living out of their lives in a private sphere. The tradition of the left was created in such groupings, by those who searched for means to implement in history the values and visions with which they had become imbued.

Many of these—and Marx was exemplary here—saw that intellectual work *per se* was insufficient as a means for influencing history; talk had to be linked to practical action. For Marx, the visions carried by enlightened intellectuals could have real historical effect only if they were taken over by the masses who remained in chains—for only if these masses awakened and entered history could democracy and equality become real, practical possibilities.

Thus the tradition of the left is constituted by the interaction between intellectuals (those free to be engaged in history but powerless to make it) and masses (those whose labor makes history possible but are powerless to direct it). Participation in this tradition provides intellectuals with identity, direction, meaning, and fulfillment—even if the practical historical results of their efforts are nebulous. For workers, too, such participation may provide spiritual meaning and serve as a secular faith.

For those still bound by the requirements of daily life, however, the left project must have some practical significance if it is to win long-term adherence or wholehearted attraction. For adherence to the left places strains on the capacity of members to live their daily lives: psychological strains resulting from opposing the customary beliefs of established culture; practical strains resulting from the demands and risks required by participation in dissident politics. The cultural and political frameworks provided by the left sustain mass involvement if they provide practical protections of, and spiritual meanings for, everyday life not available within the frameworks of established politics and culture.

The founding ideology of the United States set definite limits on the scope and meaning of democracy. The purpose of democracy was not to enable the people to make history or take control of the society, but to ensure that government would protect and not infringe on liberty. The emphasis on liberty as the core definition of freedom and the good life provides a powerful ethical reinforcement for the universal "natural" preoccupation of human beings with the maintenance of their personal lives rather than making of society.

Many leftists assume a rather crude model of socialization, saying that Americans are "taught" to be individualistic and egocentric. But they miss the point that such "teaching" resonates at a deep level with the fundamental nature of everyday life, in which what is experienced is not "society" or "history" but one's relations with definite other individual human beings to whom one is reciprocally obligated and necessarily committed. The idea of "liberty" is that one ought to be as free as possible to live in that realm and make of it what one can—an idea that was both historically liberating when first enunciated and is continuously experienced as commonsensically right by all of us as we try to make our days.

The idea of liberty, established politically in a structure of guaranteed rights and transmitted culturally through a host of socializing processes, powerfully reinforces the "natural" resistance of people, living in their everyday worlds, to the left's call to them to take part in history. From the perspective of everyday life, such a call makes sense only when one's expected liberty is threatened or denied; one's participation is therefore likely to be limited to action necessary to protect the rights one feels oneself to be entitled to. "Liberty" is, in this sense, experienced as antithetical to "democracy" insofar as the latter demands a generalized reordering of priorities, a putting of the "social," the "public," the "historical" ahead of the "personal," the "private," the "everyday."

"Liberty" immunizes Americans not only against ideologies of the left, but (as I have already suggested) against all ideologies that require sacrifice of concrete personal interest in behalf of remote or abstract collective goals, and against all intense supra-individual loyalties that are experienced as involuntary. There is strong American resistance to sacrifice in the name of national "honor" and "glory," and little popular support in our history for the varieties of authoritarian or fascistic ideologies—religious or secular—that have achieved fanatical followings elsewhere.

Belief in the moral priority of liberty thus encourages a highly pragmatic attitude toward all political claims. It is an attitude that can appear selfish and socially irresponsible from the vantage point of the left, but also anarchistic and undisciplined to those on the authoritarian right. Since, as I have argued, "liberty" narrowly defines the moral requirements of citizenship, those in authority can count on a large degree of popular indifference to their actions. But "liberty" requires those in authority to deliver on their promises to protect the everyday expectations and entitlements of the underlying population. As long as Americans have believed that liberty is not only the basis of freedom, but that it is also possible within the established political economy, they have naturally not been particularly receptive to proposals to replace it.

The simplest explanation of the American exception is, therefore, that the American system delivers the goods—a naturally abundant land coupled to an efficient political economy has provided an average living standard unparalleled in the human experience. If Americans are better off than any other people are or have ever been, why should they be at all interested in radical change?

The reason this explanation is not readily adopted is that it is too simple. Whatever the truth about average living standards may be, millions of Americans during the last century have suffered greatly from the horrors of labor in factory, field, mill, and mine, from urban squalor and rural poverty, from the wrenching dislocations of economic booms and busts. The mass experience of deprivation, insecurity, and inequality has been sufficient to generate considerable mass discontent—as demonstrated by periodic displays of mass protest whose militancy was as fervent as comparable uprisings in other industrial countries. The weakness of the left in the United States can not simply be explained by the fact that Americans have been made comfortable and complacent by material abundance—for Americans have not been all that complacent. Millions have felt themselves to be disadvantaged or oppressed and have, at times, been willing to confront authorities and employers in physical combat as well as political conflict.

Left-wing activists have often felt these confrontations to be rehearsals for revolution. Indeed, such assumptions were often made not only by radicals but by political officials as well. Such perceptions were not necessarily, in the moment, wildly misplaced, for in the heat of such struggles protesting assemblies have been eager to hear and applaud revolutionary rhetoric and have engaged in seriously meant discussion about how history could be fundamentally redirected. But such assumptions about the revolutionary character of popular protest were too simplified. As I suggested in chapter 3, militant protest can be grounded in sentiments of "resistance" and "liberation"—perspectives less universal and embracing than revolutionary aspirations. Instead of general transformation, in the United States, militant defiance has expressed forms of consciousness oriented toward the defense or emancipation of *particular* communities and the winning of *particular* rights.

To the extent that popular consciousness is guided by the pragmatic logic of liberty then popular protest will be aimed at enabling the members of a protesting group to live the everyday lives they believe they are entitled to. Each such protest puts the going system to a test: Will the practical aims of the movement be attained within the established structures of power? Will the movement's claims—material, political, legal—be substantially successful in terms of concrete changes in the lived conditions of daily life? If so, then the revolutionary gestures the movement may have emitted have done their job—not by preparing the people for long-term commitment to making history—but by scaring the relevant elites enough to compel them to keep some of their promises about liberty and equality.

Such pragmatism narrows the effective demands movements make, while it particularizes the social base of movement mobilization. In general, people band together in ways that appear to maximize the practical likelihood of mutual gain. This proposition has numerous concrete implications for collective action. It means, first of all, that protest movements are likely to begin among groups of people who have a past history of face-to-face interaction, who know each other and have with each other an ease of communication and trust. If such movements continue, they are likely to diffuse outward along lines of easiest communication and shared social understanding—i.e., among people with shared ethnicity or other subcultural membership. If people who share a common subcultural situation also discover that they share some resources that enable them to exercise some effective power, then the tendency for a movement to become socially particularized is likely to be quite strong. Put another way, if the relative ease of mobilizing with one's cultural fellows is matched by structurally provided opportunities for such a mobilized group to make gains, then such a group is likely to lack incentive to seek out potential allies among those who are cultural strangers—especially if these strangers are politically and economically weaker.

Marx himself was quite aware of these propensities toward particularization, arguing that it was precisely here that the role of left activists in mobilizing the working class was most crucial. It was the special job of socialists to teach workers that the possible short-run gains to be won by organizing along traditional national, ethnic, religious, or racial lines would prove illusory or ephemeral, that the full power that workers had could be exercised only by unified action across such lines—by acting as a class rather than a myriad of subcultures. The logic of his prediction of proletarian revolution absolutely requires that such teaching be done—and that it prove effective.

More than any other industrial society, the United States embodied conditions that fostered the fragmentation and particularization of working-class consciousness. Great waves of forced and voluntary immigration created a laboring population that is a mosaic of ethnic and racial subcultures. The American political economy was not a melting pot; the groups that came over did not randomly diffuse through the occupational landscape. Immigration occurred in successive waves; as particular ethnic groups established themselves in particular niches, they came to perceive succeeding groups as potential competitors for scarce opportunities or as willing to undercut them in the labor market. By the late nineteenth century such competition was intensified, as massive immigration was occurring simultaneously with employers' concerted efforts to reduce the need for skilled labor in industry. Meanwhile, wherever possible, ethnic entrepreneurs tried to carve out niches in the economy, using their particular subcultures as consumer and labor markets. The history of each ethnic subculture in America is fundamentally shaped by the occupational niches its members were able to open up or control. Ethnic differentiation intimately intertwined with occupational differentiation and both contributed to a high degree of geographical concentration and segregation according to ethnicity.

The result of all this was not, however, simply to fragment the developing working class. The pattern of differentiation was also a structure of stratification. One basis of such stratification was, of course, differences in skill and differential access to skilled work. Such differential access had as its starting point the fact that the earliest immigrants (from Northern Europe) came with the most skills and established themselves before the arrival of less skilled groups.

The second basis of stratification was, of course, race. A vast pool of black slave laborers entered at the bottom of the ladder when they were freed to participate in the competitive labor market. Large numbers of Asians were imported to the West to do the most onerous, backbreaking labor on the rails and in the fields. Black and yellow workers began in the most degraded work situations—at the lowest income levels—while their visibility and cultural strangeness made them, of course, the most differentiated and disparaged of all the ethnic subcultures.

The cleavages and bonds that resulted from this ethnic differentiation and stratification were fundamental to the structuring of working-class mobilization and organization. When workers looked for the most practical means to protect their livelihoods they were likely to find these in the controls their ethnic subculture had achieved over particular economic niches.

Such protection was particularly possible for skilled workers. Possessing a skill is a potentially powerful source of leverage for bargaining over wages and asserting control over conditions of work. But such leverage depends on controlling access to the skill or to the jobs that make use of it. It was, therefore, practical for ethnically homogeneous skilled workers, who had already established themselves, to perceive newly arrived aliens as potential threats and to fight to exclude them from their trades. Skilled workers organized unions not only to fight and bargain with their employers, but also to control entry to their trades. Accordingly, the dominant form of class organization among American workers in the first several decades of the labor movement was the craft union—a mode of organization that built upon, and greatly intensified, differentiation and stratification within the working class.

Ethnically based organization was equally practical in the political arena. Ethnic subcultures were concentrated and segregated in particular neighborhoods, which enabled the carrying on and elaboration of traditionally grounded life-ways in the new and otherwise hostile environment of urban America. To the extent that the political system of the city offered any potential benefits to new immigrants, it was clear that these could not be sought or even perceived if each immigrant tried to enter it as an individual. It was eminently practical for political representation and strategy to be based on the formation of ethnically based voting blocs, mobilized by ethnic political entrepreneurs, and fueled by ethnically based businesses. Accordingly, the dominant mode of working-class political organization in the first decades of effort by workers to achieve political voice was the ethnically grounded urban political machine. This mode of organization enabled subcultures to gain political representation, to take control of a piece of the political patronage pie, to ensure that some level of municipal service would be supplied, and that the individual and collective needs of the community would be mediated by those whose language and cultural style promoted understanding and trust. This same mode of organization, of course, reinforced the fragmentation of the working class, fostered political identification among workers with fellow ethnics who were politicans and businessmen, rather than with fellow workers who were of different origin.

The craft union and the ethnic political machine were practical modes of organization because they made use of the resources and natural lines of association available to people who were otherwise powerless, exploited, and subordinated. The invention of such organization testifies to the ingenuity of people whose ability to form and protect their everyday world is imperilled. The left at the time, acting in terms of its fundamental principles, quite consistently opposed such modes of organization, seeing them as retrograde, immoral, and shortsighted. Such left critiques were, of course, correct—but they failed to recognize that, in their time and place, such modes of organization actually worked to protect concrete everyday interests—something which thc left alternatives could not, as a rule, claim to be able to do for the groups who formed the craft unions and stayed loyal to the machine politicians. There is a statement (whose authenticity I have been unable to verify) attributed to Mayor James Michael Curley, the great exponent of machine politics in Boston, to the effect that, of course, redistribution of the wealth would be right, but in America the best we can achieve is the redistribution of the graft. This rather neatly captures the essence of the debate between the visionaries of the left and the practical wisdom of white ethnic workers.

Implicit in Curley's remark, and in Sam Gompers' famous slogan—"We want more, more, more—now"—is the perception that it was possible to get more from the going system. Neither Curley nor Gompers, nor any other particularistic leader of subordinated groups in the United States, was likely to believe that such gains would flow from the benevolence or inherent fairness of political and economic elites, or that the system left to its natural, market processes would automatically benefit the people for whom they were trying to speak. What they bet on, instead, was that the American system was abundant enough to provide more to those of the poor who were able to organize for effective participation in the existing arenas of bargaining. The point was not to overthrow the system nor challenge the power of those who ran it, but to find the leverage that would make it worth the while of elites to make a deal.

Thus ethnic differentiation and stratification and the resulting fragmentation and ethnocentrism of the American labor movement were the result of the objective conditions of American national development as well as the patterns of self-organization that American workers tended to undertake. In addition, these tendencies were manipulated, reinforced, and elaborated by those seeking to control or undermine the labor movement and other grassroots protest. Employers rather early came to understand that inter-ethnic competition could be fostered and that such fostering would prevent effective labor solidarity. They rather soon came to see that job structures could be organized in finely graded ways to promote aspirations for individual mobility and antagonism within the ranks of employees. They saw that they could gain immediate and long-range practical benefits from systematically using blacks and other despised ethnics as imported strike breakers. And, perhaps most importantly, they learned that protest movements could be undercut if concessions and repressions could be coordinated to reward the effectively organized while punishing those who sought to speak for and organize the most downtrodden.

Because the labor movement and other large-scale mass insurgencies were constituted by a mosaic of the skilled and the unskilled, the relatively more and less advantaged, and diverse ethnicities, the effective, classic American method for controlling these insurgencies was to institute a stratification of benefit, concession, and reform. This is a patterning of response that heightens latent cleavages. It is a method of control that reinforces the already strong tendencies of the less disadvantaged protesters to settle for practical immediate gain rather than risk these in behalf of the needs of their weaker brothers and sisters. The reason that American abundance has worked to undermine the appeals of the left is not that it has provided a progressively better life for all, but that it has provided elites with the wherewithal to concede very substantial benefits for some, so that the exclusion and repression of others would be tolerated by the "class" as a whole.

Winning these benefits quite naturally draws people back into privatized commitments, away from the risks and uncertainties of history making and from potential interst in "class," rather than particularistic, organization.

From the vantage point of the left, such processes are often seen simply as the "buying off" and the "selling out" of relatively privileged groups. Such moralism, however, fails to confront the hard fact that particularistic organization was the most practical expression of the concrete everyday needs, interests, and experiences of the working people who engaged in it.

The left's particular problem, not shared by other ideological enterprises, is that it must call on people to engage in politics not merely to defend particular interests but to advance a vision of universal emancipation. This vision inherently conflicts with the pragmatism and particularism that characterizes grassroots political mobilization in the United States. Although pragmatism and particularism may have been fostered by the opportunism of leaders and the "false consciousness" of masses, leftists have been blind to the fact that such tendencies flow from rational assessment by particular groups of the possibilities for practical gain in the ability to make life.

If the majority of American workers were able to readily identify with each other on the basis of a common cultural heritage, and if they also experienced a common and relatively equal burden of exploitation and deprivation, then the fundamental social conditions for a powerful left would be present. But the essence of the American situation is quite the reverse. When the left called on the workers to organize as a class, it was not, in the United States, proposing a strategy that could make sense as a practical route to collective power, but rather it was asking large numbers to forgo the practical advantages they were more certain of getting through more particularistic organization. When the left called on the people to break fundamentally with established structures of power and to refuse to support established politicians, it was, in effect, proposing that people risk losing the frameworks that enabled many, as individuals, to hope for a better life, in favor of a future whose benefits for individual life were, to say the least, uncertain.

We can sum all this up by saying that *none of the conditions that the tradition of the left has theorized to be requisite for the emergence of either mass allegiance to socialism, or a party representing the majority of the working class have been present in the United States.* If one had wanted to design a capitalist society to minimize the likelihood that the left (as conceived of by its European founders) would be a framework of mass participation, one could not have done much better than to implement the social development that has, mostly unplanned, constituted America.

The perspective we have so far adopted leads to one major conclusion about the fate of the left in the United States. This conclusion is that the conscious, organized, ideological adherents of the left tradition were destined to be a dissenting minority. They were not only in conflict with the status quo and the dominant elites, but also at odds with the patterns of life and consciousness that characterized the subordinated groups they sought to speak for and lead.

There is nothing dishonorable about being a prophet or a dissenter; the agonizing dilemma of the left is that its ideological commitment depended fundamentally on popular, majority adherence to the left vision and project, and therefore the dissenting role could not be accepted and lived within if the ideology was to be fulfilled. Those who are deeply committed to enabling the people to take control of history cannot be satisfied when the majority remain fixed instead on protecting the frameworks of their individual lives.

The American left's inability to be what its ideology declared it could be does not mean, however, that it has been without major historical significance. Indeed, the tragedy of the left may be, not that it failed as a historical agency, but that its adherents failed to comprehend their authentic historical roles. For, despite the weakness of the left's organizational and ideological appeal to the majority of "the people," there has, at various times, been a popular left among specific sectors of the larger mass. Moreover, despite the failure of the organized left to win power, its activity has been integral to the development of American society and culture. Out of the dismal wreckage of the left's past, some hope for renewal may be salvaged—if actual accomplishments and successful moments can be identified.

SUCCESSES OF THE AMERICAN LEFT

The Politicization of Intellectuals

As in Europe, the left tradition in the United States first emerged among intellectuals; for at least one hundred years American intellectuals have been significantly influenced by left-wing ideas and attracted to participation in various forms of left politics. Indeed, the main social and cultural drift of American development has typically been opposed by an "adversary culture" whose members included the leading writers and artists that the society has produced. The adversary culture has been "left" because its primary themes expressed strong alienation from "bourgeois" values and capitalist/industrial reality; however, this alienation usually has been couched in terms of democracy (rather than, as in Europe, in terms of nostalgia for the lost values of pre-capitalist, aristocratic culture). American literary culture was shaped by writers like Whitman, Twain, Thoreau, Melville—who contributed powerfully both to generalized critiques of American civilization and to specific protest against particular features of it, adding richly to the imagery and rhetoric of the left tradition (not only in the United States but globally). Those seeking cultural support for the free market, for business values, or for the going system in general find little comfort in their works. The critical stance toward American civilization adopted by the founders of the literary culture has continued to characterize serious American writing down to the present—even if the early optimism about "democratic vistas" has eroded.

Meanwhile, alongside the strictly creative efforts of artists, many notable intellectuals have, from the nineteenth century on, sought avenues of political engagement. We have figures like Edward Bellamy, whose *Looking Backward* inspired broad interest in socialism and a considerable amount of organizing in its name; Jack London, who helped organize socialist intellectuals and wrote political tracts as well as popular novels; Upton Sinclair, who combined a career as a political writer with many years of active participation in socialist politics; the Brook Farm intellectuals, who sought to organize a community that would attempt to practice the ideals they shared; Dashiell Hammett, who created the hardboiled detective novel and powerfully influenced literary style, and who was a committed member of the Communist Party; John Reed, whose reportage was itself a form of political action, but who also committed himself to party organization. Such engagement was of course not typical of intellectuals, but those who have sought to combine strictly cultural work with direct political action were often admired, and certainly not isolated, within intellectual circles.

Alongside such individual examples of political engagement, there have been periods of broader, movement-like, collective expression of leftism among writers and artists. At least three times in this century considerable numbers of American intellectuals have shared such collective identification.

Prior to World War I, aspiring young intellectuals were strongly attracted to emerging bohemian enclaves, of which Greenwich Village was the most celebrated and important example. In these settings, young writers, poets, and artists developed modes of aesthetic expression and shared lifestyles deliberately designed to challenge conventional constraints and forms—conventions they identified as expressions of "bourgeois" values and commercial civilization. Cultural radicalism was intimately associated with political radicalism and was expressed in terms of fashionable sympathy and also incorporated into the content of artistic work and the journals—especially *The Masses*—that provided the primary arenas for the discourse of the new intellectuals. Literary radicals rubbed elbows with Wobblies and other revolutionary types at the celebrated Village salons of patrons like Mabel Dodge; such physical contact reinforced the shared sense that avant-garde art, sexual freedom, socialism, psychoanalysis were all complementary elements of a single, modern world view.

World War I—and the issue of United States entry into it—led to a disintegration of the "new radicalism" of young intellectuals as a shared sensibility. But the prewar movement had crystallized the tendency for intellectuals in the United States to identify as an adversary culture: the view that intellectuals' fundamental social role was to challenge established structures of belief, criticize the accustomed patterns of daily life, experiment both with symbols and with lifestyle, favor political reform as well as cultural reformation, needle the bourgeoisie and discomfit the ruling elites.

A second wave of shared radicalism emerged among intellectuals during the thirties. The depression compelled many to question the viability of the established order; the rise of fascism in Europe awakened interest in the defense and revitalization of democratic values; militant labor protest provided dramatic confirmation of the idea that the people could mobilize as a progressive force. Intellectuals during the decade frequently signed on to political causes: support for the CIO, defense of Spanish loyalists, the American Writers Congress, the striking miners, the Scottsboro boys. But, as in the pre-World War I era, political engagement was not restricted to such political gestures; radical perspectives influenced the form and content of literary and intellectual work. In the thirties emphasis was less on the breaking of bourgeois moral constraints than on dramatizing the plight and the potentials of the dispossessed and the exploited. The Communist Party's effort, beginning in the mid-thirties, to construct what it called a "Popular Front," claiming to unite all groups that shared an interest in defending democracy against fascism, was paralleled by cultural work identifying with and attempting to speak to the common man. At the same time, groupings of young radical intellectuals, hostile to "Stalinism," worked toward a synthesis of the avant-garde in art and in politics in the pages of such journals as *Partisan Review*.

The sixties marked a third wave of collective intellectual leftism—a mood in which bohemian revolt was revitalized and spread far beyond the enclaves that had been its established base. Once again, cultural radicalism was linked to political protest as intellectuals felt themselves morally challenged by the civil rights revolt, romantically inspired by the example of revolutionary Third World intellectuals (Che, Fanon), and, above all, deeply disturbed by the Vietnam war. Whereas the earlier upsurges of left identification among intellectuals occurred in conjunction with the growth of left parties based among workers, the sixties left was the property of intellectuals themselves, spreading to a mass base not of workers but of students (i.e., youth looking toward intellectual careers). Cultural radicalism in the sixties resembled the "new radicalism" of the early twentieth century in its emphasis on personal liberation, the challenging of conventional morality, the celebration of the avant-garde, and the denigration of the mundane. At the same time, like the intellectuals of the Popular Front, sixties intellectuals were preoccupied with the creation of *popular* culture. But, unlike their thirties counterparts, who sought to "reach" the masses by working with highly accessible forms and symbols, cultural radicals in the sixties tried to do what previous generations would have thought impossible—fuse "avant-garde" and "mass" sensibility.

As Marx himself suggested, intellectuals are attracted to the left because they are vocationally involved with the critical reconstruction of social meaning. The social role of the intellectual has to do with the assessment of society's practices in terms of canons of rationality; to become an intellectual is to be socialized into a language of critical discourse. Like the political activist, the intellectual has consciously decided to orient his or her life to history rather than merely to the sphere of the personal. Both the intellectual and the activist seek to influence the development of the society as an ongoing theme of their lives. The activist seeks such influence through political action; the intellectual, qua intellectual, influences through symbolic action. The activist, who is guided by vision, values, and ideology, is a kind of intellectual, whether or not he or she has received formal training or is formally employed in an intellectual vocation. And the intellectual who consciously directs his or her work toward challenging the legitimacy of established authority structures, who is guided by visions of a newer world and hopes to influence social relations and practices, is a kind of activist—whether or not he or she takes part in specific occasions of political action.

When persons come to the point of seeking a role in shaping the development of society or culture, we can, schematically, describe them as confronting a fundamental choice. On the one hand, they can try to find such roles within the established career structures of political power and institutional responsibility, guided by the prevailing ideological frameworks of society. But such pathways may be objectively or subjectively blocked, either because of scarce occupational opportunities or because of eroding legitimacy of established authority and dominant ideologies.

The tradition of the left has grown out of such historical blockages; activists and intellectuals, finding their history-making ambitions thwarted by the going system, discover modes of history making and models of vocation by constructing space and locating place for opposition. It is therefore inadequate to say that intellectuals and activists are "attracted to" the left; it is more appropriate to recognize that the left is constituted by intellectuals and activists as they search for self-realization within sociocultural orders that thwart aspiration and violate moral sensibility. Karl Marx became the Marx of history because his moral sense was violated by the realities of German society, and also because he was blocked from pursuing an academic career in philosophy. His practical and moral situation was paradigmatic of the situation of many intellectuals over the last couple of centuries. The tradition of the left is continuously carried forward by significant numbers of young people in both "modernizing" and "advanced" societies who develop history-making ambitions and yet are unable to fulfill such aspirations by following the programs, rules, and models officially sanctioned in their societies. Such young people may come from the ranks of the materially oppressed classes, but more likely they were born into family situations of relative privilege and comfort.

The tradition of the left, then, may be understood as an avenue for personal fulfillment, integrated with moral coherence, for youth possessing a certain kind of ambition. That certain kind of ambition is directed not at amassing wealth or power or status in the conventional sense but at making a difference in the world, a mark in history.

The Creation of Democratic Moments

In addition to intellectuals, left organizations and belief have had impact on other sectors of the U.S. population. These are the main instances:

■ From 1905 until World War I, the Socialist Party demonstrated considerable popular success; garnering up to 6 percent of the popular votes in the presidential campaigns of Eugene Debs; winning, by 1912, some 1,200 local offices; selling hundreds of thousands of copies of its major weeklies. Debs himself won a wide popular following, drawing large and highly responsive crowds to his speeches. But the Socialist party showed its most impressive strength within particular locales. Some examples: In Milwaukee, Socialist leader Victor Berger organized an electoral apparatus whose strength rivaled that of any other urban machine. Based in the German immigrant community, the Milwaukee socialists controlled city government for several generations (even after the national party declined into insignificance) and elected Berger to Congress. Meanwhile, between 1905 and 1916, the Socialist Party won popularity among the rural populace of Oklahoma and Texas. In the Southwest, Socialist encampments were huge, festive gatherings attracting thousands for several days of speechmaking, Socialist politicians threatened the power bases of Democrats and Republicans, and Socialist agitators helped spark militant local protest.

■ During the same period, the Industrial Workers of the World (the Wobblies) achieved considerable success in organizing unorganized unskilled workers. In particular, the IWW became the political home of itinerant workers and hoboes—the men who traveled the rails in the West, working in mining and lumber camps and in the fields. The IWW was self-consciously revolutionary, preaching the moral necessity of class struggle, eschewing electoral politics in favor of direct action at the point of production. Wobbly activists led strikes for immediate improvement of conditions and wages, but explicitly declared that such strike action was a rehearsal for eventual revolutionary seizure of the production system by the workers themselves. This revolutionary stance won the Wobblies an extremely bad press, but it did not seem to alienate hundreds of thousands of itinerant workers who carried the red card and participated in Wobbly-led protest. Wobbly influence can be measured not only in the extent of its mass support in certain locales, but also in the depth of commitment demonstrated by many adherents. Wobbly rank-and-filers risked beating and death; many were habitual jail-goers and, in jail, were often subject to harsh conditions, including torture.

■ The Communist Party, founded in the early 1920s, was throughout its history, the most widely despised of American radical organizations, feared not only by its "class" enemies, but by most working people as well. Despite this, however, the CP did achieve significant grassroots support in certain specific cultural locales. In the twenties, when the CP was highly sectarian and isolated, it nevertheless succeeded in attracting sizable numbers of young industrial workers. Such recruitment did not, as a rule, occur en masse—instead, young workers in industrial communities across the country were drawn to the Party in twos and threes, in response to Party agitation or protest activity. The recruitment of such cadre became crucial in defining the CP's role and character during the later years of the depression.

In addition to attracting young workers on a more or less individual basis, the CP in the twenties and thirties was a significant force in particular working-class communities. Most important of these were the Jewish working-class communities in New York—in the Bronx, Brooklyn, and the lower East Side (where, by the thirties, the Jewish population intermingled with Italians and other ethnics). By the mid-thirties the CP also had considerable respect and following in Harlem and some other Northern black ghettoes. Indeed, the Party's strength in New York was sufficient for it to elect two members of the New York City Council, one of whom, Benjamin Davis, was the first black elected to public office in the city. The CP

also helped form and lead the American Labor Party in New York—one
of the few reasonably successful efforts in American history to create a
labor-based party independent of the two established parties. Meanwhile,
apart from electoral activity, the CP and its "front" organizations played a
considerable role in the social and cultural life of the city during the depression and World War II. The CP was a key force in the organization of a
number of New York-based unions, beginning with the largely Jewish clothing trades, and in the thirties branching out to maritime and subway workers, teachers, and other public employees. The CP led successful organization of the unemployed in the early thirties, and of tenants later on.
Public events sponsored by the Party and allied groups, such as the annual
May Day parades and frequent mass rallies in Union Square and Madison
Square Garden, typically drew very sizable crowds. Nowhere else in America
did the Communist Party achieve the kind of grass-roots base that it had
in New York, although in certain communities, notably San Francisco and
Detroit, where CP activists had been key leaders in the creation of strong
and dynamic unions, the Party did win significant grass-roots influence.

■ The Student Non-Violent Coordinating Committee (SNCC) was, in the
early sixties, the organized expression of the radicalization of black students and other black youth. Although ostensibly a civil rights organization
working for specific legal and social reforms, SNCC defined itself as revolutionary and embodied a vision, admittedly vague, of a new society—a
"beloved community." SNCC's ideological perspective included a Wobbly-
like emphasis on militant direct action and a kind of anarchist anti-
elitism, coupled with eloquently expressed faith in the practicality and
rightness of democracy. SNCC was not structured as a mass membership
organization—only full-time organizers could be members—but it clearly
was a focus of identification for large numbers of black students and for
black youth in the rural Southern counties where SNCC concentrated its
organizing. SNCC-led "parties"—the Mississippi Freedom Democratic Party
and the Lowndes County (Alabama) Black Panther Party—were popularly
based, if short-lived, organizations. As the Southern direct action movement ebbed in the mid-sixties, SNCC leaders, such as Stokely Carmichael
and H. Rap Brown, redefined their stance. Through widely publicized,
flamboyant speech-making to black student audiences in the North and the
South, they became articulators and models of radicalization, abandoning
their earlier role as relatively self-effacing organizers. By the late sixties
a new group of young black radical leaders had emerged, most notably in
the Bay Area-based Black Panther Party, who, like the SNCC leaders,
served as models of identification for large numbers of black young people.
Black radicalism was sometimes expressed in terms of a revolutionary na-

tionalism, rooted in the example of Malcolm X and elaborated by Carmichael, and sometimes in a more Marxian rhetorical framework improvised by the Panthers.

Despite such ideological diversity and internal conflict, it was clear by the end of the sixties that a large proportion of the urban black population identified with distinctly left perspectives, even if this identification was not accompanied by much in the way of organization. Indeed, the tradition of the left continues to have a mass base in the United States today within the black communities of the cities, measurable not by the strength of particular organizations, but observable in voting patterns, the rhetoric of leaders, and the content of popular cultural expression.

■ The white New Left of the sixties began among small grouplets of intellectually oriented college students at a few elite universities. Many of these grouplets came together in 1962 in the organization of the Students for a Democratic Society (SDS). By the second half of the decade, identification with SDS and the New Left had decidedly become a mass phenomenon among college students. By 1968, SDS claimed a membership of around 70,000; a Fortune magazine poll of college students in 1969 found that about 13 percent (or well over half a million) identified themselves with the New Left. SDS chapters at some major universities had hundreds of members; SDS-led protests often mobilized thousands on particular campuses. By the end of the sixties a sizable minority of American college students were consciously trying to define their life goals in terms of left values. Clearly the tradition of the left had achieved a degree of mass adherence within the relatively narrow but strategically important confines of the university.

THE POPULAR APPEAL OF THE AMERICAN LEFT

WHAT DO these instances of left popular appeal in the United States tell us about the conditions under which left organization and ideology can win popular allegiance in the exceptional environment of the United States? Let us consider the following as a set of provisional propositions:

First, material conditions are important. Certainly any group of workers whose ability to make the necessities of life is precarious, or who work in life-destroying conditions, or who are consigned to living in squalor have some likelihood of being receptive to those proposing solutions. But in the United States the left has been more readily received by those living under a special constellation of disadvantages. It has had particular appeal for *those workers who have experienced themselves as the victims of progress or who have been neglected or disdained by organized labor.* The southwestern farmers, tenants, and workers who flocked to Socialist revival meetings were suffering the results of severe economic dislocation and depression in the midst of national prosperity. The itinerant workers who sacrificed themselves for the Wobblies were regarded as thoroughly unorganizable by the AFL. The blacks who applauded Malcolm X and Huey Newton confronted lifetimes of economic marginality in the midst of the "affluent society"—in part because they were excluded from the jobs controlled by established labor unions.

Insofar as economic growth in this country has entailed new investment and development in particular regions it has created strong material bases for working-class pragmatism and accommodation. That same growth has been accompanied by disinvestment and decline in other regions, thereby creating the basis for organized resistance movements and the possibility of radicalization. Similarly, insofar as groups of workers have found it practical to form exclusive trade unions to protect their particular advantages, they have created the conditions for bitterness and a vacuum of leadership among the unorganized. These circumstances have provided reason and room for left organizers—like the Wobblies or the socialists who led the New York garment workers—to exercise leadership and articulate alternative ideologies.

Economic decline, unemployment, and exclusion not only produce poverty, but also force the physical uprooting of large groups. Most of the instances of left popular appeal have occurred among people whose lives had been disrupted in this way: the itinerant workers who roamed the West lacking the material capacity even to establish a household and family life; Jewish immigrants from Eastern Europe, thrust out of long established traditional communities into a New York whose streets did not turn out to have gold pavements; Southern blacks, pushed off the land and out of rural life into the squalor and profound uncertainty of the urban North. Such uprooting is itself a source of discontent, especially when coupled with degradation and poverty. But, by breaking the hold of tradition and the constraints of everyday life, it is also a source of painful freedom, especially for the uprooted young. The itinerant workers who formed the Wobblies thought of themselves not only as oppressed and disadvantaged, but also as uniquely free to act because they were not settled down.

A similar freedom, under less desperate material conditions, is available to "youth"—who have left the confines of their parents' households but are not yet expected to take on full-fledged adult work and household responsibilities. Such freedom is especially clear for college students, who are "uprooted" into a social setting that encourages experimentation and free expression. But is is also experienced, more painfully, by poor ghetto and slum youth, who find in the streets demands to break out of the tradition-bound constraints of their families, but little opportunity to find the resources to settle into stable work and family life. Young people, in these circumstances, searching for new meanings and identities, have sometimes found them in the organizational and ideological frameworks of the left.

Our inventory of cases of left popular appeal suggests that, in addition to these material conditions, receptivity to the left is made more likely by the presence, in excluded and "deracinated" groups, of a *cultural heritage that embodies themes of struggle, resistance, and liberation*. Socialism in the Southwest grew among people who had earlier organized in the populist movement. The Wobblies were started by Western miners who already had a legacy of militant action. The IWW attracted, as did the Socialist Party, a myriad of immigrants who had been touched by European revolutionary traditions—Irish rebellion, Italian anarchism, Christian socialism. The American Jewish labor movement had its roots in Eastern European socialist traditions. The black radicalism of the sixties drew inspiration from a century of black struggle, and from the examples of such leaders as W. E. B. DuBois, who linked pan-Africanism and socialism, and Marcus Garvey, who preached a militant nationalist vision of emancipation. And the white New Left was initiated by young people who had been raised in family climates influenced by liberal and radical intellectualism.

Thus, groups influenced by a distinctive set of material and cultural conditions were considerably more likely to be receptive to the perspectives and leadership of the left than groups of workers who were more culturally and economically integrated into the American mainstream. But the left's appeal was based not only on such external conditions but also on what the left organizations did with, and for, these groups.

It is usual for organizers to tell themselves that their success depends on their ability to offer their constituencies means to protect or improve their material welfare—means that depend on the organization and that would be lost or unavailable if people operated singly or relied on established authority. As I have been at pains to stress, however, the left in the United States has typically not been a credible practical instrument for group defense or advancement.

This seems to be true even in the cases where the left has succeeded in winning a popular base. In some of those instances, to be sure, left organization did provide some immediate practical return to its constituents. Victor Berger's Milwaukee socialist machine provided many of the same services that other urban political machines provided—and, more than most, governed the city as a whole in ways that facilitated its effective modernization. Wobbly-led strikes often resulted in improved wages and working conditions. Communist-led unionizing efforts in the thirties achieved substantial gains for workers. Perhaps most dramatic was the case of the West Coast longshore workers, organized by Harry Bridges and his fellow "reds," who won a degree of job security, job control, and living standards probably unsurpassed by any union. But such gains in immediate conditions of life do not account for the intensity or the persistence of radicalism in the groups we have been talking about. Indeed, whenever left organizers have had success in securing material gains, they have, with considerable justice, been criticized from the left for compromising the left project. When the organized left has had significant appeal, it has provided something other than instrumental value. That something I would summarize as a "framework for self-development."

By "self-development" I mean growth in the capacity of the individual to find and express meaning in his or her life, to believe that one's life counts both for specific others and for some larger, historically relevant purpose, that one is a person of worth and acomplishment. Self-development in this sense has two facets. On the one hand, it is constituted by the establishment of *identity*—the sense that one's life has a meaning defined by a heritage that one is true to and carrying forward, or by a vision of the social future that one is trying to contribute to. Second, self-development has to do with growth in the *actualization* of one's potentials— the sense that one has talents, abilities, and qualities that are valuable to others and that one is using with increasingly good effect.

In the official culture of Western industrial societies, self-development —the achievement of identity and self-worth—is, at least for men, guided and measured by vocational choice and advancement and, at least for women, by the making and raising of a family.

Economic and social marginality blocks self-development. The economically excluded and socially uprooted cannot follow the prescriptions of official culture to find meaning and self-worth. Indeed, to adhere to those prescriptions is to view oneself as insignificant and worthless. Sociologists—following Durkheim's classic work—have long understood that these circumstances foster the development of all manner of "deviant" adaptations and subcultures—frameworks of belief and collective action that permit members to live coherent and relatively self-respecting lives in the face of established social structures and cultural prescriptions that make them defeated and unrespectable. This is how sociologists have explained the growth of delinquent gangs and other criminal subcultures, of religious sects, of a great variety of spiritual and secular cults, popular enthusiasms and collective outbursts among poor people—especially the poor whose customary lifeways have been disrupted by social change and dislocation.

There are times when the organized left has been able to serve unrespectable people by providing a framework for daily life and for self-development that constituted a viable alternative to official culture.

SP AND IWW AS FRAMEWORKS FOR MORAL REDEMPTION

WHEN THE Socialist Party took hold among the tenant farmers of Oklahoma and Texas, one of its primary activities was the convening of week-long summer encampments, the largest of which attracted thousands of families. These events were modeled after revival meetings and had a good deal of their emotional tone. The encampments featured the popular Socialist speakers of the day—like Gene Debs, Mother Jones, Oscar Ameringer, and Kate O'Hare—as well as lectures and classes, carnival booths, ferris wheels. These encampments provided opportunities for socializing and communal relaxation otherwise unavailable to the people of the region. They offered information and insight about the larger world, and a taste of the world of ideas that encouraged many to expand their intellectual horizons. At the encampments one could make direct contact with history in the persons of heroes like Debs and Mother Jones; moreover, the size of these gatherings surely enabled otherwise isolated poor folk to feel the potential strength of their numbers and shared enthusiasm.

Southwestern socialism was also spread by a remarkable weekly newspaper, *The Appeal to Reason,* published by Julius Wayland—a magazine which, next to the *Saturday Evening Post* was the largest circulation weekly of its time in the United States. Its subscriptions were sold by an "army" of volunteer salespeople, who traveled into remote areas to sell the paper and spread its word. The paper was a binding force among its tens of thousands of readers in the Southwest—and its army provided, for participants, a definite avenue for finding purpose and recognition in daily life. In the encampment and the *Appeal,* Socialists had found two ingenious mechanisms for filling fundamental developmental needs of large numbers of people whose cultural life would otherwise have been profoundly impoverished.

The IWW created a rich array of practices and institutions to serve the practical and developmental needs of the itinerant workers who constituted its popular base. In numerous western towns, Wobbly meeting halls and houses served as safe havens where itinerants could find comradeship and a place to crash. The Wobbly red card became a ticket, in railcars and jungle camps, enabling one to obtain brotherly protection from police and toughs who hassled or preyed upon the hoboes. Indeed, the Wobblies were a national brotherhood of support for such men, more developed and effective than the casual mutual aid that hoboes otherwise could establish, and far more egalitarian and less sanctimonious than that provided by the IWW's major competitor, the Salvation Army. Along with such material aid, the IWW offered some remarkable opportunities for creative expression for its adherents. Wobbly publications were filled with the stories, poems, and drawings of hundreds of working stiffs; Wobbly streetcorner rallies featured the songs of its numbers of troubadours and provided platforms for an army of homegrown orators. And for the majority of Wobblies, who might not have had aspirations to artistic or intellectual expression, the movement in its heyday provided daily opportunities for members to test their courage in combat and in jail. The IWW was thus a framework in which some of the most scorned and dispossessed members of society could find voice, purpose, and opportunity for heroism.

Both the Socialists of the Southwest and the IWW provided not only institutional mechanisms but also belief systems that promoted enhanced feelings of purpose and worth. A fundamental difference between these politically expressive movements and other "deviant subcultures" was that the political groups, by definition, offered members *a conception of their role in history*. Both organizations, of course, argued and struggled for the rights of their constituencies; unlike religious or "criminal" deviant adaptations, these political movements challenged the legitimacy of a sociocultural order that denied such rights. But both groups went further. They emphasized not only that their constituencies deserved relief from victimization but that these victims had a fundamental role to play in history. "Solidarity" was a means to win protection from oppression and to enter history as a redemptive force in society, as emancipators of humanity. "In our hands is placed a power greater than their hoarded gold," sang the Wobblies, a power capable of bringing to birth "a new world from the ashes of the old." The Wobblies perceived that their very rootlessness gave them a freedom to make history that other, more settled, role-bound workers did not have. If, objectively, itinerant workers did not have the power literally to remake society, their vision and organization did give them the psychological power to transmute themselves from men and women living in desperation to persons capable of articulating and acting for the best hopes of their fellow workers.

THE CP AS A WORKER'S UNIVERSITY

THE RUSSIAN revolution seemed to provide overwhelming proof of the power of united masses to overturn their oppressors. Not only did it inspire radical activists—it challenged them to emulate the Bolsheviks, who were seen as far more disciplined and "professional" in their organization and practice than American radicals conceived themselves to be. Accordingly, many activists left the SP and IWW to help found the Communist Party in an effort to implement the Bolshevist model.

For more than a decade after its founding, the CP was little more than an isolated and generally despised sect, not achieving even the pockets of popularity that its predecessors had won. If the CP had any concentrated popular base at all it was among Jewish workers in New York. From the late nineteenth century on, these workers strongly identified with socialism—an identification that many had brought with them from Eastern Europe. Jewish socialism in New York was intimately intertwined with a host of social and cultural institutions developed within the community to cope with the pain of sweatshop, slum, and "acculturation." These included medical and burial societies, literary circles, theater and choral groups, housing co-ops, and networks of schools, publishing houses, newspapers, and magazines that promoted the use and development of Yiddish—the everyday language of Eastern European Jews. This institutional support structure, and the growth of a Yiddish literature that expressed class consciousness and radical perspectives, reinforced and deepened the sense among many Jews that socialism and Jewish identity were practically synonymous.

Socialist trade unionism and cultural expression among Jews predated the Soviet revolution by at least thirty years but, since New York Jews were predominantly Russian in origin, that revolution had an enormous and special impact on the community. Much of the impetus for the creation of a Party in the Bolshevik image came from the Russian Federation within the Socialist Party; at the same time Jewish Marxists independently were coming to similar conclusions. Indeed, the first daily newspaper in North America to identify with the Soviet Revolution was the Yiddish language *Morning Freiheit*, whose founding predated the formation of the Communist Party itself. Once the Party was established, it garnered the allegiance of the *Freiheit* as well as leaders and members of the fraternal societies, trade unions, and cultural organizations already deeply imbedded in the New York Jewish community. By the twenties, Jewish workers were served by several parallel institutional structures tied to competing groups of Communists, social democrats, and labor Zionists. These groups warred with each other, but their combined effect was to fuse the sense of being Jewish with a left-wing political sensibility. It was in this community that, in the 1920s, the Communist Party was able to find one of its few toeholds of legitimacy. But it is evident that the Party itself made little independent contribution to the development of either radicalism or the community in this case; the contribution of the Jewish Communists was enormous—but it seems likely that they would have done what they did had the Party never been founded.

Outside of New York, the CP was, for at least ten years, highly isolated and largely ineffective. This isolation had its origins, of course, in widespread fear and hatred of Bolsheviks and reds whipped up by the mass media and linked to long-standing strains of xenophobia and anti-radicalism in the culture. But the CP's isolation was enormously aided by the Party's own practices—its slavish adherence to Comintern policies, its superheated revolutionary rhetoric mixed with imported phraseology, its refusal to trust or work honestly with competing left organizations, and its repeated inability to see American conditions through other than red-tinted glasses. Yet, despite its glaring limitations as a political vehicle, the Party, during those years, managed to recruit a sizable number of new members from the mainstream of the working class.

A reading of the biographies of those who eventually became leaders of the CP suggests that for some workers the Party, in its early years, provided opportunities for self-development similar to those offered by the SP and the IWW.

In the twenties, Party organizers concentrated their efforts on industrial communities, agitating for militant strike action, preaching the gospel of proletarian revolution. Although efforts to win mass support were generally unavailing, small numbers of young workers were attracted to the Party. Some were drawn to it because they perceived the Communists as the legitimate heirs to a radical tradition in which they had been raised; others because of the clarity of the Party line and its links to the successful Soviet revolution. But the appeal of the Party was not, I think, based on its specific ideological thrust or the quality of its public work. Rather the Party had a particular attraction for some young men and women who aspired to live in a wider world, to experience more, to "be somebody"—and who could find little opportunity to pursue their aspirations within the terms of their accustomed lives or expected futures.

For such youth in those years, formal schooling was not an available route to expanded opportunity. The rapidly expanding industries of popular entertainment and sports were opening avenues for achievement and recognition for some talented youth of working-class and immigrant background. For others, there was opportunity in the underworld of organized crime. But if you were a working-class youth who was interested in the world of ideas, if you were burning with moral indignation at social conditions and, at the same time, seeking to leave your mark, the Party provided opportunities worth considering.

Party meetings were occasions for intense and serious discussion and for encountering, perhaps for the first time, young people like yourself. The Party demanded that you keep informed, that you learn to debate, to read and to study, to speak and to write. People of this background, when reminiscing about their early experience in the Party, often mention being forced to do soapbox streetcorner speaking—recalling this as a crucial event. Think of what this meant for a young woman of, say, sixteen: having to get up in front of a crowd of strangers who were potentially hostile; having to formulate one's thoughts and express them with force. It is clear that this sort of experience, if carried off with any success, was a terrific opportunity for growth.

In addition to such precious opportunity for expression and intellectual development, the Party offered the opportunity to travel to conferences in strange and wonderful big cities, there to rub shoulders with those who had made history in labor struggles, and to meet comrades from all over America. Moreover, it was not unusual for young activists to be sent to international meetings where the sense of expanded horizons and contact with history in the making was incredibly exhilarating. As one's involvement deepened, there was the likelihood of being asked to move to a new place, to become a fully responsible organizer, a full-time history maker.

In short, the Communist Party in the twenties and thirties was the functional equivalent of a university for working-class young people who were attracted to it. The Party provided opportunity for intellectual development, for the acquisition of skills, and the establishment of a vocation— opportunities not readily available to such youth in the official institutional structure of society. The CP enabled such youth to move beyond the confines of working-class life—but unlike conventional pathways to success, communism provided a moral framework that encouraged young workers to leave their homes behind while deepening their generalized commitment to their class. It provided members with resources and opportunities for self-development conventionally available only to middle-class youth, while uncoupling the conventional connection between personal advancement and material well-being. From a "middle-class perspective" the Party appeared to be a kind of trap for aspiring, intelligent youth, preventing them from pursuing the advantages that their talents might otherwise have made possible. But from the perspective of many of these youths the Party provided a sense of possibility for personal and moral fulfillment that no other structure in society could offer. In the twenties and thirties, thousands of young men and women, drawn from steel towns and ghettos, from auto plants and sweat shops, from mines and docks, were schooled in this way.

THE NEW LEFT AS A LABORATORY FOR
MORAL VOCATION

BY THE fifties and sixties, higher education had become a mass institution, still predominantly reserved for the offspring of the upper and middle classes, but increasingly open to the sorts of young people of working-class origin whose opportunities for expanded horizons had been so limited in earlier decades. Interestingly enough, the revival of the left in the early sixties was begun by, and had its greatest impact among, college youth. These clearly did not have the problems of blocked self-development confronted by earlier generations—problems of impoverishment, of dislocation and exclusion. Is there, nevertheless, any sense in which the New Left of the sixties provided means for self-development for its constituencies comparable to that provided by the earlier lefts we have been describing?

The first and most radicalized youth of the sixties were the black students of the South who initiated the sit-ins and other direct action campaigns and organized the Student Non-Violent Coordinating Committee (SNCC). There can be little doubt that black students in the sixties confronted deep dilemmas of self-development. It was now possible for them to go to college, but the black colleges were certainly not vehicles for achieving elite status—and many were poorly financed and educationally marginal. Black students in the early sixties undoubtedly knew that their likely future incomes would give them rough equality in living standards to the average white *without* higher education. They could look forward to continuing discrimination and exclusion in the occupational world. Most galling was the continuing reality of everyday structures of segregation of public life and exclusion from the political system in the South. Finally, there seemed no way to escape from the dilemma that upward mobility, as defined by the dominant culture, required the remaking of oneself in white terms, the betrayal of one's own traditions and ways in favor of a patterned blandness—a betrayal which, however, did not guarantee one's acceptance into that culture.

Black students had moved out of the frameworks of self-definition provided by tradition, but found themselves blocked—in terms both of material opportunity and of moral coherence—from finding a viable place within the dominant institutions and cultural framework. The shared personal crisis of black students was resolved as they discovered a method of struggle—nonviolent direct action—and a mission encompassing both the liberation of black folk and the redemption of white America.

The formation of SNCC enabled hundreds of black youth, drawn from northern universities, southern black colleges and high schools, to find their place as organizers of the wider community, operating in terms of a more or less coherent and dramatically effective political strategy. At the same time, SNCC was a community that served as a crucible of identity for its members. SNCC workers, garbed in overalls and blue jeans, developed, in their situation of shared risk, a camaraderie expressed not only in enormously courageous action but also in an outpouring of song, poetry, and eloquent speech. For a time, SNCC workers felt that their comradeship prefigured a future in which a "beloved community" would come into being in the South—a vision clearly echoing the tradition of the left.

SNCC did not survive organizationally, and its distinctive ideological perspective eventually was replaced by a more assertive and explicitly revolutionary nationalism. But the SNCC experience, for those who shared it, resulted not only in substantial political gains but also in personal growth in capacities for self-assertion and self-expression defining a new, liberated identity for young blacks.

Numbers of white students were also deeply affected by the SNCC experience. In 1960, hundreds of northern white students mobilized in support of the Southern sit-ins and many committed themselves to long-term involvement in the civil rights struggle. By 1964, hundreds were ready to respond to SNCC's call to spend the summer in Mississippi, in the knowledge that they risked hardship, jail, and physical danger. The white New Left crystallized out of this movement, the formation of Students for a Democratic Society having been consciously motivated by the example set by SNCC.

The founders of SDS had been reared in families of at least middle-class comfort—and quite a few were very well-off. These were the sorts of families that provided their children with a richness of cultural resources. They were excellently schooled; they had private lessons and went to progressive summer camps; they had traveled widely and lived in stimulating and self-consciously caring family surroundings. Most SDS founders, and others in the early New Left, had all the benefits to self-esteem that come from academic success. Most of them did not lack opportunities for self-expression. They had been encouraged to develop their artistic talents, they had been leaders of their classmates. Indeed, most of those who gathered at Port Huron, Michigan, to found SDS were, at the time, leaders in student government, editors of their college papers, or in other ways outstanding among their peers. Most were enrolled at elite colleges and universities and had little doubt that any careers they might choose were readily accessible to them. It is, therefore, not easy to see what left activism had to offer them in the way of self-development that they could not readily find by following the established paths of career and lifestyle that had already opened before them.

Yet, if there is one thing they had in common at the beginning, it was their extreme reluctance to go down those paths. That reluctance, for most, originated in their upbringing, for most had been raised not in "conventional" middle-class families but in families that in some way or other were "carriers" of the tradition of the left. Some were in fact "red diaper babies," as they called themselves—that is, sons and daughters of parents who had been Communists, or Socialists, or strongly identified with left-wing causes. Most, however, did not have parents whose political identifications were so explicit; they were, rather, people who had liberal sympathy—a sympathy that might have been occasionally expressed by support for various causes, or that connected to their vocation as liberal professionals. What all these family situations had in common was the emphasis given to the moral imperative that the children lead lives rooted in social purpose, rather than simply settling for material success and personal comfort. In one way or another, the white students who responded to the civil rights movement and who helped form the New Left had been raised to feel that they were morally required to contribute meaningfully to "making the world a better place." Moreover, in most cases, parents' encouragement was directed not at having their children follow in their footsteps but at being more fully and wholeheartedly "involved" than they had been. For, on the whole, these parents, representative of the generation of thirties "intelligentsia," felt that they had not really fulfilled their social obligations, that they had compromised their values in a quest for material security and career advancement, or in naive and uncritical sympathy with "old left" practices. Such parents were strongly impelled to encourage their children to seize opportunities to do more with their lives than make money and win status.

Young people, having been raised in such terms, found their already formed disposition to resist conventional definitions of the meaning of their lives reinforced and deepened by the critical intellectual traditions that they encountered in their college studies. Moreover, they had entered college in a period in which influential intellectuals were explicitly criticizing the conformism and privatism of fifties' youth—criticism that resonated with their own direct experience with their fellow students. By the late fifties, substantial pockets of "alienated intellectual" students were noticeable on many campuses, among whom "subterranean traditions" of bohemianism and political radicalism were visibly influential.

Student intellectuals in the late fifties confronted the problem that Marx himself articulated at a similar stage in his own life—how to change the world rather than merely criticize it. But they could not simply adopt his solution—i.e., join the movement of the proletariat. There was no such movement; there was no proletariat. The left of their parents' generation had long since been exhausted, its organizational framework had been morally and practically discredited, and many of its key premises—about the nature of American society and of the Russian revolution—had been invalidated. With the dissipation of their political hopes, the parents' generation had sought personal modes of fulfillment and expression—and yet those same elders were often warning that such modes were limited, compromised, even empty.

One reason the Southern student sit-ins were so compelling for young whites such as these was that the black students had invented a way for seemingly insignificant young people to make a major difference in history. The sit-ins filled a missing link between feelings of alienation and historical opportunity—a link that was not only practically effective but morally compelling. The sit-ins demonstrated to socially concerned youth that small groups of principled people could intervene in history by taking direct, non-violent action to confront obvious injustice, and that such action could be taken without the need for the sterile ideological debate and political maneuvering that they saw as characteristic of the old left. Moreover, the sit-inners and freedom riders were frequently met with physical attack and jail. Their martyr-like sacrifices created strong moral pressure on relatively privileged white youth. The sit-ins were thus a signal event in the politicization of a generation of "intellectual" youth, providing both impetus and method for transmuting alienation into action.

When white students found each other in the civil rights movement, they began a process of mutual discovery of aspirations for a shared mission. The New Left was an effort to create a new ideological foundation and political practice for the left; it was also, and equally, an effort to create new vocational possibilities for young intellectuals. Rather than allowing themselves to continue to be groomed for the academic, professional, and managerial roles their professors had repeatedly told them they were highly qualified to succeed at, the early New Leftists sought work that would be both principled and historically effective, that would permit use of their skills and talents without being avenues to privilege. There were a few models—a handful of maverick professors like C. Wright Mills; writers and artists like James Agee, who had tried to give the voiceless poor a voice; fearlessly independent journalists like I. F. Stone and Carey McWilliams; students turned organizers like the young communists and socialists of the CIO days and the SNCC people; a few free-lance radical intellectuals like Paul Goodman; a tiny number of long-time radicals who had lived lives of deep commitment while retaining their intellectual independence like A. J. Muste. But by and large New Leftists in the early sixties felt that any definitions of, and opportunities for, the vocations they sought would have to come from themselves, that the Old Left was too moribund to provide such frameworks, and the institutional structure of established society too monolithic and retrograde to provide sufficient space within which their emerging self-definitions could find support.

It was not long before SDS, aided by small grants from unions and liberal foundations, began to create such vocational opportunities. The most prestigious role was that of the full-time organizer, imagined as a carrier of commitment and skill to politically under-represented poor communities— especially poor white or ethnically mixed urban neighborhoods—helping to develop community-based, quasi-union organizations. During the mid-sixties, SDS recruited and trained several hundred students for such work, drawing on the knowledge and example of old-time labor organizers and the inspiration and experience of civil rights movement organizers who were already working in comparable ways. SDS' approach was not dissimilar from what some in the Peace Corps were developing as a vocational direction for middle-class American youth; it was strongly influenced, too, by the ideas and practices of Saul Alinsky and his Industrial Areas Foundation, whose effort to form neighborhood organizations comparable to labor unions dated back to the thirties. But the SDS effort was self-organized, exhibiting both the strengths and the weaknesses that one might expect to be produced by a band of rather naive, inexperienced, romantic, and excessively self-confident middle-class youths.

Whatever the political impact of the Economic Research and Action Project (ERAP—the official name SDS gave to its community organizing program), its personal effect on participants and on the wider SDS following was significant. The project seemed to demonstrate that privileged middle-class young intellectuals did not have to remain enfolded in the confines of their cultural situation, nor settle for the career lines defined by established institutions. Only a few ERAPers were ultimately able to believe that the specific role of organizing the urban poor was one that they could effectively and viably carry through on a long-term basis. Not a few ultimately "burned out" as a result of the terrors and frustrations of this work. But a sizable portion of a whole generation was directly or indirectly encouraged, by SNCC and by ERAP, to orient their lives as future intellectuals and professionals toward the needs of the dispossessed and the poor, toward issues of social justice and social change.

The stories I have been telling—about the Oklahoma Socialists, the Wobblies, the New York Jews, the young Communist workers, SNCC, and SDS—are intended to show that there have been times and places in this country when left organizations have made deep connection with definite communities and specific segments of the population. These were communities and segments whose material circumstances or cultural situations prevented members from relying on traditional or culturally dominant frameworks for the formation of identity and the establishment of self-worth. The quest for cultural alternatives nascent in such groups was given form and substance by left organizations. These organizations did not, as common stereotype would have it, simply come from "outside" and "recruit." Each of these organizations must also be understood as an expression of the self-organization of a stratum of society whose shared problems of self-definition could be resolved, at least in part, by the creation of an organized politics and culture of protest.

These stories suggest, then, that the "popular appeal" of left organizations has had to do not with political program or the capacity to win power and control material benefits, but with the capacity to create ideological and institutional frameworks that promote the self-development of adherents. In the American context, when previously privatized people have formed a shared and conscious identification with the left, it has been because their unfulfilled "cultural needs" have been met, in specifically defined ways, in and through left organization. If the American left has so far failed to socialize the political economy, it has nevertheless succeeded in certain times and places in socializing particular groups of human beings.

THE LEFT AS AN AGENCY OF SOCIALIZATION

Nurturing Grass-Roots Activism

How was such socialization actually accomplished? What sorts of concrete methods and processes did left organizations develop to nurture members' commitment to activism?

First of all there were the obvious ones—the meetings, rallies, newspapers, pamphlets through which the organization's general values and specific policies were propounded, explained, and defended. Less well-known, but far more effective, were efforts to undertake education of adherents by establishing relatively formal institutional structures. These included: family encampments like those convened by the southwestern socialists; party schools, which were established by socialists and communists; children's summer camps; training institutes for organizers, including the Brookwood Labor College run by A. J. Muste, and the Highlander Folk School; freedom schools, established by SNCC during the peak period of organizing in Mississippi; free universities, established by SDS in the mid-sixties.

Typically, such efforts were designed to provide members with deeper understanding of the organization's ideological foundations. In most cases, however, their most important educational functions were aimed at various kinds of training and self-development. The curricula included courses that incorporated technical knowledge—about the workings of the economy and the political system, or conditions in other countries, or the history of the movement, and technical skills—in writing and speaking, in the production of printed materials, in organizing. In addition, there were often less "practical" courses—in, say, literature, philosophy, science, and art—that served the needs of working-class members who lacked formal education, while implementing the organization's understanding of itself as an heir to, and a carrier of, the humanistic cultural heritage.

The deepest socializing impact of participating in a left organization was the result, however, of processes that transcended such formalized educational practices. The very experience of being an activist challenges individuals to expand their competences and skills, to be assertive rather than self-effacing, to take social and physical risks. To have to speak before strangers, trying to articulate abstract ideas coherently and persuasively is one set of such challenges. Being chosen to lead, to take organizational responsibility, to be a spokesperson or a representative is another. To be an activist, one discovers, requires the development of the various complex skills that go with being a leader or a public person. Moreover, one is put into intense contact with others in situations that demand a high degree of mutual support and trust. Such experiences of comradeship can build self-confidence and a sense of self-worth while widening one's circle of deep friendship.

To be a relatively committed leftist, then, has meant both that one adheres to an ideological perspective that fundamentally affects one's beliefs and values, and that one enters a framework of institutional and interpersonal ties that fundamentally affect one's self-conceptions and life choices. Indeed, in some cases, most notably that of the New York Communist Party in the 1930s, virtually every aspect of one's everyday life could be lived in relation to the Party's institutional framework. One could read the Party's daily newspaper, go to work in a shop represented by a Party-allied union, eat lunch or dinner at a restaurant run by Party sympathizers or frequented by comrades, participate in a Party organized softball or volley-ball league, sing in a Party-organized chorus or theater group, attend two or three meetings a week, send your children to a Party-allied summer camp or after-school program, get medical care through the Party-sponsored medical society, go to lectures or concerts or rallies put on by Party-related organizations, read books by writers celebrated by the Party cultural magazine or published by the Party publishing house, vacation at a

Party-owned resort, spend retirement recreating at old people's activity centers sponsored by the Party, be buried by the Party-sponsored funeral society. In those years, in New York, it was possible to find housing projects that had been developed by the Party, and neighborhoods in the city where Party members were likely to live next door and everybody was some kind of left winger. Although the left in New York was unusually elaborated institutionally, wherever left organizations have taken root in the United States, they have reinforced and enriched many members' capacity to live everyday, even if, as activists, they were often estranged from the demands and joys of conventional daily life.

All of the "mechanisms of socialization" I have mentioned served the function, for the organizations who used them, of binding members' loyalties and developing their capacities as organizational cadre. But the point I have been making is that they were fundamental sources of fulfillment and development for the individual members as well. The commitment of left activists—their willingness to make sacrifices and take risks—is thus best understood not in terms simply of passionate adherence to a cause or a system of beliefs, nor in terms of authoritarian obedience, but as the expression of an identity formed in the process of living as a member of a cherished community—a community that has given one the chance to be more than what one would otherwise have been.

From the perspective of the organizations, the purpose of investing resources in education, services, and cultural expression was to build a loyal, competent, and disciplined membership. The party did not exist, certainly, to serve its members' needs for self-development and fulfillment, but to make history. The Communist Party was most explicit about seeking the development of a disciplined, professional membership, but all the other organizations, to one degree or another, certainly tried to instill in members specific readinesses to do their organizational duty, and to implement organizational policy. Obviously, one effect of the socialization practices of these organizations was to achieve a degree of such loyalty and discipline. But this effect was probably the least successful outcome of such practices.

As we noticed earlier in this chapter, none of the organizations that have constituted the organized left in the United States was able to sustain itself as a dynamic force for more than about a decade. The evidence is that this tendency to decline was not due to the failure of these organizations to develop strong ties to significant grassroots communities. Nor was it due to a failure to bind members to strong commitment to self-sacrifice and collective responsibility. Yet, if one of the primary intended purposes of left socialization was to create an "army" of devoted followers, then in this respect all these organizations had only fleeting success.

What the left organizations did best was to develop the capacities of thousands of Americans to be political activists. Many of these were drawn from the stratum of the educated middle class and therefore already predisposed to active political involvement. For these, participation in the organized left helped crystallize activist identity and encouraged commitment to labor and other movements of the disadvantaged. But the particular contribution of the organized left was to enable many thousands of economically disadvantaged and educationally deprived people to become committed activists, training many, who would never otherwise have had the opportunity, to take on political roles.

What Activists Accomplished

Some left activists focused their political energies on efforts to build and maintain the organizations that had socialized them. However, although the logic of organization as well as the explicit ideology of most of the left parties generated expectations that organization building would be the first priority of those whom the parties had nurtured and trained, the typical activist member did not, in fact, spend his or her political life primarily as a party organizer or funtionary. Instead, most devoted primary attention to needs and opportunities for political action they found in the milieus of workplace and community.

There were, to be sure, thousands of Socialist Party members who spent much energy to promoting Party electoral campaigns, distributing Socialist papers, and in other Party support activity. In its heyday, scores of effective speakers and agitators organized for the Party and spread its gospel. These activities helped build, for a time, a vital organization that appeared destined to have major historical impact. In that period, the Party threatened the electoral base of established politicians and forced a broadening of the ideological spectrum in America. As an organization explicitly advocating an alternative to capitalist ideology and policy, the Socialist Party in those years was the most effective of any of the left organizations in American history.

A more important source of ferment in society at that time were the waves of mass strikes that periodically engulfed the nation—among coal and hard-rock miners, among textile-mill workers and garment workers, among railroad and mass transit workers, among tenant farmers, farm laborers, lumbermen. These were, by and large, unskilled workers, ignored by the AFL, or skilled workers facing attacks on their accustomed work rules and wage scales. These prewar strikes were usually "spontaneous," in the sense that they were not preplanned and coordinated by national union officials (and were often opposed by them) and often began in a particular locale, in response to a particular local situation.

A particularly illuminating documentation of the history of American mass strikes, beginning with the 1870s, appears in Jeremy Brecher's *Strike!* (Brecher 1972). Brecher argues that such uprisings were rooted in the immediate needs for resistance (to wage cuts, firings, industrial accidents, unilateral changes in work rules, and other sharp changes in accustomed conditions) experienced by groups of workers whose decisions to take collective action were mediated through networks of informal face-to-face work groups. He shows how such actions were often opposed by established union bureaucracies and, not infrequently, by national left organizations as well. But his accounts imply that such collective action did not simply and naturally flow out of the grievances of average workers themselves. Instead, it seemed to require the presence of conscious political activists.

Collective resistance depends on the shared perception that there are practical lines of action available that have a chance of succeeding, as well as on shared perceptions that the common life of a group or community is being threatened by the decisions of those in power. While such shared perceptions may occur "naturally" to members of an oppressed group, it is much more likely that they are made possible by the conscious effort of particular persons in the community to foster them.

If a practical line of action—a credible strategy and potentially effective tactics—is available to a community of excluded and disadvantaged people, it is because some in that community know about past and current forms of action that have worked, have acquired a repertory of protest forms, and an understanding of the practical measures that must be taken to implement a strategy and overcome the problems and pitfalls that accompany it.

If situations demand actions that entail risk—and such situations typically do—then initiatives may have to be taken by those who are strongly motivated to take the risks of defiance and dissent.

If such actions depend on gaining support and building alliances with groups outside of a particular locale—and they typically do—then people are needed in the community who have effective lines of communication to such centers of support.

And if such actions require the effective targeting of protest and a capacity to predict the likely course of action of the group's adversaries, then some in the community must claim to have the theoretical and practical knowledge of the workings of society to enable such prediction to be made.

If the knowledge, will, and social contact necessary for effective mobilization and collective action are not widely distributed in a given community—and typically they are not—such action is highly dependent on the initiatives of political activists. It has been the particular contribution of the organized left to have "created" such activists so that they would be available to disadvantaged and oppressed communities as catalysts of collective action.

Thus, thousands of members of the Socialist Party, informed by the Socialist press, party publications, and educationals, inspired by their identification with socialist ideology, culture, and heroic example, and connected to nationally coordinated networks of support through their membership, were able to serve as spark plugs and organizers in the mass strikes of the early twentieth century. These people were, for the most part, rooted in the communities in which they acted, although some of the party's contribution to catalyzing mass action undoubtedly was made by its traveling organizers serving as "outside agitators." The initiatives they took were not guided by national policy directives or party lines. The Socialist Party as such had no strategy for promoting mass uprisings of workers—indeed its labor policy was more oriented to working within the much tamer framework of the established AFL unions. But individual socialists, living in the midst of oppressive conditions and social unrest, found that they had the skill, the knowledge, the strength, and the moral compulsion to mobilize and organize fellow workers in moments of crisis and opportunity.

This generalization applies even more clearly to the IWW. Unlike the Socialist Party, the IWW was explicitly designed to promote direct action and grassroots organization among workers. Untrammeled by elaborated national strategies and programs, and inspired by a self-consciously revolutionary ideology and cultural climate, individual Wobblies were emboldened to seize opportunities for catalyzing collective action in their locales. The loose national organization of the IWW served as a transmission belt for information about what was happening in many localities and sought, sometimes with great success, to provide support to local struggles.

Without the presence of the Socialist Party and its predecessor socialist organizations, such as the Socialist Labor Party and the IWW and other anarcho-syndicalist style unions and organizations, such as the Western Federation of Miners, that were related to it, the periodic waves of mass strikes that mobilized masses of workers would not have been possible. It was not that such organizations designed such actions or coordinated them or even endorsed them—for in most cases they did not. Instead, they made a crucial contribution to the development of working-class organization and collective action by providing a framework within which small numbers of workers could develop the skills and the moral energy to assert various kinds of local leadership. These organizations further aided such local initiative by providing, at times, material and moral support and publicity. Meanwhile, radical speakers and writers, through muckraking journalism, visionary speechifying, and critical analysis, contributed to creating an ideological climate that legitimated militancy and a national spirit of reform.

Many of the mass upheavals of the prewar years were defeated; all were contained in one way or another. But what came to be called the Progressive Era did produce gains for social equality and democracy—including child labor laws, government regulation of trusts, consumer protection, political reform in some cities, and woman's suffrage. Perhaps more important than concrete legislative gains was the fact that the era established the legitimacy of political perspectives and policies that promoted public solutions to the social ills created by industrial capitalism and Big Business—perspectives and policies that, from that time forward, became the basis for political mobilization and intellectual discourse in the United States. The organized left of that era failed to establish itself as an independent, durable political force. But its adherents, both as activists and as intellectuals, were crucial to creating the ferment that forced new directions for American politics.

Indeed, Socialists and other radical activists not only sparked labor militancy, but also were mainstays of other reform movements. Early twentieth-century feminism was deeply intertwined with the Socialist Party. The most important black leaders of the nascent civil rights movement were members of the Socialist Party. Socialists led the opposition to U.S. participation in World War I; Socialists and Wobblies were leaders in struggles to protect and advance freedom of speech and in the formation of organizations like the American Civil Liberties Union. It was not that the Socialist Party or the IWW were foresighted enough to organizationally initiate or promote all of these causes. Indeed, often their official policies were quite half-hearted with respect to such issues. Rather it was their function as institutional frameworks for the socialization and support of democratic activism that was critical.

How the CP Nurtured—and Destroyed—Grassroots Activism

The Communist Party was even less successful than its predecessors in establishing itself as an independent popular political force. It had some limited success in this sense in the period 1936–39 as the leading left organization in the "Popular Front" it had helped create to oppose fascism and support the policies of the New Deal, only to be substantially discredited by its vociferous defense of the Hitler-Stalin Pact. During World War II the CP experienced a resurgence of membership and legitimacy, due largely to the wartime alliance between the United States and the So-

viet Union, only to plummet to the depths of political isolation during the
Cold War. But, like its predecessors, and perhaps even more effectively,
the Party did serve as an agency of socialization for a new generation of
political activists who played a vital role in the mobilization of historically
crucial grassroots collective action.

More than the SP and the IWW, the CP operated as a centralized, directive organization for its activist members. Indeed, the first significant
success of CP-nurtured activists—the organization of a movement of the
unemployed in the early thirties—was to some extent preplanned by the
Party itself. In a number of cities, Communist activists organized marches
of the unemployed and unemployed councils that aided unemployed workers in resisting eviction while agitating for government relief and unemployment compensation. Communist activists mobilized neighborhoods to
forcibly resist evictions, turn the gas back on, storm relief offices and city
halls. Similar initiatives were taken by socialist, Trotskyist and other radical activists as well. During the same period (from the mid-twenties to
the mid-thirties) Communists, who had been recruited in small numbers
out of factories, mines, and other industrial settings, were intensely active
at the local level in the labor movement. During much of that period Communist strategy was aimed at organizing militant "dual" unions that would
attempt to compete with the highly accomodationist, and largely stagnant,
AFL unions. This strategy was, for the most part, a disastrous failure.
Some militant strike actions occurred, but were thoroughly defeated and
repressed. In some cases, however, most notably that of coal miners in
"bloody" Harlan County, Kentucky, Communist-aided uprisings won national attention to the plight, and the courage, of brutally exploited groups
of workers.

More fruitful, however, were efforts by Communists and other working-
class radicals to form "rank-and-file" caucuses within existing union locals
and agitational groups among unorganized industrial workers, to promote
the vision of industrial unionism. By 1934 a full-fledged mass strike wave
was underway, sparked by such locally rooted radical activists. Communist-led longshoremen in San Francisco struck, and the result was a general
strike that engulfed the city. Trotskyist-led Teamsters in Minneapolis waged
a pitched battle with their employers. Workers in many mass-production
industries besieged the AFL with demands to form industrial unions. Small
farmers in the midwest organized to forcibly block mortgage foreclosures
and demand fair prices.

This turmoil was the political impetus for New Deal reforms, including
the adoption of social security and unemployment compensation measures,
agricultural policies to support small farmers, and the passage of the Wagner
Act. That Act, for the first time in American history, provided legal pro-

tection for the right to form unions, to strike, and to engage in collective bargaining. By the mid-thirties FDR and congress had substantially rewritten the social charter, by obligating the Federal Government to protect the subsistence of those whose lives were destroyed by economic crisis, to intervene in the economy and social life to "solve" such crises, and to guarantee the right of working people to organize their power vis-à-vis their employers.

These enactments were soon followed by a decision by some established leaders of the AFL to support and coordinate the grass-roots movement for industrial unionism. That decision led, of course, to the establishment of the Congress of Industrial Organizations (CIO), headed by United Mineworkers leader John L. Lewis. Lewis had the foresight to understand that the age of the craft union had passed, that organized labor's power now depended on the organization of the semi-skilled industrial workers in some degree of unity with the skilled crafts, and that the Wagner Act now provided the practical means to fulfill the decades-old dream of a "grand industrial union." He also understood that industrial unionization could not be organized by traditional union representatives. These men, by and large, had become routinized in the practices of business unionism and habituated to lives made comfortable by the collection of sizable union dues. What was needed were young people, with roots among the unorganized, who were willing to take the risks of open battle with fiercely recalcitrant corporations—who were in it not for the money but for the dream. And so Lewis turned to the reds—the assorted radicals who had been agitating the unemployed and the unorganized for years now. Most particularly, he turned to the Communist Party, the largest and best organized of such groups—and proposed that the CIO would now employ its activists as organizers, provided, of course, that they would serve the CIO loyally and operate within its policy framework. The Party welcomed this proposal, even though Lewis had, throughout the previous decade, been among the most ruthless of labor leaders in suppressing leftists within the Mineworkers Union and had long been regarded as one of the major "labor fakers."

Lewis' offer coincided with an important shift in Party policy, based on the decision of the Communist International to promote the formation of a "Popular Front"—that is, an alliance among all "democratic" forces in the face of the threat of fascism. The Popular Front was a fundamental turn away from the notion that the immediate aim of the Communists was the promotion of revolution, and from the practices that flowed from revolutionism, of fighting against social democrats, reformists, and other non-Communist influences in the working class. It was a turn toward the notion that various forms of unity and coalition, in the interest of democracy and progressive reform, were more important than ideological purity. American Communists had always believed that industrial unionism was a fundamental strategic priority; now they had the ideological freedom to work for that goal without needing to couch it in revolutionary terms—terms that many Party activists, well before the Comintern's announcement of the Popular Front, already knew from their experience to be profoundly self-defeating.

The CIO could not have been created without the Wagner Act, and without the decision of Lewis and other top labor bureaucrats. But also it could not have been created without the knowledge, will, and organizing skill of left activists out in the field. Workers were spontaneously rising, but their rising had to be mobilized strategically if gains were actually to be won. Workers were ready to strike and to fight, but such direct action had to eventuate in forms of stable organization if the provisions of the Wagner Act were to be of use. Communists and other radical activists provided the day-to-day leadership that helped spark collective action, that guided it toward strategically effective channels, that focused it toward durable organization.

Like their Socialist and Wobbly predecessors, rank-and-file Communists in the thirties were empowered by their identification with the organized left to catalyze historical intervention by their less ideological fellow workers. More than their predecessors, they carried out their initiatives in relation to policies of national organizations—the Party and the CIO leadership. Insofar as such centrally formulated policies were congruent with their direct experience, the coordination and direction that resulted greatly expanded the historic impact of their local activity.

The Communist Party in the second half of the thirties encouraged its membership to build and work for external movements and causes, rather than simply for the Party itself. The CIO was the most dramatically effective instance of this, but it was hardly the only one. For example, thousands of Party members worked in behalf of the Spanish Loyalists fighting a civil war against a fascist army supported by Hitler and Mussolini. Hundreds of young Communists fought in Spain, and half of those who went died on the battlefield. The Party sponsored the formation of dozens of "front" organizations, including relatively influential groups such as the Negro National Congress, the American Student Union, the American Youth Congress, the League of American Writers. These organizations typically had a formal leadership of non-Communists, but were effectively controlled by the Party because its members served as full-time staff and active volunteers—and the non-Communist leadership were typically "fellow travelers" (i.e., leftists who tended to recognize the Party's claims to "vanguard" leadership, despite their unwillingness to formally submit to its discipline). Although the character of such organizing was manipulative, the Party's emphasis on building "mass organizations" during this period contributed significantly to the mobilization of support for specific causes and reforms, and to the general atmosphere of democratic ferment that characterized the era of New Deal and the Popular Front.

In addition to channeling the energies of activist members into dedicated union and "mass" organizing, the Party, in some locales, began to encourage members to participate actively in mainstream electoral politics. The most notable instance of this was in New York, where CP unionists and activists joined with others in the labor movement to establish the American Labor Party. The ALP was an independent party that endorsed the New Deal and FDR nationally, while running independent candidates for state and local office with the aim of simultaneously strengthening the left wing of the Democratic Party nationally and undermining the control of the Democratic Tammany Hall machine over New York politics. New York City then had a proportional representation mode of electing city council members, which was designed to ensure that independent parties could win seats on the Council, and the concentration of minorities and left-wing subcultures in New York meant that ALP candidates for congress and other district-based offices had a real chance of election. Beginning in the late thirties, the ALP showed a rising curve of electoral success. Congressman Vito Marcantonio of Spanish Harlem was the ALP's leading politician—an extraordinarily popular figure who eventually served seven terms in Congress. ALP-backed candidates were elected to a variety of other offices, and the CP itself succeeded in electing two candidates to the New York City Council—the only official Communist Party candidates elected to public office in the United States. During and immediately after World War II, it appeared likely that the ALP would remain a strong force in New York politics.

In addition to this local electoral base, Communist activists were becoming effective electoral workers in a number of other localities. This involvement reached its peak in the 1944 presidential campaign, when the CIO, under the leadership of Sidney Hillman, organized the Political Action Committee, designed to build grassroots support for labor-backed candidates for Congress and for FDR's fourth-term candidacy. PAC was undoubtedly the most ambitious grassroots electoral effort organized in the United States to that time. It represented a fundamental break with the tradition of leaving voter mobilization to the party machines and regulars. Just as Lewis found it necessary to hire reds to organize the CIO, so Hillman sought out Communists to serve as workers in CIO-PAC, despite his long history of animosity to their influence in the labor movement. Once again, the socialization supplied by the Party—the training and the motivation its adherents had received—provided the grassroots leadership needed for social reform.

Thus, by the end of World War II, under the tutelage of the CP and other left parties, a new social type had emerged—the professional grassroots organizer. There were thousands of these by then, people who had been drawn from the ranks of aspiring working-class and minority youth, and who had been trained primarily on the job, in the midst of struggles to organize the CIO and to mobilize popular support for social reform. Their training had been supplemented by more formalized institutes, schools, classes, and workshops sponsored by the Party and other left organizations and unions. As the industrial unions and the network of cause organizations that had been created in the thirties stabilized, these organizers anticipate long-term careers as staff members. Meanwhile, alongside these full-timers, there were tens of thousands of others who worked at conventional blue-collar or professional jobs, but who had, under the influence of the organized left, internalized a deep commitment to undertake activist responsibilities as a regular feature of their daily lives.

Wherever parents organized to demand new schools and better education for their children, or tenants formed tenants' unions, or neighborhoods mobilized for public housing, or opposition to Jim Crow laws was voiced, there one was likely to find in the midst of such organizing somebody who was a red. These were people who willingly volunteered time and energy to help organize a union in their workplace, help build an interracial children's summer camp, organize support for a strike or for a progressive political candidate, or pass a petition for a federal anti-lynch law.

Unlike their Socialist or Wobbly predecessors, the left activists of the forties did not devote their energies to proseletyzing for socialism or recruiting members for the Party, nor did they expect to stimulate mass uprisings in rehearsal for revolution. Instead, at the war's end, they devoted themselves to the development of ongoing grassroots organization designed to implement the visions of the New Deal and the Popular Front. Such "reformism" or "gradualism" was, at first, conceived as a necessary accommodation to the threat of fascism. In 1944, however, under the leadership of Earl Browder, the Party formalized this stance as a long-term perspective. "Browderism" attempted to redefine the Party as a "political association," whose goal was to work with all reform forces in the society, including centrist labor leaders, liberal politicians, and progressive capitalists, to fulfill the promise of the welfare state and the wartime alliance between the United States and the Soviet Union. This position assumed that the postwar world would be structured in terms of a symbiotic relationship between these two great powers: Soviet needs for postwar recovery and development would mesh with U.S. needs for expanded markets; Americans' needs for expanded social equality and rational economic planning would find impetus from the model of societal organization provided by the "land of socialism."

Browderism was not imposed on Party-influenced activists. Their own experience, on the battlefronts of industrial conflict and the war, made them feel that it was far better to join the mainstream of popular consciousness rather than to confront it. As Party activists increasingly made intimate contact with fellow Americans, they came to believe that the possibilities for grassroots organization were considerable. In effect, they learned that people were not likely to live for history, but would fight for the right to live, and that politically aware, skilled, and energetic activists could be of aid in such a fight. Browderism permitted the Party, for a brief moment, to incorporate this experience into its policy, promising thereby to serve as the center for coordinating left activist energies, while permitting individual members to find ways to deepen their connections to the everyday experience of their communities.

The great tragedy of the American Communist experience was that, having fostered a generation of grassroots democratic activists, the Party abruptly turned in directions that resulted in the political disintegration and disillusionment of most of these people. Within a year after its promulgation, Browderism received withering criticism from international Communist sources—an attack that signaled the impending breakdown of the wartime alliance. True to their historical form, the American Party leadership immediately capitulated to such criticisms from abroad, expelling Browder and repudiating his line. This step began the Party's long slide into total political isolation.

From its beginnings, the relationship between the Communist Party and its activist members was fundamentally contradictory. The Party was socializing its members to seek effective leadership roles in everyday work and community situations and become creative initiators of popular protest and organization, while it was demanding from these members total fidelity to policies and "lines" promulgated by a top-down, centralized leadership. All organizations are characterized by fundamental tensions between the concrete experience of members and the demands of central authority; but this problem was not simply a more or less manageable "tension" for American Communists—it was a profound and destructive dilemma.

First, Party membership demanded a discipline far more rigorous and self-effacing than that normally expected in political organizations. Its organizational doctrine implied that the experiences and perceptions of individual members were bound to be imperfect, that "correct" ideas were held by those who were masters in their knowledge of Marxist-Leninist theory, and that such mastery could be claimed only by those at the top of Party leadership. If individual members found themselves to be subjectively at odds with the established Party line, it was because they were inexperienced, theoretical, and political novices, or, if they were not themselves industrial workers, because their class origins or locations made them susceptible to "petit-bourgeois" feelings and thoughts. Thus, fundamental to the Party's socialization process was the internalization of the idea that the true test of revolutionary courage was readiness to accept and implement the Party line in the face of private doubts, to recognize the superior validity and reality of the leadership's positions compared with one's own immediate perceptions and judgments.

The political dilemmas that derived from such authoritarian subordination were enormously magnified by the fact that the Party leadership itself felt an absolute duty to conform to the expressed and perceived policies of the Soviet Union. Even if, as was often the case, adherence to such policies destroyed the American Party's ability to respond to American political realities, it was absolutely predictable that the Party leadership would resolve its own doubts by defending and supporting the Soviet line. Thus, individual Party activists were repeatedly confronted with the burden of trying to organize politically passive people for collective action while having to argue in behalf of the policies of an alien State—policies that were, to put it mildly, highly controversial.

Almost by definition radicals are subject to public attack and fear—their nonconformity and dissent set the stage for possible social sanctions; because they are in the business of opposing powerful, entrenched interests and habits of mind, the application of such sanctions is practically guaranteed. But Communists in the United States, since the Party's founding, have had to deal with scorn, hostility, and organized repression to a far greater extent than any other breed of radical. Party members might console themselves by believing that the ferocity of opposition to them was due to their effectiveness—and this may, at times have been true. But anti-Communism is not simply a reflex to radical dissent; it was fueled by the negative image and reality of the Soviet Union and by the willingness of American Communists to support every one of Stalin's moves, refusing to recognize the possibility that the values and promises they claimed to stand for were in any way betrayed or contradicted by Soviet conditions or policies.

Anti-Communism took many forms: it was embodied in crude prejudices and stereotypes of average working people; in blunt reactionary antiradical propaganda of conservative media; in sophisticated critiques of the Soviet Union by non-Communist left-oriented intellectuals; in brutal techniques of surveillance and harassment employed by local police "red squads," the

FBI, and private company spy outfits; in resolutions, adopted by unions and liberal organizations, excluding Communists from leadership positions. The combined weight of anti-Communist sentiment and practice made it difficult, even in the times of greatest Party legitimacy, for rank-and-file members to work effectively if they were identified publicly as Communists. Accordingly, many Party activists experienced a fundamental split in their identity. On the one hand, they were publicly respected as dedicated leaders in workplace or community; on the other hand, they were, secretly, members of a stigmatized and arcane group.

These contradictions of Party membership boiled over into crises of conscience and organization on several occasions in the 1930s. The first was provided by the Moscow "purge trials" beginning in 1936, when Stalin accused many of the foremost leaders of the Bolshevik revolution as traitorous agents of Trotskyism and Nazism. These events certainly provided evidence of the sickness of Stalin's regime, and strong support to the "Trotskyist" and other left intellectuals who had already found sufficient grounds for hostility to the Soviet Union.

Some Communist Party-oriented intellectuals were affected by the Trials, disturbed not only by what they implied about the USSR, but also by the venomous attacks that the American Party launched against those who had presumed to question them. However, most rank-and-file Party members were probably unaffected by this controversy, since it occurred, ironically, at the high-water mark of international Communist moral legitimacy. For this was the period of the Spanish Civil War, the moment when Communists could claim to be the most resolute resisters of fascism—in Spain, in China (where Mao and his followers were organizing resistance to the Japanese invaders), and in the developing European anti-fascist movement. Meanwhile, in the United States, Communists could take justifiable pride in their leadership of militant labor struggle and in helping, through the Popular Front, to stimulate the renaissance of democratic spirit that was sweeping through the culture and the polity. Criticisms of the Soviet trials, sponsored in large part by "renegade" Trotskyists, could not, in this climate, have had much effect on Party members and sympathizers.

The next trauma was the Hitler-Stalin nonaggression pact, announced three years later. The American Party leadership now defended the Pact as necessary for Soviet reasons of state, and it also enunciated a fundamental change of line. Reversing the Party's strong support for collective security among the British, Americans, and Russians, the Party now declared that there was no fundamental difference between the Axis powers and the British "imperialists," urged that the United States stay out of the war, and declared that FDR was manipulating the United States into it. This policy reversal, and the horrifying symbolism of the Nazi-Soviet Treaty, hit some rank-and-file Party activists hard—for it struck at the heart of their activity and their moral commitment. The very anti-fascism that had defined their politics was now to be put on the back burner; their understanding of the Soviet Union as a uniquely moral state, as the legitimate repository of human hopes, was now challenged. Some members withdrew from the Party in this period; others experienced considerable disorientation. Meanwhile, the Pact, and the way in which it was reacted to by the Party leadership, generated an enormous degree of mistrust toward the Party among those liberal groups and individuals who had been willing to make common cause with Communists during the Popular Front period.

The Pact was a major impetus to the crystallization of anti-Communism as an ideology that liberals could embrace. Communism could be redefined now as "red fascism," as another species of totalitarianism, rather than as an embattled, militant variant of socialist democracy. Worse still, the Pact created a warrant for assorted professional anti-Communists to experiment with ways to root Communist rank-and-filers out of the labor movement and other mainstream milieus—using legislative hearings, such as those of the newly created Un-American Activities Committee; new laws, such as the Smith Act, which banned the teaching and advocacy of the violent overthrow of the government; the FBI, which now had Roosevelt's consent to actively seek prosecution of Communists; and exclusionary provisions in organizational constitutions, most notably one adopted by the ACLU banning Communists from leadership posts in the organization. In short, the post-Pact climate made it much harder, both emotionally and politically, to be a Communist.

This climate seemed to be overcome when, in June 1941, Hitler invaded the Soviet Union. Overnight, the Party leadership rejoined the anti-fascist crusade, renounced its opposition to war preparation, and gave its eager support for a U.S.-Soviet alliance. This turn, despite its incredible inconsistency with the immediate past, was a tremendous relief to the Party rank-and-file. It permitted them to return wholeheartedly to the anti-fascism that was the authentic inspiration of their political energies, and to bury the doubts about the Soviet state that had been eating at many of their hearts.

As the Grand Alliance took form, Party members became thoroughly committed to the war effort, finding previously unimagined ways to unabashedly join the American mainstream as wholehearted patriots. Veterans of the Spanish Civil War volunteered for front-line duty (a position they often had to fight for against lingering government suspicion of their subversive intent). Party members sold War Bonds, organized for civil defense, and salvaged tin cans. Party policy actively supported the wartime no-strike pledge, and union activists worked assiduously to enforce it.

Communist-oriented artists wrote popular patriotic songs, radio plays, and movies.

Communist enthusiasm for the war effort was remarkable—given the left's historic opposition to war and militarism. It can be explained in large part by recognizing the unique character of the Nazi threat—the sense that Nazism represented unmitigated evil, an evil that could not be stopped except by military defeat, an evil whose triumph would surely mean the extinction of all Jews and Communists in particular, and of democratic possibility in general. But for individual Party activists, participation in the war effort provided, for the first time, a solution to the contradictions of their politics. It was a way of being good Party members while simultaneously overcoming their isolation from the American mainstream. Browderism, articulated in 1944, was an effort to project this resolution into the postwar years. It was an expression of what I take to be a longing, on the part of many Party activists, to find a way to make the slogan of the Popular Front—"Communism is twentieth-century Americanism"—a working principle of their political activity.

The Party's slavish subservience to the Soviet line derailed these hopes after the war. Repudiation of Browderism meant that the Party no longer operated on the premise that U.S.-Soviet rapprochement was a likelihood, or that center-left coalition-building was the main strategic goal of Party strategy. In the context of a developing Cold War, the Party leadership, true to its entire history, decided to give first priority to defending the Soviet Union, even at the cost of breaking up working alliances with more moderate forces in the labor movement and other arenas of progressive reform. Once again, Party activists at the grass roots experienced a split between their capacity to work effectively as local organizers and the demands of the Party line.

Meanwhile, various political forces in the country that had been on the defensive through the New Deal and war years, now found, in the Cold War, opportunities for resurgence. Conservative corporate and right-wing groups perceived that a way of delegitimating the Democratic Party, the labor movement, and other liberal organizations was to charge that the New Deal forces had been soft on Stalin's Russia, had harbored Communists and been manipulated by them. Versions of a revitalized and newly focused anti-Communism emanated not only from the traditional right, but also from anti-Communist liberals and social democrats who had been bitter about the strength of the Communist Party since the days of the Popular Front, and who now saw a way of destroying its influence.

It was not long before anti-Communist theory found practical application in demands for a purge of Communists from positions of influence throughout the society. The Truman administration established a sweeping "loyalty" investigation to remove Communists and "fellow travelers" from government positions. Congress passed the Taft-Hartley Act, a measure designed to weaken and contain the organizing ability and leverage of the labor movement, which included a provision barring Communists from holding union office. By 1949 the CIO, the stronghold of Communist activists' career hopes and grass-roots effectiveness, was voting to purge Communist-led unions (constituting one-third of its membership) from its ranks. Similar, if less dramatic, purges of Communists occurred in other liberal and reform organizations.

Meanwhile the Un-American Committee and other congressional inquisitorial bodies were holding almost daily public hearings, at which undercover FBI agents and former Party members recited long lists of the names of suspected Communists living in numerous communities, working in many diverse sectors of society. Many so named were hauled before the committees to suffer further exposure and demands that they "clear" themselves by cooperating in the inquisition. Failure to cooperate typically led to loss of jobs and other forms of personal misfortune; in addition to the personal costs of such exposure, however, the significance of "McCarthyite" witch-hunting was to destroy the grassroots work of activists, and spread fear and suspicion through the ranks of those who had been organized in behalf of progressive reform.

For these activists, it was bad enough to be exposed as a Communist, to have years of dedicated, honorable effort in behalf of social justice and equality undermined or ruined by publicity about a stigmatized affiliation that one had, typically, tried to keep secret or play down. But the Cold War years added to the long-standing bad stereotype of the Communist some new and more evil dimensions. Communists could, it was now said, literally be spies (not just misguided or servile apologists for Stalinism). They could be conscious members of a Fifth Column designed to turn the United States over to the Russians. By the early fifties Communists were defined as participants in a criminal conspiracy, rather than simply as members of a disliked political movement, by courts that convicted the Party leadership under the Smith Act, and by congressional legislation that effectively outlawed the Party and required the registration of its members.

In the early days of the Cold War, the CP searched for a political strategy that would enable it, despite the burdens of its new line, to sustain the political influence and legitimacy it had begun to achieve during the war years. In the immediate postwar period, large numbers of non-Communist leftists shared with Communists considerable trepidation about the Truman administration and the shape of America in the period to come. There were widespread fears of a return to prewar economic depression. There was a general recognition that the promises of the New Deal to labor and minorities had to be redeemed, that fundamental reforms in housing, in health care, in education, and in economic planning were desperately needed, and that "Jim Crow" remained firmly entrenched in the South. Despite U.S.-Soviet tensions, there was continuing broad support for good relations with the Russians, and hostility toward the Truman administrations's turn toward a hard line.

Indeed, doubts about Truman fueled considerable discussion in the labor movement and among liberals about the need to start a new party—a party that would be true to the vision and program of the New Deal. Henry Wallace, who had served as Agriculture Secretary and Vice President under FDR, and who had been replaced as Vice President by Truman in 1944 as the result of a revolt led by Southern Democrats, was asserting outspoken leadership of these sentiments, even as he served in Truman's cabinet as Commerce Secretary. After resigning under fire from the cabinet in 1947, Wallace began to be seriously discussed as a liberal alternative to Truman in the 1948 presidential primaries. Since it was then considered impossible to run against an incumbent President within his own party, Wallace eventually expressed readiness to lead a third party effort. Although liberals of many stripes had earlier declared an interest in opposing Truman, the new party effort rather quickly split liberal-left ranks. Despite some reservations, the Communists decided to throw themselves fully into the Wallace effort; he was, after all, the last major American politician advocating the preservation of the U.S.-Soviet alliance. Wallace drew support from a fairly wide variety of others on the left, but in the end his expected support from leftish labor leaders and other New Dealers failed to materialize.

The Wallace campaign, in fact, marked the crystallization of a kind of establishment liberalism—what historian Arthur Schlesinger called the "vital center"—that was assertively anti-Communist, consciously integrated into the Democratic Party, explicitly reformist, rather than visionary, and eager to abolish the influence of "Stalinism" in American life. This liberalism had roots among those, in the thirties, who had been disillusioned by the purge trials, the Hitler-Stalin Pact, and had felt stifled by the Popular Front, but it did not fully crystallize until Wallace's candidacy forced everyone on the left to make clear-cut choices. Establishment or "cold war" liberals, led by the newly formed Americans for Democratic Action, stuck with Truman, as did most leaders of organized labor and most of the politicians claiming to be in the FDR mold. Some were guided by ideological considerations; others by practical worries about the fact that a left-wing Third Party would ensure the election of conservative Republicans.

In the end, the Progressive Party was powered by CP activists, a fact that gave it considerable organizational capability, but made the Wallace effort extremely vulnerable to red-baiting from the right wing and from Truman's supporters as well. Still, despite these liabilities, opinion polls during the campaign, coupled with massive turnouts for Wallace at his campaign appearances, led to predictions that he would end up with at least 10 percent of the vote. But when the actual balloting was counted, Wallace ended up with only 1 percent; millions of left-oriented voters decided, at the last minute, to go with the "lesser evil" of Truman rather than allow a return to power of the Republicans (led by Thomas Dewey). Truman had won back many New Deal supporters during the campaign by articulating strong support for rather far-reaching welfare state reforms (including socialized medicine) and for Federal initiatives on behalf of civil rights for blacks. He thereby isolated Wallace both by tying him to the reds, and by taking over a good deal of his rhetoric and program on behalf of domestic reform.

These events, in 1948, marked the end of the era of the Popular Front and the New Deal, an era during which, despite many tensions and conflicts, ideological radicals and pragmatic reformers of many varieties had worked together in a loosely coordinated coalition, and during which, under the tutelage of the Communist Party and other left organizations, a stratum of leftist activists had begun to catalyze grassroots action and build popular organization in many American communities and milieus.

In the years that followed many of these activists became disillusioned and withdrew from political action. The disillusionment had its basis in the loss of faith in the Party. It had so often betrayed both its principles and its analyses that it became harder and harder for adherents to see the Party as anything like what it claimed to be—and what it claimed to be was nothing less than the repository of the best moral impulses of humanity and the most "scientific" approach to political action. Disillusionment was reinforced by the fact that postwar America did not experience a new economic slump, but instead an unprecedented burst of economic growth, an opening up of opportunity for career and consumption that few in the depression years could have imagined.

Many who had been left activists thus felt the ground cut out from under them because the issues that had focused their emotions and actions—the failures and human costs of capitalism—no longer seemed pressing. Workers in large numbers were now finding that everyday life could be lived, and that it made sense to enjoy the fruits of past struggle rather than press on with the fight. Meanwhile, left activists themselves found that careers in education, social work, communications, planning, social research, human service professions were now available because of the growth of the public sector that the New Deal had stimulated. Such careers provided ways to do some good while making a normal life—offering opportunities that had obviously moral, as well as practical, appeal.

Despite this widespread political withdrawal and the collapse of its political fortunes, the Communist Party managed, through the darkest days of the McCarthy era, to hold on to a substantial fraction of its activist core. A primary reason for this continuing adherence was McCarthyism itself. The whole point of McCarthyism was that the "witches" who were being hunted could save themselves from public burning by confessing their crimes and renouncing their faith.

For principled political activists within the Party orbit, the choice was quite clear. To act in such times in terms of one's private doubts about the Party's viability was to sell out; however much the Party may have lost the ability to influence the American mainstream, adherence to it was now (perhaps for the first time in a long time) an honorable thing to do. Moreover, in the context of McCarthyism, many found a new focus of political concern—the question of civil liberties provided a way of reorienting one's political identity. If one paid both a personal and a political price for continuing fidelity to the Party, this was made worthwhile by the conviction that by so doing one belonged to the saving remnant who were resisting McCarthy. One stuck with the Communists precisely to preserve the right to be a Communist, because otherwise dissent in America might be totally obliterated.

But such sentiments masked undercurrents of internal alienation from the Party's modes of operation—undercurrents that became evident after the release of Khruschev's revelations of Stalin's crimes and the Soviet crushing of the Hungarian uprising in 1956. There ensued an unprecedented free-wheeling public debate within the Party, raging in the pages of the *Daily Worker* and other Party publications for several months. The debate encompassed the entire character of the Party's past, its structures and strategies, and, for the first time in its history, a full discussion of the character of the Soviet Union and the Party's relation to it. This debate, which resonated with similar ferment in some European Parties (especially the Italian), produced perspectives that anticipated by a couple of decades the ideological formulations that came to be called "Euro-Communism."

For a year or two, it seemed possible that the American Party would break its dependence on the Soviet Union and adopt a reformist socialism and an internally democratic structure. But the Party reformers ultimately lost the struggle for control and overwhelmingly departed the Party to take up life courses similar to those who had quietly, and individually, left in earlier crisis periods. The collapse of the reform faction, and the withdrawal of thousands of its members from politics, marked the end of the "thirties generation" as the decisive core of grass-roots left-wing activism. These events coincided with the beginning of the end of the McCarthy era. The Old Left (as the radicalism spawned in the thirties came to be called in the sixties) had died.

The Communist Party left a legacy of failed hopes, of disillusionment with political commitment as such, of deep bitterness among many who had been socialized by it. In long retrospect, reflective veterans of the era are likely to share the assessment I have suggested in my discussion of the period: Beneath the incredible blindnesses and political failures of the Communist Party as an organization, there had been a rather remarkable achievement—the socialization of a large band of people who had learned to be effective catalyzers of popular struggle. These people had played a critical part in the revitalization and extension of democracy in the labor struggles of the thirties, in the beginnings of mass action against racial segregation in the thirties and forties, and in resistance to McCarthyism in the fifties. In the end, most abandoned commitment to activism; still many former activists tried to sustain some sense of social responsibility through the professional careers they entered.

The career paths of Old Left activists have not, to my knowledge, been systematically studied, but I have the strong impression, based on personal knowledge of large numbers of individual cases, that former left activists of the New Deal era became the backbone in the fifties and sixties of what came to be called the professionalization of reform. They took up careers in the burgeoning bureaucracies of social service, public education, public planning; they became leaders in such academic disciplines as sociology, social psychology, anthropology, and history; they became professional labor bureaucrats and staff members in a host of voluntary organizations. A few escaped the blacklisting that drove many former comrades out of the entertainment industry and the universities; when the blacklist was undermined, others were able to return. Not a few became politically active at a local level again when the New Left of the sixties restored the possibility of political hope and popular movement and when their own children or their students presented them with a moral challenge. Thus, despite the death of the organized politics of the Old Left, its socializing effects were considerably more durable, helping to shape the individual life courses of a generation of professionals and intellectuals.

The Old Left was organizationally dominated by the Communist Party. This dominance, however, did not mean that the left in the thirties and forties was exclusively defined by the CP. There were other organized forces during the period that paralleled the Party as agencies of socialization. There were, for example, radical splinter groups who had split from the CP to follow Trotsky. There was the Socialist Party of Norman Thomas, and its youth wing, the Young People's Socialist League—organizations that eventually welcomed some of the Trotskyists into their fold. There were small bands of radical pacifists, most notably those influenced by the remarkable A. J. Muste. And there were grouplets of independent Marxist and Socialist intellectuals, such as the editors of the *Monthly Review* and *Dissent*. During the heyday of the Party, these groups rarely had significant national impact, although they provided leadership in particular local struggles. Despite their relative invisibility, these groupings shared in the fundamental positive function of left organizations, namely the socialization of grassroots activists. Of particular importance was a band of young pacifists who gathered around A. J. Muste. Muste had been an active radical since World War I, as a pro-labor minister, then as the leader of the Brookwood Labor College—one of the most important training institutes for labor organizers, and, later, as the leader of a Marxist splinter group called the Worker's Party. Late in the thirties, he turned toward Gandhian nonviolence and became the full-time leader of the Fellowship of Reconciliation. In this role, he began to encourage pacifists to train for disciplined nonviolent direct action, advocating the strategic use of civil disobedience as a primary weapon for social change. These efforts eventuated in the establishment of the Congress Of Racial Equality (CORE), which pioneered in the use of direct action by small interracial groups to violate boundaries of racial segregation. In the fifties, Musteites formed the Committee for Non-Violent Action which sponsored small group direct action forays against nuclear testing and nuclear submarines.

Muste's insight was that activists need not be restricted to efforts to organize large numbers. They could catalyze popular feeling by taking exemplary actions that directly confronted injustice. They could physically intervene in history by putting their bodies in the way of engines of injustice and war. Young people influenced by Muste in the forties, men like Bayard Rustin and David Dellinger, became key leaders in the civil rights and antiwar movements that began to emerge in the late fifties and flourished in the sixties. Muste's synthesis of Marxian social analysis and Gandhian social action was a fundamental influence on the New Left, although he was so self-effacing that few were aware of his name or his contribution. Indeed, although the Communist Party shaped the identity of ideological leftists during the thirties and forties, the teachings of Muste, largely unnoticed during that period, had more fundamental and long-term influence in the sixties, and, as I suggest in chapter 6, still contain profoundly useful clues to the possibilities of the left in the future.

By 1960, the organized left was virtually nonexistent, and the great majority of those who had been socialized to activism within it had withdrawn to more privatized pursuits. Prominent social commentators (many of whom

had once been socialists) declared that the left as an independent ideological force in "advanced" industrial capitalist societies was finished.

Such commentary assumed that the problems of capitalism that the left
had emerged to combat had now largely been solved, in part because the
fundamental proposals of the left—for a welfare state and government regulation of the economy—had in fact been incorporated into the "mixed"
political economies of the advanced industrial societies. These mixed economies were clearly superior to the "socialism" of the Soviet bloc; workers
in the West were now sufficiently organized to defend their interests as
actors in the pluralist polities their past struggles had helped create. Socialism was obsolete, as was the Marxian interpretation of capitalism; politics, henceforth, would be characterized by conflict and bargaining over
technical issues of administration and problem-solving rather than embracing social visions and mass mobilization. In modern societies, it was argued, mass withdrawal from politics was desirable—it made sense for people to be preoccupied with the quality of their lives; the remote issues of
social administration were better left to the wisdom of politicians and experts, aided by an increasingly sophisticated social science that would free
policymakers from reliance on nonrational ideologies.

The Revival of Activism in the Sixties

Anticipations of an end to ideology (and, in particular, an end to the
tradition of the left) were rather rudely shattered in the sociocultural climate of the sixties. Beginning with the student sit-ins in 1960, the decade
was marked by a steadily rising curve in the numbers of young people who
adopted activist identities. In a sense, the "end of ideology" perspective
was relevant to understanding the organized New Left. New Leftists, by
definition, endorsed the argument that the ideological politics and organizational forms of the Old Left were obsolete. Their fundamental challenge
to the anti-ideological intellectual consensus of the fifties was instead to
dedicate themselves to the revitalization of democratic, popular *action,*
counterposing this quite explicitly to both party politics and the technocratic model.

More than any of their predecessors in the organized left, SNCC and
SDS emphasized the socialization of activism as their primary function, rather
than the building of organizational strength, the recruitment of members,
or the spreading of gospel. SNCC, in fact, was a pure case of a "cadre"
organization; membership was possible only for those committed to full-
time organizing work. Only a few hundred belonged to this organization of
organizers, and the primary purpose of membership was the mapping of
strategy, the allocation of resources for organizing, the communication and

mutual support that front-line activists need to keep going. SNCC organizers were self-consciously catalysts of community-based action; their job was defined as helping people to act for themselves and to construct their own community organizations. SNCC field workers engaged full-time in voter registration, and in mobilizing direct action protests against specific targets of segregation and repression. These workers lived on bare subsistence stipends, under constant threat of police harassment and physical injury. Their vision of a "beloved community," a "band of brothers standing in a circle of love" was reinforced by the intense bonds of community that most found within the organization, and by the exhilarating sense that they actually were giving poor folk opportunity for voice and dignity.

The Southern movement of the early sixties was a mass movement. It was made possible by the charismatic leadership of Martin Luther King, Jr., and by the space, legitimation, and resources provided by many local black churches. But equally indispensable to the mass mobilization was the daring daily work of the SNCC staffers. This work reached a culmination in Mississippi, where police-state conditions prevented the kinds of mass action that King and his SCLC fellow ministers had been able to lead in other locales. In Mississippi, SNCC workers operated for several years against great odds to try to break white supremacist control over the electoral process. Then, in a brilliant strategic move, SNCC and other civil rights organizations decided to recruit and train a small army of white activist volunteers to join with an expanded corps of black students and youth in a concerted drive to register black voters and create an alternative to the white supremacist Democratic Party structure in the state. In addition to door-to-door canvassing and organization building, SNCC established "freedom schools" designed to bring black young people together to study their heritage, learn their rights, and develop literacy skills. A state-wide political structure, the Freedom Democratic Party, was created, whose goal was to challenge the seating of the Mississippi Dixiecrats at the Democratic convention to be held at the end of the summer. SNCC painstakingly nurtured the development of "indigenous" activists in the impoverished communities of the state. They initiated self-help projects, bringing Northern white and black professionals in health care, child care, economic development, and education together with community-based groups. Although the Mississippi Freedom Democrats did not succeed in winning the recognition they sought from the national Democratic Party in 1964, the Mississippi Summer was instrumental in laying the organizational and psychological groundwork for what eventually was achieved—the political enfranchisement of the black population there.

Unlike SNCC, SDS was a general membership organization, admitting as members anyone who agreed with its goals, whether or not they were committed to activist work. But SDS was deeply inspired by SNCC's activist example. The SDS Economic Research and Action Project, like SNCC, recruited and trained students to work as full-time organizers in poor communities. Responding to SNCC's challenge, ERAP was aimed at fostering, in Northern urban poor neighborhoods, a movement that might parallel and converge with the upsurge of Southern rural blacks. SNCC and SDS theorists argued that the economic needs of poor blacks could not be served without the achievement of economic reform in the whole society, and that poor whites and blacks shared a common interest in such reform. Although the readiness of poor whites for collective action was hardly as developed as it was among blacks, SDSers hoped that their efforts could have a significant catalytic effect. Indeed, while their work was profoundly frustrating, the combined efforts of community organizers sponsored by both groups did help create the climate that led LBJ to announce a "war on poverty" soon after he took office. ERAP notions about the potentialities for organizing "community unions" in urban poor neighborhoods became the basis of a considerable amount of community-based organization, sponsored by Federal poverty programs and by private foundations as well.

In the era of the IWW and later the CIO, the fullest realization of activist commitment was embodied in the role of the labor organizer. SNCC and SDS carried that tradition forward into the sixties by fostering the development of the community organizer. By serving as frameworks of personal development and schooling, the New Left organizations, like their Old Left predecessors, empowered activist members to find full-time roles that were indispensable to the achievement of the potentials for social change that were present in the society at the time.

Activists thus empowered were able to provide politically excluded groups and communities with human resources that these communities otherwise lacked—resources that enabled such groups to crystallize the perceptions and modes of actions that were necessary for collective historical intervention. Socialists, Wobblies, and Communists usually thought that by performing such work they were building the popular base for socialism, or undertaking rehearsals for revolution. Their New Left counterparts in the first half of the sixties were less burdened by such ideological preconceptions; for them, the articulation of popular demands and the self-organization of disenfranchised communities were sufficient ends in themselves. For both SNCC and SDS the left tradition had come to be summarized by such slogans as: "Let the people decide," and later, "Power to the People." Taking such slogans seriously meant that self-conscious left activists ought not to try to impose any elaborated programs or models or answers on their communities. Instead, the New Left faith rested, first, on a belief that participation, collective discussion, and action were intrinsically valuable, and second, that once such participatory processes were set in motion, their outcomes would be determined not by preexisting ideologies but by the dynamic of historical struggle itself.

By the mid-sixties, however, New Left efforts to socialize community activists and coordinate their work had largely ended. There were several reasons for this. First, the Federal Government, through the War on Poverty, Vista, and the Peace Corps, was developing a much larger and more systematic framework for organizer training. Since these government programs were supposed to be administered with the "maximum feasible participation of the poor" in locally based projects, many of the community-based organizations that had been initiated by New Left organizers entered into effective relationship with them, and not a few SDS- and SNCC-trained organizers were hired onto the poverty programs. This development was not, on the whole, resisted by SNCC and ERAP. Despite many reservations, they tended to see the poverty program as a promising way to institutionalize the democratic participation they had been trying to foster.

Second, by the mid-sixties the Southern movement had entered a new phase. The basic legislative reforms sought by the movement (the abolition of legalized segregation, Federal protection of voting rights) had been won. These reforms now had to be used by Southern blacks themselves—the movement had to shift "from protest to politics"—and this meant concentration on voter registration and the building of long-term political organization. Some SNCC leaders, most notably James Forman, argued that SNCC should take the lead in organizing the new black politics. Such a role was quite possible in theory, but it required a fundamental psychological shift for many SNCC workers. They would have to become permanently rooted in depressed rural small towns, functioning in terms of long-range strategic perspectives, rather than in the context of dramatic, emotionally intense confrontation. In any event, many SNCC workers were, by then, feeling mightily "burned out." They had lived in fear and in deprivation, they had agonized over the ambiguities of their encounters with poor rural people to whom they were reluctant missionaries, they had experienced considerable turmoil in their relations with established liberal organizations that had failed to fully deliver at the Democratic convention and on other occasions when their help was desperately needed, and there were severe tensions between black SNCC workers and the "middle class" white youths that had joined them. Forman's rationalistic perspective, which demanded that SNCC assert its leadership at a higher level of discipline and energy than it had yet been called upon to exercise, could not prevail.

The "internal disorder" (as Forman termed the condition that SNCC was in by 1965) was also linked with developments in the black community nationally. Northern blacks were taking collective action, in the violent, spasmodic ghetto uprisings, that contradicted the nonviolent, patient organizing that had characterized early New Left strategy. The ghetto riots, although unorganized, did far more to win the promise of economic reforms than had the efforts at organization that had preceded them. Moreover, it appeared that the urban black ghettos no longer needed the catalytic efforts and organizing skills of specially trained and motivated "outside" activists. In the aftermath of the riots, a burst of indigenous organization and creative leadership emerged from within the ghettos. These indigenous activists may have been inspired by the earlier SNCC efforts in the South, but they were more attuned to other voices, such as the black nationalist rhetoric of Malcolm X. In the climate of black power and revolutionary nationalism, there seemed little use for the SNCC-style community organizer.

SDS was undergoing a parallel reordering of its priorities. ERAP projects that had succeeded in taking root in their communities (and many had not) were integrated into War on Poverty frameworks. Meanwhile, by 1965 SDS campus chapters had inevitably become focused on the Vietnam War and on their newly discovered potential for organizing a mass student movement. ERAP had been the SDS priority in the first years of the organization's development because most white New Leftists believed that the great mass of students were bound to be politically apathetic or conservative, so that the best role for the small number of left-oriented students was to work off campus on fundamental issues of social injustice. The Free Speech Movement in Berkeley in 1964, however, showed that large masses of students could unite for collective action—and events soon demonstrated that the Berkeley uprising was not an isolated case. In the spring of 1965, campus protest against the escalating war in Vietnam was gathering force (most notably in the rapid spread of "teach-ins" organized by concerned faculty and students). SDS, in April 1965, organized the first national protest against the war—a march on Washington that proved to be the largest student demonstration in the United States since the thirties. SDS suddenly achieved national media publicity and was swamped by new members.

From that point on, the character of SDS was changed. It was no longer a small, cohesive organization of radical student intellectuals experimenting with ways to express activist commitment at the grass roots. It had become the organized core of a mass movement of students who were responding to the threat of the war and the draft. Moreover, it was, inescapably, a very loose organizational structure, given its lack of resources, the rapidity of its growth, and the inherent fluidity of the student membership. No single ideological perspective characterized the organization; indeed, more than any previous left organization, SDS was explicitly open to a pluralism of ideological tendencies. It was, in short, a kind of antithesis to the Communist Party—completely reversing the Party's emphasis on organizational discipline, hierarchical leadership, ideological conformity, and centralized strategic direction.

In the second half of the sixties, the real life of the New Left occurred not in the national offices and meetings of groups like SDS, but in hundreds of local chapters, informal friendship circles, ad hoc committees, educational and cultural projects. These locally based radical communities were loosely connected by SDS' newsletters, traveling organizers, and national meetings, and by the growth of other national communication structures as well. For example, an important development in the student antiwar movement was the emergence of draft resisters—young men who publicly refused induction and thereby faced trial and jail. SDS was never able to agree on a full-scale policy of support for draft resistance; instead draft resisters, whether SDS members or not, formed their own local support groups and outreach efforts, coordinating nationally through an unformalized communications network. Antiwar coalition structures grew up during these years for the purpose of mobilizing national protest events; SDS was never able (or even interested in trying) to control such national demonstration activity after its initial success in April 1965. Meanwhile, on any given day during the second half of the decade, there was likely to be some campus protest taking place. But these were the result of localized dynamics of conflict and decision, sometimes initiated by an SDS chapter, sometimes by ad hoc or independent groups—but all of it occurring without the guiding hand of a central, national organization.

By the late sixties thousands of students were identifying themselves with the tradition of the left and were defining themselves as activists. In this period the number of leftist activists was probably comparable to that in the heyday of the Socialists, Wobblies, and Communists, although New Leftists were drawn from, and operated within, a much narrower range of social milieus than these earlier lefts. But the late sixties left activists were no longer being socialized primarily in the context of organized, institutionalized frameworks created by national left organizations. Instead, their commitment was being shaped, in the context of localized patterns of interpersonal and informal association, as well as by a national cultural climate promulgated as much by commercial mass media as by the channels of communication and expression controlled by the organized left.

SDS was accordingly riven by a fundamental contradiction. Its base consisted of thousands of student activists, locally oriented and autonomous, whose emotion and energy were bound up in resistance to the war. Its national structure recruited a small proportion of that base, who, more than the local membership, were compelled to think about the longer term political and personal implications of the movement's actions. SDS was a student organization in composition and day-to-day orientation. But it operated in a situation in which there were no other general "adult" organizations that could serve as centers for sustaining and carrying forward the left tradition. Despite considerable discussion about its desirability, there was no concerted effort by SDS founders (who had now "graduated" from active SDS leadership) to create an "adult" counterpart to the student organization. Thus, the SDS national staff, already cut off from its student roots, had the burden of operating not just as the leadership of a national student organization, but as a kind of surrogate leadership for a more general left, a role they had neither the resources nor the experience to effectively play.

Both publicly and face-to-face, national activists were trying to confront such questions as: What were the long-term prospects of the left? What kind of program, apart from ending the war, could the left put forward—especially as events in the late sixties seemed to signify the exhaustion of liberal reformism? What role could radicals of middle-class white background play in reconstructing an American left? How to understand and deal with the apparent conservatism and racism of the established labor movement and masses of white workers? What was the long-term political meaning of the youth revolt and the student movement?

In the late sixties these questions could not be discussed in an atmosphere of calm and rational deliberation. The whole world seemed engulfed in a turmoil of youthful revolt. Black ghettos were exploding in physical combat; these uprisings were being framed by a rhetoric advocating Revolution Now, a rhetoric that young white radicals, always vulnerable to the moral pressure of black oppression, felt impelled to try to match. SDS leaders were in continuous struggle with well-organized Maoists who challenged their revolutionary credentials. By 1968, both the world situation in general and their close-up organizational situation led SDS leaders to adopt a "revolutionary" ideological perspective. The content of that perspective was in hot dispute, but all leadership factions tended to agree on at least two things: first, the founding perspectives of the New Left were too reformist, gradualist, and "intellectual" to suit a revolutionary organization, and second, the mass student base of SDS was too narrow and "privileged" to serve as shock troops for revolutionary combat. These convictions characterized the outlook of the national staff and permeated the debates that occurred at national meetings. The structural separation between SDS membership and the organization's national leadership was now powerfully exacerbated by the ideological perspectives that were crystallizing within that leadership—perspectives that were only dimly reflected among rank-and-file members.

SDS disintegrated at its convention in 1969; those there assembled splintering into several warring factions, each claiming to be more revolutionary than thou. By the time of its disintegration, however, the national organization had little relevance to the fostering of campus activism. One indication of this is that in the year following SDS' demise, the scope and intensity of campus protest were much greater than ever before. After the Cambodian invasion and the killings at Kent State and Jackson State, there occurred an unprecedented general strike of students. This was one of the largest protests in American history, involving millions, who engaged in days, and even weeks, of organized protest activity in May and June of 1970. Yet this activity took place with only minimal, ad hoc national coordination. It was made possible by the presence, on hundreds of campuses, of large numbers of young people who had come to an activist commitment during the preceding period, who were capable of undertaking creative initiative and of building cross-country communication links, without the guidance or resources of a preestablished national organization.

In the years that followed, the mass student movement receded; meanwhile New Left activists were graduating from college and also from the political frameworks within which their activist commitments had formed and focused. The disintegration of the sixties New Left and the larger movements that it had helped catalyze did not prevent large numbers of ex-student activists from undertaking self-initiated efforts to sustain and develop their commitments as they entered adulthood.

Unlike the generation of the thirties, the generation of the sixties was not burdened by feelings of bitter disillusionment. Having never been dependent on a Party for guidance, they were not likely to be disoriented by the demise of SDS. Many were unable to make the "transition to adulthood" with their activist commitments intact; many others gradually became less politically involved after a period of intense activism in their immediate post-student years. Like their predecessors of the thirties generation, many former sixties activists refocused their activist identities into professional careers in human services, education, communications, planning—seeking in these ways to find institutionalized channels for the implementation of their values. Still, thousands, in one way or another, retained their commitment to activism.

We have seen that CP-oriented activists, by the end of World War II, had come to be rooted in a wide range of locales and milieus, and had begun to work effectively as local organizers and catalysts of diverse collective activity for democratic and egalitarian reform. The promise of this permeation was dashed by the Party's ideological blindness and by the repression of the Cold War era. In the postwar world of the seventies, a new generation of left activists became similarly rooted, becoming the catalysts of feminism, environmentalism, and other locally based "populist" and citizen action efforts. The main legacy of the New Left of the sixties was this decentralized diversity of locally based activism.

In the years after the demise of the organized national New Left, no new national organization arose to replace it. No national group today exercises authority within the community of left activists, the way the Socialist Party, the IWW, the Communist Party, or SDS each did for a time. The absence of a national organized left creates a vacuum and leads the casual observer to think that the left tradition is dead in America. Such a conclusion, however, fails to notice the persistence of the tradition in the identities and work of thousands of democratic activists. Moreover, it misses the point I have tried to make in reviewing the history of the organized left—namely that the reality of the left, its fundamental role in American politics, has *always* been embodied by such activists—even when they thought it was their Party that was the embodiment of their meaning.

Promulgating Ethics of Social Responsibility

The left's socializing impact has not been restricted to the development of several generations of highly committed activists. In addition, left activity has, over the decades, fostered what I want to call "ethics of collective responsibility" that have been taken up by millions who remain committed to nonactivist everyday lives.

A social movement of any duration and scope requires a band of highly committed activists, as well as a much wider constituency willing to take specific actions that support the movement's strategies. The labor movement must enforce norms against scabbing and crossing picket lines. It must achieve the participationg of nonmembers in consumer boycotts. No strike can be won, nor union preserved, unless members and nonmembers share the strikers' refusal to cooperate with the employer. Strikers, like any group engaged in serious combat, will often try to enforce adherence by explicitly or implicitly threatening potential violators. But mere force is rarely an effective way to win active support, and it typically can be neutralized by the intervention of the police and the courts. Much more than force, the labor movement has had to establish the legitimacy and sanctity of the strike among workers and labor sympathizers. In other words, it has needed to articulate an ethic of collective responsibility, a set of principles and rules for individual action that are morally binding on members, and that are capable of becoming obligatory for ever-widening circles of nonmembers as well.

The need for an ethic of collective responsibility is equally evident for other social movements. For example, the contemporary environmental movement has as a goal as well as a strategy the promulgation of rules for ecologically valid everyday living. Such rules, couched in moral terms, include emphasis on recycling of household waste, the conservation of energy through the use of efficient and renewable modes of energy generation, conservation of water, the avoidance of practices and products that increase dangers of environmental pollution, and, generally, the examination of every aspect of daily life in terms of its implications for resource conservation and environmental preservation.

Similarly, the women's movement has fostered an ethic of collective responsibility that focuses on the moral imperative that women (and men) reshape their everyday roles and relationships, actively refuse to cooperate with traditional interpersonal modes that enforce gender inequalities, assert rights and interests in arenas hitherto regarded as male dominated preserves. The ethic of the women's movement includes rules about the minutiae of daily speech as well as the most profound dimensions of human relations.

Because male-female relations are the most fundamental ones for human beings, the ethical framework expressed by the women's movement is more elaborated than that of any other social movement—but many of its rules governing interpersonal interaction have many parallels with other liberation movements. For example, the black liberation movement placed similar demands on blacks for active self-assertion and noncompliance with traditional modes of subservience, and similar demands on whites for changes in forms of address and other symbolic gestures recognizing black equality and self-determination.

In short, all movements have strategic needs to exercise moral claims on their organized adherents and numbers of nonmembers alike. The more a movement can get others to feel a sense of responsibility to it, the more it can call up a wide variety of resources.

But, as the examples of the environmental movement and the women's movement suggest, ethics of collective responsibility have more than strategic utility for a movement. Liberation movements seek the institutionalization of such ethics as goals as well as means. For such movements make history not just by redistributing political power in the formal arenas of its exercise, but also by encouraging relatively privatized people to actually live their daily lives in terms of the movement's definitions of what is rational and right. The practical and symbolic activities that such movements encourage in the wider population, while signs of support for the movement, are themselves the movement's central goals.

One basis for perennial splits in movements between "radical" and "moderate" leaderships has to do with controversy over the extent to which the movement should seek to engage the collective moral responsibility of "masses." On the one hand, there are leaders emphasizing the practical gains to be won by focusing on particular reforms and concessions, on bargaining and dealing with established authority. On the other hand, there are those arguing that "the issues are not the issue," that the real meaning of the movement is its democratizing thrust, its capacity not only to win some improvement in everyday life for its constituents, but also to change the ways history is made. It is the latter emphasis that provides the grounds for articulating the universalistic moral claims of the movement as well as, or more than, its pragmatic, particularistic demands.

A crucial historical role of the American left has been to do that kind of articulating. This role has been carried in part by left activists involved in mass movements. These people have not been mere catalysts and organizers of mass action and popular struggle; they have frequently sought to influence the direction, rhetoric, and style of movements in the moral directions to which I have been referring.

Parallel to these intra-movement dynamics has been the contribution of left-oriented intellectuals and artists, especially when they have gone beyond critique to try to call out social responsibility: by dramatizing injustice or social irrationality; by articulating a previously unspoken, shared sense of grievance; by symbolizing potentialities for solidarity and community; by typifying positive models of heroism and moral purity and negative models of betrayal and moral compromise; by providing examples of concrete principled action that can be emulated; by expressing utopian hopes in such a way as to undermine the moral foundations of present realities.

There have been times when writers and artists have been strongly influenced by a particular left organization. Many intellectuals were at least nominally members of the Socialist Party during its heyday, and some who later became major ornaments of the established culture (Walter Lippmann was a major case) devoted some concentrated energy to the SP.

The Wobblies were to a considerable degree designed as an organization to encourage working-class members to develop themselves as artists and writers. Wobbly songs by writers like Joe Hill were undoubtedly crucial in the development of the ethical principles of the labor movement, with their cutting, satirical attacks on scabs, "Scissor Bills" (boss-oriented workers), and their celebration of working-class heroism.

The Wobblies inspired that band of radical writers and artists in Greenwich Village—such as the people around the *Masses*—who helped crystallize the "adversary culture" before World War I. These people were not Party-minded, but, in their peak years, they did much to expose social ills, and legitimate militant protest. An excellent example was the famous Paterson Strike Pageant, directed by John Reed—an ambitious theatrical event in which the Wobbly-led silk-workers of Paterson, New Jersey, dramatized their struggle and their revolutionary sentiments in Madison Square Garden.

The most important instance of organizational effort to mobilize intellectuals was that undertaken by the Communist Party in the 1930s. The Party, from the early thirties on, recognized the publicity value of having famous intellectuals endorse specific causes; it was always after names for letterheads and public petitions—as are most cause-oriented groups down to the present day. More important, however, was the concern that the Party had to support the emerging social consciousness of intellectuals in their work and to promote the development of social space within which radical intellectual work could be done. In the early thirties the Party line emphasized independent revolutionary action; accordingly, the Party's cultural efforts were dedicated to the development of what was called "proletarian literature"—the encouragement of working-class artists and writers, and the support of themes that emphasized the oppression of workers and their revolutionary potential. During the era of the Popular Front, both the general intellectual climate and the Party's own literary criticism encouraged a more eclectic, populist, and broadly democratic kind of content.

Party-sponsored frameworks for artists were largely superseded by a variety of New Deal programs that were able to give financial support as well as free opportunity for artists and writers. That era was the high point of left consensus among American cultural workers—it was the time of Clifford Odets' *Awake and Sing*, Steinbeck's *Grapes of Wrath*, Sandburg's *The People, Yes*, Ben Shahn's social realist lithographs, and Refrigier's post office murals.

Perhaps the Party deserves some credit for creating, in the years before the Federal Projects, some significant opportunities for working-class young people to become artists, and for helping foster the political and social climate that set the stage for the enormous outpouring of socially concerned cultural work that occurred in that time. But it is abundantly clear that, on the whole, the Party's interventions on the cultural "front" did much to eventually undermine the Popular Front cultural consensus. All too often, the Party's official literary periodicals criticized work of intellectuals if they had taken the wrong line on some political issue. Someone who was politically "incorrect" could not possibly be artistically valuable. Moreover, Party literary criticism typically adhered to fairly philistine standards—even those who were politically correct were suspect if their work was avant-garde.

In general, the CP had a cultural line. It demanded that intellectuals and artists who were Party members be subject in their work to the line, and to the Party functionaries who had the authority over that line. "Culture is a weapon," said the Party, meaning that it was a means to an end, and that its value should be measured in such terms. This view, owing much to Stalin and little to Marx, could not be imposed for very long on self-respecting intellectuals and artists. The effort to impose it contributed not only to dramatic defections from the Party and disgust with its leadership, but to disillusionment with political engagement as such among American intellectuals and artists in the aftermath of the thirties.

I think that except for the relatively brief (although historically significant) period of the Popular Front, the influence of the left on American writers and artists has come much more through conscious identification with the tradition on the part of individual intellectuals rather than because of the mobilizing efforts of left parties. That tradition embodies very diverse ideological strands; it includes not just Socialists and Communists, Wobblies and Marxists, but all kinds of anarchistic perspectives, a variety of Christian faiths and theologies, and, in recent decades, a generalized anti-authoritarian, humanistic or democratic set of sentiments often willfully unlabelable.

Indeed, it makes sense to see that the tradition of the left in the United States has run along two more or less parallel streams. One stream is made up of the organizations and parties, their public activities and programs, their institutional structures, and the political activists they socialized.

The second is made up of intellectuals: of novelists, poets, painters, musicians, actors, photographers, historians, sociologists, educators, philosophers, journalists, film-makers, dancers, psychotherapists, architects, who have, in one way or another, sought in their work to criticize and socialize American individualism and privatism. Some of these took their cues at least in part from the organized left, but mostly they did not. Many have been conscious of an affiliation with the left as an ideological and political tradition, but many have not (or have not openly professed it if they have).

The Historical Impact of Left Intellectuals

The left stream in American culture, like the left stream in politics, has had its main historical impact in "socializing" Americans for collective action. In the years before World War I, the work of left-oriented artists and writers fed off of and fed into labor organizing, and socialist voting, antiwar feeling, women's suffrage, and municipal reform. In the depression years, it interacted with the CIO and with struggles for Negro rights, with opposition to fascism, with the rebellions of farmers and sharecroppers, and with New Deal reform.

In the sixties, critical intellectuals helped arouse opposition to the Vietnam war and were in turn influenced by the mass antiwar protest. Intellectuals helped set the stage for public concern with "poverty" and helped frame the thrust of the official "war" against it. The "counterculture" was pioneered by social critics and poets, publicized by journalists, and fundamentally influenced the sensibility of writers and artists. The black movement drew its ideological themes from the work of various intellectuals and helped create a whole generation of poets, playwrights, and artists. The rebirth of feminism began with certain key writings; indeed, feminism has been as much an intellectual/cultural movement as it has been a social/political one. The environmental movement depended on testimony of technically trained people without whom environmental dangers would not be perceived nor their inevitability questioned. Nor could it exist without systematic efforts to formulate a coherent public philosophy based on ecological values.

It is by no means clear how such intellectual and artistic production actually gets to influence the ethical perspectives of large numbers of people. The politically engaged intellectual and artist is inescapably frustrated by the feeling that his or her work lacks social meaning or historical effect. I cannot here even begin to develop a theory that might help solve this problem, but I think it is possible to throw out some probes and suggest some clues that can be of use.

The problems of the left intellectual include the following:

1. The situation of the intellectual is sharply divergent from the everyday experience of those he would like to communicate with—by reason of social background, everyday routine, and formal education.

2. The established means of communication—the various mass media and the academy—are controlled by those interested in perpetuating, rather than opposing, established values. Left intellectual, therefore, cannot count on these media to transmit their work nor depend on them as a reliable source of livelihood.

3. Assuming that channels of communication have been found, the artist or writer confronts the problem of what to say and how to say it—to be appreciated, and to have a historical effect.

Marx, as we have seen, thought that these problems were soluble if intellectuals participated in the movement of the working class. That movement would provide the means of connection and communication that intellectuals need, its problems and experiences would provide the subject matter for their work, and the consciousness of its members would be both guide and pupil for intellectuals.

If, indeed, there were a movement of the working class as a whole, and an emergent collective consciousness among a "proletariat," then Marx' advice to left intellectuals would, quite obviously, have force. But these conditions do not exist. In their absence, some intellectuals have thought that organized left parties could serve as adequate surrogates for the proletarian movement as such. By joining the Party, one would make the social and political links that would provide an audience; the Party's cultural apparatus would provide channels—and even a livelihood; the Party's ideological framework and political strategies would provide guidance about content. Furthermore, some American intellectuals have felt that submission to a Party was a clear-cut way to overcome a privileged individualism about which they had come to feel guilty.

But Party discipline and bureaucratic control are fundamentally at odds with artistic creativity and intellectual honesty. Moreover, even if this were not a problem, Party-oriented intellectuals found that the political weakness and isolation of their organization contradicted hopes they might have of "reaching" and affecting large numbers. To work in the context of a left organization frequently meant that one was spending one's time preaching to the converted.

Some artists and writers of the left found solutions within the looser institutional frameworks provided by the subcultural pockets of radicalism that emerged in various ethnic and work communities. The Southwestern radical farmers, the itinerant workers of the West, the New York Jewish community, and the black communities of both the rural South and the urban North provided both audience and stimulus for creative, and often highly influential, popular and "high" cultural production.

The work of such "Party" and "subcultural" intellectuals was a vital part of the process of radical identity formation and movement building. The songs of Joe Hill and other Wobbly minstrels deepened the emotional bonds of their movement—and Joe Hill's songs undoubtedly taught many the basic ethics of the labor movement: There is strength in union; don't scab; don't count on the "pie in the sky" of the preachers; don't shake the bosses' hand. Jewish left poets, writing in Yiddish, helped reinforce the ethnic identity of their community while articulating the grievances and ennobling the condition of sweatshop workers. Paul Robeson, despite his identification with the Soviet Union, became a symbol of the potentialities for human brotherhood; his singing and his presence had a sizable impact on popular culture in the thirties and forties.

Of all the arts, song and poetry are the most democratic, the most readily capable of symbolizing and communicating collective identity. The songwriter and poet can express their individuality in their work, but the song and the poem can be easily remembered and readily repeated by others.

In all cultures, songs are an integral part of collective mobilization; a fundamental way of recalling and expressing shared identity; a basis for group rituals symbolizing unity, power, and shared belief. It is not surprising that one of the main ways that the tradition of the left has influenced American popular culture has been through song. The most important single influence on American popular music is black culture; jazz, blues, and gospel elements pervade American music. The content of these genres is rarely explicitly political protest; still, these forms articulate the emotions and experience of people who are oppressed, celebrate the creativity and dignity of common folk, and reject the genteel modes of expression of official, WASP, respectable culture. American popular music, having such roots, has for decades had undertones of social criticism and democratic feeling.

To these roots, left artists have tried, since the thirties, to add further influences. In the late 1930s a small group of young performers, led by Pete Seeger and Alan Lomax, became intrigued with the idea of reviving American folk music as an antidote to the commercialized pablum of Tin Pan Alley, and as a way of symbolizing the persistence of the democratic spirit. They discovered and publicized contemporary folk singers whose work carried on folk traditions while embodying explicitly political themes. There was Huddie Ledbetter, discovered by Lomax in a Texas prison, who had in his memory hundreds of Negro work and prison songs and who wrote songs with clear protest themes. There was Aunt Molly Jackson of Harlan County, Kentucky, who sang radical union songs she and her friends and family had written, using the musical traditions of Appalachia. And most important, there was Woody Guthrie, who came out of the Oklahoma dust bowl, had been a hillbilly singer on Los Angeles radio, and who was an astonishingly prolific and creative songwriter with conscious radical politics. By the late thirties, a folk song revival was going on in New York, and Guthrie and Seeger had formed a singing group to work in union organizing drives.

Although the folk song revival in the thirties and forties never made a big splash in the mainstream of popular culture, it did create a national audience of folk music fans and a sizable collection of songs that were crucial in reinforcing left-wing identity in the years that followed. By 1960 the folk music constituency had produced a new generation of singers and songwriters—and, most unexpectedly, commercial record companies took an interest. It did not take long for the work of performers like Bob Dylan, Joan Baez, Phil Ochs, Tom Paxton, and other proteges of Seeger and Guthrie to become highly popular, and eventually to help shape the sensibilities of the emerging youth revolt.

The folk song revival turned out to be the most notable instance in which consciously left artists, working within the cultural apparatus of the organized left, ultimately influenced mainstream popular culture. Despite the effects of blacklisting and commercialization on the original project, its political impact was nevertheless substantial. From the thirties to the sixties a widening stream of popular music with protest themes was produced; and this stream undoubtedly affected the consciousness of audiences that were attentive to it. Indeed, the movements of the sixties are hard to grasp unless one recognizes the ways in which music helped crystallize the identities of many "alienated" youth, and provided the occasion and emotional underpinning for numerous collective gatherings. Moreover, in the years since the sixties protest themes continue to be heard in popular music oriented toward youth, and mass protests continue to be powered by politically minded musicians.

The story of the folk music revival helps us see how cultural radicalism, spawned in relatively encapsulated social settings, can eventually percolate outward, penetrating the everyday experience of large numbers. A mass culture industry such as the recording business may be imagined as a kind of voracious octopus, searching everywhere, and indiscriminately, for material to spew across the landscape. It tries to program the production of its material, through institutions like Tin Pan Alley in the thirties, but the result is typically banal and quickly stale. Wherever there are subcultural pockets of creativity, there the octopus is likely to find fresh "product" that can revitalize consumer interest. Without realizing quite what they were doing, Seeger and his comrades in political song had brought about such a creative pocket, and songwriters like Dylan had discovered how to rework the material so that it could be of wide commercial use. On the other hand, the record industry, without quite realizing it, had provided a medium for expression that challenged official values and helped dispose audiences to alternative perspectives.

Is this an isolated instance of left cultural influence on the popular mainstream? In certain respects I think it is, because, as I have suggested, song is the cultural form most easily and directly relevant to collective mobilization. It is also a form that is uniquely capable of being created outside of institutionalized structures of cultural production. The songwriter does not require a lot of equipment to create his work, he does not need a theater within which to present it, or a publisher to print and distribute it. In short, songwriting is a way of creating culture that is relatively free of the kinds of problems that intellectuals and artists typically have when they want to fuse their creativity and their political commitment. It is not surprising that song has been the most effective medium by which the tradition of the left has permeated American popular culture.

Typically, however, whenever the organized left or unaffiliated left artists and intellectuals have tried to foster the development of an opposition culture, their success has depended on the degree to which such projects have been carried on within relatively closed and cohesive communities.

It was in more-or-less self-contained ethnic communities and isolated groups of workers that left preachers and teachers could make face-to-face contact with subordinated people, and could inject their ideas and visions directly into their everyday processes of interaction.

It was with such communities that left writers could most readily make mutually intelligible contact.

It was in such locales that cheap, simple communication media were most likely to be effective: the street corner, the barn, the church, the campground were places where people who already shared common frameworks of belief and a common fate could readily gather to be touched by moral appeals addressed to them in terms that fitted their experience.

It was in such communities—of miners, timberworkers, Southwestern farmers, and Jewish garment workers—where the tradition of the Left penetrated most deeply into everyday life, and where ethics of collective responsibility were most fully shared.

Ironically, the very achievement of intimate connection with minority cultural enclaves tended to preserve and reinforce the American Left as a minority current that could not readily merge with the mainstream.

To reach the mainstream, Left intellectuals and artists have had to try to find linkages to the institutionalized cultural apparatus, rather than rely solely on the means of direct cultural transmission found in self-contained locales and within the organized Left. Each of the periods when large numbers of intellectuals identified with the left began with the formation of relatively self-contained circles of writers and artists who strongly sympathized with grassroots protest, actively seeking ways to express their sympathies in their work and to make their work historically relevant.

In the pre-World War I era, the primary locale for such ferment was Greenwich Village, to which aspiring writers and artists flocked, passionate to break conventional constraints on personal expression, moved by the plight and struggles of the workers, thinking of themselves as socialists, eager to make a difference. Out of their coffeehouses and salons came a flowering of "little magazines" (most notably the *Masses*) that expressed their quest for ways to link social revolution and personal freedom, socialism and psychoanalysis, progressive politics and avant-garde art. For a few years the bohemians were able to see all these concerns as facets of a single, modernist synthesis, in which Gene Debs and Big Bill Haywood, Sigmund Freud and John Dewey, Emma Goldman and Jane Addams, Pablo Picasso and Isadora Duncan were all symbolic leaders.

But it was not long before this synthesis fragmented, as many of the young intellectuals found ways to work within established institutions. A notable case in point was the establishment of *The New Republic* by the young socialist intellectual, Walter Lippmann. Lippmann saw that the Progressive wing of the "Establishment" provided avenues of influence and channels of communication far more effective and historically relevant than those provided by the Socialist Party and literary bohemia, and came to believe that reformist intellectuals would have far greater influence by trying to talk directly to the powerful than to themselves or to communities of the downtrodden. Progressivism splintered the radical intellectual community because it suggested that the "system" was open to reform from within, and that those intellectuals who sought to articulate their critiques and proposals from within would have real effect. Insofar as being a socialist meant staying in continuous opposition to, rather than engaging in dialogue with, established elites, progressivism forced radical intellelctuals to choose between staying left or being "effective."

These matters were brought to a head in the debate over U.S. entry into the war; the organized left in the United States opposed such participation and actively agitated against it, but many intellectuals, identifying with Wilson's Progressive rhetoric, joined the war effort. The case of John Reed, Lippmann's Harvard classmate, dramatized in the movie *Reds*, was not at all typical. As most of his fellow bohemians moved toward institutionally connected reformism, or maintained a detached sympathy with revolution, or engaged in aesthetic, spiritual, and psychological innovation, Reed became more radicalized and politicized—ultimately helping to found the American Communist Party. But Reed did not think of himself as sacrificing historical relevance. For just as Lippmann had gravitated toward Wilson, so Reed had become attracted to Lenin. Both men found that indigenous American radicalism was a framework insufficient to their ambitions to be historically significant intellectuals.

Most in the World War I generation, as they searched for ways to connect to history and to mainstream audiences, ended up in locations far removed from their radical political origins. Still, that generation had a transforming influence on American culture. It introduced "modernism" in literature and the arts. It was the seedbed of new ideas about child rearing, education, mental health, and social control—ideas influenced by psychoanalysis and related perspectives favoring the overthrow of "Victorianism" and the restructuring of the frameworks of individual development in society. It provided an ideological foundation for fundamental changes in the role of government in the United States—changes directed at ameliorating the human costs of industrial competition and growth and recognizing rights of workers, immigrants, and women to participate more fully in society. This ideological foundation had roots in socialism, but Progressive intellectuals (many of whom had been socialists) eventually defined the social reforms they advocated as measures that would represent an antidote to socialist agitation. The Progressive generation found that the newly emerging mass media were willing to provide them with publicity and audience, provided their critiques could be reframed as efforts to improve rather than overthrow the system.

Cultural radicalism in the thirties had much of its origin in circles of young writers, attracted to the John Reed clubs and to upstart radical journals such as *Partisan Review*. Like their predecessors in the prewar years, young radical intellectuals of the early thirties were caught up in a revolutionary spirit. Many thought their mission was to work specifically in behalf of "proletarian" struggle, while others, such as the *Partisan Review* group, sought to restore the synthesis between aesthetic modernism and revolutionary politics that had been lost in the twenties. But New Deal cultural programs—the Federal Theater Project, the Writers Project, the commissioning of public art, documentary film, and photography—gave large numbers of artists unparalleled opportunities to express social concerns in mainstream institutional contexts, just as the New Deal era was providing left activists with unprecedented opportunities to work effectively in grass-roots reform movements. Moreover, given the organized left's emphasis on the Popular Front and "broad" democratic ideology, the move by left intellectuals into the mainstream did not seem to require them to break their affiliations and identification with the left.

In those years, individual left artists and left-wing perspectives gained entry into the two emerging centers of commercialized mass culture—Hollywood and network radio. Left writers, directors, and actors migrated to Hollywood from the Group Theater and the Federal Projects. Some—most notably Orson Welles and Norman Corwin—worked creatively to develop radio drama and documentary forms oriented to social themes. The left in Hollywood had little freedom to innovate in terms of either content or form, and most of its product is indistinguishable from the work of nonleftists. The left screenwriters' most distinctive achievement was the production of a large number of war movies, portraying World War II as a struggle for democracy. Indeed, in the climate of national ideological unity of the war years, leftists working in popular culture fields were involved mainly in reproducing generalized patriotic and anti-Fascist themes that were hardly controversial.

This situation presumably led many left intellectuals to assume that they had won secure positions within the institutionalized cultural apparatus without having to abandon their sympathy with the organized left. Such assumptions were utterly smashed by the rapid escalation of the Cold War. Among the first victims of the anti-Communist purge were, of course, the members of the Hollywood and radio left; the "kosher" content of their work did not protect them from being blacklisted by the entertainment industry they had helped to shape.

During the Cold War years, there were basically three alternatives for those artists and intellectuals who had identified with the left. One could continue to maintain one's affiliations, sympathies, and ideological perspectives (or at least refuse to renounce them)—in which case one would be assured of being blacklisted out of films, radio, and the university, and quite restricted in finding opportunities in more marginal arenas as well. Or one could follow the lead of those who explicitly renounced their pasts and their politics and denounced their former comrades, framing one's actions as a moral choice dictated by the horrors and failures of Communism. Finally, some left-sympathizers were somehow able to avoid being "named"; these therefore escaped blacklisting by putting their political concerns on the shelf, at least for the duration. Each of these paths led to the same cultural outcome—the virtual obliteration of the left from the mainstream of cultural expression in the United States.

During the time of the Popular Front, the cultural left had glimpsed the possibility of becoming an established force in American culture. Leftists found themselves in the ironic position of helping the development of major forms and genres of popular culture—contributions that were quite ambiguous in their political and social meaning. So, for example, the Hollywood Left produced some of the best prowar movies and some of the most stirring patriotic propaganda art ever done in America. Dashiell Hammett created the hard-boiled detective story. Left-wingers like E. Y. Harburg helped increase the sophistication and social relevance of Broadway musical comedy. By the fifties, artists who had started out in the circles of the cultural left had come to dominate American theater, film, and literature —men like Elia Kazan, Arthur Miller, Norman Mailer, John Houseman, to name randomly a few key figures. Similarly, many of those most influential in academic social science and social criticism in the fifties had been student radicals in the thirties. Thus, even though the thirties cultural Left was wiped out during the Cold War, some of the artists and forms it had spawned shaped the intellectual and popular culture of the Cold War era.

The course of twentieth-century American cultural development could be seen as a series of "radical" waves followed by the "selling out" of those able to make it, coupled with the repression of those who remained true to their left-wing commitments, but to take such a view ignores the many intellectuals and artists who abandoned the political Left yet continued to take critical stances toward the society and the culture. Even at the height of the Cold War consensus in the fifties, both serious and popular culture embodied a considerable amount of social criticism. The focus of that criticism, however, had shifted away from the issues of the Depression, emphasizing not the exploitation of the proletariat and enthusiasm for mass action, but the personal and social costs of competitive individualism. If the key literary work of the thirties was the *Grapes of Wrath,* then its fifties counterpart was *Death of a Salesman*—a play that hardly endorsed the American way of life. There is little doubt that the Joad family could find solutions to their problems through collective action and social reform; it is practically impossible to see how the Lomans could find political answers to theirs. But, at least in retrospect, Miller's play turns out to have been as "radical" in its critique and its political implications as Steinbeck's novel—and it spoke more directly to the everyday experience of the mainstream of Americans. The critique embodied by *Death of a Salesman* paralleled themes present in many other popular works of fiction and social criticism during the fifties that challenged the terms of everyday life in relatively affluent society and the assumptions of those who had escaped "proletarian" oppression.

The culture of the Fifties helped in surprising ways to prepare the ground for the radicalization of the Sixties:

■ The "privatization" in the fifties of the New Deal generation was, by definition, a move toward political resignation. But, as they concentrated on family life and childrearing, many of these people became conscious of trying to apply "humanistic" and "democratic" values in the personal sphere, a concern strongly stimulated by the post-thirties orientation of popular social analysis toward "psychology." As a result, many "middle class" families, produced offspring predisposed to question conventional values and authority, to search for frameworks of meaning and identity alternative to those provided by official culture.

■ The popular social criticism directed at "suburbia," "conformity," and "status-seeking" reinforced such discontent in middle class kids who grew up in the Fifties, even if such criticism looked, from a "Left" perspective, like avoidance of big issues of power, exploitation and social change.

■ The popular culture of the Fifties embodied a rather vibrant semi-underground current of anarchistic mockery of conventional authority, carried by the "Beat" poets and writers, by popular satirists like Lenny Bruce and Mort Sahl and *Mad* magazine, by rock and roll performers. By the late fifties, these themes had become part of the currency of everyday banter in not a few adolescent friendship circles.

What was subtext in the fifties, became the main text in the Sixties.

Perhaps the most striking cultural development of the sixties was the incorporation of avant-garde perspectives and styles into many arenas of popular culture. Music was the preeminent mode of popular cultural expression during that period, and its main characteristic was the creative fusion of the content and tone of avant-garde poetry with rock and roll and other established genres of popular song. The pioneer of this fusion was Bob Dylan (Robert Zimmerman), whose nom de plume derived from Dylan Thomas, and who self-consciously sought to follow in the footsteps of such diverse culture heroes as Woody Guthrie, Allen Ginsberg, and Elvis Presley. Dylan found his first audience among the exponents and fans of the folk-song revival; for several years his songs were faithful reflelctions of the tradition of left protest music and were avidly taken up by the young activists of the civil rights and peace movement. During that period, in addition to readily accessible anthems and topical ballads, his work included a number of surrealistically toned, "poetic" pieces as well.

In the early sixties music and protest were more deeply intertwined than at any time since the days of the Wobblies. Not only did the Dylan and other New York-based folksingers help inspire support and recruit activists for the civil rights movement, but the movement itself, based in the black churches, was producing its own songs, rooted in the rich soil of gospel singing. The interpenetration of these two cultural streams can be illustrated by the story of "We Shall Overcome"—the great anthem of the civil rights movement. This was a song first learned by Pete Seeger from the singing of Southern unionists in the early forties. They in turn had adapted it from a traditional gospel hymn, "I Will Be All Right." "We Shall Overcome" was sung in left-wing circles during the forties and fifties, and was carried to the Highlander Folk School, a left training school for civil rights workers, by a Seeger disciple, Guy Carawan. Carawan taught the song to the first group of student sit-inners in 1960, and it immediately caught on—finally being brought back into the black churches and restored again as a gospel-style hymn. There can be little doubt that the song played a crucial role in binding people together in the face of fearful threats; singing "We Shall Overcome" with thousands of others—its melody permitting rich, spontaneous harmonizing, its lyrics simply and directly addressing fears and announcing hopes—was an emotional experience that surely helped sustain mass involvement in the movement. Indeed, the song is now sung worldwide in an astonishing array of diverse protest contexts.

Thus activism in the early sixties was nurtured by and provided the audience for Bob Dylan and his fellow "protest singers" and for the Southern freedom songs. It was not long, however, before songs by Dylan began to hit the pop music charts. His first big hit, "Blowing in the Wind," was the most popular song in America in the summer of 1963, as recorded by Peter, Paul, and Mary, a trio who themselves were on the way to huge popular success, and who had also had their start in the folk music world of Greenwich Village. From that point on, "folk music" ceased to be the property of the political/cultural left.

As the forms and styles of the "folk revival" became commercialized and televised they also quite rapidly became banalized, although a number of songs with rather pointed protest themes became popular in the process. The tradition was perhaps saved from complete absorption and digestion by the mass media by the continuing blacklisting of its most seminal exponent, Pete Seeger. His exclusion led others, most notably Joan Baez, to refuse to appear on network television shows that were exploiting the folk revival.

The transformation and incorporation of the left-wing folk revival into an element of popular commercial culture was signaled by the turn taken by Bob Dylan—namely, to abandon the acoustic guitar and his Huck Finn-like solo stage persona in favor of an electrified rock band—a turn first exhibited at the Newport Folk Festival in 1964. From then on, Dylan sought to write and perform in every genre of American popular music. He played rock, he did a country album in Nashville, and later, in the seventies, he professed to be an evangelical Christian and recorded several gospel-style albums. If one were to judge by his public performances and his work, Dylan was simultaneously hungry for the heights of pop stardom and at the same time saw himself as the epitome of the romantic, alienated poet—Elvis Presley fused with Rimbaud.

Interestingly, the search for this sort of fusion was not idiosyncratic to Dylan. By the mid-sixties, it was evident that the most popular singing group of all time, the Beatles, were interested in the same sort of thing. By the later years of the decade, the predominant themes and forms of youth-oriented music derived directly from the traditions of "romantic" art (rather than the traditions of popular music genres). Songs were filled with symbolism, surrealism, and literary allusion. They expressed apocalyptic visions, strong hostility to industrial society and encroaching technology, explicit paranoia about official authority, deep antagonism to conventional morality, and affinity with a variety of non-Western spiritual and religious traditions.

Dylan had demonstrated that a fusion of the avant-garde and the pop was aesthetically and commercially possible. It was commercially possible because the youth "market" now included millions of college students— i.e., young people with "educated" tastes who themselves would not have been content with the unsophisticated styles characteristic of "teen"-oriented music up until Dylan's emergence. The performers—like the Beatles, the Rolling Stones, the Doors, et al.—could "relate" to such aesthetic ambitions because they, unlike most in previous generations of pop performers, had been to college or had come from educated backgrounds. The new generation of singers were self-consciously "artists," schooled in traditions of popular culture as well as traditions of "serious art"—and they interacted with mass audiences who were ready to be addressed in such terms.

The new music thus was central to the so-called "counter-cultural revolution" of the sixties. I am not here going to attempt to assess the cultural "meaning" or impact of that "revolution." Suffice it to say that the climate fostered by the music, by the use of marijuana and hallucinogenic drugs, by the growth of new bohemian enclaves in major cities, by celebratory "be-ins" and "love-ins" and pop festivals, by "happenings" and other forms of "street" and "guerrilla" theater, by "black humor" and fantasy in novels and films—and by the magazine and newspaper stories and advertising that further popularized these already popular forms—encouraged young people to challenge conventional cultural repression, hierarchical authority, bureaucratic rationalization, and all forms of institutionally directed rationality. Such challenges were intensified by the Vietnam war and the draft, but "countercultural" stirrings were evident before the large-scale involvement of American troops in Vietnam.

Such "stirrings" had roots that were decades old—dating back to the days of Greenwich Village bohemianism. What was culturally new in the sixties was that themes of cultural protest that had previously been "subterranean" expressions of critical intellectuals and artists were now carried in the mass media and consciously adopted by large masses of young people. The massification of the avant-garde meant of course, that experiment and protest were inevitably turned into relatively trivialized fashion.

Still, for several years the popular forms of cultural radicalism had real historical impact. For a moment, youth in the United States—and internationally—were culturally united as a distinctive social force, with a strongly felt, shared interest in questioning authority. This collective spirit was confronted by the direct threat of a war whose means and ends could not be justified. The results of this collision between collectively mobilized youth and authority seeking cannon fodder were, of course, explosive. The antiwar movement was catalyzed by the organized, politically conscious New Left, but it could not have become a popularly based mass movement simply as a result of the exertions of SDS and other ideological leftists. The cultural climate made mass protest possible by creating a widely shared ethical framework for resistance and solidarity among young people.

Young intellectuals and artists who had been radicalized in the sixties did not simply repeat the patterns of earlier generations, seeking mainstream acceptance by shedding their politics. The sixties had demonstrated to mainstream communications media that openings to the left were strategically necessary if audiences were to be held. As a result the main story of the intellectual/cultural left in the post-sixties period was not that it lost its soul by becoming absorbed, but that it continued to develop while finding some institutional niches.

This was most evidently true in academia. By the late sixties most of the socially relevant academic disciplines were in considerable ferment over their material relationships with the "military-industrial complex" and their dominant intellectual frameworks. Radical caucuses, promoting left politics and left theoretical perspectives, had substantial effects in a number of fields. These included substantial widening of the range of acceptable discourse, redefinition of the dominant subject matters of research, and heightening professional sensitivity to issues of corporate and state "cooptation." A flock of New Left oriented journals were started—and quite a few of these became established. A sizable number of radicalized graduate students and young faculty got employment, and eventually tenure.

In addition to those representing the Marxian tradition and related theoretical perspectives, academic radicalism, beginning in the late sixties, was constituted also by those who identified with feminism and with minority liberation movements. The academic movement for affirmative action and for ethnic studies and women's studies affected the institutional priorities and practices of universities and, perhaps even more important, the content of scholarship and teaching as such.

By the eighties, the tradition of the left was rather well-entrenched in American academia, having come to have a taken-for-granted influence on the curriculum, on dominant outlooks of the social sciences and humanities, and the micro-politics of academic life. This academic left is diffuse and uncoordinated. It is certainly not "revolutionary," and its links to political movements in the outside society are surprisingly weak. Still, it is a definite institutionalized force in American intellectual life.

Whatever the long-term impact of an institutionalized left in the universities will be on American culture and society, American cultural life now more closely resembles that of other industrial capitalist societies. That is, at least in the major universities (if nowhere else in this country), it is intellectually respectable to express an affinity with "Marxism" and to be some kind of socialist. What is more important, this layer of radicals, neo-Marxians, feminists, black and Latino intellectuals, despite its fragmentation and political ambiguity, and despite the manifold career pressures and institutional constraints on its members, is positioned to carry forward the tradition of the left as a social critique, as an ethic of collective responsibility, and as a framework for the socialization of identity.

Meanwhile, outside of the university, members of the sixties generation have created a number of other institutional frameworks for the cultural transmission of the left tradition. Scores of former student activists looked toward work in mass media, once they realized that they had to settle in for the long pull. In the early seventies hundreds of weekly "alternative" newspapers were established around the country. Many of these have survived by cannily contriving to surround politically reformist and radical journalism with thick layers of cultural "features" designed to appeal to the tastes and fashion consciousness of young adults. The combined circulation of the alternative weeklies today is well over a million; although these papers are designed to be read by anyone, regardless of their ideological affinity, they typically serve as primary organs of communication and information for left-wing political activists, supporting community-based movements and populist local politics while providing critically oriented writers with outlets and opportunities for career.

There have been many other cultural developments flowing from sixties alumni. For example, radical filmmakers have made an effort to document social history cinematically. For the first time in the United States, the labor movement and the organized left have begun to receive detailed, sympathetic, and illuminating treatment in film, beginning with such justly celebrated documentaries by young filmmakers as *Harlan County, USA,* and *Union Maids.* The National Endowments for Humanities and for the Arts and Public Television, especially during the Carter years, served some of the functions of the New Deal arts programs in supporting the work of filmmakers and others interested in popularizing social history and documenting social problems. These independent film projects apparently had some effect in Hollywood; despite the film industry's enormous emphasis on escapist blockbusters, there were a number of commercial films in the seventies and eighties dealing with politically controversial subjects (*Norma Rae, The China Syndrome, Reds,* and *Daniel* are some notable examples).

In the aftermath of the sixties, left cultural workers compared with earlier post-radical eras, had considerably greater freedom and self-confidence to express their perspectives rather than compromise or abandon them. As a result, American cultural life in the seventies and eighties was far more pluralistic and ideologically contentious than in the fifties.

The cultural climate, from one point of view, thus appears incoherent and anomic: no values or institutions are sacred, no anchoring beliefs or perspectives are secure. Nevertheless, in the aftermath of the sixties, Americans have an unparalleled range of alternatives for identity, an unprecedented richness of resources for self-development, and a degree of freedom for self-expression that brings us closer to the ideal of liberty than we, or anyone else, have ever been. This more open and pluralistic cultural situation was one of the main historical effects of the New Left and movements of the sixties.

THE LEFT AS AN AGENCY OF HISTORY: A SUMMATION

WHAT, then, can we say about the historic meaning of the left in twentieth-century America?

1. The tradition of the left (defined as action and belief directed at replacing elite authority and impersonal markets with frameworks of public discourse as the basis of historically relevant decision making) has been carried forward along two channels. On the one hand, there is the organized, political left, constituted in the United States by a series of organizations ostensibly aiming at political power. On the other hand, the tradition of the left has developed as an intellectual and cultural current, constituted by artists, writers, teachers, and other cultural workers, who have engaged in concerted critique of established conditions, institutions, and values, and have tried to foster in popular consciousness what we have called "ethics of collective responsibility."

2. The political left is usually seen as a dismal failure. This assessment is obviously correct when the achievements of the left organizations are measured against their own strategic goals and self-understandings. No left organization succeeded in becoming the political voice of the American working class, nor was there any point in time when any of these organizations had the chance of winning majority support for the ideological perspectives they tried to espouse. Each of these organizations made some headway in implementing shorter-term political strategies, but ultimately failed to fulfill them.

Thus, the Socialist Party did begin to win some control in some local governments and elect a number of public officials who carried the party's banner—but these electoral successes were short-lived.

The IWW did succeed in mobilizing mass strikes among the unorganized and the unskilled, but these did not eventuate in the establishment of a viable structure of industrial unionism.

The Communist Party did succeed in fostering a "center-left" coalition within the labor movement and in reform politics, but this did not survive the end of World War II.

SNCC succeeded in mobilizing the struggle for voting rights in the South, but it was never able to create the South-wide independent political organization that its more strategically minded leadership hoped to bring into being.

SDS succeeded in mobilizing masses of students against the war and the draft and in sparking student protest for university reform, but it failed to witness the establishment of the national union of students that, at least briefly, its leaders had hoped for.

Not only did the left organizations fail dismally to achieve their strategic ambitions, they also were unable to sustain themselves for very long. Each disintegrated or passed into thoroughgoing obscurity after their brief period of dynamic leadership.

3. Although the left organizations failed to be frameworks of popular initiative or vehicles for effective struggles for power, none of the major left organizations can be thought of as merely the expression of a relative handful of marginal malcontents; each had roots in definite sectors of the population, and each achieved a definite popular base.

The problem for the organized left in the United States is not that it has never been "popular," but that its popularity has always been grounded in minority subcultures, communities, and sectors. This situation provided each of the organizations with enormous energy and vitality at a particular moment, but contributed further to the isolation of the organization from the mainstream. The American left, from this angle, is part of the general story of American inter-ethnic and sectoral struggle. Left organizations served as vehicles for advancing the interests and crystallizing the collective identity of various subgroups and sectors of the working and "middle" class, but never were able to fulfill their asserted mission of uniting workers as a class and crystallizing class-based identification.

4. Instead, the fundamental historical contribution of the left organizations was in the "socialization" of political activists, providing the experiences that enabled many of their members to develop the will and the competence for effective political participation and leadership. The activists' effectiveness rested not on the capacity to serve the goals of the organizations that had nurtured them but to become catalytic agents of grassroots social movements.

The organized left recruited to political activism many who, by virtue of their social location in the working class and other excluded strata, would otherwise never have taken such roles. It inspired many in the "middle class" who were already predisposed toward political concern to direct their energies in behalf of democratic and egalitarian reform. Without the presence of these grassroots activists and organizers, socialized by the left, the great twentieth-century movements of resistance and liberation that helped reshape the American social charter would not have been possible. For without the leavening of some members committed to history making, the grievances and discontents of those committed to the living of their lives are dissipated by the manipulative and coercive practices and processes of controlling elites and institutions. Even though left organizations often became fetters on grassroots activists, they enabled many oppressed

and exploited communities to acquire leadership necessary for their mobilization and provided this activist leadership with knowledge and material
support that enabled such mobilization to develop and win important gains.

5. *The left has had more meaning in the United States as a cultural than
as a political force.* A sizable proportion of American intellectuals and artists
have spent formative periods of their lives within the orbit of the political
left, even if their mature work departed widely from its perspectives. The
major periods of popular upsurge and left political influence had strong impact on the perspectives and content of the formal culture; to a considerable degree, the key works in both "serious" and "popular" culture in
United States reflect that impact.

Cultural expression is often thought of as a substitute for effective action; elite tolerance of cultural opposition is regarded by some analysts as
a powerful tool of social control, since it creates the illusion of freedom
without granting its substance. But such views are one-sided; clearly, the
expression of critical and alternative perspectives in intellectual discourse
and in art is itself historically relevant, since such expression has the potential of changing the meanings people employ in their everyday lives even
if it does not directly affect the material conditions and the legalized terms
of daily existence.

Such changes in consciousness may quite clearly eventuate in historical
action as well. In the American case, the left as a cultural force has had
at least three kinds of historical effect:

■ It has provided the ideological frameworks and the spiritual/emotional
resources that have sustained democratic activism. Such activism depends
not only on having the will and the skills to act, but on what might be called
the "faith" and the justification as well. The music, the literature, the social
philosophy, and the social science produced within the left tradition constitutes the identities, shapes the discourse, and fosters the faith of those
activists and intellectuals who have tried to be catalysts of change in American history.

■ It has provided the ideological and symbolic materials that have enabled oppressed, disadvantaged, and excluded communities and strata to
achieve shared identification, justify demands for rights, identify shared
sources of oppression and targets of opposition, formulate proposals for
reform. The formation of collective consciousness and the recognition of
collective responsibility cannot occur solely on the basis of immediate experience and face-to-face interaction. Collective consciousness depends also
on the preservation of collective memory, the transmission of a relevant
heritage, the existence of legitimating ideological perspectives, the formulation of political programs. All of these are both antecedent and parallel

to collective mobilization. To the extent that such collective consciousness has developed among depressed and excluded working-class communities, among blacks and other ethnic minorities, among students, and women, it has been because of the availability of ideas and ideologues, of symbols and artists carrying forward the tradition of the left and making that tradition relevant to these groups.

■ It has provided a continuing "adversarial" thread in our culture that has counterbalanced cultural themes that promote conformity to the logics of capitalism and the nation-state. It is simply not the case that American culture is unambiguously shaped by the "hegemony" of the capitalist class or that American nationalism straightforwardly structures popular attitudes toward authority. Alongside "capitalist," authoritarian, and "patriotic" themes in the culture and in consciousness are many strands of opposing belief. Americans, for example, are likely to be quite ready to "put human rights ahead of property rights." They are likely to believe that the environmental commonwealth should be protected against the claims of private interest. Americans are at least as likely to admire those who obey their conscience as those who obey the State, and more than a little disposed to question rather than accept the widsom of those at the top. Such themes are inherent to the general cultural tradition, but they have been continuously revitalized and reformulated in more critical and embracing terms by those cultural workers who have been influenced by the left. The presence of such "adversarial" themes in the formal culture and in popular consciousness is what enables social movements, starting largely in minority enclaves, to gain support and acceptance from those in the mainstream.

Anti-authoritarianism as a theme in both culture and consciousness helps explain why Americans are more "ready" for protest than most other peoples. For example, despite the absence of an organized majoritarian left in this country, the American labor movement was more militant in its actions (even though less radical in its stated goals) than that of any of the other industrial capitalist societies. In the 1960s, it was evident that the United States was typically the pioneer society in generating social movements. It was here that the mass student movement began in that decade; it was in the United States that feminism had its rebirth, and that environmentalism was first articulated as a basis for collective action. American movements have often provided the concrete techniques and modes of mass action and collective resistance taken up in other industrial societies. American movement leaders have often attained a degree of international symbolic significance rarely matched by popular leaders from other capitalist societies.

The international impact of American protest movements is ironic, given the weakness of the left in American politics. That impact has something to do with the quasi-anarchist elements of American culture. For one effect of American individualism has been to enable Americans to be more assertive and innovative in their relations with authority than others are likely to be.

The individualism in our cultural tradition resonates deeply with the anti-authoritarian elements in the tradition of the left, but it has made it difficult for left cultural expression to transmit what I have called an ethic of collective responsibility.

Left-influenced cultural expression has encouraged mainstream skepticism toward established institutions, helped the continuous reinvigoration of criticism, promoted tolerance for nonconformity, and extended both the definition of and the space for free expression. Gains made by social movements in winning new rights and by left cultural efforts in opening up the culture for critical and alternative perspectives have increased the possibilities for liberty. Such efforts revitalized, in the sixties and seventies, Americans' quest for freedom defined in terms of self-development.

The cultural left has had much less success in stimulating popular concern for the common good. Except for somewhat radicalized subcultural enclaves and for the relatively small number of democratically oriented political activists, the cultural left has had as little effect as the political left in fostering in popular consciousness a generalized awareness of, let alone commitment to, the vision of history made democratic.

We can summarize the left's story by saying that it has influenced American history by serving (often unconsciously) as an agency, not of socialism, but of socialization—that is, of nurturing, among individuals, in disadvantaged communities, and in mainstream popular consciousness, of perspectives, aspirations, and values that permit popular protest and grassroots organization to emerge and grow. As a force for socialization the American Left has been a crucial element in the evolution of the American social charter—the bargains and understandings about rights and obligations made and remade between elites and masses. That evolution has provided each of us with rights and opportunities for personal development and fulfillment that were previously undreamt of.

Without knowing it, each American is indebted to the often despised left for helping keep the flame of liberty burning, and compelling it to shine in corners it had never before reached. Each American today, therefore, has more control over his or her life than would have been true in the past. But the weakness of the left has made it possible for history increasingly to be made in places far removed from where these lives are lived.

Today, the left as an organized force is barely visible, its ideological foundations seem crumbled, its historical limitations seem to have overwhelmed its possibilities. Realism suggests that the left's vision of a fully democratized society will always be a utopian goal. Yet should the tradition of the left cease to have vital relevance, the space available for such democracy and liberty as we now have would surely constrict. So in the remainder of this book I want to define the left's troubles and see whether there are indeed realistic prospects for its revitalization.

5

Someday We've Got to Get Organized
Why the Left is Not a Party

Jim Jim
Where is our party?

—*Bob Dylan*

THE ABSENCE of socialism in America can adequately be explained by those American conditions—economic, cultural, and social—that immunized the majority against socialist gospel while transmuting protest movements into vehicles for social renovation rather than precursors of revolution. What is harder to account for in this way is the inability of left activists to sustain their own organizations even as holding companies for the left tradition. The relative unpopularity of radical ideology does not, in principle, explain why radicals in the United States have never been able to hang together in formal organization over the long pull. Government repression certainly took its toll—but communist parties, and other left organizations, have survived elsewhere in the face of far more severe repression than that experienced in the United States.

DILEMMAS OF ORGANIZATION

THE SOCIALIST Party and the IWW were dynamic centers of left initiative for about fifteen years. Many of their most militant members went over to the nascent Communist Party, but the Party did not become publicly significant until the early thirties (ten years after its founding) and it, too, led the left for about fifteen years. SDS and SNCC each lasted no longer than seven years.

Each of these five organizations, then, experienced a period in which its leadership defined the left. During that period, left-oriented activists were either drawn to membership in the organization or recognized its authority to define activist priorities. The Communist Party, more than any of the others, created many enemies on the left—but even these could not act without taking the Party into account. In each case, however, the organization's authority was eventually lost, and it either disintegrated or passed into a moribund obscurity.

Each new left generation in America has tended to rebel against the organizational format that preceded it. Thus, those who organized the Communist Party in the early twenties believed themselves to be the rightful heirs of the pre-World War I left, claiming leadership of the left from those who had been made outdated or irrelevant by the success of the Bolshevik Revolution. From their perspective, the demise of the SP and the IWW was progressive, because a "party of a new type" was needed. This perspective certainly felt itself vindicated by the Party's growing influence in the thirties.

Similarly, by the late sixties, some SNCC and SDS activists had become convinced that these organizations were obsolete. Certainly, neither could claim to be national leadership groups, since their membership base—and their very names—were largely restricted to "students" (and to those whose political experience was rooted in the student movement). The energy to try to create a new "party" came from those most attracted to the Chinese revolution. Their efforts to create a "new communist party" to replace the New Left and the old CP looked very much like those of their Communist predecessors in the aftermath of the Russian revolution in 1920. Parallel attempts to create a black-led revolutionary party, supported by some former SNCCers, were launched by the Black Panther party and other revolutionary nationalist groupings. But these efforts in the seventies, unlike those in the twenties, did not culminate in the establishment of a viable "Leninist" organization.

Accordingly, the demise of SDS and SNCC in the late sixties did not clear the ground for the creation of a more effective national left organization, but instead marked the beginning of a period in which no national organization exercises authoritative influence over left activists. Today, when leftists bemoan their failings and diagnose their ills, they often conclude that the problem lies in the "lack or organization," by which they usually mean the absence of a single national "party" that people on the left generally recognize as their center.

Why is a national "party" felt to be a need?[1] What do political activists think such an organization would do for them?

First, left activists usually express sharp needs to be represented in national arenas of debate and publicity. No matter how effective or satisfying particular local activity may be, it is experienced as historically limited because of its localism. A national organization with an identifiable set of national leaders can serve as the voice of grassroots leftists in the national media and other national political contexts, providing left critiques and alternatives to the policies and practices of national elites.

Second, a national party is the most obvious way to symbolize and define left political identity. Membership in a party provides continuous reinforcement of one's particular political commitment, and a ready at hand way of identifying oneself to others. The fortunes of one's party provide a straightforward measure of the historical impact of one's personal commitment—a kind of everyday validation of its meaning.

Third, a national organization is a mechanism of coordination. It helps rationalize the necessary political division of labor, helps members and local groups to define priorities, to see the relevance of particular work to larger, more encompassing projects, and therefore utilize energy and resources efficiently. By providing identifiable channels through which locally needed resources are allocated, the national organization enormously simplifies activists' problems in finding the means to carry out their political tasks. The newsletters and mailings of the national organization and the travels of national organizational officials are not only the most efficient way for members to know what is happening, but also provide ways members are rewarded by recognition in the network for their own accomplishments.

Fourth, a national party is a mechanism of consensus. At any given time, numerous ideas and proposals for strategy and program are proffered on the left. It is a particular feature of a party that such proposals are debated not simply as interesting ideas but as options for action—and such debate is consequential in that it eventuates in choices and collective decisions. The public ratification of strategic and programmatic proposals then becomes the means for unifying and coordinating the activities of adherents. This process puts pressure on individual members to seriously consider such proposals and discuss them as live options; the achievement of con-

---

1. "Party" is in quotes because the organizational need described is not fulfilled by an electoral party of the American type. The word "party" here refers to an organization that invites membership on the basis of shared principles and social vision, hammers out a political program for which it seeks popular support, develops a strategic perspective for achieving that support and fulfilling the program, and expects members to act in terms of that strategy. By this definition a left party *may* have an electoral strategy, but it need not. Thus, the IWW, the CP, SDS, and SNCC were all "parties" even though, unlike the Socialist Party, their strategies did not center primarily on running in electoral campaigns.

sensus then frees members from interminable and paralyzing concern with
deciding what is right to believe and to do.

Fifth, national organization provides continuity. The organization is charged
with carrying forward the tradition of the left, so that the fate of that tradition is not dependent simply for its survival on the actions of particular
individual members. Organizations record their history and consciously
transmit it to members through written literature, ritual, and formal educational arrangements. Organizations actively recruit new members, send
organizers into "virgin" territories, establish youth sections to attract the
new generation. They are the most systematic means by which the tradition of the left is conveyed and passed on.

Finally, the party is a framework of social control or "discipline." It provides means for members to hold each other accountable and to engage in
reciprocal evaluation of their common work. To know that one's political
work is being observed beyond its immediate social context is to give that
work a significance and a shape that it might not otherwise have. If, as is
usual, such accountability is accompanied by additional incentives, then the
organization can be a very powerful instrument for calling on members for
sacrifice, for dedicated energy, for self-improvement.

All of these are compelling reasons for establishing and maintaining a
national organization; to list them is to wonder how left political activism
can exist at all without such a structure. Why then the continual inability
of American leftists to sustain such organizations over the long run? Why
did no durable left organization come out of the New Left of the sixties?
Why have the great majority of left activists, for the last fifteen years,
been hesitant about the creation of such a national party?

To commit oneself to an organization is to risk infringements of one's
freedom of thought and action. Despite this risk, people participate and
support organizations insofar as they are thereby aided in achieving some
purpose they otherwise could not obtain. Politically active people hope that
through organization they can increase their political efficacy—that is, that
the organization will deploy resources in such a way that the course of
history will be influenced in directions they favor. I want to suggest that
resistance to national organization among leftists is rooted in the perception
that, historically, *left parties reduced members' freedom without increasing
commensurately their capacities to be politically effective.*

Here are some examples of the ways in which organizations infringe on
freedom:

■ Active organizational membership defines one's identity. The identified member wears the organization's label and is inescapably linked to and

held accountable for the policies, activities, and reputation of the organization.

■ Active organizational membership restricts freedom of thought. The loyal member must be something of an apologist for the organization, something of a romantic about its potential achievements, something of a chauvinist vis-à-vis competing groups, something of a factionalist in organizational disputes. Just as a salesperson cannot afford to be open-minded about the virtues of competing products or the flaws in what he is selling, so the party member cannot readily be objective about his or her commitments and is inclined to suppress rather than entertain negative evidence and private doubts.

■ Active organizational participation infringes on private space. Organizations engaged in ongoing political struggle tend to have needs for members' time and energy that continually threaten to become all-consuming. These pressures in left organizations are experienced as deriving from *practical* requirements of goal attainment and as *moral* obligations—against which "personal" needs and wishes are felt to be selfish and trivial.

■ Active organizational commitment can limit personal options and define personal priorities. Organizational imperatives can not only affect day-to-day activity, but also fundamentally shape longer term life goals.

■ Organizational participation limits freedom of political action. Nationally formulated programs and strategies are usually intended to compel locally based activists to put organizational priorities first, even when their experience and "instincts" must thereby be overruled.

All such infringements are likely to occur even under the most democratic kinds of organizational circumstances, to the extent that the development and maintenance of the organization is a high priority for its members. All organizations are ostensibly means to some ends; all are merely instruments. But a fundamental dilemma of organizations is that they can never be merely means. Their sustenance requires some diversion of energy, some rechanneling of motivation, some commitment by members to the organization as an end in itself. Such commitments require members to sacrifice private wishes, individual perceptions, and locally grounded interests in favor of organizational imperatives. The more that such imperatives are enforced through structures of hierarchical leadership and explicit disciplines the more intense is the infringement on freedom.

There is a resistance to organization that political activists tend to share with less politicized people—the resistance based on the desire for personal "free space"—a desire that pulls people away from political engagement itself. Even highly committed activists cannot forever suppress the parts of themselves that respond to the obligations and joys of everyday personal life—the caring for one's children, the pursuit of private enjoyments, the peace of letting go of History.

Organizations depend for their long-term effectiveness on developing means for managing these inevitable personal conflicts. The ways, described in chapter 4, by which members of the CP and the SP could find opportunities for everyday leisure and self-development within the orbit of the party enabled many to see the organization as aiding self-fulfillment rather than just requiring its sacrifice. In addition, of course, most political organizations stress the moral necessity, and celebrate the heroism, of self-denial. Such appeals obviously are efficacious to the degree that members continue to feel that the organization does embody their highest ideals.

The most serious personal dilemmas faced by members of left organizations have had to do with organizational infringements on their *political* freedom. Such infringement results when organizational imperatives come into conflict with demands arising from workplace, community, or other social networks within which activists are doing their day-to-day political work. Even more distressing of course are circumstances in which organizational practices conflict with members' consciences. When a national organization adopts policies, priorities, and lines that members are expected to implement even against their own political inclinations, they set the stage for member disaffection and disillusionment.

If a national party were likely to enhance the political efficacy of activists or of the wider constituencies for whom they claim to speak, then the infringements on personal and political freedom that membership entails would be accepted as necessary costs. But the left parties have had very spotty records as vehicles of effective political leadership. Instead, members repeatedly found that they had to pay a heavy *political* price for party loyalty:

■ Membership itself was frequently self-isolating. To be publicly known as a member often threatened members' legitimacy and credibility as organizers in workplace, community, or movement settings. One typically hid one's party affiliation not only as a protection against political reprisal but also to keep the trust of fellow workers.

■ Members repeatedly felt at odds with central party leadership, saw them as bureaucrats, out of touch with political reality. Such tensions between the functionary leadership and grassroots membership were a continuing theme in all the left organizations, breeding factionalism, disaffection, and cynicism.

■ The history of the U.S. left is shot through with interorganizational rivalry and bitter infighting; often the primary organizational preoccupation was the defeat of other left groups rather than the advancement of wider social goals.

Such experiences were regular features of daily life within left parties. No surprise that many members came to doubt whether their organizational loyalty was really an aid to their political work, coping with such doubts by surreptitious efforts to evade demands emanating from the leadership. Such feelings contributed to the high membership turnover of the Communist Party. They had a lot to do with the eventual demise of all of the national organizations.

All organizations, left-wing or not, political or not, make demands on members that infringe on freedom of thought and action, demanding the sacrifice of personal inclination in the interest of collective goals, rules, and consistency. Member alienation is therefore an inherent feature of voluntary organization. Accordingly, the problem of restoring members' commitment is integral to organizational dynamics, especially when members can exit. The primary way commitment is maintained is by providing specific, more-or-less material benefits in return for conformity and committed performance. Such incentives are maximally effective to the degree that they are "selective"—that is, uniquely available from the organization.

Left organizations, however, did not have an abundance of such material incentives to offer. Indeed, they rarely provided such a good deal for anyone who tried to calculate the value of membership on the basis of a personal cost/benefit ratio. As we have seen, the CP and the IWW did provide unique opportunities for self-development—for education, skill-development, travel, and adventure—to impoverished working-class young people. The gratitude many felt for such benefits undoubtedly impelled them to face enormous risk—of jail, physical danger, loss of livelihood; it also accounts for the deep sense of loyalty and obligation that these organizations were able to maintain.

But such individual benefits cannot be the basis of integration and commitment in left organizations. It is not just that these organizations lack the practical capacity to provide such opportunities on a big scale. Their *raison d'être* is, after all, ideological; members must expect of each other a high dedication based on principle. Members validate their ideological commitment to themselves and to each other by self-sacrificing actions that justify and are justified by their shared ideology. The emotional rewards and moral pressures that derive from membership in a close-knit band of comrades—and in a wider tradition of shared belief and struggle—are the primary means by which members' commitments are maintained and deepened.

The opportunities for self-development, for community, and for moral coherence provided by left organizations sustain commitments in the face of sacrifice and risk. They also help blunt members' doubts about the organizations' efficacy—and blind them to many failures and weaknesses. But the more effective such binding mechanisms are, the more they fundamentally contradict the public, historical goals of the parties. These were not organizations whose purpose was to create a community for members or to be islands of true faith. They were organizations whose meaning depended on the capacity to influence history, to lead "masses," to gain power, to affect popular consciousness. Such goals require that members be loyal to the organization and defenders of its faith, and that they be actively engaged in the mainstream arenas of political action. The source of disillusionment of left activists with their organizations was their continuing inability to reconcile such active external engagement with their organizational commitments. All too often, organizational commitment tended to undermine activist effectiveness rather than aiding it.

There are, it seems to me, two main reasons for this inescapable dilemma. First, the organizational need for ideological consensus and closure contradicted members' continuous discovery that the society they had to deal with was more complex than any organizationally serviceable ideology could encompass. Second, the organizations' orientation toward the development of their power fundamentally conflicted with members' efforts to act in either principled or effective terms.

IDEOLOGICAL ORGANIZATION VS. SOCIAL REALITY

IDEOLOGIES inevitably simplify social reality. Ideologies embody models of society abstracted from complex reality so that the causes of social ills can be identified and targeted and lines of action formulated. To a considerable degree, the simplifications characteristic of ideologies are similar to those of any theory, including scientific theories that model aspects of the natural world. That ideologies simplify does not distinguish them from other forms of conceptualization. Simplification and abstraction are necessary to permit us to cognitively process reality and to decide what to do about it.

In general, cognitive simplifications are treated either by lay individuals as they go about their lives or by scientists as they do their work, as beliefs and hypotheses that are subject to revision as they are matched against reality. Individuals who adhere to their beliefs in the face of contradictory reality may get regarded as stupid, neurotic, stubborn, or otherwise irrational. The processes and social organization of scientific work are designed to enable contradictory realities to overcome established beliefs. Ideologies, however, characteristically persist and even flourish in the face of reality—and accordingly we often use the word to refer to just those forms of thinking that evidence such persistence.

I think that the relative immunity of ideology from reality is due not to the ideas that are ideologized, but to the fact that ideological perspectives are embodied in organizations whose survival and growth is fundamentally intertwined with them. To the extent that an organization espouses a single ideological perspective, then those who have a stake in the organization also have a stake in maintaining faith in its ideology. I use the word "faith" advisedly here, because ideological commitment linked to organizational loyalty does become a kind of religious faith which cannot be permitted to be readily subject to empirical test. Adherence becomes a matter of principle, a test of commitment to ideals, and therefore adherence as such is more important than fidelity to empirical reality. Conversely, to the extent that members confront realities that cannot readily be fitted into the established ideological framework, the organization faces the problem of losing support, especially among those most in tune with the real world.

These are not problems for religious sects for whom faith is explicitly recognized as the dominant way of knowing. But left political organizations do not define themselves primarily as communities of faith. Instead they claim to be rationally based, indeed "scientific," in their orientation to society, and justify their existence on evidence that they are practically effective vehicles. Thus, in the long run such organizations cannot rest simply on ideological commitment and loyalty; they have to be able to interpret and predict reality with a reasonable degree of validity, at least in the eyes of members and potential recruits.

From one point of view, the very complexity of social reality gives added power to ideological simplification. Adherence to an ideology is a way to end confusion, to find an anchor of clarity in an otherwise incoherent world. Insofar as an ideology provides an overall mapping of the society, a general set of guidelines for how to think about the social order and large social issues, a broad interpretation of history and a vision of a possible future —and insofar as it is a widely shared belief system that has stood the test of time—it is not easily going to be falsified by particular events.

Indeed, the great ideological frameworks that have dominated social action in the modern world are sufficiently flexible to handle a great many

potential setbacks. Not only do they embody plausible models of the society, but they also provide moral justifications for the claims and demands
and reflect the experience and situation of significant social groupings. As
broad frameworks of perception and action—as "traditions"—they are not
going to be proven "false" by empirical reality. "Socialism," "liberalism,"
"anarchism," "conservatism" may embody simplifications that partially blind
adherents to the full complexity of social reality, but each of these is sufficiently "true" so that commitment to them need not preclude "rational"
thought and action.

The problem lies in the linkage of these broad perspectives to the fate
of particular organizations. Insofar as a particular organization claims to be
the true inheritor and interpreter of the tradition it is upholding, then cognitive flexibility of members is to that extent narrowed. Insofar as the specific strategies, policies, and programs of an organization are taken to be
directly derived from, and uniquely expressive of, the ideological tradition,
then rational discussion, analysis, and validation of strategy, policy, and
program are thereby limited. Insofar as the organization is hierarchically
structured so that some members have more authority than most to interpret the tradition and define policy, then the capacity of the organization
to learn from and respond to the full range of members' experience in the
real world is thereby limited. Insofar as certain issues are ruled out of
bounds for legitimate questioning and discussion within the organization, then
members are compelled to defensively manage their cognitive dissonances
rather than seek their effective resolution. Insofar, then, as organizational
loyalty is made equivalent to ideological commitment, and both are defined
as fundamental tests of moral worth, there is little room for the dissent
that is necessary for rational consensus.

These sorts of observations have been relatively commonplace for at
least several decades. Many of them derive from the experience of the
Communist Party in the United States and elsewhere—an organization that
claimed to be the true inheritor of the tradition of the left and the first
truly scientific political organization in history. Despite these claims, of course,
the Party, was, more than any other left organization, subject to continuous schismatic splintering while it seemed woefully unable through most
of its history to formulate a strategy or a modus operandi that was adapted
to American reality. It seems likely that one of the main reasons for the
Party's inability to develop on the basis of rational understanding of its
situation was its insistence on ideological uniformity, structured by a highly
centralized process of idea formation and decision making.

If there is a typical member's story about the Party experience it would
run something like this: The Party provided me with wonderful opportunities for self-development, for education, for comradeship. The ideological

clarity and moral commitment gained through Party membership empowered me to make sacrifices, take risks, and dedicate enormous energy to political work that proved to be very beneficial to the communities with which I was involved. I will always be grateful for these opportunities and proud of the work I did. But eventually I found that I could not reconcile the demands and expectations that came to me from the central leadership with the work I felt was necessary in the locale I was in. Time and again, these demands threatened to undermine that work in one way or another. Time and again, the Party line swerved in directions that contradicted my local situation. On became increasingly mistrustful of the Party "bureaucrats" and their good sense; increasingly, one felt that one's Party membership was a drag on effective work and was frustrated at the failure of the Party publicly to be a credible organization. I learned that despite the official line that said that the Party was run on a "democratic centralist" basis, it was all centralism and no democracy—and that was fatal to its ability to reflect and learn from the experience of its rank and file organizers in the field.

The same situation has prevailed in all of the left parties that followed the "Leninist" model of ideological uniformity, centrally determined "lines," and claims to "vanguard" leadership. That model, which was supposed to maximize the efficiency and effectiveness of Party cadres, turns out, in practice, to be remarkably immune from reality testing, fundamentally incapable of adapting to the complexities of social life.

The other major left organizations in the United States—the SP, the IWW, SDS, and SNCC—followed quite different organizational logics. The SP was ideologically diverse and consisted, throughout its history, of several distinct factions and tendencies. Consensus was arrived at through open debate and voting at national conventions—and these debates had more to do with planks in the party's public platform than with arguments over ideological principle. The SP was organized like a circus tent, which housed a great variety of action-orientations, ranging from the strictly conventional electoral politics of a Victor Berger to the insurrectionary actions of the Oklahomans. The IWW embodied a more definite ideological framework than the SP, but its central leadership was always weak, and local members had a high degree of autonomy.

Still, even these organizations insisted on certain principles, violation of which was grounds for expulsion. The Socialists, for example, forbade members to cooperate with any other political party in election campaigns—if you were a Socialist you had to run under the party label or leave the party. Similarly, the IWW forbade locals from entering into signed contracts with employers; an IWW local that won a strike could not formalize its gains in a legal arrangement; any local that did this was expelled. These principles of noncooperation with capitalist employers or politicians were regarded as moral imperatives; their formulation in such terms prevented members from responding to their understanding of what might be politically effective in a given local situation, forcing members to choose between continued party membership and local effectiveness. Many chose the latter, thereby weakening the organizations, removing from their ranks activists who had actually been successful in achieving some local base. In retrospect, given the fact that the left eventually came to recognize the validity of center-left coalitions and collective bargaining agreements, these SP and Wobbly "principles" seem neither moral nor practical; the dysfunctions of ideological rigidity are clearly evident in these cases.

The SP and the IWW were ideologically committed to the notion that the independent organization of the working class was an absolute priority that ought not to be compromised. Such a perspective, however, failed to acknowledge that the working-class constituencies of these organizations were committed, as a first priority, to their lives rather than to the historical mission of their class—and that, therefore, the opportunities to win specific reforms or to obtain contracts would very likely be welcomed by these constituencies. Members who understood this gap between party ideology and popular consciousness and who sought to remain integrated with their constituencies were thus faced with wrenching choices between adherence to "principle" vs. staying responsive to the needs of the people they purported to lead.

Both SNCC and SDS learned a great deal from the flaws of their predecessors. Indeed, one of the reasons the New Left thought of itself as "new" was precisely that its initiators were consciously and explicitly opposed to the establishment of ideological uniformity and the encrustation of dogma. Since SNCC never developed to the point of becoming a full-fledged party-like national organization and was so focused on the achievement of particular goals, it never really confronted the problem of reconciling ideology and reality. SDS, however, although it was predominantly a student organization, was the closest thing to a national party that the New Left ever developed during the sixties.

SDS was open to all who wanted to join, provided they professed acceptance of its general value framework. It was organized explicitly to encompass diverse ideological perspectives. Chapters were completely autonomous—and there were no rules or procedures by which any member or chapter could be disciplined or expelled. In its early years, whenever there were major segments of the membership who disagreed over strategy, SDS adopted the practice of permitting each alternative strategy option to go forward as an experimental "project," providing organizational sponsorship and (to the limited extent possible) resources. Thus, in 1963–

64, SDS was divided over strategic priorities: some favored active participation in electoral politics, while others favored the development of SNCC-
like organizing in urban poverty areas. Rather than decide among these
priortities, SDS established two projects: the Political Education Project
to work electorally, and the Economic Research and Action Project, to
initiate the neighborhood organizing effort. This sort of experimental, project-
oriented approach to strategy was quite innovative in left history, since it
had been much more usual for left organizations to debate strategic options
and try to choose among them on the basis of internal organizational pol-
iticking. SDS' approach recognized the need to give space for alternatives
to be tested in the real world rather than simply in the crucible of intra-
organizational debate.

Despite the early New Leftists' self-consciousness about avoiding ideological rigidity and their emphasis on learning from experience, in the end
SDS was overwhelmed by the very "mentality" its founders had hoped to
avoid. The organization's openness to all comers allowed the entry of ideological dogmatists—particularly cadres of the Progressive Labor party. PL
was the first "Maoist" party in the United States, and operated very much
on the Leninist model. PLers challenged New Leftists for leadership of
SDS, organizing disciplined bands to turn out at national conventions, with
the result that SDS national meetings became arenas of intense ideological
dispute. Meanwhile, a "new guard" of SDS leaders had emerged to replace
the old guard founders who had "graduated" from the organization. This
new guard was itself less committed to "open" nondogmatic styles than
the founders had been, and, in the atmosphere of 1968 (a time of world-
wide turmoil and revolutionary rhetoric), more interested than its predecessors in finding a definite ideological direction. Under the pressure of the
PL challenge, ideological lines hardened among all of the national leadership
elements of SDS. Distinct factions developed, each claiming superior truth
and contending for organizational control, and each characterized by astonishingly simplistic models of society and perspectives on strategy. The
last convention of SDS in 1969 became a battle ground between slogan-
chanting factions, each proclaiming their revolutionary superiority, and none
bearing much relation to external political reality. SDS itself died on that
battleground, and members of its founding generation continued for many
years after to wonder how their commitment to experiential rather than
ideological bases for radical politics could have been replaced by a wild
caricature of ideological politics at its most simplistic.

All of the American left organizations were thus undermined by tendencies to enforce certain kinds of ideological conformity at the expense of
members' direct experience. Particularly damaging were efforts to insist

that strategic perspectives adopted at the center were morally binding on members, irrespective of their own reading of either external reality or of the ideological texts from which the strategic lines were said to flow. Such insistence tended to lead either to the disaffection of individual activists, who lost respect for the central leadership, or to bitter factional dispute over strategic options, whose correctness should have been judged on their practical utility rather than their moral validity. The Communist Party and other Leninist sects exemplified these propensities in extreme form, but they were nevertheless present also in groups that were less disciplined and hierarchical.

The problem of ideological rigidification cannot therefore be solved simply by creating an organization that is democratically structured or that is open to ideological heterodoxy. The problem lies in the very idea that the tradition of the left is best implemented by the building of a single national organization that stands as its authoritative representative. For it seems likely that so long as American society is able to reproduce itself, so long as the established institutional structures continue to function, and established patterns of differentiation and stratification continue to be sustained, the society will be—as it always has been—too complex to be effectively defined by a single model or changed by a unitary strategy.

The complexities that the left confronts have first of all to do with the extraordinary pluralism of American society. The traditional working class is itself internally divided by deep racial cleavages and further differentiated into a continuously changing profusion of ethnic subcultures. Ethnic and racial differences are strongly undergirded by associated differences in occupational location, and reinforced by the physical clustering of subcultures. Added to the complexity of the traditional working class is the rapid growth of large and strategically situated strata of so-called "new," "white-collar" and "educated" workers. Further, American society is characterized by patterns of "uneven development" that produce major differences in experience and interests from region to region and vast shifts in population through internal migration. The considerable decentralism of the political system results in further complexities—significant variation in the character of state and local political structures, in the degree to which formal democratic rights are respected by local elites, and local power structures are subject to popular intervention. The pluralistic and uneven development of the society fundamentally affects the way localized groups perceive their shared situations, define their common interests, and mobilize politically. Thus, the American left has had to confront not only a class system that it has never succeeded in adequately comprehending, but also a complexity of social movements whose character and thrust typically affront the models and categories of established left ideology.

The irreducible assumption that leftists must hold on to is that all subordinated groups in society have a common interest in the expansion of democracy. But it is plain that the multiple complexities in the social composition, economic situation, and political position of the underlying population make it practically impossible to conceive, let alone implement, a single, uniform strategic perspective capable of unifying that population.

Virtually all of the debates about strategy that have divided the American left in the twentieth century were rooted in false dichotomies; most of the sides in most of these debates were expressing valid understandings of partial truths. These debates—about "politics" vs. "direct action," about "confrontation" vs. "permeation," about "independent political action" vs. "coalition," about "dual unionism" vs. "boring from within," about "integration" vs. "black power," about "reformism" vs. "revolutionism"—occurred not because some leftists were morally pure and others were "revisionists," nor because some were "crazy" and others "rational," but because there were fundamental differences in the perceptions leftists had of social reality, differences made inevitable by the complexity of that reality. What was mistaken, then, was not this view or that, but the assumption that only one pole of each of these debates could be right, or that there was one "correct path" that all organized leftists had to find and follow.

SOCIALIST IDEAL VS. "SOCIALIST" REALITY

THERE ARE still further complexities that weaken the capacity of the left to sustain a national organization. These have to do with the cumulative global experience in the twentieth century with revolution, socialism, and capitalism. To put it simply, the experience of these decades has repeatedly undermined the ability of the left to claim that it had ready answers to humanity's problems.

There was a time when left parties could argue that they knew how to reorganize the society so that human freedom and material well-being would be guaranteed. The success of the Bolshevik revolution provided proof of this claim for some, but caused considerable disquiet in others—a disquiet that, of course, grew as the Soviet Union pursued the building of what it called socialism. Such doubts were voiced on the left during the thirties, but were relatively isolated by the apparent contrast between a capitalist world wracked by profound economic depression and social crisis and a socialist country that was rapidly lifting its population out of social backwardness and economic misery.

In the last forty years, however, it has become progressively harder for

any on the left to claim that a revolution that overthrows an established
class system in the name of socialism will usher in a classless society, or
that the social ownership of the means of production wedded to centralized
economic planning ensures economic productivity and equitable distribution, or that the coming to power of Marxists in several states results in
the supplanting of interstate domination and rivalry by internationalism, or
that the popular forces who made a revolution will control the society after
the revolution, or that parties imbued with Marxist and socialist ideologies
will be incorruptible, humanistic, democratic. In short, the left in the industrial capitalist countries can no longer retain credibility by asserting any
identity with the Soviet model—nor can it define its vision by pointing to
the examples of socialism in practice. What "Western" leftists mean by
socialism has been profoundly complicated by the "socialist" revolutions.
Indeed, no party has been able to redefine its socialism in such a way as
to restore the purity of the old-time faith.

    Nor can Western leftists simply adopt the mantle of the rival left pole
to revolutionary socialism—namely, European social democracy. The first
disillusionment of Western leftists was not with the aftermath of the Bolshevik Revolution—it was with the succumbing of the German and French
social democrats to the logic of the nation-state during World War I. The
collapse of "socialist internationalism" at that time, and the subsequent long
history of social democratic willingness to administer capitalism rather than
carry forward the struggle to transcend it, permanently underminded the
early, simple notion that the democratic election of socialists to governmental office was the way to achieve social transformation. That history
makes it clear that parliamentary success is not an adequate alternative to
revolution. In recent years, the electoral achievements of social democratic
parties have created new grounds for disillusionment with social democratic
strategies and with the credibility of left programs as solutions to capitalism's ills and crises. Social democratic parties that have won governmental
office have typically made a difference in implementing policies that aided
working people, but they have not been more able than conservative parties in achieving the revitalization of sagging national economies.

    The declining credibility of socialist solutions in Europe and the United
States is, then, partly the result of the perception that "actually existing
socialism" can have frighteningly authoritarian and barbaric dimensions—
thereby forcing Western socialists to engage in defensive arguments to try
to disassociate their goals from the realities of the socialist states. But the
effort to create a nonrevolutionary, "democratic," programmatic socialism
in the West has foundered in the face of the logic of the capitalist world
economy. Social democrats in government discover that their power to
institute alternative policies is fundamentally limited by the dependence of

their national economies on multinational corporations, world markets, and "international finance." At least in the period we are now going through, genuinely socialist reforms, when instituted or even suggested, are checked by flights and strikes of capital. Socialist politicians typically find themselves favoring restrictions on working-class demands and paying other obeisances to private capital in order to prevent economic destabilization.

Accordingly, the "socialist" label conveys less and less about the substance of one's proposals and visions, while carrying with it a great many burdens of meaning that are discrediting. The emptying out of the meaning of "socialism" is occurring world-wide; in the United States, where the word has never had popular resonance and where socialists cannot claim to be heirs of a long tradition of representing popular needs, the problem of legitimating socialism is even more severe.

At some level of awareness, activists sense that their political effectiveness depends on remaining tentative and experimental about political strategy and remaining free to openly express their reservations and skepticism about vision and program. Rather than committing themselves to a national organization, whose practices and labels might foreclose such openness to experience, their overwhelming preference for the last years has been to participate in local organization, oriented to particular constituencies, working for specific issues, committed to specific social movements.

MAKING HISTORY VS. BUILDING ORGANIZATION

THERE IS still a further basis for the resistance of left activists to party-style organization, rooted in the experience that organizational demands conflict with members' effective participation in external social struggles. Insofar as this conflict leads members to measure their effectiveness in terms of organizational growth and influence, they tend to be pulled away from assessing their effectiveness in terms of authentic historical impact.

The goal of the left, as we have reiterated, is to enable the people to make their own history. But the goal of a left party is more immediately to gain members, expand its resource base, recognition, and influence. To put it crudely, the logic of party organization fosters a view that it is the party that ought to make history, and gain credit for doing so.

This logic derives, in part, from the structural facts of existing society —the fact that, on a day-to-day basis, the people are making their lives and therefore must be represented, rather than continuously involved, in history. Consequently, left parties work constantly to legitimate their claim to be authentically representative. Such legitimation can be measured by growth in membership, in the numbers of people who read the party-oriented press, participate in its institutions, vote its ticket in elections. It is asserted by the formulation of programs that are thought to reflect popular sentiments or needs, or that are hypothesized to be capable of capturing popular imagination. At bottom, left parties say to mass constituencies choose us, support us, follow us rather than the established elites—because by giving us power, by letting us represent you, by putting our people in office, your lives will be better, your values will be implemented in history. Insofar as the politics of representation is operating, then the organization is taken by its members to be the fundamental repository of their political hopes, the primary vehicle for defining their political goals, an end in itself.

Organizations become ends in themselves for additional reasons as well. To the extent that an organization becomes a full-time enterprise, it requires a staff of functionaries who must be paid, offices that must be supported, a range of operations that require financing. Acquiring such financing becomes a fundamental organizational goal—and, given the obvious fact that left organizations cannot depend on a membership having sizable discretionary income, activity that directly or indirectly contributes to maintaining the organization's resources becomes a fundamental, continuing priority. Thus, issues may be chosen in terms of their fundraising potential, rather than their political or social meaning. Organizations needing to maintain themselves must aim for visibility, must claim credit for victories, or claim to be threatened by sinister enemies.

In short, the logic of organizational maintenance creates a competitive struggle among groups seeking scarce resources. Some organizational rivalry within a movement framework can be a spur to heightened organizational effectiveness and dynamism, but quite often it is the source of destructive infighting, of efforts to dominate and control political turf, of deceptive self-promotion and moral decline.

The existence of a full-time staff is a condition for the operation of that classic sociological proposition—the "iron law of oligarchy" first formulated by Robert Michels. Michels' observation—that party leadership developed a vested interest in perpetuating itself in power—was based on the experience of the first great left party in the world—the German Social Democratic Party in the period before World War I. The party's tendencies toward top-down control and practical political conservatism were rooted, said Michels, in the fact that the leadership had an inescapable wish to remain in office, having come to enjoy the status, power, and everyday experience associated with their positions. Internal opposition had, therefore, to be controlled so that it would not threaten to overturn the leadership—and, consequently, organizational resources were increasingly dedicated to such self-maintenance. Moreover, the party could not, under these conditions, afford to let the unrest of its working-class constituency be mobilized in excessively militant or revolutionary directions—since such directions would threaten the existence of the party, providing pretexts for repression and creating social instability. Thus, the development of a bureaucratic internal structure in a left party enhanced its tendency to serve as a surrogate for popular involvement in history—and its tendency to be defined by leaders and members as an end in itself rather than a vehicle for social change.

There is no "iron law" of oligarchy (or of any other social propensity), but certainly Michels identified a fundamental feature of organizational dynamics. It is a feature common to all bureaucratic organizations, but it is particularly damaging to the organized left, precisely because the left is uniquely committed to popular participation as its stated means and end. Michels was showing that organizational structures create propensities that violate fundamental ideological principles, and cannot be overcome by ideological criticism.

There are two kinds of activist orientations in left parties. There are some whose political activity is directed toward the development of collective action among fellow workers and neighbors, the sparking of self-directed organization, democratic consciousness, and collective action in relation to the everyday life of communities; there are others whose activity is directed at the building of the party—recruiting members, raising money, promoting party-sponsored events, selling the party's papers, arguing for its policies.

Insofar as the organization is an end in itself, it is the second type of activist member who is drawn into the party leadership, locally and nationally. These are the people who run the local chapters, who become delegates to party conventions, and from whom are drawn the staff and leadership. But it is the first type whose lives and experiences are more closely integrated with the everyday worlds of the constituencies the party is trying to "reach," while the second type are more likely to include members whose daily lives are relatively closed off from these worlds. As a result, the party is continually threatened with becoming a kind of closed system, run by people whose perspectives, personal styles, interests, and beliefs are relatively out of touch with those prevailing in the "outside" world. Propensities to make the party an end in itself are thereby continually reinforced. Capacities of party leadership to act with "intelligence" or to speak intelligibly are thereby undermined. The potentialities for sectarianism, already latent in the ideological radicalism of the party, are thereby increased.

Thus, an organization that claims to be a vehicle to promote the self-determination of subordinated peoples comes to follow instead a logic of domination. Claiming to be selflessly devoted to the interests of the "masses," it comes to focus on its own self-perpetuation. Claiming to be the voice of the politically voiceless, its strategies and policies are shaped by those having least contact with the people for whom it is trying to speak.

These tendencies are made more manifestly contradictory to the extent that the party employs a rhetoric of power. That rhetoric is most evident among groups that follow the Leninist "vanguard" model. Within that framework, the party is likely to claim that it is the embodiment of the cumulative experience of the working class and its most "advanced" activist members, and that it has special insight into the direction of events and "correct" strategies by virtue of its command of Marxist theory. The "vanguard" party seeks to establish its "advanced" leadership over popular social movements and, implicitly or explicitly, claims to be the nucleus of the group that will take power over the society comes the revolution.

Parties of the Leninist type are likely to employ ways of speaking that are particularly jarring to the ears of the nonmember. Part of their rhetorical problem comes from the use of terms taken directly from "foreign" sources—arcane usages from Marxist theory coupled with invectives found in the propaganda media of various successful revolutionary parties. Such usages are good indicators of the sectarian character of the group—the use of arcane language making it clear that one has to be an initiate to share the party's wisdom, or, alternatively, dramatizing the degree to which party spokespersons are out of touch with the sensibility of their target audiences.

But even if the vanguard party learns to use the idioms of the larger culture, its rhetoric is likely to seem inauthentic, because it is likely to be a hard-to-digest mixture of claims to power coupled with claims to superior moral purity. It is characteristic of the vanguard party that it presents itself as the embodiment of revolutionary consistency, adhering to "principles" of uncompromising struggle against an evil system, never participating in the "betrayals" characteristic of the many misleaders of the people to be found in other parties, in the labor unions, and in other social movement organizations. At the same time, the party claims to be striving to "take power." But since any serious effort to "take power" would inescapably require any number of "compromises," bargains, and trade-offs with all sorts of other leadership elements, party rhetoric seems anomalous. Even if one were to take seriously the idea that any of these parties had particular wisdom, their credibility is typically destroyed as they try to claim revolutionary moral superiority while simultaneously claiming to be masters of political strategy.

The Communist Party was the last of the Leninist style organizations to achieve significant leadership among left activists; in the years since, such activists have overwhelmingly resisted such formations. In the aftermath of the sixties, however, a significant number of young people who sought to develop long-term activist commitments were attracted to the notion that the Leninist model provided a framework for effective revolutionary action. Influenced by the apparent revolutionary purity of Maoism, there was a flurry of effort to create a "new communist party" in the early seventies—resulting in the formation of several groups competing with each other for the mantle of the "true vanguard," and all resembling the old Communist Party in its most sectarian phase. One outcome of these efforts was that a number of former student radicals went into industrial work. Although a few were effective in becoming rank-and-file leaders of opposition caucuses within some unions, the goal of creating a viable new Leninist-Maoist vanguard party was not achieved. It was still another instance in which left organizations served as socializing agencies for the development of activist commitment, while utterly failing as coherent centers of leadership—and burning-out quite a few young activists in the process.

The Leninist model constitutes the extreme case of organization as an end in itself. Its logic compels members to measure the meaning of their activity in terms of the power and influence of the organization. Instead of finding meaning and deriving satisfaction from having helped foster democratic, grassroots action, the member of a vanguard party is encouraged to push the party line within the larger movement and to criticize established movement leaders who refuse to follow it. Both organizationally and ideologically, the vanguard model assumes that democratic upsurge and popular organization are insufficient and must be controlled and channeled down the "correct" path. The real victory—the real historical gain—in the perception of the good party member, comes when the party and its leadership is recognized by "the working class" as its authentic voice and guide.

Despite its continuing attraction for some, this model has been quite thoroughly rejected by most left activists for at least the last twenty five years. Indeed, even in the heyday of the Communist Party, large numbers of Party activists who were effectively involved in grassroots organizing developed considerable private skepticism about the competence of the Party bureaucracy. The New Left was "new," in large part, because it explicitly rejected this model. Both SDS and SNCC searched, during their brief organizational lives, for alternative organizational approaches that could preserve the crucial functions of national organization while avoiding tendencies toward oligarchical leadership and "organization as an end in itself."

After the demise of both groups, some members concluded that they had failed because the pendulum had swung too far in the other direction. According to this analysis, New Leftists had been so hostile to "leaders," so resistant to committing themselves to organizational maintenance, so "anarchistic" that they were unable to be organized. Actually, however, in the case of SDS, the unwillingness of most activist members to focus on organizational maintenance did not leave a complete vacuum at the center. Instead, national decision making was gradually taken over by those willing to engage in factional dispute and intra-organizational debate—and these tended to be members least involved in the practical world of grassroots organizing.

SDS, toward the end, experienced a profound split between its tens of thousands of rank-and-file members, whose activity was locally based and issue oriented, and a thin layer of national leaders, who were largely isolated from the student movement and were increasingly living in a fantasy world of imminent revolution. In this case, the split between national leadership and activist members did not derive from Leninist ideology and structure, but from a consciousness and structure that fostered "anti-organizational" perspectives in the majority of members, while permitting a more power-oriented and organization-minded minority to control national affairs. The result, in the end, was a Frankenstein monster whose death was mourned by no one.

DILEMMAS OF ORGANIZATION: CONCLUSIONS

THEREFORE, some fundamental dilemmas are inherent in the logic of the left party. These dilemmas are most dramatically evident when the party conceives itself as a "vanguard," but they are present in any effort to create an organization aiming to unite ideological leftists and direct their political efforts.

The first dilemma derives from imperatives of organizational maintenance as such. Left activists seek to stimulate popular movement and organization when they are involved in the milieus of daily life. This goal comes into conflict with the need to sustain and build the national party. Frustrating details of framing the organization's constitution, solidifying its leadership and staff, and formulating its policies and priorities divert time and energy from ongoing political work. "Party-building" involves interminable meetings, writing of position papers and resolutions addressed to fellow members rather than the larger world, mobilization of support for particular intra-organizational goals—activity making sense only in the closed space of the incipient organization. Once the early phases of organizational development are passed, party demands shift to concern for accumulating resources, recruiting membership, enhancing visibility—all of which may be tangential to, or in conflict with, the activist member's ongoing political commitments. Thus, even when party policies are reasonably attuned to larger political realities, and even when members feel able to have a direct voice in influencing the party's directions, the demands it makes can threaten the grassroots work and established commitments of activist members. Nor can the organization refrain from making such demands if it is to survive—the staff must get a salary, the office must be financed, organizational growth must occur.

In addition to the role conflicts that derive from the logic of organizational survival, further dilemmas flow from the logic of what might be called organizational aggrandizement. A political organization is successful when its members feel that they are empowered to make history in and through the organization. But this very feeling, when acted upon, creates the basis for a split between the organization and the wider movements it seeks to influence. Left organizations that come to define their own growth (in numbers, in recognition, in influence) as the measure of historical achievement are inescapably perceived by those with whom they seek to ally as potentially aggrandizing, as "using" issues for self-promotion, as having "ulterior motives" for supporting a given cause or participating in a given coalition. The tensions that already exist in any mass movement between activists and those with "everyday" commitments, between "reformists" and "ideologues," are enormously reinforced when the activists and ideologues are members of an "outside" organization that, in the nature of the case, has its own agenda of interests. This situation is, of course, played upon by those who oppose and seek to suppress the movement, but the existence of such tensions cannot be attributed simply to such external manipulation. Each activist who belongs to a national, ideologically oriented organization is confronted by the question of whether his or her actions are to be shaped first of all by the local imperatives of the movement or by the opportunities presented for organizational gain.

This dilemma is reinforced to the extent that activists define themselves as the political representatives of mass constituencies, thereby accepting the political passivity of the majority as a given rather than as a problem to be faced and overcome. Politicians and activists of the center and the right have no particular problem wearing such an elitist mantle, for it fits comfortably the political perspectives within which they operate. If freedom consists of the right to be left alone and democracy is the right to choose those who will govern you, then those who are politically active within the terms of such political conceptions quite naturally define their politics as the making of claims to leadership and representation. The mak-

ing of such claims inevitably involves the exploitation of issues, the opportunistic use of alliances, the aggrandizement of organization, the quest
for followers, the manipulation of symbol and slogan.

It is exceedingly tempting for ideological leftists to enter this representational mode, seeking to become the embodiment of popular aspiration
and the voice of mass grievance, competing with centrist and rightist organizations for mass support and following. The signs of such temptation
are evident whenever left organizations discuss such questions as What
issues are most likely to get us support? How can we change our rhetoric
so people are not so turned off? What movements or campaigns are most
likely to provide us with opportunities for visibility and approval? What will
we do about "x" when we take power?

When left organizations seek to compete with established elites in the
marketplace of political allegiance, they risk falling into an intellectual delusion and a strategic trap. The delusion is that the victory of "socialism"
can be measured by the numbers of people who believe in it or who support the parties that claim to be its embodiment. "Socialism"—or more
broadly, the full realization of the democratizing vision of the left—is not
achieved when socialists occupy the seat of power or when the "masses"
become socialist converts. The tradition of the left is realized instead only
and whenever the people are making their own history, not when history
is being made in their name or with their consent. Thus, the representational mode, however necessary it may be at a given historical juncture,
cannot be the defining strategy of leftists if they mean to achieve in history
what they say they are about. The role conflicts that activists experience
when they try to orient both to popular movements and to their own national parties are not simply practical dilemmas. They are experienced as
moral conflicts as well.

In the United States, the organized left has never been able to compete
effectively with established elites for positions of leadership and authority.
One of the main points of this book has been that the stability and legitimacy of established authority in the United States has rested on its capacity to "deliver the goods"—that is, to provide the material basis for
viable daily life. As long as this remains largely true, it is hard to imagine
why the majority would take a left organization seriously as an alternative
national leadership.

As a result, leftists are prone to fantasize about the possibility of large-
scale social breakdown that would seriously delegitimate established authority. It is often supposed that in a highly disruptive economic crisis, in
which accustomed everyday security became deeply eroded, the left would
then be in a position to become an authoritative national alternative. But
even if we assume that such a crisis could happen, the notion that the

majority would turn to left political leadership to restore economic order seems dubious, to say the least.

In countries like France or Italy, where the Communist and Socialist Parties are remembered for having provided effective leadership in struggles of national resistance against fascist and traitorous national elites, left parties could justifiably claim that they spoke for the majority of workers, and effectively compete with other elite groups for national leadership. The American left has no such legacy on which to build; moreover, it cannot plausibly claim the ability to mobilize the power, resources, and expertise to restore the social order in a time of crisis. Thus, to construct a national left party in the United States whose aim is to compete as an independent leadership force for "state power" seems an exercise in delusory futility.

What I am trying to suggest is that the effort to create a national left organization is not only "objectively" problematic, but also that *its inherent contradictions have been sensed by the majority of left activists for several generations.* These contradictions today constitute a dimension of the consciousness of left-wing activists, a dimension that is now a fundamental barrier to the creation of such organization in the United States.

The entire history of the organized left was colored by the experience of these contradictions, in one form or another, among left activists. It is this experience that has led them to repeatedly and restlessly abandon or split their organizations, continually experimenting with new proposals for a revitalized "new left." The Socialist Party and the IWW were efforts to replace the sectarian and dogmatic Socialist Labor Party and respond to the demise of populism. The Communist Party was designed to replace the loose, undisciplined, and factionalized old left of the SP and the Wobblies, with a disciplined, "professional," and revolutionarily pure party of a new type. The Popular Front was designed to replace the sectarian, dogmatic, isolated CP with a party capable of playing a leading role in a "center-left coalition" that would reform America—and, for a brief moment in the mid-forties it seemed that such a new left had actually been created. The sixties New Left was designed to sweep away all of the dogmatic, authoritarian, and bureaucratic political styles of the Old Left in favor of models of organization that emphasized decentralization, personal engagement, and ideological openness.

In the 1970s, for the first time, American leftists operated without any significant "party" type of organization at all. The absence of such organization has been interpreted by some observers as meaning that the left has died in America, or that it is unprecedentedly weak. Such an interpretation is quite mistaken, in my opinion. It neglects the rather extensive organized left structure in the United States, the continuing dynamism of left-wing activism in American life, and the influence of the tradition of the

left within the institutionalized intellectual arenas of the society. This is not
to say that the left is wonderfully healthy; it is to say that conventional
measures of its presence—based on *organizational power*—are fundamentally misleading.

HOW IS THE LEFT CURRENTLY ORGANIZED?

A PARTY is any organization (whether it calls itself a party or not) that
articulates a comprehensive program for social change and seeks to advance that program by means of a strategy that members are expected to
implement; a left party typically claims to derive its program from a set of
principles to which its members are committed and from a social analysis
that is fundamentally critical of the social order; principles, analysis, and
program cohere in terms of a shared vision of universal human emancipation.

By this definition, except for some marginal sects, there is no left party
in the United States. But the absence of a party does not mean that left
activists are unorganized.

The most important framework of their organization is local. In most
localities in the United States, one can today find a variety of organizations,
groupings, and institutions that, implicity or explicit, carry forward the
tradition of the left. In some communities there are multi-issue organizations that have some of the functions of a local political party—taking stands
on a broad range of issues, running candidates for local office, sponsoring
cultural and educational activities with a left orientation. More commonly,
there are a variety of organizations that focus on particular issues, sectors,
and constituencies. Within a typical city one finds: one or more groups
concerned with "peace"—opposing the arms race, opposing U.S. intervention in the third world; a tenants' union; one or more environmentalist
organizations focusing on problems of pollution, land use, alternative energy; one or more consumer organizations focusing on such issues as utility
rates; labor unions or other workplace-based organizations concerned with
broad political issues; black and Latino organizations working to increase
minority political representation and to voice community grievances; one
or more feminist organizations concerned with aiding women to cope with
violence and sexism and with increasing women's political power; a gay
rights center providing services to gays and lesbians; an ACLU chapter;
a local Democratic Party club with a "reform" or "left-liberal" orientation;
a community "alternative" newspaper; an FM radio station; organizations
of health workers, teachers, social service workers concerned with sup-

porting the quality of local public services; a variety of cooperatively organized services—food coops, health clinics, housing coops, legal service centers, coffeehouses; a variety of cultural groups with alternative perspectives—theater groups, film clubs, artists' cooperatives, concert promoters. These groupings may have somewhat overlapping memberships. It is likely that they have come to form a loose network that could be, but rarely has been, mobilized for unified action.

In addition to such locally created and supported organizations, there are several supra-local organizations interested in developing locally based "citizen action." The form was pioneered by ACORN—the Association of Community Organizations for Reform Now—which systematically developed membership organizations aimed at voicing the grievances of working-class and middle-class neighborhoods in about twenty states. ACORN-like organizations have developed in a number of other states—Massachusetts Fair Share, the Ohio Public Interest Coalition, similar groups in Illinois and New Jersey. In California, Tom Hayden's Campaign California (formerly called Campaign for Economic Democracy) has established chapters in a number of cities; while across the country, Public Interest Research Groups (PIRGs), begun on college campuses under Ralph Nader's tutelage, have established significant community bases in a number of locales. By the early eighties these state and local citizen action groups had begun to form explicit national networks to share strategy and resources.

In addition to such locally rooted organizations, the American left is embodied in a number of national structures. These include a host of single issue or sectoral groups whose primary political function is to engage in lobbying and public education in their issue domain, and whose support derives from contributions solicited through systematic direct mail campaigns. Such national issue organizations characteristically do not have a grass-roots membership that is reliably ready to respond to the organization's appeals to action or that has any channel for participating in the organization's policymaking. Instead, the national left lobbying and educational groups operate almost exclusively in a representational mode, with a full-time staff and a board deciding on policy and strategy in the name of a generally diffuse constituency. The existence of a sizable "constituency of conscience" on the left—i.e., a relatively affluent stratum of people who support fundamental social reform—enables such organizations to participate as pressure groups in the legislative process on a day-to-day basis. Without such structures, the grassroots environmentalists, feminists, antinuclear and other left-oriented and reform-minded people would have few ways to have their views heard at the national level, and few channels through which they could learn about the details of national decision making that affect their interest.

The centralization of such decision making in the national government, the narrowness of the policy options supported by coventional politicans and the two major parties, the need for professional expertise in order to comprehend and participate in the details of policy formation are some of the structural factors that make such lobbies politically necessary. Some of the lobby organizations of the left are relatively long-established groups—like the AFL-CIO and individual labor unions, the NAACP and other civil rights groups, the ACLU, the Sierra Club, SANE and a few other peace organizations—that have an authentic and active grassroots membership and a capacity to directly mobilize large numbers. In the sixties and seventies, such organizations increased their skill and effectiveness as national lobbies, and in recent years, having recovered somewhat from the bitter divisiveness of the Vietnam War era, have found ways to work in loose coalition.

To these established organizations have been added many newer lobby groups that tend to be more specialized and less connected to a definite membership base. This development has given the social movements more resources for influencing day-to-day policy than there have ever been.

The thrust of this left lobbying apparatus is, of course, not "militant," "radical," or confrontational. By definition, it operates to achieve incremental gains, or to resist rollbacks of gains already won. Furthermore, this organizational structure tends to reproduce the gap between "everyday life" and "history" that the left seeks to close—because it establishes full-time functionaries and experts as the primary participants in the national decision-making process while consigning grass-roots constituents to the relatively passive role of providing reflexive financial support. Moreover, because of the pragmatic issue- and sectoral-orientation of these groups, their work is not guided or integrated in terms of a comprehensive political philosophy or vision and therefore does little to counter prevailing official ideological perspectives.

Accordingly, the structure of the organized left today replicates classic pluralist models of political process. A myriad of interest groups participate in a variety of specific local and national issue arenas. These groups compete with each other for the scarce resources that left constituencies and audiences have to offer—although their competition is nowhere near as conflictful or disruptive as were factionalisms in the American left in earlier eras. If there is a left consensus that encompasses this profusion of activisms it is lurking implicitly somewhere behind them, since none of the organizations I have discussed is willing or able to articulate a comprehensive strategic perspective or explicit social vision.

Still, the situation I have described is not quite as atomized or diffuse as it may seem. There are a few mechanisms of integration of the left.

First, although much of the financing of local and national organization occurs through the dues and contributions of thousands of individuals, most of the national, and a good deal of the local, activity depends to some degree on grants and seed money from some wealthy philanthropists and private foundations. Priorities and criteria established by these funding sources—most of whom have evolved ways of consulting with people with grass-roots connections—shape to some unknown degree the strategies of left activists and organizations.

A second way the left is integrated is through its periodicals and the writings of some left intellectuals. A variety of journals of serious analysis and reflection promote discussion of left strategy, program, and vision. These include weekly magazines of information and comment, especially *The Nation* and *In These Times;* monthly and quarterly journals, especially *Mother Jones, Dissent, Socialist Review, Social Policy, The Progressive.* The combined circulation of these periodicals is small (around 500,000), but they are primary means through which proposals are debated and analysis articulated. In addition, there are a sizable number of left intellectuals whose books, articles, and teaching make continuing contributions to the synthesis of political experience, the analysis of social development, the clarification of ideology and vision, and the formulation of strategic possibilities. A handful of "think tanks"—most notably the Institute for Policy Studies —provide a few arenas for the face-to-face discussion of ideas. Opportunities for strategic and programmatic integration of the left are today certainly meager, but they are not absent.

More than earlier generations, today's left activists and intellectuals have adapted to milieus other than those provided by traditional left cultural enclaves. In these milieus, they have been free to act without the constraints of party line and label, and to give central priority to grass-roots organization and mobilization (rather than proseletyzing and party-building).

As a result, some of the fundamental reasons for the historic isolation of leftists from the American mainstream are disappearing. Left-wing activity is no longer as geographically concentrated as it once was. Left activists are less likely to present themselves as deviants, or to appear as outside agitators. Radical ideas and actions are likely to pop up in places once thought most unlikely—in midwestern small towns and Sunbelt cities, in Catholic churches and in evangelical magazines, in blue-collar industrial neighborhoods and in silicon valleys. These ideas are now expressed in rhetorics and terms that would be quite strange to radicals of earlier generations.

Since there is no national organization around any more that can set doctrinal boundaries for the left, there is today more room for expressing and acting upon the full range of issues and perspectives that actually con-

stitute the radical, democratic, critical tradition. Once can more easily be
a Marxist in the morning, a pacifist in the afternoon, an environmentalist
at dinner, and a feminist in the evening while going to church on Sunday
and voting Democrat on election day.

The diffuseness and heterogeneity of the activist projects I have enum-
erated certainly prompts the question—why call all of this the "left?" If
those involved are not oriented toward a common set of goals, and if there
is not explicit ideological framework that unites them, what justifies the
claim that they all belong under the same political tent?

WHAT IS LEFT?

IT IS TEMPTING to share the view that political labeling referring to
"left" and "right" or to "socialism," "liberalism," "conservatism" is obsolete. All of these traditions have been undermined by their common failure
to adequately comprehend or guide the development of any society, and
by the fact that, in their name, monstrous crimes have been committed.
Further, society faces fundamentally new problems for which none of the
historic ideological perspectives appear relevant. On the other hand, all of
the ideological traditions have contributed some truths to political
understanding—by now, the valid elements of each have assimilated into
contemporary political consciousness. On such a reading, the fragmentation
of what we choose to call the left is not due to the failures of "leftists"
but to the reality that the left itself is obsolete.

There is much to agree with in such sentiments. Indeed, one of the main
themes of this work has been to demonstrate that popular political consciousness cannot be mapped in terms of conventional ideological labels.
In addition, I have stressed the degree to which activists, even when they
identify with the left, have increasingly resisted adherence to strongly defined ideological frameworks—a resistance evident since at least the beginning of the New Left (and probably felt, if not often articulated, by large
numbers of activists during the peak years of the old left as well).

I have insisted on talking about the "tradition of the left," rather than
making use of more specific ideological terms like socialism, Marxism, pacifism, anarchism, to emphasize that beneath the differences in belief defined by these words, more fundamental values, sentiments, and principles
have been shared by American leftists across parties and generations—
whether or not they recognized it. These shared values, I have argued,
have been more animating than particular doctrines and party lines in guiding the practice and justifying the commitments of activists. The deep

structure of left thought and action has never been adequately defined by terms such as "socialism"; explicit ideology has always had only limited "relevance" as either a usable map for, or an explanation of, American radicalism.

Implicit in my central argument, however, is that there is a fundamental political division that, in both the past and the present, has determined political discourse, conflict, and consciousness in this society. This division has to do with the question of how individual life and history ought to be interrelated. The prevailing American perspective has emphasized that the good society is one in which individual lives are insulated from history, in which persons are as free as possible from external constraints and obligations so that they can make their own lives—that freedom is equivalent to liberty.

Contrasting with this view has been another—that the good society is one in which the people make their own history, that they share in the responsibilities and benefits of social development—that freedom is equivalent to democracy. The "tradition of the left," I have said, is constituted by those currents of thought and action that have tried to advance democracy—criticizing social conditions and practices that blocked non-elites from participating in historically determinative decisions, stimulating and justifying popular efforts to intervene in history.

To refer to the "tradition of the Left," then, recognizes a distinctive oppositional political and cultural current in American history constituted by diverse and contradictory ideological perspectives, and that beneath the surface of these clashing perspectives there has nevertheless been an underlying unity. However obsolete any particular ideological perspective on the left may be, the underlying, animating principle remains valid and distinctive. In short, as long as history is experienced as being made in a realm remote from daily life, as long as there are elites positioned to define the conditions of life for the great majority, terms like "left" and "right" remain meaningful. They cannot be obsolete until those without power cease aspiring to gain some control over history, and those in power cease seeking to hold on to their control.

It is useful, from this perspective, to think of the left as having two components. First, there are the social movements—the collective efforts by powerless groups to intervene in history. Such movements are oriented toward historical action with the goal of restoring or achieving the ability to live life "normally": they seek either to resist threats to accustomed patterns and meanings of everyday life or to liberate members from conditions and practices that prevent them from having rights they claim to be entitled to. The consciousness expressed in social movements is therefore grounded in particular experiences of encroachment and oppression and aspires to win the kinds of freedom the established culture has already promised. Social movements have not asserted new definitions of the relation between history and everyday life. They have sought to expand the scope of established definitions so that previously excluded groups were included, or to win formal guarantees that rights promised will actually be recognized and practiced.

Thus, social movements are regarded as "reformist," since they appear to seek nothing more than that the "system" actually work so that its promises will be fulfilled. Social movements do not attempt to overthrow established national elites, but to forge new relationships between these elites and those who are trying to live their own lives. They typically do not try to articulate an embracing, universal vision of a new social order, but instead express aspirations for a more secure or liberated life for the groups that constitute the movement.

Despite this expressed reformism and particularism, however, the major movements of American history have each compelled fundamental restructuring. Their main achievements have been to expand the meaning of democracy in both theory and practice:

The labor movement did not simply win better living and working conditions for workers—it expanded the power of workers within enterprises and within the larger political system, thereby fundamentally changing the structure of "industrial relations," the character of the political parties, and the ideological justifications of capitalism.

The women's movement did not just win votes for women or improve women's access to economic opportunity—it has fundamentally affected power relations between the sexes and the ideological frameworks that govern those relations.

The black movement did not just win the extension of the U.S. Constitution to the Southern states, but fundamentally challenged the ways in which power was organized in cities, the ways in which public welfare was distributed and administered, the ways in which the cultural apparatus dealt with minority cultures.

All of these movements have had meaning, not only as expressions of particular grievance and disadvantage but also as forces that have propelled processes of general social democratization; all of them have continued or been periodically revitalized, because their fundamental "business" remained unfinished. Even when they had won the reforms around which they had mobilized, they had not yet won the degree of democratic control that had been implicit in the demands they had raised.

Thus, if the "tradition of the left" in the United States means the tradition of efforts to democratize the society and its institutions, then that tradition has been carried, to a very considerable extent, by popular movements that have sought to empower those who were powerless, even if those who were making that effort did not adopt the language and symbols promulgated by socialists and other ideological leftists.

The second component of the left tradition is constituted by organizations, activists, and intellectuals who explicitly adhere to ideological perspectives alternative to those of the dominant culture. It is they who are conscious of being carriers of a vision of universal emancipation, who view each movement of popular protest not as an end in itself but as a kind of pre-conscious stirring that could eventuate in a generalized conversion to such a vision.

The ideologically conscious left is composed of people who seek a historical role not so as to return to ordinary life but as an end in itself. What differentiates conscious leftists from other political specialists, ideologues, and elites is that leftists claim to be working for the dispersion of power to the people themselves, rather than the reproduction of existing power relations. Although conscious leftists disagree among themselves about the degree to which particular democratic reforms ought to be worked for or supported, their specific role has been to try to foster levels of popular consciousness that go beyond particularism, pragmatism, and reformism. The committed leftist is at odds with what we have called "commitment to everyday life" and with the notion that individual liberty is the equivalent of freedom. Leftists want people to become fully responsible not only for their own individual lives but for the development of the society as a whole. They want people to view history not simply as an alien territory that threatens life but as a realm of opportunity for shared self-realization.

The ideological left therefore has difficulty accepting the popular left of social movements as the embodiment of its hopes, even though consciously left-wing activists have played major roles in stimulating the development of such movements. As long as such movements remain sectoral in their composition and particularistic in their demands, and as long as they ebb and flow in relation to particular gains and losses for the groups who constitute them, they appear to be limited vehicles for full-scale democratization—and their specific achievements are often said to divert members from the "larger," more "revolutionary" possibilities. That is why, historically, the organized left has sought to do more than organize protest, why it has tried to proseletyze for socialism, build its own independent base, formulate strategic lines for movement activists—and why it has hoped for the creation of an independent "mass" party to unite the working class and coalesce the movements and communities of the disadvantaged.

Yet what the organized left has been able to do is to nourish capacities for collective action and organization at the grass roots—by encouraging adherents to develop themselves as activists and by fostering in the wider

population awareness of shared threat, collective possibilities, and responsibilities. The authentic mission of the American left has always been
"socialization"—not of the economy, but of the people it has been able to
touch.

In sociology and psychology, the word "socialization" is often used to
refer to those processes that shape individuals so that they can play the
roles instituted for them by society; such usage implies that socialization
is primarily a process of learning to conform to established norms and roles.
But sometimes the term has been used to refer to processes by which
individuals develop capacities to transcend role conformity, to develop capacities for critical judgment and action with respect to the established
culture, to become centers of initiative and innovation, capable of recognizing the gap between particular cultures and universal human needs and
potentialities, capable of responding to the split between cultural ideal and
societal reality. It is this second meaning of "socialization" that I use when
I talk about the left as a "socializing agency."

One of the primary contradictions in American culture is that it stresses
so strongly that the good life is made by individuals, each pursuing his or
her own needs within the framework of his or her immediate social ties
and role obligations—while claiming to be a "democracy"—i.e., a society
in which all members have the right to participate in the collective processes of self-government. Moveover, even if there were not this fundamental value contradiction between self-centered "liberty" and democratic civic responsibility, there are other compelling grounds provided by
our common experience for challenging American individualism. Threats to
human survival posed by environmental degradation, by gross disparities
in life chances both internationally and within the society, and by national
rivalry require of Americans more awareness of their interdependence, more
concern for the social consequences of their individual activities, more social responsibility than that which is encouraged by the established culture
and the dominant institutions of socialization. Finally, it is plausible that
human beings are not fully developed (and therefore unable to be "happy"?)
if their social concerns are restricted to the maintenance of their own particular sphere of direct interaction, if they are blocked off from considering
their own activity in light of what they owe to their ancestors and to future
generations, if they are aware that others are suffering needlessly while
(and perhaps because) they complacently enjoy relative comfort.

These cultural contradictions provide the warrant and the social space
for the repeated revitalization of left political and intellectual currents. It
is the left, in its manifold guises, that seeks to resolve these contradictions
by promoting democratic collective action, by offering models of social
commitment, by heightening awareness of social irrationality and proposing

ways to counter it, by articulating a social ethic and a democratic and egalitarian political philosophy—in short, by continuously utilizing whatever
channels are available to remind people of their shared fate and responsibility and, when social creativity is on the loose, by showing people new
possibilities for making a historical difference.

The left as an organized force has thought it was a party, a vehicle on
the road to power. What it has more nearly been, however, is a network
of schools, of churches, of theaters, and arenas. Other metaphors also
apply: a training ground, a launching pad, a crucible, a potting shed.

PROBLEMS OF THE CONTEMPORARY LEFT

National Invisibility

Today, the tradition of the left is being carried in a thousand fragments
through the activity of numbers of locally rooted activists and relatively
specialized intellectuals, cultural workers, and professionals. We can see
that the democratic flame still burns. Despite the mass mediated image of
a society in the throes of political apathy, the local reality throughout the
seventies and eighties, is better understood as a continuously oscillating
rise and fall of grass-roots participation, focused usually on particualr issues, often directed at defending gains, but sometimes at advancing claims.
Despite the alleged "trend to the right," the political culture has perhaps
never been more inclusive of diverse perspectives patterned in a fragile
balance of uneasy tolerance. Today's left-wing activist and intellectual is,
therefore, likely to have found a niche that provides some sense of individual, local effectiveness.

Despite this sense of personal efficacy and coherence, however, the typical leftist cannot help but feel deeply inadequate. For the discovery by
activists of ways to be locally relevant has not meant that they have found
ways to affect the overall historical drift. If history were merely the sum
total of local activities, then the present localism of activists would represent a resolution of the gap between history making and everyday life.
But the fundamental social problem of our time is precisely that history is
dominated by decisions at the center of the nation state and at the pin-
nacles of the corporate economy.

These centers of elite control do not exercise absolute power; some
capacity for shaping the conditions of life remains at more local levels. But
the overall direction of society and the boundaries within which local initiatives can be effective are the result in large part of decisions made by

national and corporate elites. The arms race, the military buildup, interventions in the third world, intensifying international tensions—the continuing orientation of the society toward war—persist in the face of a proliferating variety of local resistances.

Local opposition to environmental degradation has frequently been effective in vetoing a large number of specific projects—but the overall orientation of the society toward evironmentally destructive "hard" rather than "soft" paths continues.

Local organization of economically disadvantaged groups and community development make little headway in the face of national economic stagnation and deindustrialization, the private concentration of economic power, and steady increase in global inequality.

The establishment of local cultural and political pluralism helps make daily life somewhat freer, but does not stop the overall social drift toward increasing concentration and centralization of political, economic, and communication control.

Insofar as history can be made by elites, insofar as decisions can be made—such as those having to do with war and peace or economic priorities—that have vast impact on the way daily life can be lived (and whether it can be lived at all), no one who is politically oriented can remain satisfied with merely local influence. In this situation, there is a felt need for a left political thrust and strategy, for an effort to counter the power elite at the "national level." Such a thrust is now virtually absent. Although strategic proposals are often presented in national left periodicals, there are few forums within which such ideas can be fully debated, and few organizational vehicles through which they can be implemented. As a result, activists interested in national strategies are drawn, in rather atomistic fashion, toward projects that interest them. Such projects compete for support on the basis of publicity, rather than in the context of rational deliberation of alternatives and priorities.

Sometimes, a national consensus among left activists can be achieved in these ad hoc ways. A recent example is the nuclear freeze—as both a policy proposal and a framework for directing activist energies. The freeze provided a focus for a wide range of locally based activity that has had national impact—and achieved the revival of popular awareness and broad political involvement with respect to the arms race and the threat of nuclear war. But even this important strategic thrust has been considerably blunted by the inability of its leadership to define a long-term strategy for actually changing national policy.

Meanwhile, no similar focus or consensus has been achieved in most other issue domains. Particularly striking has been the absence of a concerted left initiative with respect to economic stagnation and unemployment, despite the obvious need for such an alternative, the circulation of a number of left-oriented ideas about economic policy, and the readiness of sizable numbers of workers to mobilize.

Along with the difficulty that the decentralized and fragmented left has in establishing strategic directions and priorities for activists is its invisibility in the mainstream arenas of national debate over particular issues and with respect to broad political philosophy. The absence of a national left organization or leadership means that the media are free to ignore the possibility that, with respect to any public controversy, there are positions other than those staked out by the official leaderships of the Republican and Democratic parties. Anyone who experienced the political culture of the fifties is likely to feel that controversy and challenge are now more often present in the media than then, even over such previously sacred issues as the defense budget, Presidential commitment of American troops abroad, and the nature of the "communist threat." Journalists' skepticism in the face of official postures is helpful; the "Establishment" is itself divided over key policy issues; "bipartisanship" is no longer the only rule in foreign policy. But it is also clear that whatever debate does take place is highly circumscribed by a framework of shared assumptions, and that left-of-center Democrats are more often heard when they cave in to conservative policies than when they articulate resistance. Even if there were highly visible spokespersons of the left available to be presented, they probably would not be—but their total absence means that the boundaries of acceptable debate are not tested or breached.

Beyond debate over particular issues and crises there is the absence of fundamental discourse with respect to public philosophy. For the generation after the New Deal, the philosophical foundations of mainstream political rhetoric was derived from that peculiarly American brand of "liberalism" that had more affinity with European social democracy than with classical liberal doctrine. This perspective legitimated claims to political and social equality, and propounded the view that the state ought to be responsible for managing the economy and implementing social policies to offset the instabilities and social costs of the private enterprise economy. Of course, this perspective was honored far more in rhetoric and symbol than in practical policy—but it provided an ideological framework for activism that few on the left, including convinced socialists, felt the need to fundamentally challenge.

The issue for the left after the New Deal was to struggle to fulfill liberalism's stated promises—for full employment, for an end to racial discrimination, for an end to poverty, for a redistribution of wealth toward public goods and social equality. To be a socialist in the heyday of the welfare state was to question whether its promises could be fulfilled within the framework of capitalist political economy—but to be unable to prove that they could not.

As a result, the New Left never announced that it was "socialist"— emphasizing instead the contradictions between domestic welfare and international imperialism and the threat to democracy and individual freedom posed by the growth of massive corporate and state bureaucracies. Indeed, the New Left had begun to articulate a public philosophy that reached beyond both socialism and liberal statism, emphasizing principles of community control, local self-organization, and participatory democracy.

The New Left, to the extent that it articulated a coherent social vision (and it did this more than it has generally been given credit for), did not so much address matters of public policy as attempt to formulate a set of standards that could be internalized by citizens at the grass roots, within which demands could be expressed, claims put forward, and action guided. The forms of action that typified the New Left—draft resistance, student power, community organization—were ways of communicating principles of decentralization and participation through action; the principles were embodied in their very form. Moreover, for a brief period, there was considerable mass media interest in these ideas, and no dearth of publicists ready at hand to articulate them in varying degrees of deformation. No formal mechanisms for presenting left alternatives seemed urgently needed; in the sixties, publicity, slogans, actions, symbols, and popular literature spawned by the New Left and the counterculture seemed quite adequate for catalyzing shifts in popular consciousness.

The trouble was that New Left principles were to a considerable extent derived from what was often called "post-scarcity consciousness." They were most salient for those who were freed from preoccupation with fundamental issues of economic survival and security, and most applicable to a society in which minimally adequate standards of living were promised by the official social charter. New Leftists assumed that the basic principles of the welfare state were accepted by national elites and fully internalized in popular consciousness, and that economic growth was a more or less automatic feature of modern capitalism. Let the "corporate liberals" take care of economic stability and protect the welfare state, they declared— these were no longer progressive and anyway were primarily instruments of control rather than authentic foundations of emancipation.

Such views presented a political problem that New Leftists only gradually took cognizance of. They prevented those influenced by the New Left from finding common ground with traditional working-class constituencies —i.e., with those who had less reason to believe that economic scarcity and insecurity were no longer problems. In the long run, this itself might not have mattered, since many young workers were coming to share countercultural perspectives and were receptive to anti-authoritarian impulses. But by the early seventies it was becoming clear that "post-scarcity society" was not arriving, that economic growth had ceased, and that problems of scarcity, state fiscal crisis, and unemployment were emerging.

The return of economic trouble and class oppression as political reality provided avenues for left organizing largely unavailable in the sixties. This situation, coupled with the rapidly eroding legitimacy of "liberalism" as a public philosophy, compelled most on the left to rethink the nature of their public stance. A new conservatism was on the rise, aiming at the destruction of the post-New Deal ideological consensus and the dismantling of much of the state's role as a protector of living standards and the guarantor of collective goods. In the last decade left activists have had to mobilize defense of such living standards and goods, rather than continuing to emphasize New Left perspectives on authority, bureaucracy, and self-realization.

The movements sparked by the economic conditions of the last ten years typically appear to be protests by particular interest groups pressing for a piece of the pie, rather than expressions of a general movement embodying a broad vision of the common good. Thus tenants fight for their rights, women for theirs; public employees organize for themselves, and so do embattled farmers and unemployed steelworkers; here we have a community upset about a toxic waste dump, there a neighborhood protesting gentrification, and somewhere else a group resisting a nuclear power plant. Students protest impositon of tuition, mothers protest the closing of a daycare center, blacks fight to preserve an affirmative action program. If there is anything all these forms of mobilization have in common, one would not be able to discern it from their rhetoric, nor would it be clear what the moral grounds are for the claims and demands being made.

No general public philosophy now legitimates the feelings of injustice and claims to entitlement that such protests express. For the first time since the pre-New Deal era *attacks* on these entitlements are couched in terms of a coherent public philosophy—the neo-laissez-faire doctrines of the Reaganites and other "conservatives," "neo-conservatives," "libertarians," and "new rightists." Thus, ironically, the left, previously the most explicitly ideological current in the American political culture, now operates in pragmatic, piecemeal fashion according to the rules of pluralist interest group politics, while the right presents itself as the moral, visionary force. Meanwhile, the politicians and intellectuals of the "center"—having shaped the ideological consensus of the post war years—now lack ability to articulate any coherent perspective in behalf of either social reform or retrenchment.

There is, accordingly, a decided vacuum in the political culture, and, conceiveably, a widespread hunger for intelligible alternatives to the view that market competition and property rights define the good society. There is an opportunity—not available since the thirties—for the tradition of the left to be carried forward in terms of a public philosophy that the majority might find plausible. But the left as presently organized is in a weak position to fill this vacuum.

Problems of the Contemporary Left: The Loss of Continuity

We have seen that the particular contribution of left organizations was their capacity to embody and transmit the tradition itself, thereby enabling new generations to find ready frameworks and models for identification. The existence of coherent organizations served as constant reference points, even for those leftists who refused to join them. The Old Left parties, upholding the banners of commitment in the face of repression and public scorn, were something like a superego for those who professed left-wing identification. The absence of such organizations today threatens the erosion of left identity.

Can the continuity of the left tradition be sustained without a national party or similar institution? How can members of the new generation come to know and identify with that tradition? Some may, by being raised in left families—a mode of transmission of left identity that has always been of fundamental importance. Some may find it by participating in particular movements; it seems characteristic that, for example, participation in antinuclear and peace movement activities fosters more general concern about the nature of society and the need for fundamental social change. Movement participation can lead members to awareness of potentialities for long-term activism and can bring them into contact with older people who can serve as models. Left-oriented cluture—literature, film, theater, music— provide further materials for identity formation. Local and single issue organizing provides avenues for vocation and long-term commitment that continue to attract significant numbers of youth.

An entire generation of young people has come of political age since the demise of the organized New Left. These young people appear markedly less political than the generation that preceded them. Still, on most college campuses and in most communities, one is likely to find contingents in their teens and twenties who are taking on activist commitments. Left continuity is being carried forward in these grouplets. Yet one has to feel that the entirely "voluntary" character of the present-day left—the absence of any effort to systematically bind people to commitment—means that this minority of left-oriented youth may have only fragile ties to the tradition.

The party type of organization provided a generalized framework for expressing and reinforcing activist commitment. Those who were locally active could believe that their activity gained historical meaning because it was systematically linked to the work of many others in diverse locales. Moreover, party membership permitted commitment to be readily transferrable from one locale to another; the student activist, after leaving the campus, could find, through the national organization, new avenues for activist participation ready at hand.

The absence of such ready-made roles for "adult" activists in the early seventies was one of the primary difficulties many sixties student activists faced when they tried to find ways to express their youthful radicalism in their post-student lives. The lack of a coherent national structure for the left continues to present the same sort of problem for young people disposed to activist identity.

If there were a left party today, it would be actively seeking the establishment of youth and student chapters aross the country. It would be sending out organizers and speakers to spread the party gospel, disseminating literature designed to win recruits, striving to create a public image of left commitment. Young people already disposed to such commitment would find their identities validated and reinforced, their arguments amplified, their activity given a kind of "professional" support, and their connections to like-minded youth across the country more readily established. The existence of such an organization would help many such youth see how one can enter adulthood and its routines and obligations while, through party membership, retaining activist commitment.

In the absence of national organization, the left, decentralized and fragmented, lacks objective definition. For one to become an identified leftist is, therefore, very much a matter of self-construction. The left one identifies with tends to be the left one happens to see—and there is a good chance that one will not see the left at all, or see only a portion of its potentialities.

Left organizations not only socialized young people for activist commitment, they also served as a superego for those members and sympathizers who were established in "adult" rounds of life. The classic situation is that of the left-wing professional or intellectual embarked on a conventional career path or working in a mainstream institutional setting. In the inevitable conflict between careerism and principle, the party organization had some capacity to hold members and sympathizers accountable, to promulgate and enforce a social ethic, or to demand of its affluent and successful supporters conscience money or other signs of continuing fealty to ideals.

The problem of reconciling professional career and left commitment has never been more central than it is today. It is the "intelligentsia" that today are the primary conscious carriers of left ideological traditions. Yet, much

more than in the past today's conscious leftist is likely to have some possibilities for advancement in an established career due to the strategic economic and social position of educated workers and to the political gains of
the left within the university and the knowledge industry that have made
it more possible than it used to be for left-wingers to get ahead.

"Getting ahead" obviously entails enhanced ability to live in personal
comfort (insulated from everyday threats that revitalize radical commitment) and to exercise authority over others. In addition to these obvious
and classical conditions for deradicalization and "selling out," there are also
more subtle incentives for political disengagement built into professional
life. Professions reward "objectivity" and "detachment," the capacity to
separate one's personal values and emotions from the fulfillment of the
role. Professional detachment, intellectual skepticism, a tendency to be
cynical about claims to selflessness, and ability to distance oneself from
emotionally involving commitment, a readiness to accept truths even when
they undermine one's own cherished beliefs—these are all qualities necessary for membership in intellectual circles.

Intellectual and professional work is highly demanding of time and energy
and in our society is organized so that *individual* creativity and achievement are regarded as the only valid definition of excellence. Few career
involved professionals and intellectuals can avoid the feeling that their work
is profoundly important, that their personal needs and claims are vital, that
they have the right to fully determine the uses of their time and to seek
service and deference from others in order to fulfill their goals. In short,
the life world of the aspiring professional promotes egocentrism to a very
high degree; political disengagement, disillusionment, and cynicism are, accordingly, definite occupational hazards.

Sometimes such disaffiliation is loudly and dramatically rationalized by
the disengagee; such rationalization is encouraged by the professional obligation of intellectuals to articulate justifications for their actions. Consequently, each generation of ex-leftists has produced its literature of re-
nunciation and disillusionment. For most, the abandonment of past idealism
is rarely so complete, public, or conscious; instead, one observes among
career-oriented former radicals signs of increasing self-centeredness, a
growing privatization of life-style and of work, a bittersweet and amused
acceptance of one's material well-being.

Today, more than ever, the tradition of the left as a body of belief and
a framework of conscious identification is alive only to the extent that individuals voluntarily construct it or internalize it. There is no longer a left
church having powers of absolution and ex-communication, or a left army
trying to make culture a weapon. This situation is an advance over the
past, for it permits adherents much wider latitude to live creatively in terms

of the tradition and to be self-determining and self-disciplining. But one price of this freedom and diversity is a seemingly inevitable fragility of commitment and responsibility. Another is the decline of the left as a coherent community of solidarity that can serve as a moral alternative to the individualism and careerism of mainstream society.

Today's left activist, lacking a party, feels invisible and unrepresented. He or she finds it hard to see the strategic relevance of local work and is uncertain about the reliability of existing political networks as frameworks of support and coordinated action. The activist, thrown back on his or her own self-constructed political identity, often feels the need for some overarching moral authority, some systematic mechanism for transmitting and externalizing the tradition. Finally, he or she is likely to regret the absence of frameworks for discussion in which strategies could be collectively analyzed, vision articulated, programmatic priorities examined, and personal roles scrutinized.

Left activists thus are profoundly ambivalent about problems of organization and leadership. They reject top down leadership and refuse to participate in constructing a new party—yet, at the same time, recognize that they confront deep problems of impotence in the face of elite dominated history. Many of their recent accomplishments have resulted in the opening up of space for grassroots activism and for left-oriented cultural work—but this space often seems more like a reservation or a museum than an open field.

The burden of this book, however, is that these dilemmas cannot be resolved by a new attempt to start a national party or by reawakened effort by leftists to compete for national political power or control over American consciousness. If the goal of the left is to achieve a society in which the people themselves make their own history—in which the opportunity to participate in history making is an integral feature of everyday life for all of society's members—then this goal cannot be attained by attempting to assert leadership over people, or to compete for their allegiance, or to convert them to an alternative belief system. Elitist practice—even if grounded in democratic consent—logically and morally undermines the left vision. And even if these moral objections were put aside, such practice would not be practical.

Left activists and intellectuals who are true to their identity and their tradition do not want to lead others, or convert them. Instead their goal is to empower and enlighten. The post-sixties left is in a better position than its predecessors to do such work. Having abandoned in practice the pretensions to power that so frequently trapped earlier lefts, today's leftists are freer to act creatively and are more in touch with the everyday worlds of their fellow Americans than were earlier generations of American radicals. In what follows I want to suggest how the apparent powerlessness of the American left can become a resource for affecting American culture and consciousness and suggest some ways that left activists might organize that could enhance their historical effectiveness without falling, once again, into the snares and delusions that have plagued the organized left in the past.

6

Making History Democratic
Revitalizing The Tradition Of The Left

I pondered all these things . . . how men fight and lose the bat-
tle, and the thing they fought for comes about in spite of their
defeat, and when it comes turns out not be what they meant, and
other men have to fight for what they meant under another name.

—William Morris

HOW CAN the making of history be democratized when Americans are
committed to the making and living of their private lives? From the perspective of the left that commitment represents a profound resistance to
political engagement and social responsibility. There are two principal ways
that leftists have sought to deal with that resistance. On the one hand,
they have tended to stand outside the mainstream as prophets and critics,
bemoaning the emptiness of daily life, attacking the "false consciousness,"
the selfishness, the conformism, the bigotry of Americans, calling on them
to wake up and to change their lives. Alternating with this prophetic, moralistic stance, leftists have often adopted an opposing strategy deemed more
practical. Pragmatic orgnizers suggest working with people "where they
are," finding the issues that actually bother them, organizing them around
immediate "bread-and-butter" problems, rather than addressing them in
moral terms. Neither of these stances is particularly satisfactory. The
prophetic posture tends to be self-isolating and elitist; the pragmatic approach often appears opportunistic (gives the appearance that the organizers are "using" issues to recruit people for ulterior purposes) or else
exceedingly reformist (the demands made are so limited and particular that
no development of consciousness or political commitment results from the
campaign).

Furthermore, both stances reinforce the experienced gap between everyday life and history. Both perspectives take it for granted that what people are actually doing in their lives lacks political relevance, and define the left as that force that will get people to stop their ongoing lives in favor of a larger cause. The moralistic perspective says that the way to do this is to attack these lives and disturb popular complacency; the pragmatic approach is directed at more gently seducing people into organized activity by appealing to their immediate interests.

Both prophecy and bread-and-butter organization are needed, and there are circumstances under which each may win a considerable popular response. Radical moralism can certainly appeal to those who feel oppressed or guilty or stifled in their daily lives; unions, neighborhood action groups, and other community institutions do grow out of the everyday grievances of their constituencies.

These perspectives however neglect the ways that people can participate in history in and through their daily lives, rather than simply outside of them. A primary trouble for the left tradition has been the failure of its intellectuals and activists to see the potentials for social change and cultural innovation that are present in the lives of people who may otherwise appear to be "apolitical." The discovery and development of such potentials is one key to the revitalization of the left tradition.

EVERYDAY LIFE AS A TERRAIN
FOR HISTORY MAKING

NEW LEFTISTS and feminists often say that the "personal is political." That slogan seems to be in the spirit of what I want to advocate, but not completely. For what has usually been meant by this phrase is a criticism of the ways in which personal life robs people of political will and reinforces the structures of domination in the society at large. From this point of view the family is a political arena because it is patriarchal, authoritarian, a framework of social control that instills conformity in children and obedience in women. The "radical" conclusion to an argument of this sort seems to be that, if we discover that the "personal is political"—i.e., that we are oppressed in our intimate relations as well as by impersonal institutions— then we will overthrow the personal in order to be more fully political.

Despite the experience that all of us share, of everyday impotence in the face of "world events," it may be possible for people to see that their own lives can be a source of historical initiative. When the left defines history making as the antithesis of everyday life, emphasizing only the powerlessness, conservatism, and egocentricity of private individuals, it contributes to, rather than contradicts, the prevailing ideological climate.

How, in existing society, can ordinary people contribute to social change in and through their daily lives? I think the history we have reviewed in this book provides some clues, as does a close examination of everyday behavior:

■ "Wherever worlds are laid on, underlives develop," remarked the late Erving Goffman. He was talking about the ways in which inmates in mental hospitals, prisons, and other total institutions organize social relationships and make use of physical space to evade rules, avoid surveillance, resist arbitrary impositions, and retain a sense of personal identity. The same principle applies in all hierarchical setups—especially workplaces—in which persons are compelled to spend major parts of their day under rules and authoritative controls not of their own making.

These informal, "spontaneous" daily struggles for liberties that are not authorized enable people to adjust to their subordination. But is such adjustment all there is to such informal, often unnoticed, often taken for granted self-organization? Or is it not the case, as Jeremy Brecher in his study of the history of mass strikes has suggested, that such organization establishes networks of identification and communication from which more conscious, directed collective action may eventually arise? Is it also likely that such self-organization is not merely defensive and adjustive, but also a way that many bureaucratic institutional setups are made more practically responsive in their day-to-day operations than they appear to be from their formal, explicit structures?

In short, even the most powerless people in the society exercise some control over the conditions of their lives by informal organization and everyday resistance to authority. Leftists, correctly, want people to "go beyond" such "primitive" organization and gain formal, legitimate power to control their work. But might there not be a potential for socialization at the level of informal resistance? Can people be encouraged to take more advantage than they do of available space for self-assertion in the workplace and other bureaucratic settings? Can such self-assertion be enhanced by teaching and publicly advocating it?

Perhaps left activists could take a leaf from mainstream cultural entrepreneurs. What would be the effect of trying to disseminate, alongside all the books and videotapes and courses on self-improvement, coping, and fitness, material that instructed Americans in the arts of everyday resistance? What if such "training" were coupled with insistent public advocacy of the rights of people to have a say in workplace, school, and neighborhood? Can the currents of anti-authoritarianism that already flow through

American daily life find democratic channels? Quite possibly—but not without spadework by conscious activists.

■ The women's liberation movement provides us with the clearest framework by which everyday activity can be seen as history making. For the achievement of sexual equality requires that women assert their claims directly, in their relations with individual men, in the organization of family life and household, in the rearing of children, in the workplace, and in every other arena of daily life. Such assertion entails the conscious rejection of many conventional role expectations, through repeated episodes of conflict and renegotiation. In the process, the most intimate, private occurrences now carry historical implications.

When lovers quarrel and spouses fight, they are today deciding not only the fate of their particular relationship, but also the question of how women and men are to relate to each other in society at large. Every woman's assertion of a degree of autonomy, or of a recognition of her needs, or of a restructuring of the division of labor and the decision-making process in the household today represents not only a change in her personal condition but also in the social position and role definitions of all women. Every man's recognition of the legitimacy of such claims, every change individual men make in the exercise of their traditional dominance, similarly contributes to the social reconstitution of sexual power relations.

Because of the degree to which sexual inequality is carried through informal norms, reproduced in face-to-face interaction, and embedded in individual character, self-assertion by individual women can have historical impact. Feminism provides an ideological framework that enables women to interpret their personal discontents as social issues, and to declare, to themselves and to their intimate others, that change is morally right as well as personally necessary. The movement projects models of everyday equality and liberation that serve as guides and standards for individual action. The movement provides, in both its face-to-face small groups and through the mass media, publicity about the fact that personal change is taking place. Thus even when women are doing the most mundane things, many are today likely to know that they are contributing to history.

■ It is not unusual for Americans to say that the most important way they contribute to the improvement of society is in the rearing of their children. The reproduction and socialization process is not necessarily merely a way of ensuring that the status quo is perpetuated, or that fodder and cogs are produced for the cannons and wheels of history. One of the primary routes to radicalism in America is through the conscious efforts of socially concerned or left-wing parents to pass on the tradition of the left. But the belief that the society can be made better by bringing up children better is held by many more people than simply those who are consciously on the left. It animates the writings of Dr. Spock and the progressive educators and the child psychologists—indeed most of those who, in the twentieth century, have thought that childrearing could be made more scientific so that people would be healthier and more humane.

Today's conscious parents are likely to want their children not only to have the personal attributes deemed requisite for competitive success and emotional well-being, but also (or even instead) to be socially concerned, democratic, capable of standing up to authority, nonsexist, anti-macho, anti-racist. Such parents believe that to raise children in such ways is to contribute to social change—even when they, in other contexts, adhere to a social analysis that says history is made through political action rather than personal development.

The evidence is that such beliefs have validity. Childrearing matters politically. There is no other way to explain the emergence of a New Left in the early Sixties than to recognize that a proportion of those then coming of age had been raised to need and to be able to create such a politics. Similarly, feminism must be transmitted as an integral, internalizable dimension of the childrearing process if it is to have durable social impact. In general, capacities to question authority, to resist demagogic appeals, to refuse military mobilization, and to feel the obligations of citizenship depend for their development on the early experience of individuals.

■ Social movements are constituted not only by an activist core, but by a much larger penumbra of supporters who may never step out of their daily lives to engage in visible action, but whose everyday allegiance is a vital resource. These are the people who send money, put on buttons and bumper stickers, support a boycott, refuse to cross a picket line, sign a petition, and cast their vote. But beyond such obvious support activity lies a range of behaviors that actually constitutes aspects of the historical transformation being sought by the movements.

The women's movement—and the black movement—called on people to change the ways they interacted with each other. They encouraged changes in language and modes of address, in appearance and modes of dress—changes that both symbolized demands for equality and at the same time reinforced and reproduced these demands in daily life. Thus to adopt "nonsexist language" was to recognize the legitimacy of women's liberation and to aid the process of its reproduction. Similarly, the environmental movement advocates and instructs changes in personal lifestyle that both symbolically and concretely implement the need for conservation of scarce and fragile resources. To recycle paper, to become a wary consumer with respect to chemically adulterated goods, to take concrete steps to conserve energy, to reduce dependence on the private car—all of these are activities that not only express commitment to environmentalism but also actually constitute social change.

All of these examples indicate ways in which persons can take conscious action in their everyday roles and relationships that have historical meaning. These examples illustrate that defiance, renegotiation, and initiative are integral features of daily life—and that such nonconformity can have real historical effect.

Left activists and intellectuals, influenced by Marxism, know that such personal action is not enough to change history. The actions of individuals, even when paralleled by those of many others, do not necessarily affect the core structures of domination and exploitation. These structures, by definition, set limits on the freedom of individuals to live according to their values; they are moreover organized to be as immune as possible from the moral inclinations of individual actors. Structural change, the left knows, requires mass action, strategic mobilization, politics, and public conflict.

The left "knows" these truths too well, and therefore neglects the fact that changes in what people believe, say, care about—and what they refuse to believe and do—are part of what constitutes the processes of historical transformation. Such changes may be achievable even when possibilities for large-scale structural change are blocked. Indeed, such possibilities may become less blocked by such personal change. One way to resolve the left's deep dilemma is to take seriously the ways in which history can be made in daily life—despite the structures of domination that set limits on the ability to do this.

Taking such potentialities seriously means working on ways to enable people to use them more effectively—by providing models of right action and manuals on ways to live so that one's life matters. It means learning to measure the historical significance of the left, not simply in terms of organizational membership figures, voting statistics, and mobilization turnouts, but also in terms of the far less visible activity, embedded in the fabric of daily life, that signifies that social turns are being taken. It means, above all, that the tradition of the left be understood and transmitted as a *cultural* framework as much as—and perhaps more than—a political one.

From a cultural perspective, the anarchist heritage can help people find models and moral warrant for their felt resistances to hierarchy and their quests for autonomy. As a cultural force, socialism expresses the interdependence of human beings, calling them to take account of the social effects of their individual lives. Such understandings are internalized and become features of identity when they are expressed in the songs people sing, in their myths and rituals, in their models of heroism, in their literatures of fact and fantasy. Such internalized understandings enable people to break through privatizing conventions, to perceive and act out the connections between their lives and history. If conscious leftists want the people to make history, then the point is not to lead them, but to continuously create a culture through which such making can be understood as morally and practically right.

SOCIAL MOVEMENTS AS THE REAL LEFT

IN ADDITION to developing a deeper appreciation of and a methodology of support for the ways in which history can be constituted by everyday activity, conscious left activists and intellectuals need to reexamine their assumptions about the historical meaning of social movements.

The left's view of mass action is contradictory. On the one hand, guided by socialist vision and precepts, conscious radicals have always assumed that social movements were not to be valued in themselves, but as hopeful harbingers, or possible precursors, of full-fledged, class-conscious revolutionary mobilization. Movement leaders who concentrated on particular reforms were condemned by the left, and each generation of left activists has been disappointed by the "failure" of the movements they gave themselves to—meaning by "failure" that the movement receded after winning some gains rather than radicalizing and broadening its demands.

On the other hand, it has been in and through such movement involvement that conscious leftists in the US have always found their historical meaning. They have understood their political accomplishments in terms of the building of such movements and have assumed that these movements were in fact valid in their own terms, even if they did not culminate in "higher" consciousness or "revolutionary" mass action. Still, the capacity of leftists to fully savor popular victories they have helped to bring about and to see these as the measure of their success has been strictly limited by the deeply held belief that such victories were both logically and psychologically incompatible with the task of persuading the people that the "system" had to be overthrown.

Such beliefs are emotionally debilitating to the individuals who hold them. They are at the heart of the left's political isolation and impotence. For, by holding them, the leftist claims to have a special knowledge and a morally superior set of motives unavailable to the masses who struggle for goals the left knows, in advance, to be false. These claims are inherently self-isolating and are made all the more so when they actually guide action. To actually implement the logic of these claims in one's work as an activist is to put oneself in a position where one can be charged, with justice, with using the movement in behalf of an ulterior ideological purpose.

In practice, each generation of left activists has found itself deeply immersed in "reformist" struggles that became ends in themselves, whatever activists may have believed they believed about the reasons for their involvement. The irony has been that such immersion has typically been regarded as a sign of weakness, a postponement or diversion from the real struggle—the struggle for socialism. Such theorizing has made leftists feel guilty or inadequate because they did not in fact successfully use or manipulate the movements they helped organize, or because they devoted themselves too much to immediate, rather than long-range efforts.

Leftists have shared with their critics the notion that the real left is something quite apart from popular protest. That such protest has rarely had explicitly socialist content has been taken, by both left and non-left observers, as evidence for the immunity of American popular consciousness from radical ideology and for the weakness of the left as a historical force. By defining their stance toward social movements in such ways, leftists have repeatedly caught themselves in a double bind. If they work in movements in order to radicalize them, they are damned as elitist manipulators. If they work in movements as whole-hearted participants, they are demonstrating the historical irrelevance of their ideological commitment. I want to propose that the way out of this dilemma begins with an effort to re-theorize the historical meaning of social movements.

Movements are rooted in commitment to daily life, in efforts by people to overcome threats to their accustomed collective life or to claim rights they have come to believe they are entitled to. Movement participants, so committed, are therefore disposed to return to their lives once such return is made possible as a result of movement gains. This disposition is what frustrates conscious leftists.

Conscious leftists, entering movements not simply in behalf of their own lives but in order to make history, are inescapably at odds, motivationally, with the majority of their fellow participants. The latter are often glad there are some among them who are historically ambitious—and who are therefore willing to shoulder some of the burdens of movement leadership and responsibility and able to provide some expertise and skill needed for successful action. Activists wish that more of their fellow participants would undergo a motivational transformation; they try in various ways to encourage this, and some nonactivist participants do come to see the ways in which activist commitment can be self-enhancing, despite its many burdens and risks. For the most part, however, such conversions are relatively rare; mass withdrawal from participation is the overwhelming feature of the aftermath of mass movements.

Conscious leftists have often tried to overcome this situation by trying to foster ideological, rather than motivational, change. They attempt to demonstrate through argument that the achievement of a movement's immediate goals will not be enough, that the logic of the political economy and the state will result in the falsification of these gains, making them temporary and insufficient as means to protect the life that participants are trying to make. However "correct" such argument may be, argument by itself cannot persuade large numbers to forgo the chance to return to everyday living once that chance presents itself. For analysis must resonate with lived experience if it is to be effective as a goad to action. Indeed, many participants may readily acknowledge the validity of radical argument and nevertheless return to their lives, because it is now practical to do so. It is reasonable to suppose that movement participants never withdraw from participation because they believe they have won everything they have been fighting for, or because they now fully trust the system to work in behalf of their values and interests. Instead, such withdrawal occurs because participants see practical possibilities for making life, and weigh these against the likely costs of continuing to sacrifice the everyday in order to make history.

Radical arguments are activating, then, to the extent that established elites resist accommodation in favor of repression. Movement participation may decline when repressed, but the movement tends to live on. In the face of repression, participants may prudently avoid public action, but many are likely to be involved in keeping its flame burning—through song and story, through forms of symbolic gesturing, through subterranean talk and action. Sooner or later, broad popular movements that have been repressed burst again into historical flower, and usually with more radical, far-reaching agendas for change. Movements around the world have radicalized, then, not because the left participants in them have been more effective than American radicals at transforming popular consciousness or motivation, but because these movements have faced elite rigidity and repression.

There has been plenty of repression in American history, and, accordingly, movements whose participants have experienced this have tended to become more radical. A half-century of corporate intransigence with respect to the labor movement culminated in the radical upsurge of the thirties. A century of southern white resistance to and repression of the civil rights movement resulted in the radicalism of the sixties. But it is characteristic of American history that elite intransigence has tended to rather rapidly give way at the point that mass radicalization seems most ready to explode. At such moments, the particular "genius" of American politics comes into play and popularly demanded reform and accommodation occur in doses just sufficient to undercut radical argument. At such moments, participants are likely to feel, with some relief, that ordinary life is now possible for them—and that if more far-reaching struggle is needed, it would be prudent to leave it for the next generation. Meanwhile, they implicitly declare, let us see whether the promises we have got can be fulfilled for us in our lives.

Conscious leftists bemoan such attitudes but they are wrong to do so. If the cause people fight for when they fight is their lives, then it is right that they should try to actually live those lives when they have won some ability to do so. To ask something else is not only to fly in the face of "human nature," but really to contradict the human ground of the left tradition. The disposition of people to return to their lives and abandon their "historical mission" may look as if it is a readiness to consent to domination, but it is not simply that. It is an assertion that a new social contract has been worked out—not that the old one is back in force—and that contract binds elites as well as "masses" to a new set of social arrangements. These new arrangements are supposed to provide people with better guarantees for their accustomed lives, with a firmer foundation of material security, with more equality, voice, and dignity than they had before.

The popular return to everyday life is also a critique of the left. For when the left insists that history takes precedence over life, it is (like the ruling elites) pushing people to sacrifice their lives in the name of goals that go beyond their experienced needs. Isn't it perilous for leftists to label as "false consciousness" the desire of people to make their own lives rather than submit to the historical projects of the powerful? Especially when that desire is directed at living through the possibilities achieved by popular struggle?

The left theorizes social movements as symptoms of popular unrest, and therefore as possible signals of "real"—i.e., "revolutionary"—upheaval, as rehearsals for the main insurrectionary event. Some left theorists, moreover, recognizing the strength and flexibility of American elites, have joined with liberal analysis to view movements as forms of social leavening that provide impetus for societal modernization. In this view, movements, whatever their intent, are functional for the going system rather than symptoms or harbingers of its decline. From this perspective, movements are part of endlessly repeating historical cycles—mass involvement alternating with mass withdrawal—that reflect the "system's" ongoing capacity to maintain or restore its equilibrium.

These perspectives are not the only possible ways to interpret the historical meaning of social movements in this society.[1] Occasionally, some of the left have come to see that the great mass movements might be viewed as aspects of a unified narrative, and that this narrative has no end outside of itself. In other words, it is possible, as a leftist, to theorize movements as ends as well as means, to understand them as loosely interlinked rather than as discrete processes, and to see movement participation and outcomes as the fulfillment of the left's vision.

The left rightfully wants the capacity to participate in history-making to become an integral feature of daily life, so that people will not have to sacrifice life in order to enter history. I want to suggest that leftists need to rethink their belief that such everyday participation can only be realized after the revolution, "under socialism." Instead, it seems more fruitful to recognize that each of the great mass movements has sought, and won, a measure of democratization of existing society, so that in the aftermath of each it became more possible for formerly powerless people to exercise voice in some of the decisions that affect them.

The theme of democratization is the thread that runs through the history of each of the popular movements and that links each of them to the others. When these movements are viewed as discrete fragments, then each of their gains tends to be viewed as a fragmentary "procedural reform" that served to dampen, "coopt," channel the movement in ways that restored social stability and preserved the established structure of power. But if we focus on the common, unifying theme, framing our understanding of the meaning of the popular movements as if they were all episodes in a narrative of democracy, we would see the gains of particular movements as partial *but cumulating* societal and institutional restructurings that do in fact change the relationship between daily life and historical action.

It is true that the "powers that be" in this narrative are not fundamentally changed; it is true that from one angle the plot line can be read to mean that the capacity to make history is more and more monopolized by economic and political elites. That is certainly what C. Wright Mills thought, discerning the "main drift" of history to be represented by the concentration of control in the Federal Executive, the boardrooms of giant international corporations, and the command centers of the expanding military machine. The capacity of elites to make history has grown not only because of the growth of these national hierarchies, but also because of their control

---

1. It would of course be possible to suspend any effort at interpretation until history is made. For example, it is only after a revolution actually occurs that we feel confident in believing that all the struggles that preceded it were really part of its process. If a revolution accomplishes nothing else, it seems to validate all of the suffering and defeat that preceded it. But to think this way is to perpetuate the notion that people's lives are historically meaningful only as means to some final end — and it is just this perspective that psychologically traps leftists into postures that are self-isolating and morally contradictory.

over technologies of weaponry, mass communication, and information. The left has learned this historical reading exceedingly well, and it is sufficiently resonant with everyday experience to have permeated the consciousness of most Americans. Indeed, this way of looking at history has itself come to be a contributing factor in reinforcing mass privatization.

The centralization of power and its concentration in elite hands is only one side of the story of twentieth-century America. During these same decades, popular upsurge achieved a diverse set of reforms that have contributed to a decided widening of democracy in America. These reforms provide, at least in principle, means for people to influence the conditions of their lives where such means did not previously exist.

Some of these reforms strengthened the democratic features of the formal political system. The most dramatic of these have had to do with the right to vote—extended to women as a result of the struggles of the women's suffrage movement, to Southern blacks as a result of the civil rights movement, and to 18-year-olds as a result of the youth protest of the sixties.

Less elemental, and less dramatized, has been a considerable array of reform measures that, formally if not in practice, widened the ways in which voting could be used to influence governmental decisions, or otherwise democratized aspects of the electoral process. Thus, early in the twentieth century progressive reformers achieved the establishment, in various states, of the initiative, the referendum, and the recall. Beginning in the thirties, a variety of activists drawn from various movement and ideological contexts initiated efforts to democratize the functioning of the Democratic Party—by opposing the power of entrenched urban machines, by drawing labor and other movement leadership groups into active party participation at the local level, and by seeking a variety of procedural reforms that would democratize candidate selection and party operations. These culminated in the late sixties and seventies to create a situation in which candidates are far more subject than in the past to primary election, and a variety of previously excluded groups have formal voice in Democratic Party affairs. Still another democratizing reform has been the effort to restructure campaign financing.

The results of these reforms have been ambiguous in practice (and I will return to the question of the electoral process below); still, it is clear that many anti-democratic features of the formal political system have been abolished or modified as a result of popular protest and the reforms that sought to allay it.

But social movements are typically about more than simply the strengthening of conventionally defined political democracy. Movements assert, explicitly or implicitly, that democracy ought to be extended to arenas of decision making and frameworks of institutional control that are thought to be "nonpolitical," "private," or otherwise taken for granted as authoritarian. The most socially significant case is the labor movement's demand for workers' rights to participate in aspects of the management of firms—i.e., that they ought to have a voice in setting wages, hours, and working conditions. The achievement of "collective bargaining" rights, and the establishment of governmental machinery to oversee their exercise, was thus a major gain in extending the meaning of democracy. The labor movement has not pressed beyond collective bargaining to try to implement the wider vision of industrial democracy that has been circulating among intellectuals and workers since the beginnings of the factory system; furthermore, collective bargaining, as it has been institutionalized in the US, has had decidedly mixed results as a vehicle for workers to directly influence the conditions of their work. But despite the limited vision of the leadership of organized labor, despite the weaknesses of the union format as a democratic mechanism, the principle that the "private" corporation is not simply private property, and that its operation has to take account of a variety of rights of workers and others affected by its operations, was established and legitimated by reform measures such as the Wagner Act.

Gains similar in form, though hardly comparable in social meaning or historical significance, were won by the student movement of the sixties. Universities today routinely include students in most aspects of governance, including areas long thought to be the sacrosanct preserve of the senior faculty. Although students are not well-organized to take advantage of the formal representational rights that were achieved, campus life today is far more democratic than it was twenty years ago. Students are no longer burdened by authoritarian rules restricting their freedom of expression in politics and in social life, and they have far more leverage to advance their collective interests than they formerly did—leverage that has so far been rarely used.

Similar kinds of democratization have been achieved, in many localities, by the diverse and decentralized thrust of "environmentalism." A primary achievement of the environmental movement has been the establishment of mechanisms of public environmental impact review of industrial, commercial, and land development. Such review processes, coupled with extensive use of the judicial process as well, permits environmental organizations to play something like the role of the labor union in representing grassroots interests. Not only do these processes place some check on "private" development, but typically they compel processes of publicly visible negotiation with respect to issues previously decided in smoke-filled rooms by businessmen and their close political allies.

The democratization of institutional life has been aided by a variety of

other movement-sparked reforms as well. "Affirmative action" not only
opens up some opportunities for upward mobility for women and minorities, but perhaps more importantly also compels a degree of accountability
in institutional personnel practices not previously present. "Freedom of
Information" legislation has been an important resource for opening up the
operation of government agencies, including those, like the FBI, with repressive functions. A variety of mass-communications mechanisms have
increased public access to information and diverse opinion—e.g., the establishment of public television and radio, the creation of a large number
of nonprofit community-based radio stations, and the development of public
access channels in cable television. Occupational health and safety legislation provides some means for workers to have voice and leverage in
workplace conditions. "War on poverty" programs in the sixties required
that they be implemented with the "maximum feasible participation of the
poor." This established a precedent that has encouraged the continuing
growth of community-based organization and community participation in aspects of physical and social planning.

The left has always maintained that democracy requires, in addition to
structures that promote public awareness and participation, material conditions in daily life that enable people to be concerned with issues beyond
mere subsistence. The case for social welfare, for public subsidy of minimum living standards, for aid to those unable to work has, for the left,
never been couched simply in terms of "compassion for the needy." Instead, leftists have tended to argue that such support is essential for
democracy.

Social democracy—the effort to equalize the life chances of society's
members, to provide all the chance to develop their potentialities even
when these chances are denied by the operation of the market economy
—is, of course, one of the primary thrusts of the great social movements.
Social security, unemployment assistance, medicare, family assistance: all
these welfare entitlements, in one degree or another, provide the promise,
if not yet the reality, of a degree of social democracy. Even more important
from the point of view of democratization has been the growth in public
investment in education and the production and distribution of culture. Public education was one of the first demands of the nascent labor movement
in the early decades of the nineteenth century; the extension and improvement of public education, including mass higher education, has been a fundamental issue for all of the great social movements ever since.

The concessions and reforms won by each movement have expanded
the capacity of formerly powerless people to have voice in many social
arenas and compelled a greater degree of public discourse and accountability concerning hosts of decisions that affect the conditions and terms of

daily life. Moreover, in addition to such reforms, the movements have, in the aftermath of popular upsurge, built a variety of institutional structures whose purpose is to represent movement constituencies in these newly opened processes. Movement organizations (unions, civil rights organizations, etc.) provide the personnel and resources for representative participation; movement originated technical apparatuses (legal services, research centers, publications) enable a degree of ongoing monitoring of public processes and disseminate information to constituencies about relevant public issues. The professionalization and institutionalization of movement activism thus provides, at least potentially, channels for awareness and voice among the previously voiceless and unrepresented movement constituencies.

All of the things I am saying movements have achieved have been subject to the most withering critiques from the left. These critiques have made the following points:

1. Reforms won have been decidedly partial—far more modest than those sought by the movements themselves. Public sector investment in social welfare has been exceedingly stingy, rarely even approaching adequacy in dealing with the need. Procedural reforms are always compromised at the outset so that the established structure of power will not be fundamentally disturbed.

2. Such reforms are even more diluted in the process of their implementation. Established interests invariably find loopholes that enable them to take advantage of reforms to restore and even increase their power. Enforcement procedures are invariably inadequate, half-hearted, or corrupted. Potential beneficiaries of public programs very often find them hemmed around by bureaucratic fences.

3. Such reforms result in the dampening of democratic action rather than their stimulation. Instead of serving as independent representatives of popular constituencies, activists are coopted by the established elites. The opening of channels for participation means the creation of formal rules and bureaucratic processes that severely constrain popular expression and undercut the real power of the powerless—namely, the capacity to disrupt—without providing substantive power in return. The welfare state buys off popular discontent without enabling its beneficiaries to obtain the means for authentic self-development.

4. If reforms are actually effective in redistributing power, in curbing the freedom of dominant elites in a particular arena—it is predictable that these elites will find ways of circumventing these gains in the long run. Thus, the stronger the union, and the more effective it is in winning short-run improvements in living standards, the more likely it is that the em-

ployers who confront it will seek ways to move away from the union's zone
of influence. If capital can move more freely than the democratically expressed will of the people, then efforts to impose democratic control over
capital must eventually prove abortive.

Such arguments make up a large part of the radical critique of American
society as such. That critique asserts that democratic gains are largely a
mirage because they are granted by the very corporate and political elites
who are supposed to be controlled by them. If these elites write the terms
of the contract, if movements operate only to pressure (rather than overthrow) them, then these terms will be written in such ways as to undercut
the democracy they appear to be extending.

This critique is fundamentally valid. But, ironically, it is contradicted by
the practice of left-wing activists as they engage in political organizing and
advocacy. In the midst of concrete political action, struggles for reforms,
for partial gains in material well-being and voice are recognized as necessary and justified. As theorists, American radicals are Marxian—emphasizing that the "system" is dominated by the logic of capital, or they
are "elitist"—emphasizing the overwhelming control over history by those
in charge of the key institutions of society. But as activists, American leftists have implicitly been "pluralists"—emphasizing that grassroots mobilization and popular pressure can offset the power of entrenched interests,
that the self-organization of disadvantaged groups can increase their voice,
and that such increase in voice is itself worthwhile.

Somehow, American leftists have to learn how to hold in their heads an
analysis that recognizes the relevance of seemingly contradictory models
of the workings of the society. America is both class-dominated and pluralistic. Its elites do make history, but in so doing they are never free from
the need to take account of popular reaction, and are often (and perhaps
increasingly) significantly constrained by it. C. Wright Mills' depiction, in
The Power Elite, of American society in the fifties failed to even glimpse
the sixties and the scope and intensity of mass intervention in history that
succeeded the mass apathy of the fifties. His elitist perspective helped
clarify the structures of established power, but it tended to blind him with
respect to the potentials for history making available to the powerless. Yet
his style of thought and the content of his critique have tended to characterize the articulated understanding that most American leftists have of
how the society works.

The legacy of the American left appears as a failure if success is measured by the degree to which the left was able to organize the American
working class in terms of its ideology, program, and leadership. But if,
instead, the tradition of the left is understood as a long-term project to

steadily expand the capacity of the people to influence history, to democratize structures of power, and to enhance the capacities of powerless groups to exercise voice, then the historical record looks a good deal more positive.

Viewed from this angle, social movements are the main popular expression of the tradition of the left. Rather than being precursors, or recruiting grounds, for a "socialist" movement that will really be the popular left (as organized leftists have usually hoped) *the movements are themselves the primary vehicles of democratic restructuring in America.* They are such vehicles although they have been only sectoral, and despite the "reformism" of their demands, and their having typically been directed at pressuring elites rather than seeking to topple them. Despite the apparently nonrevolutionary character of the movements, their fundamental historical impact has been to extend democracy. Their cumulative effect has resulted in real structural change.

Such democracy as now exists can, I think, be evaluated by saying that formerly powerless groups now have much more capacity to veto policies and decisions that infringe on their interest. Resistance can now be accomplished through routine political processes more readily than ever before. What remains largely out of reach is the power to initiate positive change against the will of dominant elites. The innovation that does occur in response to routinely expressed popular demand is overwhelmingly symbolic.

The Marxian model predicted that workers would soon discover that fragmentary movements of protest were inadequate, and that their common interests could be served only by uniting within a political party that would be the primary means for mobilizing popular involvement in the struggle for democracy. That prediction has been borne out in the political development of all the industrial capitalist societies, except the United States. In all of these countries, the labor movement became closely linked with a working-class-based party or parties, the building of which constituted the main thrust of activist energy.

Such parties remain the primary focus of left hopes (and frustrations) in Europe. Under these circumstances, when left-oriented social movements arise outside of the control of the party, there are strong tendencies to subordinate them to the party's strategic requirements. My argument suggests that *in the United States the movements themselves have played many of the political functions that a labor party would have played had one been successfully formed.*

The tragedy of the American left lies not in its failure to have directed these movements toward "socialism" but in its failure to comprehend these movements as the primary vehicles of history making—as embodying the very social development that conscious leftists all along have been after. As Michael Harrington has suggested, American socialism has been carried as a popular force not by the parties that have adopted the name, but, invisibly and implicitly, in the actions and demands of self-organized mass movements. Or, as James O'Connor has proposed, beneath the fragmented, diffuse protests of discrete movements can be discerned the "Democratic Movement."

SOCIAL MOVEMENTS
AND ELECTORAL STRATEGY

ALTHOUGH LABOR and the other great social movements in the United States never seriously tried to build an independent party, movement strategies have always included efforts to influence established parties and politicians. Even though mass protest and direct action are the sources of their power, movements can hardly ignore established political processes. The capacities of movements to mobilize support and to formulate effective strategies are related to the degree to which state power is oriented toward their repression or encouragement.

In the days of Eugene Debs, American socialists believed that they could create a vehicle that would represent American workers and other disadvantaged groups in the political process. In the years before World War I, the labor leadership debated whether labor could and should lead such an independent politics or continue Gompers' policy of staying aloof from party politics while "rewarding friends and punishing enemies" within mainstream politics.

This debate lost much of its relevance during the New Deal era, as FDR formulated a rhetoric and a set of policies giving the labor movement legitimacy and material aid. From 1936 on, the mainstream of labor began to reject both the socialist dream of a labor party and Gompers' pretense of abstention from all party politics, responding instead to the opportunities provided within the New Deal coalition to directly participate in the Democratic Party.

This strategic move was pressed not only by mainstream labor leaders, but by CP labor activists as well. By the end of World War II, left activists were envisioning the possibility that the Democratic Party would be the home of a progressive coalition; labor leaders in many states mobilized union efforts to build up moribund party organizations, or develop reform organizations to fight entrenched party machines.

Liberals and leftists were momentarily optimistic in the immediate postwar years that the New Deal could be carried forward as a long-term social democratic program (comparable in scope to that of the newly ascendant British Labour Party), and that the right-wing elements in the Democratic Party (including the white supremacist Southern wing and the big city machines) could eventually somehow be eliminated. But such hopes were soon dashed by the triumph of the Republican Party and the conservative climate of the fifties. In those years, the spirit of reform stagnated, and popular consciousness settled into the privatized terms of the postwar social charter that had been inscribed by the social conflicts of the depression era.

The sixties revival of grassroots protest put new pressures on established Democratic politicians. Both Kennedy and Johnson made successful Rooseveltian efforts to embrace the civil rights movement. LBJ presided over the great wave of legislation implementing the basic demands of the Southern movement and putting state power behind the enforcement of voting and other civil rights. His "war on poverty" program boldly went further. By requiring "maximum feasible participation of the poor" in developing local poverty efforts, the war on poverty, like the Wagner Act, provided a legal basis for grassroots organization of the disadvantaged and for the recognition of such organization by the state.

Both the New Deal and the Great Society were designed to contain protest, to move it from the streets to the courthouse, to channel protest energies into political resources for professional politicians. Thus welfare state programs facilitated the transformation of collective protest into a quest for individual security, the winning of voting support for the Democratic Party from both disadvantaged and socially compassionate constituencies, and the development of a multiplicity of interst groups whose fate would be deeply intertwined with the fortunes of the party. Moreover, it seems important to remember, the architects of such policies did not believe that they would be financed by robbing hardworking Peters to pay shiftless Pauls. Instead, they assumed that the welfare state would be funded by capturing a portion of economic growth for public purposes, and that the expansion of the public sector would, together with a dynamic private sector, ensure steady economic growth indefinitely. Indeed, some argued that the maintenance of steady growth in a "mixed economy" would make social protest a thing of the past, reducing democracy, happily, to a process of public choice among slightly competing programs of social engineering designed by increasingly sophisticated social scientific experts.

From the perspective of the grassroots movements, however, the thirties and sixties had provided more than merely manipulative and technocratic opportunities to participate in a federally funded barbecue. The movements of those years never simply demanded that disadvantaged people ought to be financially supported by the state. Their primary concern was that state authority recognize and defend rights—rights to organize, to exercise voice, to strike, and to vote. Some of these were rights guaranteed in the Constitution but not enforced by constituted authority; many were claims for empowerment and voice not granted by the Constitution itself. From the point of view of the movements, the main gains of the reform wave were benefits that enabled people to function as workers and as citizens when they were denied the ability to do so by the inequities and failures of the private economy. Rather than "compassion for the needy" or the buying off of protest, what the movements sought (and partially won) from the Democratic Party was the recognition and protection of their legitimacy as the public voice of the disadvantaged constituencies.

In the seventies and eighties, the welfare state strategy collapsed because it had resulted in an unmanageable "fiscal crisis"—i.e., it had created a tax and wage bill that the capitalist and propertied classes were unwilling to pay. As a result mainstream party politicians and professionals have found it increasingly difficult to continue the Rooseveltian embrace of popular movements while defining a program that would be both electorally popular and credible as a solution to problems of economic stagnation.

Meanwhile, in the post-sixties era, a conservative strategy, designed to rewrite the social contract on terms much more favorable to the corporations and the wealthy, was taking shape. The Reagan administration was the high water mark of that strategy. During those years, government policy and administration rhetoric aimed at demonstrating that labor and other movements of the disadvantaged no longer had the ability to represent their constituencies effectively and no longer would have more than a small, marginal voice in defining the social contract. Such state perspectives were implemented throughout the economy, as employers successfully compelled unions to accept wage and benefit rollbacks and developed effective strategies to undercut local organization.

The disintegration of the postwar arrangement and the effort to stabilize the Reagan version of the social contract impelled the major movements to search for a new political strategy. They were no longer able to rely on an alliance with established politicians, or to rest comfortably on their clout within the party. The time when the pressures of the movements and their constituencies could be reconciled with corporate interests had passed.

The elements of a possible new strategy for the movements have been evolving for at least fifteen years. Since at least 1972, when antiwar and civil rights activists sought direct influence in candidate election and platform writing, one can discern increasingly conscious efforts by the movement leaderships to participate directly in party decision-making. The decline of the party machines, the rise of the primary and other "open" forms for candidate selection, the transformations of political campaigning wrought by television—all of these have hollowed out the established party organization as a mechanism for decision-making and vote getting.

Movement organizations have come to see this vacuum as a potential opportunity for developing power within the Democratic Party. For movement organizations can supply the troops, and some of the financing, that candidates need. They can mobilize supporters at conventions and caucuses in behalf of favored candidates and issues. Party rules requiring affirmative action in selection of delegates, passed in the seventies, provided opportunity for the women's and minority-based movements to gain unprecedented presence at the national party conventions.

By 1984 these developments had resulted in a situation in which each of the major movements had become mini-parties themselves. The AFL-CIO and NOW both had nominating conventions before the regular party one was held. A large part of the activist core of the black movement tied itself to Jesse Jackson's campaign—and he himself, of course, was a movement activist. Similar party-like structures were developed by the environmental and nuclear freeze movements. In each case, movements, using the framework of the PAC, established independent mechanisms for fundraising, voter registration and mobilization, convention delegate selection, issue development—in short, most of the functions that the political party organization itself is supposed to play.

The forms created in 1984 were not necessarily permanent, and at this writing it is not yet clear how the movements will organize themselves for the 1988 campaign. The 1984 experience was successful in the sense that the movements made concrete political gains within the Democratic Party as a result of their exertions: Mondale—labor's chosen candidate—was the party nominee; Ferraro, as the first woman to be a major party's vice-presidential candidate, fulfilled a principal demand of the women's political caucus; Jackson succeeded in mobilizing the black vote and in dramatizing the continuing reality of the black movement; rhetoric supporting the nuclear freeze concept was widely adopted by Democratic Party pols. But Mondale's shattering defeat overshadowed such largely symbolic gains, and, in the aftermath, party professionals tried to explain the loss as due in part to the excessive influence of the "special interests" represented by the movements.

The results of the 1984 campaign demonstrated that the technical ability of the movements to create party-like structures is not sufficient to define an effective political strategy. Although the combined constituencies of the labor, women's, black, peace, and environmental movements would, on paper, represent an electoral majority, the movements as such do not yet have the capacity to actually mobilize these numbers.

The constituencies of the movements themselves are quite variable in their readiness to form a voting bloc. At one pole there is the black community. Blacks, having overcome their historic low participation at the ballot box, do vote in concert—they are the most politically conscious of the "disadvantaged groups." On the other hand, the results of the 1984 elections made clear that large numbers of union members do not feel identified with or obligated by the political orientations of union officials. Mondale won a bare majority of union members—and this appears to be because of the support he received from blacks more than because white unionists were effectively mobilized. The now famous "gender gap" signifies the possibility that a potential voting bloc is present among women, but that "gap," in 1984, was not sufficient to change the presidential outcome. The ability of cause-oriented movements, like environmentalist and anti-arms race groups, to organize bloc voting among their demographically diffuse constituencies is weak in national elections. In short, however well-organized movement activists may be, their organizational ability alone is insufficient to deliver a majority in a presidential race even by intensively working their own putative constituencies.

Beyond these constituencies are vast numbers of Americans who are even less identified with the interests and causes that are represented by the major social movements. For Americans in the great middle, as I tried to suggest in the first part of this book, the meaning of politics has to do with potential threats to their ability to make the lives they believe they are entitled to. This attitude connects to a view of voting as a means mainly of vetoing or warding off such potential threats, or a means of registering one's established political loyalties when such perceived threats are not salient.

This perspective leads to considerable ambivalence toward social movements and the left. On the one hand, privatized consciousness can be mobilized by resistance movements that address threats shared by the majority; both environmentalism and the nuclear freeze movements find much popular support on this basis. On the other hand, movements are frequently perceived as threatening to established patterns of everyday life. Movements are threatening in the first place because they must employ tactics that disrupt the social fabric; in so doing they always risk hostility from those who perceive themselves to be innocent bystanders. Second, of course, movements may make demands for redistribution of power or income that threaten the position of elites and the rich and of relatively advantaged groups in the middle. Accordingly, one of the fundamental problems of political strategy for movements is that their own activity mobilizes electoral support for their opposition. This problem is exacerbated to the degree that the movements are framed as "special interests," seeking power and privilege at the expense of the common good.

Such framing is a regular feature of contemporary political discourse. Despite the erosion of labor union membership and the weakening of its leverage, opinion polls suggest that the majority is willing to believe that unions have too much power and that their leadership lacks social responsibility. Large numbers believe that government social programs are designed to favor blacks. Environmentalists are regularly described as "elitists"—although, interestingly, James Watt's effort to advance an anti-environmentalist program on this basis met with a wave of popular revulsion.

Resistance to the political thrust of the movements has not only been exploited by the Republicans but has also solidified within the Democratic Party itself. Party professionals argue that to have a chance of winning the party must put the movements in their place, restore the power of the professional politicians and speak to the great middle.

Such views may sound like the essence of "practical politics," but they are probably not. Democratic candidates might win back the votes of some who voted for Reagan if they followed this course, but they cannot win election without the whole-hearted support of blacks, grassroots liberals, and others on the party's left wing. The party's dilemma runs deeper than most current diagnoses seem to be suggesting. Its base includes large constituencies who are at odds with each other and who probably cannot be reconciled through symbolic gesturing. Most fundamental is cleavage between blacks and those whites whose votes are influenced, implicitly or explicitly, by racism. The old New Deal coalition between such constituencies was sustained by shared economic interest. A semblance of that coalition can occasionally come together, but only when whites are threatened by major increases in unemployment. Clearly, however, New Deal rhetoric and programs will not bridge these cleavages. Appeals to "compassion for the less fortunate" are not likely to persuade relatively advantaged Caucasian blue-collar and white-collar workers to return to the party fold.

It may actually be to the Democratic Party's advantage that the major social movements have embarked on a systematic strategy to exercise influence on its policies and selection of candidates. In 1984, despite Mondale's overwhelming defeat and the failure of the movement strategy to achieve truly impressive gains, there was some increase in voter participation among disadvantaged constituencies, effective support for locally based progressives, and, perhaps most important, the energizing of movement activists and networks for future electoral efforts. Moreover, despite its flaws and handicaps, Jesse Jackson's experiment in voter mobilization and coalition building may have opened promising paths for the revitalization of the party. The Jackson effort demonstrated that disadvantaged constituencies of the Democratic Party can be reached.

Rather than try to disassociate the party from these movements and their activists and constituencies, party professionals would be better advised to figure out how to respond to their pressures—and thereby make use of their energies—by formulating a rhetoric and a program that can build some bridges between them and the disaffected middle.

Today's economic and social conditions could provide the context in which such bridges can be constructed. For if present policies continue in force, budget cuts will continue to threaten major grassroots constituencies; a new economic turndown is likely; the threat of war will likely increase; and the drift of working-class and other traditional Democrats to the Republicans could reverse itself as economic conditions deteriorate.

In such a climate grassroots resistance is likely to grow, providing continuing impetus for a movement-based politics. It does not seem far-fetched to imagine that over the next decade a kind of "party within a party" will emerge that would represent a loose coalition among the major movements. Such a coalition seems a practical necessity given the movements' common interest in opposing a continuation of Reaganism and Democratic efforts to move the Party toward the "center."

There is probably sufficient will and technical ability among movement leaderships—and professional politicians based in movement constituencies—to bring such a coalition into being. But organizational alliance may not be enough to overcome the political impasse the movements are experiencing. Equally needed if such a coalition is to have a chance of turning the country around is the articulation of a coherent new "public philosophy."

By a public philosophy I mean a vision of the good society, a set of standards against which established institutions and practices can be judged, a structure of beliefs about the conditions for human freedom. A public philosophy can inform the development of a political program—a specific set of proposals and a definition of social priorities to address the experienced social problems of the day. In the postwar United States, the absence of ideological conflict meant that political programs were devised as pragmatic means for garnering votes, rather than being derived from coherent philosophical premises.

It has been one of Reagan's historical functions to compel attention to public philosophy for the first time since the New Deal, because he and his policy circle insisted on challenging the premises that had prevailed until his advent and claimed to be basing their program on a coherent ideological alternative. If public opinion polls are any guide, Reagan's popular success was largely in spite of his professed ideology rather than because of it. But his ideological coherence has certainly solidified the base of the Republican Party, facilitated the emergence of cadres of right-wing activists, and undermined the legitimacy of traditional liberal perspectives and programs.

If the movements are to achieve the political strength and social space to protect their gains and fulfill their agendas there is a need for a public philosophy and program that can provide the focus for movement alliance, find common ground in the great middle, and influence the rhetoric and policies of the party professionals.

DEMOCRATIZATION AND DECENTRALIZATION OF THE STATE

IMPLICIT IN the actions and demands of the social movements is a shared agenda for social change. That agenda ought to be formulated as a political program capable of winning majority support at the ballot box . But equally it is a set of goals that cannot depend on the electoral process as such. For social movements cannot depend solely on routinized politics; their potential power often lies elsewhere. Moreover, no matter who is in office, no matter what the label they carry, government policies are shaped by forces and contexts that arise out of the ferment and conflict of the wider society. What would the shared agenda of the movements look like if it were spelled out? I suggest that its central thrust would be to promote the democratization of institutional life and the empowerment of people at the level of communities, workplaces, neighborhoods, and regions. Instead of building up the authority of the central government, that authority could be directed toward deliberate decentralization and toward elimination of state constraints on democratic discourse. *The main political goal of the social movements is to turn the national government into a vehicle for societal democratization.*

How might the national government come to be such a vehicle?

First, by simply *implementing the logic of the Bill of Rights and eliminating governmental institutions and practices that contradict it.* A new democratic politics ought to deeply commit itself to the full meaning of civil liberties. Institutional threats to freedom of expression—including government domestic intelligence operations and secrecy policies—need to be eliminated. Freedom of information and privacy laws need to be guaranteed and strengthened. Public access principles with respect to broadcasting

ought to be protected and strengthened; publicly supported foundations in
the field of culture ought to foster the fullest vision of cultural and political
pluralism. Free speech rights for workers in the workplace ought to be
constitutionally recognized. In short, the American government ought to
be unambiguously committed to a vision of a society based on freedom of
expression and information; to libertarianism and pluralism with respect to
culture and politics. It ought to promote such principles internationally,
while recognizing that the best way to create a world movement for human
rights is to provide a model in America of what a genuinely free society
would look like.

Second, by *ending the arms race, the militarization of society, and the
quest for international hegemony.* There is little doubt that the principal
danger to conventional political democracy—as well as the principal barrier
to democracy's expansion—is the war system. Militarization fosters a climate of political conformity; it justifies the development of authoritarian
institutions and of government clampdown on freedom of information and
discussion; it provides the rationale for the manipulation of patriotic symbols to silence dissent; it fundamentally distorts and limits economic development and socially desirable investment. The "nuclear balance of terror" and the cold war do not simply increase the danger of war itself, they
corrode the culture and politics of the society. Moreover, the notion that
these policies somehow advance the possibilities for "freedom" in the Soviet bloc seems obviously false.

If a new left electoral politics achieved nothing more than an end to the
arms race and the beginnings of the conversion of the society to an economy and politics oriented toward peace, it would have been a great ac-
complishment. Indeed, it may well be that such a politics would be more
broadly popular than a political effort based on the economic reforms that
have been the focus of the left in recent years. At this writing, the American majority seems ready to resign itself to living within the framework
of pro-corporate economic policies—either because these are felt to be
inevitable or because many believe them to be in their interest. Reagan's
successes in building consent to his economic policies was not, however,
matched with similar success in gaining support for his global agenda.

Because his policies appeared to heighten the threat of war, they suggested profound danger to the daily lives of everyone, no matter how comfortable they may otherwise believe themselves to be. Although, as the
1988 campaign was taking shape, both established liberal politicians and
the popular left believed that the best strategy for taking back national
leadership was to develop a credible program for dealing with economic
problems, it appeared more plausible that efforts to define a program aiming toward peace and authentic national security might have greater polit-

ical potency in the immediate political context. In the long run, of course, vision, language, and program that can restore popular support for social equality and for an economy that serves the common good will be needed. It seems evident however that the traditional welfare state and state socialist formulas no longer provide frameworks for building that support.

Instead, what is needed is a vision of *the state as the guarantor of social, economic, and legal measures that foster the democratization of institutional life*. The Wagner Act suggests a model for this: its provisions protected the right of workers to form unions, established administrative machinery permitting workers to choose a union as their official representative, required employers to bargain in good faith with such representatives, and legalized the workers' right to strike and engage in other forms of direct action—under controlled conditions. The Wagner Act was certainly a mechanism for controlling industrial conflict and channeling protest. But its passage was also a victory for the labor movement, because, for the first time, it provided a way for unskilled workers to organize and effectively press their claims. It was clearly an advance in the democratization of the economy; it represented a substantial redistribution of power in economic organizations.

The Wagner Act committed the authority of the state to protecting the rights of a previously powerless group to have a voice in the decisions that affected it. Since then, the major movements have won a number of similar commitments. The voting rights act of 1964 committed Federal authority to the protection of black voting in the South. Federal legislation concerning affirmative action enabled minorities and women to challenge hiring and personnel practices of employers. Occupational health and safety legislation provided a legal basis for workers to gain some voice in working conditions. Laws concerning environmental quality in California and other states contribute to the democratization of planning land and industrial development by providing environmental groups and local communities with channels for contesting environmentally damaging projects. Federal poverty programs provided a basis for grassroots organization of poor communities by requiring "maximum feasible participation of the poor" in their administration. Rent control laws that provide an elected administrative board encourage the growth of tenants' unions.

All of these forms of legislation gave impetus to the self-organization of previously powerless constituencies by providing legal avenues for such organizations to gain a voice in decisions previously controlled by an exclusive elite. From the perspective of social control, such measures induce powerless people to "get off the streets and into the system." But from the perspective of movement activists and the groups they represent, such measures provide an opportunity to engage in historically relevant decisions *without having to disrupt the fabric of daily life.* It is true that the routinization of movement participation can enmesh activitists in a maze of bureaucratic maneuver, and that such maneuvering can undermine the capacity of activists to mobilize their constituents. But the opening up of legitimite channels for direct participation has aided movement organizations' growth, has resulted in measurable gains, and has raised the awareness of substantial numbers of movement supporters.

These experiences could be the foundation for a new era of democratic reform. Indeed, in recent years movements have attempted to develop programmatic proposals that illustrate ways that the state can be an instrument of community empowerment. Some examples: Inclusion of worker and consumer representatives on corporate boards; requiring utilities to provide consumer organizers with access to their customers; strengthening workers' control over workplace conditions affecting safety and health; the Equal Rights Amendment as a constitutional foundation for feminist challenge to all forms of institutional sexism; administration of health and welfare programs by locally based boards representative of client populations; compelling corporations to be accountable to workers and impacted communities with respect to decisions concerning plant closings. Although such ideas have won considerable support at local levels, they have not become subjects for debate in national political arenas. Nor have they been articulated as elements in a coherent vision of democratic control. Yet such notions promise an agenda of reform based not on expanding federal expenditures or state power, but instead on using the state as a positive means to support the capacity of citizens to influence decisions that affect them in ways that connect to daily routine and experienced milieus.

Moreover, *the state can be a vehicle for democratization by serving as a source of capital for decentralized democratic development and enterprise.* A central theme of a new democratic politics ought to be that neighborhoods, communities, and regions be empowered to determine their own futures, to reduce their dependency on both the national government and the multinational corporation.

The decentralization of the economy requires the development of public investment in activities and enterprises that are democratically defined at the community level as necessary but that are unattractive to private investors. It requires the formation of a mix of community owned public enterprises, producer and consumer cooperatives, nonprofit corporations, and locally based private enterprises developed through a democratic planning process.

Thus, to illustrate: Communities ought to be free to decide the merits of public ownership of locally serving energy utilities—and they ought to be able to mobilize the capital to assume such ownership. Capital ought to be available to enable tenants to buy out their landlords on a cooperative basis. Communities ought to be able to realistically envision the creation of locally based cooperatively owned cable TV systems—and such a possibility requires that capital be available. Workers ought to be able to consider buying out their private employers.

The role of the Federal Government in such endeavors would be to facilitate the creation of public banks or other mechanisms of public credit and investment and to provide the means for local communities to obtain the technical expertise needed to test and implement such visions. The essential point would be to get communities to think through their futures, using the widest possible array of means to promote public discourse, and to greatly broaden the powers of communities and unpropertied people to take economic initiative.

Instead of focusing on the welfare state and central planning, a new "liberal" or "social democratic" politics should emphasize policies that enable people collectively to be empowered to solve their problems themselves. The route to social justice does not lie primarily in taxing relatively advantaged workers in order to support the disadvantaged, but in social investment in enterprises and activities that address community needs and provide a measurable return to the public as a whole.

Decentralization means that national politicians and policy experts no longer could claim the capacity to set the main social priorities or define the content and pace of social reform. Instead, the processes of planning, of reform, and of social melioration would devolve on localities. Such devolution would not only reduce the power of national elites; it would have the pragmatic value for them of reducing their responsibility for the nature and impact of social change.

In an earlier era the struggle of disadvantaged groups was blocked by entrenched local business and political elites. Today, democratic possibilities seem to spring from localities and find resistance at the national level. Decentralization—once opposed by progressives concerned about labor and civil rights—now seems crucial if economic revitalization, environmental values, and democratic participation are to be advanced.

In the aftermath of the sixties, left activists began to devote their energies almost entirely to locally rooted political and cultural projects. There has been a tendency to bemoan the localization of the left, since it seemed to draw energy away from the main arenas of history and into its byways. But a politics of decentralization, pressed nationally, validates that local turn. It says that the political and cultural changes that have been achieved in communities can now become the basis of real historical initiative, that people, acting where they live and work, will have a chance to shape the future, rather than seeing it controlled by elites whose actions are checked only by desparate assemblies of people in the streets. Moreover, it seems evident, on both strategic and moral grounds, that leftists should not try to compete with national elites for control over history. Instead, the appropriate goal is to build a politics that seeks, over time, to return historical initiative to self-organized communities.

The social movements share a common interest, then, in four interrelated goals: free speech and expression, a demilitarized economy, the democratization of social institutions, community control over capital. The movements need the help of ideologically conscious left intellectuals and activists in translating these goals into articulated vision and concrete policy. In the process, democracy itself could come to be understood as a morally and practically superior framework for daily life when compared with prevailing conceptions of "liberty" based on possessive individualism. The advancement of these goals, and the formulation of vision and program in these terms, seem to me to be worthy tasks for those who are now conscious heirs of the tradition of the left.

I am both arguing for and predicting the revitalization of what in Europe would be called the "social democratic" Left—i.e., that expression of the Left tradition that concentrated on building up the support of a popular majority, in order to advance social justice and win workers effective representation in the capitalist state. I am suggesting that a new social democracy could develop in the U.S. based on the capacity of each of the major social movements to mobilize electoral strength as quasi-independent organizational forces, and on their shared need and opportunity to form working political coalitions. It could be spurred by the widespread impulse of local communities and constituencies to protect threatened ways of life and gain control over their development. It is likely to concentrate on developing cadres of professional politicians in localities and regions of movement strength, rather than on challenging established "liberal" politicians directly at a national level, preferring instead to develop working relationships with the latter.

The unfolding of such a "new democratic politics," and its chances of gaining majority support, are fraught with obstacles. These have to do with the predictable opposition between powerful corporate interests and the deep-rooted ambivalence toward socioeconomic reform that millions of Americans, embedded in their everyday lives, are likely to feel. Despite these obstacles, however, such a new politics could fundamentally transform the political landscape over the next decade. Such a new politics will not happen, however, without concerted, strategically oriented activity of a large number of activists and intellectuals who see its promise as the best fulfillment of their hopes and the best use of their lives.

THE REVOLUTIONARY DIMENSION

BUT SUCH a politics does not exhaust the meaning of the left tradition and is not the only action project worthy of left activists and intellectuals. Alongside the social democratic dimension of the left tradition runs another—sometimes called the "radical" or "revolutionary" one—another way to be "left" than to operate within the frameworks of formal politics and institutional reform.

The tradition of the left has been carried not only by those who have sought to mobilize a popular majority, but also by those who have stood against the majority by standing for unpopular principles and positions. In the United States, what is "left" has often been defined in terms of dissent, nonconformity, the defiance of convention, the disturbance of public peace and of the smooth surfaces of daily life. The left has always included those seeking to challenge and confront popular consciousness, as well as those who have sought to articulate it; those who have been actively hostile to the everyday lives of the majority, as well as those who have sought to secure majority well-being; those who have taken direct action in behalf of change without waiting for majority support, as well as those who have sought to mobilize the majority in behalf of change. There is, in short, an "elitist" dimension to the left tradition, meaning by this all efforts by left activists and intellectuals to undertake direct historical intervention without claiming the validation of popular support and without relying on the processes of mass mobilization as a means or measure of historical impact.

Such elitism is an understandable and to some degree inevitable outcome of the sociology of left activism. Activists tend to be drawn from special subcultural milieus, their daily lives are fundamentally different from those that generally prevail in the society, and they inhabit an ideological and cognitive world that is quite removed from the mundane. In such circumstances activists are encouraged to feel that they have special moral insight and social awareness, that they have a moral duty and right to take immediate action, that they constitute a saving remnant, a chosen few.

Left elitism has appeared in many forms. There is the legacy of those who, emulating the biblical prophets, have cried out against the unjust institutions of their day—slavery, the oppression of women, war, racial segregation—insisting on expressing their views in the face of mob hostility, of anti-sedition laws and the disapproval of polite opinion. There are those who have challenged conventional morality and advocated radical cultural change—particularly with respect to sexuality, reproductive rights, religious expression. There are those who have advocated revolutionary transformation, heaping scorn both on the oppressors and on all those who believed that capitalism could be reformed from within, that the conventional political system could be made to work democratically, or that the nation-state had to be respected.

Radical dissenters have for at least the last 150 years subjected all institutions to fundamental critique and all prevailing popular religious and political and social belief-systems to fundamental challenge, advocating in the process a wide range of reforms and alternatives that have disturbed the minds of both the privileged and the general population. Such dissent has an elitist quality when it is couched, as it often is, in tones of moral or intellectual superiority, or framed in a rhetoric designed to outrage and appall rather than appeal.

In addition to verbal dissent and criticism, of course, leftists have engaged in a wide range of elitist actions. These include: forms of "witness," that is, nondisruptive efforts to symbolize one's stand against prevailing winds, efforts to practice one's beliefs by creating countercultural communities; forms of civil disobedience, that is, deliberate refusal to comply with unjust laws or authoritative commands; forms of direct action, that is, small group efforts to disrupt institutional processes, occupy or invade public space in unauthorized ways, attack property or persons that stand as targets of grievance or injustice; forms of revolutionary organization and action, that is, small group efforts to advocate or organize the overthrow of established authority relations.

A variety of ideological perspectives undergird such forms of advocacy and action. These include religious traditions deep in the American experience; indeed, to assert one's conscience in the face of authority and popular feeling is fundamental to Protestantism and has been central to such groups as the Quakers, who have produced a disproportionate number of dissenters against slavery, war, and other oppressive institutions. A major theme in the Jewish tradition is the readiness to assert one's identity and to identify with the ancient prophets even if one is met with scorn, stigma, and hatred.

Anarchism is, by definition, an ideological framework that mandates active personal resistance to hierarchical authority and that exalts direct action and countercultural experiment. Pacifism, both religiously and secularly grounded, demands personal refusal to participate in, or support, authoritatively organized violence, and, in its Gandhian form, sanctions small group use of civil disobedience and nonviolent direct action. Leninism is an ideological framework that encourages revolutionary socialists to organize a revolutionary elite and to serve as a vanguard for a popular consciousness that, Lenin argued, would never come to revolutionary conclusions without such special tutelage and leadership. Teachings and the example of Che Guevara ("The duty of a revolutionary is to make the revolution") and other third-world revolutionaries appeared to sanction forms of revolutionary terrorism.

"Elitism" is usually a pejorative; to use it in referring to leftists is to appear to be trying to discredit them. Leftists, after all, claim to be acting in the name of democracy and in the interests of the people—it would seem to be a fundamental contradiction for people so claiming to be acting as an elite. And, indeed, it is not unusual for such claims to be justifiably questioned by critics. Nor has such criticism originated solely from those hostile to the left; one of Marx's own fundamental political aims was to replace the elitism of Blanquists, anarchists, and utopian socialists with a socialist practice rooted in the actual movement of the working class. The social democratic themes in Marx's work helped foster an ideological framework that compelled many left activists to discipline their impulses toward elitism, their concern with principle and moral purity, in the interests of building a popularly based left.

Such discipline is necessary; if activists are seeking to fulfill a historical mission while the "masses" seek to fulfill their own lives, then activists are, motivationally and structurally, a kind of elite. To say this is not necessarily to speak pejoratively; in a society and a culture that is not democratically organized, historical initiatives of all kinds must begin with specialists in history making; leadership, tutelage, exemplary action are fundamental requisites for stimulating and shaping democratic action. The conventional wisdom that says that avant-gardes, gadflies, saints, and heroes are needed to catalyze changes in consciousness is surely correct.

When leftists are true to their historical mission, however, they define as the goal of their elite practice the achievement of a situation in which their leadership will no longer be necessary. A main difference between elitists of the left compared with other elites is that the former seek, in principle, to make themselves obsolete.

Social democracy provides one way to try to do this—by seeking an integration of the left, ideologically and organizationally, with the world views and self-organization of the people. But the reformism, gradualism, and moral compromise that is inherent in such a practice sets limits on the effectiveness of social democracy as a framework for democratic change. Without the disruptive potential of "extra-parliamentary" mass action, the catalytic effect of radical dissent, the exemplary action and experiment of small groups of romantic idealists, the corrective criticism of moral purists, social democracy becomes ossified, routinized, bureaucratized; its organizations lose connection with their traditions and principles; its programs dissipate as technocratic, incremental reforms; its leaders become entrenched, hack-like time-servers and oligarchs.

All elitism—not least elitism of the left—poses fundamental dangers to democracy and to the everyday well-being of the people. These dangers arise when an elite arrogates to itself the right to make history against the popular will, when it presumes to embody that will without being accountable to it, or when it claims to understand what the people need better than the people themselves.

When it lacks the means to effectuate its presumptions, such an elite is likely to be doomed to self-isolation as an impotent sect of believers. Such self-isolation has often been the fate of Leninist-style "vanguard" parties in the United States who have claimed to be the embodiment of revolutionary truth while simultaneously claiming to be the authentic leaders of the working class. These parties have rarely had the capacity to undertake historically meaningful action, but they often have been a source of divisiveness and emotional turmoil within social movements. Typically, they have tended to enter movement organizations with the aim of challenging established leaderships and strategies, hoping to turn the movement in "correct" directions, to control movement organizations and to win recruits from the ranks of movement participants. The result has often been considerable internal disorder, as movement organizations wrestled with the dilemma of preserving their openness while protecting themselves against divisive internal conflict. One reason members have become disaffected with the organized left has been the disheartening and draining effect of factionalism. One root of such factionalism is the elitism—characteristic of Leninist parties—that combines postures of moral and political rectitude with a striving for power.

Self-proclaimed vanguards have been destructive within the American left, but historically impotent. The danger they have posed has been largely to themselves—by locking themselves into a fatal rigidity they have wasted the energy of members who might otherwise have been politically effective. But they have also poisoned the atmosphere within movement circles they have sought to control, thereby bearing much of the responsibility for those many participants over the generations who have retreated from involvement because of the factional rancor they found on the left.

Terrorism is a considerably more dangerous form of radical elitism. Instead of engaging in political discourse and persuasion, terrorist groups are defined by their intention to intervene directly in history, by physically attacking targets that embody or symbolize the oppression or injustice they seek to overthrow. Such actions may be justified by their perpetrators in a variety of ways—as retaliation for crimes committed by the authorities, as a morally justified way of making powerful groups pay a price for their actions, as a way of galvanizing passive masses into action by demonstrating the vulnerability of authority. They are inherently morally dubious, however, because they risk human life, including the lives of innocent bystanders, while rarely, if ever, having a demonstrable effect in improving the human condition. Beyond their immediate consequences, terrorism endangers the popular movement that it purports to be advancing. Terrorist acts provide the authorities with justification for escalating repression against the movement and against the society as a whole. They stimulate popular feeling that the movement is a threat to everyday security, and therefore tend to heighten popular resistance to the movement. And rather than galvanizing mass action, terrorism tends to generate feelings of paralysis among movement supporters, who are led to feel that they are spectators of history being made in their name. This passivity is further reinforced by the fear of repression—and sometimes by fear of the terrorists themselves.

Terrorism has been relatively rarely used by American leftists—indeed, the late sixties was probably the only time in American history that any significant number of radical activists turned toward its use. If terrorism has been used at all systematically in American political conflict, it has been by right-wing vigilante organizations, typified by the Ku Klux Klan, to attack efforts to organize popular protests. The left has not infrequently suffered repressive reprisals because of trumped up charges that it was harboring terrorists; this scenario for repression was perhaps first used by the police in the famous Haymarket incident in 1886 and has been repeated a number of times since. But the temptation to terrorism represents a potential whenever a small group has become imbued with the feeling that history must be short-circuited and that they have the moral duty and the right to connect the wires.

Vanguardism and terrorism are, then, possible anti-democratic results of uncontrolled left elitism. But to condemn them does not satisfy the need to find morally coherent and practically effective ways for radical dissent, witness, and principle to be expressed. The capacity of individuals and small groups to push beyond the boundaries of popular consciousness, to insist on principle at the expense of short-term popularity, to exemplify standards of conduct that are morally superior to those taken for granted in daily life, and to criticize the compromises and betrayals of those engaged in the politics of reform must be nurtured if social and cultural change is to happen.

The pacifist tradition constitutes a framework for channeling left elitism in the service of democratization. Pacifist activists are elitist in the sense that they claim a special moral sensitivity and a capacity for morally coherent action that average people lack. Whereas ordinary people are reflexively given to violence, or are likely to submit to the domination of violence-oriented authorities, pacifists strive to discipline their reactions, resocialize their action orientations, train themselves to refuse violence and resist immoral authority. By so doing, they deliberately set themselves apart from the common run of everyday routine and role and try to embody in their daily lives patterns of action and thought that fully mesh with their values. A considerable degree of self-righteousness is a not unusual result of such exertions.

There is a strain of pacifism that verges on passivity; some religious pacifists are no doubt satisfied with preserving their personal purity through moral witness and noncooperation with evil, hoping for a kind of modus vivendi with the state in which their conscientious objection will be tolerated provided it is maintained as an insular, sect-like posture unlikely to contagiously contaminate the larger population. But there is a long tradition of historically active pacifism, in which nonviolence and noncooperation are directed toward influencing the wider population and interfering with the violence-breeding and humanly destructive projects of the powerful. It is this tradition of nonviolent resistance and direct action that is profoundly relevant for contemporary left activists.

In this form pacifism is not just a set of convictions and moral principles, it is also a set of hypotheses about the sources of historical power. Some of these are:

■ State power is inherently grounded in violence; ruling elites by controlling state power can typically be expected to be able to overmatch the capacities for violence available to those who lack state power. Therefore, the key to effective struggle on the part of subordinated masses cannot depend on improving capacities for destruction and killing or on armed self-defense. *The best strategies of democratic action are directed at disarming the powerful rather than meeting them on their own ground.*

■ The organized violence controlled by the authorities can only be used if those who are assigned to deploy and employ it carry out their assigned roles. The fundamental sociological insight of pacifism is that human beings can be addressed apart from their roles, and that such address can undermine role compliance. *The key to disarming ruling elites is to find ways to weaken their capacity to command subordinates to commit violence.*

■ The capacity of elites to command the use of violence depends first of all on beliefs—held by the general population, by the members of the armed forces, and by the elites themselves—that such commands are legitimate. Such legitimation of official violence rests on beliefs about those targeted for suppression—that they and their demands fundamentally threaten the social fabric, that they are an alien Other rather than recognizable human beings, that they are themselves bent on violent or otherwise malign ends, or are otherwise "criminal." Legitimation also, of course, depends on beliefs that the commands being given are lawfully grounded, and that they are intended to preserve a social order that serves the common good (or which is taken for granted as the only one possible).

■ These beliefs can be challenged in verbal argument, but such argument, if it is possible to engage the authorities in it, is at best likely to result in very slow-moving change. Moreover, one of the main reasons that collective action is felt to be necessary by participants is that such dialogue with the powerful is not only ineffective but also unavailable as an option. Nonviolent protest and resistance is an effort to compel role-players to question the legitimacy of their roles by providing them with direct evidence that legitimating beliefs about the protesters and the authorities are false.

Under pacifist discipline, protesters approach their adversaries as fellow humans, opposing their actions but respecting or loving their persons. The protesters present themselves as "innocent," as unarmed claimants of ordinary dignity, as faithful truth-seekers. They attempt to speak a language shared with the human beings who are occupying the oppressive roles, insisting on rights already recognized as legitimate or as derived from principles given lip service by the authorities. Nonviolent protest is an effort to get those who represent authority to face the human consequences of carrying out repressive orders: to compel them to suffer a conflict between their human values and their role demands, to get them to see the common human bonds they share with those they have been assigned to hurt, to create uncertainty in the minds of persons in authority about the rightness of their directives, to win sympathy from uncommitted bystanders.

Nonviolent resistance is thus a practical strategy for disarming one's powerful adversary, but its effectiveness depends on its being more than just a strategy. Those who employ it have the most chance of being persuasive if they are authentically committed to nonviolence as a world view. Such authenticity probably requires a belief that those whom one is confronting can and should be redeemed rather than destroyed, loved rather than hated.

■ Actions based on such philosophical and strategic premises can, of course, fail, in the sense that the adversary will not be disarmed but will persist in his repressive course. But pacifists are likely to argue that one of the advantages of nonviolence is that even defeat ends up, historically, as victory. *In the long run, repression of the unarmed results in the delegitimation of the repressive authorities.*

■ The ideal act of nonviolent protest is one that both "speaks truth to power" and at the same time materially changes an existing power relation. Thus, the sit-ins at segregated lunch counters were more powerful than a more conventional protest such as picketing the segregated facility. The draft resister is acting more powerfully than the peace marcher. *Direct action that disrupts an ongoing institutional process compels those in authority to react, to choose whether or not to repress, to defend their legitimacy—or to concede the need for change.* Direct action therefore aims to be coercive, but when carried out in the spirit of nonviolence the coercion involved is moral rather than physical.

When undertaken by a small group claiming the right to make history without the prior consent of the majority, such actions are by definition elitist. But unlike other forms of left elitism, the nonviolent elite deliberately leave the historical choices in the hands of the majority, rather than presuming to make them in its name. The pacifistically disciplined activist seeks to lead by example rather than by exercising control. He or she is not trying to dominate a following, but to catalyze self-determined action by providing models or moral inspiration.

Pacifism is thus a way of preserving the creativity and moral coherence of a highly committed elite, while deliberately, self-consciously stripping such elites of their pretensions to power. In addition, it provides an intellectual framework for criticizing other forms of Left leadership and action. For, to internalize its core insights, is to become highly skeptical of justifications for immoral means that claim that they serve moral ends, and of arguments in favor of undemocratic modes of organization that presume to advance democratic goals.

Creative nonviolence is not made obsolete as a strategic direction for Left activists by the emergence of an effective "majoritarian" social democratic popular force. By its very nature, a "parliamentary" left must mobilize around programs that speak to the perceived shared interest of the majority, give short shrift to the interests of minorities, and focus on the defense of everyday life rather than on support for the unconventional and the avant-garde.

Moreover, given the logic of the state system, no majoritarian left can go down paths that seem to weaken the state's military defense capacity, or that threaten conventional assumptions about how internal law and order are to be protected. Indeed, the European parliamentary lefts often have had to make special efforts to prove their commitment to conventional patriotism and domestic order. Not only is such proof demanded by the institutional controllers of the military and police forces (whose control over violence is a constant threat to left regimes), but is also often expected by large sectors of the general population, for whom international threat and domestic chaos are primary sources of political anxiety.

The left's historical meaning must go beyond mere defense of the everyday lives of workers and other disadvantaged groups, and certainly it is not coterminous with the strengthening of the nation-state. Indeed, the lefts within the boundaries of the superpowers have no more important mission than to struggle for demilitarization, for alternatives to the war system, and for the dismantling of machineries of domestic repression. Accordingly, alongside a majoritarian left there must be another—oriented toward transcending the logic of the nation-state, toward internationalism and communalism, toward the abolition of war. The historical record suggests that such goals, being "visionary" and highly unsettling, have to be carried initially by small minorities, unafraid of being unpopular, engaged in delegitimating conventional wisdom and challenging established lifeways, and capable of providing models in action of alternative ways of being and acting.

Several generations of leftists thought that the answer to social democracy on the left was "Leninism." I am arguing instead that the appropriate counterposition is rooted in pacifism—as a philosophy to guide extra-parliamentary activists and as a practical framework for deriving strategies for radical action. Activists who choose a radical path and an elitist practice must begin their journey by refusing absolutely to reach for power, seeing instead that their mission is to serve as exemplars of moral being and action. They must refuse absolutely the belief that history can be short-circuited through violent intervention. They ought to study Thoreau, Tolstoy, Gandhi, Muste, and King as models of history making, rather than Lenin, Trotsky, Mao, Che, and Fanon.

ON NATIONAL ORGANIZATION

THE TRADITION of the left is today embodied in social movements that struggle for democratization, in community-based organizations of many kinds that represent and empower grass-roots citizen action, in some loose, largely informal, national networks of activists and intellectuals interested in various issue domains, and in a variety of periodicals, think tanks and foundations. On the periphery, there are remnants of the old "party" form—the Communist Party, the Socialist Party, and the IWW still exist as pale shadows of their former selves, as do several Trotskyist and Maoist parties and splinters.

In this chapter I have tried to inventory the modes of action and belief that seem to me necessary for left activists to adopt if the left tradition is to be revitalized. Most of these do not require a national center of leadership and strategy. But at least one project does have to be centrally directed, namely the effort to build up a left-wing coalition in the Democratic Party. Such an effort requires plans, strategies, coordination; it requires the formulation of policy perspectives and platform planks; politicians have to be cultivated, bargained with, and developed; movement leaders coalesced; activist energies mobilized and channeled. Consider that it took the "new right" that emerged in the Goldwater campaign of 1964 about fifteen years to redirect the Republican Party and create the base for the Reagan triumph. The "democratic left" will need a similar concerted, long-term effort if it were to create a comparable national politics.

If there is a pressing need for a national organization of the left it lies in that project. There are some precedents for that type of organization. For example, the formation of the Americans for Democratic Action during the Truman administration was an effort by anti-Communist liberals to exert influence in the Democratic Party. Similarly, in the forties and fifties in California and other states liberal Democrats organized effectively in behalf of progressive policies, candidates and party reforms of various kinds. At present, conservative Democrats have an organizational center in the Committee for a Democratic Majority. Although DSA tried in the seventies to create a structure called the Democratic Agenda—this was a sporadic effort, not a long-term strategically oriented national organization—nor did it seek a grass-roots base.

Most electorally oriented left activists and intellectuals do not want to form a third party. They have developed some skill and experience in local politics, issue campaigns, and policy formulation. What they obviously lack is an organizational structure through which goals can be defined and national strategies developed. Such a structure is needed if there is to be a serious project to contest for the soul of the Democratic Party.

A new left version of ADA would fulfill such specific strategic needs, but unlike organizations of the "party" type, it would not itself compete for national power. If it were actually to serve the purpose of developing a new democratic politics its functions would be aimed at coordination, resource development, and advocacy—not building itself as a power center. Moreover, such a structure would not define the left; it would be one important, but limited, expression of the left tradition.

Such a structure is not the only framework of national organization that might fruitfully be developed by conscious leftists. There is a need—and I suspect a hunger—for something else, some format for coming together that can nourish the identity and enhance the historical relevance of the work of contemporary left activists and intellectuals—a format of a new type.

THE COLLECTIVE INTELLECTUAL

THE PROBLEM is to create sufficient structure to facilitate coordination; sharing of resources and information; mutual clarification of vision, strategy, and program; the maintenance of collective memory and identity— while avoiding the encapsulation, rigidity, intellectual deceit and distortion, interpersonal abuse and personal alienation that have been the plagues of the organized left throughout its history. I have argued that the "party" form—however democratically it is structured—is inescapably plagued in these ways. Is there another way to think about organizational form that might help?

Let us listen to the reflections of one who shares the tradition of the left, but who confronted even more impossible problems of sustaining it. He is Rudolf Bahro, once a Communist in East Germany, writing as an activist/intellectual in opposition to the official Party, struggling to imagine how the tradition of the left could become an organized presence in a society that had totally absorbed and destroyed it. Here are some of his thoughts about how the left ought to be organized:

> What is needed . . . is that the party . . . must be organized as the *collective intellectual,* which mediates the reflection of the whole society and its consciousness of all problems of social development, and which anticipates in itself something of the human progress for which it is working . . . [I]ts achievement is subject to precisely the same criteria and has also the same general conditions as the work of a group of scientists . . .
>
> The concept of a collective intellectual is in no way aimed at representing the special interests of the intelligentsia. Since all people have emancipatory interests, which cannot be sufficiently realized under the conditions of the traditional division of labor, the attempt to reflect the problems of realizing these must in principle be a universal one. [The organization] must therefore be open to all those having the need to go beyond the pursuit of their immediate interests, having recognized that the barriers to their self-realization bear a social character . . . It assumes that all thinking people are at least potential intellectuals and can acquire the ability to think dialectically beyond the hierarchy of social connections and intervene in these as active experimenters and constructors . . .
>
> In as much as the intellectuals still form a traditional stratum or group, they must become conscious of their special interests with the aim of restraining these as far as possible . . . Now that there

are millions upon millions of intellectualized people, who are moreover not held back from solidarity by any constraining barriers of
interest, and finally are themselves hungry for a more comprehensive
social communication, it must already be possible to *work out through
discussion* the necessary compromise of interests and carry it through
primarily with the "gentle power of reason" . . .

A successful work of knowledge requires the access of all participants to the totality of significant information, the "horizontal" and
non-hierarchical coordination of investigation on the basis of the self-
activity of those involved, the admission of hypotheses that break
through the customary frame of ideas, unreserved discussion of different interpretations . . .

What Bahro envisions is an organization for political work that is consciously modeled on the ideal of scientific work organization—the community of scholars engaged in free discourse, without censorship, in which
whatever consensus is achieved is based on reason and in which conformity
is neither imposed nor expected. Its members share one fundamental
commitment—to contribute to a common vision of general emancipation
—and each member is therefore accountable to him- or herself and to the
others in the light of this vision. But the "discipline" of such accountability
is entirely voluntary; each member is expected to speak and act in terms
of truth and conscience.

What is the historical role of the collective intellectual? It is, says Bahro,
the role of prophecy:

There have always been times in which people pressed beyond existing arrangements without being subordinated to the rule of a
priestly caste, times of movement, times of a people led by *prophecy* . . . It is hope that leads the people and its prophets are nothing
more than interpreters who give the deepest emancipatory needs a
concrete, articulated and historical expression, in which the totality
of what is promised is not lost . . .

What ties people to a movement [differently from to a firm that
"gives work"] is the promise of connecting the details of their lives
with a meaningful whole, of opening up to them a space for self-
realization in trans-personal and historical dimensions.

Individuals are already organized around their particular interests . . . where can we find that union in which they can commit
their emancipatory hopes?

The party Bahro envisions is a "revolutionary community with an open
periphery that lets society in . . . the ideological inspirer . . . enabling

the majority of members of society to take control of all processes of decision making from within . . . Its major function . . . will be the unification, coordination and direction of intellectual and moral efforts for elaborating a strategy and tactics of cultural revolution" (Bahro, 1978, pp. 361–376).

Whatever the chances of such a community surviving in "existing socialist" societies—and these seem slim indeed—it seems to me that Bahro has articulted a vision of organization that seems applicable to left activists and intellectuals in the United States. Today's leftists are organized—but not in terms of their shared identity or in conscious and explicit relation to their collective purpose. As a result, the continuity of the left tradition is in danger as never before. Activists become increasingly focused on narrowly circumscribed issues, arenas, and constituencies. Professional intellectuals are seduced by the manifold temptations of careerism. The left's historic functions—of socialization, of cultural renewal, of prophecy—are accordingly undermined. Bahro's vision depicts an organizational form that can restore these functions in a framework that would be far less restrictive or damaging than the organizational forms of the past.

In my opinion, Bahro's vision expresses the deepest shared hope of my generation of leftist intellectuals and activists. It is the hope of inhabiting a community through which one's talents and energies could effectively be utilized for social transformation, while, simultaneously, one could be free for authentic self-expression. Such a quest—to live in terms of both self-sacrificing social responsibility and self-determining autonomy—was at the heart of the early New Left, but no sustained organizational framework for continuing it survived the sixties. The sixties experience made most members of the generation deeply wary of renewed organizational entanglement—but the yearning for coherent connection remains.

For example, in the summer of 1977, about one hundred former SDS actives gathered in reunion near Ann Arbor, spending five days and nights in remarkably intense discussion, sharing not only memory of the past, but analysis of self and society in the present. The experience turned out to be an emotionally profound one for most who were there. To some extent, it was an opportunity for deeply significant emotional release and relief; there were strong currents of bitterness running through the group, for many in attendance had been on opposite sides of rending conflicts in the latter years of SDS. The reunion provided a time for confessions of hurt and admissions of guilt, for working through of hostilities that had torn the organization—and many of its members—apart. Thus to a great extent the reunion was a kind of group therapy (facilitated by the fact that a sizable number of those present had actually become professional therapists, and many others had had therapeutic experience). In their Revolutionary days, most of these people had participated in a collective climate characterized by intense "guilt-tripping," "macho" one-upmanship, self-righteous recrimination and bravado. In those days, members deeply feared the revelation of self-doubt, personal weakness, and "bourgeois tendency"; in the ensuing decade most had, on their own, learned to overcome those fears and had abandoned the self-righteous patterns of thought and personal styles they had adopted during the time of Revolutionary Apocalypse. At the reunion, most discovered what they had not fully known—that their fellow SDSers had all traveled similar paths, that all shared a hunger for mutual support, and a burden of regret for the mutual pain of the late sixties. The result of this discovery was an exhilarating sense of healing.

But there was another discovery as well. The hundred attendees found that they retained a shared identity—despite the passage of time, despite their earlier conflicts, and despite the fact that a great many were no longer politically active. It was hard to articulate the substance of this shared identity. To the dismay of some, many of their former comrades were no longer focused on "politics" as a full-time preoccupation. They were, instead, dedicated to some work—as artists, writers, or therapists, or as activists in quite local or sectoral context—and not, therefore, ready to devote major time to political entrepreneurship. Nor was it clear that there could have been a solid ideological consensus among those present if they had attempted to hammer one out. Still it seemed clear that most there felt nearly in love with everyone else, dying to talk, to sing and dance, to probe each other's experience. Moreover, the talk seemed wonderful; I felt, repeatedly, that I had never been even half so stimulated intellectually in all my years in the university, nor ever found academic colleagues there as insightful, as articulate, as self-aware as my former comrades, who seemed more genuinely intellectual than most of the people I normally encountered in academic life.

What was the shared identity of these people? It seems to me that what they had in common in 1977—and in 1962—was that they were each intellectuals hoping to connect their work to historical transformation. Most had settled into something like a career (though a large number remained outside the institutional structures of intellectual careers), but all were profoundly disturbed with the notion that they would settle for nothing more than careerism. Instead, they perceived themselves to be struggling to ensure that their work—and indeed their total way of life—had a meaning in history. What was shared, then, was not a political ideology or affiliation, but, instead, a tradition and an aspiration.

At the reunion, one felt that the structure of the event provided those present with a rare opportunity to collectively advance this purpose. Unlike most social occasions, participants in this situation had tacitly agreed to suspend reciprocal judgment in favor of "openness," to listen and to be vulnerably expressive rather than debate and confront, and understood that no consensus or resolutions need be achieved at the end. The result was a degree of freedom for expression and exploration that is rarely attained when groups of intellectuals assemble. It is this "free space" that accounts for the impression of remarkable intellectual power that one felt in the room in comparison with conventional academic occasions. It was not that these former SDSers were smarter or "better" than my academic colleagues, but that a social setting that drew from people their best intellectual and moral discourse had somehow been created. As a result, one felt a moment of genuine growth, of renewed commitment, of authentic revitalization.

Fitful efforts to establish an ongoing network of relationships among former SDSers after the meeting were unsuccessful. The moment was only that—and this seems strange. For if those present had "sincerely" renewed their commitment and had been so exhilarated by their reunion, why not try to continue the association? Perhaps one factor was a kind of fear—a fear that the moment could not be reproduced and that its wonder would be destroyed by the effort to sustain it in the face of mundane and routine reality. But there was perhaps a more fundamental problem, evidenced by the difficulty those who came together were having in articulating their shared identity. If neither ideology nor political priorities were any longer consensual, what was it that constituted the common bond?

What I suspect was lurking in the background, but which participants held back from accepting, was that all present were "intellectuals." In the sixties, most New Leftists adamantly refused to adopt this label. The word connoted the very things that they were trying to overcome in themselves. For "intellectual" conveys a separation from action, from material reality, from struggle, from whole-hearted commitment. Moreover, not only do "intellectuals" inhabit "ivory towers," but they do so in privilege, claiming exemption from physical labor, claiming also a capacity for understanding the world superior to that of the unlettered, demanding deference even though refusing to share the deprivations and sacrifices of the common folk. New Leftists knew that they had been raised to be some kind of intellectual (indeed, many of their parents were practicing intellectuals). They aspired, instead to be *activists,* believing that as organizers they would, by definition, be engaged in moral action (rather than just preachment) and, thereby, gain a better understanding of the world than that achieved by those remaining in the sheltered sanctuaries of intellectual work. Although there were some fitful efforts during the sixties to develop New Left proj-

A Final Word

I had *promised my children to end the war before they grew up.*
—*Grace Paley*

OUT OF THE chasm between History and our own lives grows the fantasy that we can escape History or the dream that we can make it for ourselves. For each person, each morning, the hope of escape is the more rational one because it is far more manageable. How can we get out of bed unless we assume that we can make our own day, or at least make it through the day? Such assumptions are the core of average American political sentiments as well as the background assumptions of mundane experience. Accordingly, the alternative dream—that today we can make History—is inescapably not going to be spontaneously experienced or readily accepted by very many (especially if, as is often the case, entertaining that alternative might actually ruin your day). Yet, that alternative is at the heart of the left tradition. Because it is incongruent with the logic of daily reality, the left dream is consciously held by only a minority.

Despite this, the tradition of the left does not disappear. It persists in part because some elements of the dream are imbedded in the prevailing culture. Although Americans on the average would rather ignore History, the very fact that the nation is founded on principles of formal democracy means that we are all raised to believe we have some voice and responsibility in it. The tradition of the left consists of those who have called people to exercise such voice and responsibility. In this sense, the left is the conscience of the constituted political culture.

The left tradition persists also because inequality persists; in the framework of a professedly egalitarian culture, those groups denied equal rights have learned that they cannot afford to escape History, have grasped the rationality of historical intervention, have mobilized to make it. Doing this, they demonstrate that the people can make history, thereby renewing the dream that the people will continue to develop the will and capacity to do so.

The left tradition however does not simply embody the egalitarian and democratic promises of our official culture. It is, even more, a critical tradition, not only affirming people's rights but also attacking the structures, practices, beliefs, and principles that perpetuate forms of domination, exploitation, oppression, and inequity. That critical stream persists because it has been carried by generations of writers, artists, preachers, teachers, and the like, whose words and images are deeply embedded in both serious and popular culture.

Moreover, American life contains a variety of "subcultural" streams, largely originating in various ethnic groups, that carry explicit memories, ideological perspectives, and ethical principles that help constitute what we mean by the left. Thus the left persists because the tradition is explicitly transmitted from generation to generation in some cultural pockets in the United States—for example, in the black community, in many Jewish families, among a few religious groups. Such "socialization" practices, which are sometimes amplified by mass participation in large-scale social movements, help create succeeding generations of "activists"—people who, when they get out of bed, despite their distance from the seats of established power, are likely to feel that History could be made by themselves.

One of the stories I have been trying to tell is that such activists, faced with the agony of being cut off, by virtue of both background and outlook, from the majority of Americans, have made many false steps down many blind alleys in trying to "reach" the mainstream. I have suggested that the practice of left activists over the generations has been damaged by some of the very resources they thought were of most use—namely their ideological perspectives (that supposedly provided them with a "scientific" map to the future), and their organizations (that supposedly provided them with the leadership and strategy to influence history). Yet, I have argued, the actual practices of many activists did make significant historical contributions; their reflections on their own experience often provide solid clues about what left-wing activism is actually all about.

Those reflections, combined with my own effort to read the left experience, suggest that activists, if they are not to be dangerous to society and to themselves, ought to be people: (1) whose skills and talents enable them to contribute to social movements—i.e., concrete collective efforts by the people themselves to influence History; or (2) whose skills and talents enable them to contribute to the development and dissemination of culture—i.e., the ideas, visions, models, and myths that help people see

how they might make History, why they should, and what might come of
trying. These sorts of things are what generations of activists on the left
have actually done with some "success."

What is wrong with America is not that we do not have a "mass party
of the left," or that only a very few profess to be socialists, or that people
are too conservative, nationalistic, or individualistic. What is wrong, from
my point of view, is that people lack the historical awareness and the language to articulate a generalized vision of democracy. Little in our culture
or politics enables us to ask how life would be enriched and institutions
improved if every morning we all woke up knowing that some of our day
would involve us in decisions that affected the social future. Little in our
culture and politics encourages us to think about our opportunities and responsibilities to make a difference in the "public" life of society.

The lack of democratic spirit in the everyday outlooks of Americans is
not only morally troubling but dangerous. What is perilous about the absence of democratic vision is symbolized, of course, by the Bomb (and
lesser but more likely war dangers), and by the manifold other ways in
which days are being ruined, wasted, and shortened by institutional practices, public policies, and elite decisions. Such decisions, in every sphere
affecting life, often produce anger and some resistance—and hence are
sometimes vetoed and mitigated. But such popular reactions are just
that—reactions—which permit the structural basis for life-destroying forms
of domination to continue.

If "the people" actually governed, there would be no guarantee that better decisions would be made. But if people took seriously that they ought
to govern, then many structures would have to be reevaluated.

The very size and scope of institutional control would have to change
—for collective self-government does not seem possible on the scale of
the national state and the multinational corporation.

New sensitivity to social interdependence would have to be cultivated,
since people would increasingly know that their own local actions had potential effects on other places and future people.

If the community could replace the nation-state and the mega-corpora-
tion as the center of social initiative, then what we mean by History—and
daily life—would be transformed in ways that would likely be experienced
as freer and more secure.

It is currently fashionable to believe that whatever "left" there has been
in America is now finally and permanently washed up, and that the main
trend in public consciousness in the foreseeable future is toward the "right."
Such claims, however, ignore the possibility that there is a definite sociological basis for the left's revitalization—and that this is likely to expand
in the next few years. This social base includes:

■ The social movements of the disadvantaged whose gains have been seriously eroded and power weakened during the Reagan years, but which represent large numbers whose daily lives have deteriorated or will, because of this erosion.

■ Industrial workers and others affected by the massive deindustrialization of the economy—the "newly poor," newly unemployed, dislocated millions, the communities impacted by plant closings and disinvestment.

■ Communities affected by pollution and other consequences of uncontrolled growth.

■ Those, particularly in the educated classes, who are disturbed, disgusted, or scared by the militarization of the economy and of social life, the arms race, and the immorality of foreign policy.

■ Workers, including white collar and professional, who seek more autonomy and control in their work, who sense that top down bureaucratic controls are irrational as well as oppressive.

These sectors, interests, sentiments, and anxieties are hardly reflected today in the rhetoric and program of either national party. They provide the potential base for the creation of a new left-wing coalition that seeks influence in the Democratic Party nationally, as well as electoral gains at more local levels. The existence of such a force would provide an impetus for restoring serious political debate in the United States. The emergence of such a coalition could prefigure a new era of democratic reform in the society and democratic expression in the culture.

If a new politics of the Democratic left were a visible factor, here are some of the things that would be on the agenda of public life:

Conversion of military industry to peacetime production; normalization of relations with Cuba, Vietnam, Nicaragua, and efforts to win these societies to closer links with the United States; a freeze on the nuclear arms race; private initiatives—by intellectuals, scientists, movement organizations, religious groups—to open up Eastern Europe to freer discussion; active support by such groups for free trade unions and other free space in the Communist countries; a shorter work week; expanded investment in education to reduce class size from kindergarten through college; the formation of community banks and development corporations to promote job development and community-based planned growth; expanded public investment in community-based television and radio programming; community-controlled child care; expansion of ecologically based growth—solar energy, conservation, and other "soft energy" developments as a source of jobs as well as environmental preservation; worker controlled occupational health and safety regulation; the right to adequate, food, shelter, and health care . . .

I've deliberately written this as a sort of randomly organized laundry list of reform in order to suggest, not that "neo-social democrats" have solutions to fundamental economic and social problems, but rather to illustrate the ways in which a changed political and cultural climate might foster institutional and policy changes that actually could make a difference in the daily lives of most people. Not only are such ideas missing from the national agenda of serious policy, they are not even being discussed today in mainstream national forums. The reason they are not is that, for the most part, they seem so "out of phase" with the "prevailing climate."

Instead of taking that climate as inevitable or permanent, it seems clear that what is needed—by Leftists and by the country—is for activists to agree on a strategy, such as the one sketched in the last chapter, that seeks to change the dynamics of party and "parliamentary" politics. I've suggested that both the popular base—and many of the programmatic elements—for such a strategy are evident; what's missing is a determined initiative to lead it.

Such a development would probably be the most rapid route to a revitalized left spirit, but such a revitalization does not depend on national political developments. One of my underlying goals in this work has been to try to encourge political activists to think of politics as happening in ways and places that are not restricted to official arenas and governmental processes. Indeed, if Americans are to rethink the terms of their freedom and their relationship to History, such alternative meanings of politics—and of how History actually is made—will have to be articulated. The fundamental work of those who identify with the left tradition is to show how "private persons" are in fact implicated in history, to illuminate how private acts ramify through time and space, to nourish the spiritual resources that enable the "powerless" to make History.

The shriveling of America's left-wing is not a triumph for the American Way, but a crippling of our politics and culture. Yet the demise of the left's traditional organizational forms, and the exhaustion of many of its specific ideological perspectives, clears the way for new possibilities. We can now see that the left project does not involve the winning of masses of adherents, the building up of a party, the rallying of forces. Instead, the project is fulfilled in every act that encourages people to make History their own instead of trying to escape it.

Bibliographical Notes

1. History and the Everyday

THE QUOTES at the head of this chapter are from Konrad, 1984, p. 103; and from John Berger, "In Opposition to History, In Defiance of Time," *Village Voice,* October 6, 1980, p. 88.

The formulation I've sketched in this chapter has been influenced by a number of rather diverse sources. Works that helped stimulate or clarify my perspective include: Arendt 1958; Bensman and Lilienfeld 1979; Brecher 1972; Clecak 1973, 1983; deCertaux 1980; Goodwyn 1981; Habermas 1970; Hirschmann 1982; Konrad 1984; Kraditor 1981; Marris 1974; Mills 1956; Olson 1971; Pitkin 1979; Root and Branch 1975; Sennett and Cobb 1972; Wellman and Matza 1980; Waters, ed. 1970; Erikson 1968; Janeway 1981; Sallach 1972; Smith 1972.

My discussion of "liberty" and liberalism has been aided by Friedman 1962; C. B. MacPherson 1962, and Schumpeter 1942.

Lenin's views on the issues of consciousness were propounded in *What Is To Be Done* (Tucker, ed. 1975). Examples of efforts by Marxists to develop adequate conceptualizations of consciousness and action are described in Howard and Klare, eds., 1972.

2. Making Life Not History

I HAVE taken the quotations that head this chapter from the book by John P. Diggins, *The Lost Soul of American Politics* (1984), a work that was published too late for me to reflect on how its interpretation of American political thought bears on my own. The passage from Washington appears on p. 23; from Henry Adams on p. 57. and from Thoreau on p. 218.

Some key references on political participation rates include: Dreyer and Rosenbaum 1976; Jennings 1983; Robinson 1977; Smith et al. 1980; Milbrath and Joel 1977; Verba, Nie, and Kim 1978; Nie, Verba, and Pietrocek 1976; Burnham 1982. Studies of Americans' time use are summarized in Robinson 1977 and Smith et al. 1980. Data on television watching are summarized in Comstock et al. 1978.

Pioneer studies of American political consciousness that served as models for my own empirical work were Riesman, *The Lonely Crowd* (1950), and Lane, *Political Ideology* (1962).

Observations on Americans' tendency to blame themselves for unemployment and economic disadvantage may be found in Chinoy 1955; Sennett and Cobb 1972; M. Komarovsky 1940; E. W. Bakke 1940. The most important recent study of the impact of unemployment on political attitudes and behavior is K. Scholzman and S. Verba 1979.

Lipset and Schneider 1983, Brody and Sniderman 1977, and Sniderman 1981 document both the increased political alienation of Americans in the seventies and the ways in which such feelings failed to get channelled into collective political expression.

In addition to the work by Campbell et al. cited in the text, another recent survey, focused on stability and change in Americans' conceptions of their well-being, is reported in J. Veroff, E. Douvan, and R. A. Kulka 1981.

Key examples of widely influential criticism of everyday life and consciousness include: E. Fromm, *Escape from Freedom* (1941), D. Reisman, *The Lonely Crowd* (1950), H. Marcuse, *One Dimensional Man* (1964), P. Slater, *The Pursuit of Loneliness* (1970), C. Lasch, *The Culture of Narcissism* (1978), Bellah et al., *Habits of the Heart* (1985).

For recent survey data on Americans' attitudes toward work see Campbell et al. 1976 and Veroff et al. 1981. The latter find, for example, that less than 5 percent of Americans mention their work as a source of identity (p. 254).

How workers exercise informal control in the workplace is discussed in Aronowitz 1973; Brecher 1972; Garson 1977; Brecher and Costello 1976; Lipsitz 1981; Montgomery 1979; deCertaux 1980. A classic description of workers' perceptions of mobility as a framework for accommodation is Chinoy 1955.

The trade-off between work alienation and high wages and benefits is discussed in H. Swados 1957; Aronowitz 1973; O'Connor 1973; and Wellman and Matza 1981.

My discussion of identity is of course deeply indebted to the writing of Erik Erikson, formulated in *Identity Youth and Crisis* (1968), and developed in such works as *Young Man Luther* (1962) and *Gandhi's Truth* (1969). See also Keniston (1965).

James O'Connor's recent work, *Accumulation Crisis* (1984), traces the interactions and contradictions between individualistic culture and political economy in an interpretation that resonates with the one presented here. Peter Clecak (1983) has documented in detail the growing cultural pluralism of the seventies and what he calls the "democratization of personhood."

My discussion of the postwar labor-management contract is strongly indebted to James O'Connor (1973).

The argument made here about the origins of the sixties youth revolt is developed more fully in Flacks 1971a, 1971b. See Bell (1973, 1978) for examination of the social transformations and cultural conflicts that have eroded the "Protestant Ethic."

3. Making History To Make Life

THE QUOTATION from Rosa Luxemburg comes from *Rosa Luxemburg Speaks* (Waters, ed., 1970:189).

For review of recent literature on social movements, see: Wilson 1973; Oberschall 1973; Zald & McCarthy, eds., 1973; Garner 1972; Gamson 1975; Marx and Wood 1975.

My discussion of resistance movements has been influenced by Brecher 1972; Rubenstein 1970; Marris 1974; Piven and Cloward 1977; Montgomery 1979; Stiehm 1972. Certain films have helped me see the essential ingredients of the dynamics of resistance. Two particularly useful examples: *The Organizer* (Monicelli, 1965) and *Viva Zapata!* (Kazan, 1953). A little noticed case study that helped focus my understanding is provided by Fred Gardner in his book *The Unlawful Concert: An Account of the Presidio Mutiny Case* (1970). Instances in which resistance efforts among workers generated liberation consciousness are extensively documented by Brecher 1972.

The origins of the civil rights movement of the sixties is carefully traced by Aldon Morris 1984. The events and processes that led to the emergence of the women's liberation movement are discussed in Freeman 1975 and Evans 1979.

Lawrence Goodwyn is responsible for distinguishing the "democratic movement" from other forms of grassroots mobilization. See Goodwyn 1978, 1981. Many issues of the short-lived journal *democracy* can be fruitfully gleaned for discussion about the potentialities for and barriers to popular democratic movement. See, for example, Boyte 1981; Wolin 1982; Williams 1981; Bachrach 1982.

The standard works defining a social science perspective on public opinion include: Converse 1964; Lane 1962; Lipset 1981; Campbell et al. 1960; Nie, Verba, and Petrocik 1976; Hamilton 1972. Helpful interpretations of voting behavior include: Brody and Sniderman 1977; Burnham 1982; Downs 1957; Nelson 1977; S. Popkin et al. 1976; Niemi and Weisberg, eds. 1976.

4. Struggling for the Better Day

THE QUOTATION from Debs is from his famous speech at Canton, Ohio (reprinted in Debs 1948:417–433)—a speech for which he was prosecuted under the Espionage Act of 1917.

Discussion of the "end of ideology" and of Americans' relative immunity from ideological politics became a major theme in discussion of American exceptionalism in the late Fifties. See, for example, Lipset 1981, among others.

One of the best coherent statements of the conservative perspective on political action is to be found in Schumpeter's *Capitalism, Socialism and Democracy* (1942). Most of the main ideas of contemporary "neo-conservatism" can be found therein.

The literature on "American exceptionalism" is extensive. An excellent compendium of classic and contemporary formulations is Laslett and Lipset 1974. One of the most comprehensive reviews of this literature is Lipset 1977. My own interpretation, emphasizing racial and ethnic divisions in the working class as a primary factor is based on the writing of Aronowitz 1973 and Bonacich 1976.

A major recent critique of prevailing approaches to "exceptionalism" is that of Kraditor 1981. There is considerable convergence in our analyses—for example, we both place central emphasis on the space in the United States for privatized and ethnic solutions to workers' problems. For Kraditor, the existence of such space, and the preference shown by workers for the pursuit of individual liberty and sectoral interests, invalidates the entire left project and justifies her turn toward "neo-conservativism." Obviously I have drawn quite different conclusions from a rather similar interpretation of the historical record.

My understanding of labor history in the craft union era is based on the following:

Aronowitz 1973; Destler 1966; Dick 1972; Dulles 1949; Green 1980; Greenstone 1969; Harrington 1972; Kraditor 1981; Laslett 1970; Livesay 1978; Mandel 1963; Montgomery 1979; Resek 1967.

Principal sources on labor history in the industrial era include: Aronowitz 1973, 1983; Bernstein 1960; Cochran 1977; Davis 1980a,b; Green 1980; Kraus 1947; Lynd and Lynd 1974; Mann 1973; Mills 1948; Milton 1982; Panitch 1981; Peck 1963.

On the radicalism of intellectuals, the following are basic sources: Gilbert 1968; Gouldner 1979; Kadushin 1974; Kempton 1955; Langer 1984; Lasch 1965; Lipset 1963: chapter 10; Pells 1973; Rieff 1970; Swados 1966; Ware 1965; Parrington 1927; Buhle et al. 1972; Sussman 1984; O'Neill 1982. For an evaluation of the intellectual/artistic efforts of the sixties, see Dickstein 1977 and Sayres et al. 1984. On the social role of the intellectuals, see Gouldner 1979.

The following general histories of the U.S. left have been helpful: Bell 1967; Buhle 1978; Boyer and Morais 1970; Cantor 1978; Destler 1966; Dick 1972; Goldberg 1957; Green 1980; Harrington 1972; Kann 1982; Kraditor 1981; Lader 1979; Lasch 1969; Laslett and Lipset 1974; Weinstein 1975; Rubenstein 1970.

On the history of the Socialist Party, the following are key sources: Ameringer 1983; Bell 1967; Dick 1972; Ginger 1962; Green 1978; Laslett and Lipset 1974; Levin 1977; Salvatore 1982; Stave 1975; Weinstein 1969; Yorburg 1969; Swanburg 1976.

The main sources on the history of the Wobblies include: Dubofsky 1969; Foner 1965; Conlin 1969; Chaplin 1948; Haywood 1929; Kraditor 1981; Boyer and Morais 1970; Brecher 1972; Cahn 1980; Golin 1983; Kornbluh 1964.

On the history of the American Communist Party, the following are major sources: Buhle 1980; Claudin 1975; Draper 1957, 1960; Glazer 1969; Howe and Coser 1962; Isserman 1982a; 1982b; Kempton 1955; Klehr 1984; Lader 1979; Liebman 1979; Lyons 1982; Markowitz 1973; Matles and Higgins 1974; Milton 1982; Naison 1983; Richmond 1973; Shaffer 1979; Starobin 1972; Walton 1976; Waltzer 1980; Weinstein 1975; Zalburg 1979.

SNCC's origins and development are documented in Zinn 1964; Carson 1981; Forman 1972; Raines 1978; Sellers 1973; Morris 1984.

SDS' development can be traced in the following: Sale 1973; Vickers 1975; Breines 1982; Cohen and Hale 1966; Stolz 1971; Flacks 1971; Gitlin 1980; Miller 1987; Useem 1973. The personal backgrounds of the New Left activists are documented in Keniston 1968; Flacks 1971; Leibert 1971; Lipset and Altbach 1969; Sampson and Korn 1970. "Subterranean traditions" of youth are delineated by Matza 1964.

See Alinsky 1971 for a discussion of the ideological foundations of community-based radicalism. The "alternative institutions" movement of the seventies is documented in Case and Taylor 1979.

Biographical materials on left activists used in this chapter include: Aronowitz 1979; Belfrage and Aronson 1978; Buhle 1983; Cantarow 1980; Chaplin 1948; Cole 1981; Crossman 1952; Cruse 1967; Decaux 1970; Dennis 1977; Eliot 1979; Flynn 1973; Forman 1972; Gerson 1976; Ginger 1962; Gitlow 1965; Goldberg 1957; Goldman 1977; Gornick 1977; Haywood 1929; Kann 1981; Lamont 1968; Lasch 1965; Lens 1980; Lipsitz 1981; Lynd and Lynd 1974; Lyons 1982; Mandel 1963; Meeropol and Meeropol 1975; Mortimer 1972; Nelson et al. 1981; Painter 1979; Potter 1971; Richmond 1973; Salvatore 1982; Sellers 1973; Swanburg 1976; Williamson 1969; Wright 1977; Zalburg 1979.

The half-hearted attitude of the Socialist Party with respect to racial equality is documented by R. Allen 1975. The organizing efforts of radical activists in the thirties among the unemployed and among industrial workers is analyzed in Piven and Cloward 1977.

A full-scale history of the development of American anti-communism has yet to be written, but the following works, focusing largely on issues of disillusionment and repression, are helpful: Belfrage 1973; Bentley 1971; Brown 1976; Cantor 1978; Caute 1978; Cochran 1973; Crossman 1952; Cruse 1967; Donner 1980; Gitlow 1965; Goldman 1960; Goldstein 1978; Griffith and Theoharis 1974; Howe and Coser 1962; Kempton 1955; Klehr 1984; Lamont 1968; Lasch 1969; Laslett and Lipset 1974; Lessing 1962; Lipsitz 1981; Macdonald 1948; Markowitz 1973; O'Neill 1982; Packer 1962; Sigal 1962; Starobin 1972; Swanburg 1976; Theoharis 1978; Walton 1976; Weinstein 1975; Wright 1977; Navasky 1980; Schlesinger 1949; Brock 1962. Attitudes of left activists during the McCarthy era and in the aftermath of the Khruschev revelations are documented in Belfrage and Aronson 1978; Dennis 1977; Gornick 1977; Isserman 1982a, 1982b; Lader 1979; Lipsitz 1981; Meeropol and Meeropol 1975; Richmond 1973 and the documentary film *Seeing Red,* directed by Julia Reichert and Jim Klein, New Day Films, 1984. Clecak 1973 provides a detailed discussion of the work of key radical intellectuals in the fifties. The life and work of A. J. Muste is described in Robinson 1981. The "end of ideology" was a theme developed by Bell 1962 and Lipset 1981 among others. Daniel Bell's analysis of the adversary culture appears in Bell 1978.

For samples of Joe Hill's songwriting see "The Little Red Song-book" (IWW 1970). On the folk-song revival: Klein 1980; Dunaway 1981; Denisoff 1973; DeTurk and Poulin 1967; Greenway 1963. The politicization of folk-song traditions has become an international project by left artists; see for example Jara 1984.

New Deal sponsored cultural projects are documented in O'Connor and Brown 1978; O'Connor 1975; Pells 1973; Salzman and Wallenstein 1967; Swados 1966.

5. Someday We've Got to Get Organized

THE QUOTATION from Bob Dylan originally appeared on the liner notes for the album *The Times They Are A-Changin'.* See Dylan 1985:109.

My understanding of the dilemmas of left organization has been greatly aided by the following: Belfrage 1973; Bell 1967; Berger 1981; Bittner 1963; Breines 1982; Cantor 1978; Case and Taylor 1979; Clecak 1977; Crossman 1952; Dellinger 1975; Dennis 1977; Dubofsky 1969; Evans and Boyte 1982; Forman 1972; Friedland 1982; Fruchter 1971; Goodwyn 1981; Gornick 1977; Harrington 1972; Kann 1982; Lakey 1973; Lipset 1981; Michels 1959; Piven and Cloward 1977; Poulantzas 1978; Richmond 1973; Root and Branch 1975; Ross 1978; Rothstein 1972; Starobin 1972; Tucker 1975; Vickers 1975; Weinstein 1975; Williams 1981; Wright 1977; Yorburg 1969; Zald and McCarthy 1979.

Description of contemporary left activity and organization may be found in: Aronowitz 1983a, 1983b, 1983c; Boyte 1978, 1980; Capra and Spretnak 1984; Carnoy, Shearer and Rumberger 1983; Carnoy and Shearer 1980; Case and Taylor 1979; Flacks 1977, 1981; Herbers 1983; Howe 1984; Kann 1982, 1983; Piven and Cloward 1982; Wolfe 1984, Williams 1981. See Bellah et al. 1985 for a detailed critical analysis of American individualism that resonates with and enriches the perspective developed here.

6. Making History Democratic

THE QUOTATION from William Morris was cited by Sean Wilentz, in a piece memorializing Professor Herbert Gutman. (*In These Times*, August 7, 1985, p. 15).

Information about and analysis of left and movement electoral strategy can be found in: Aronowitz 1983a, 1983b, 1983c; Atlas, Dreier, and Stephens 1983; Bowles 1982; Boyte 1981; Carnoy, Shearer, and Rumberger 1983; Davis 1980a,b; Domhoff 1977; Herbers 1983; Howe 1984; Jennings 1983; Kann 1983; Piven and Cloward 1982; Wolfe 1984; Wolin 1981. Periodicals such as *The Nation, The Progressive, Social Policy, Dissent, In These Times* carry ongoing discussion of the left's electoral prospects and problems. The development of locally based left-wing politics is described in Boyte 1980; Carnoy and Shearer 1980; and Clavel 1986.

The following are some key works providing the outlines of and arguments for a new economic program grounded in "economic democracy": Alperowitz and Faux 1984; Bowles, Gordon, and Weisskopf 1983; Carnoy and Shearer 1980; Carnoy, Shearer, and Rumberger 1983; Hayden 1980; Howe 1984; Kuttner 1984.

The rise of "neo-conservatism" in the seventies is described by Steinfels 1979. The pacifist tradition is described in: Eagan 1981; Gaylin 1970; Lakey 1973; Robinson 1981; Stiehm 1972; Useem 1973; Zinn 1964; Dellinger 1975; Sibley 1963.

The following writings have contributed to the perspectives on left strategy and organization advocated here: Alinsky 1971; Arendt 1965; Aronowitz 1983b, 1983c; Atlas, Dreier, and Stephens 1983; Bachrach 1982; Bahro 1978, 1982; Bookchin 1984; Bowles 1982; Boyte and Evans 1984; Capra and Spretnak 1984; Carnoy, Shearer, and Rumberger 1983; Cohen 1982; Domhoff 1977; Eder 1982; Feher and Heller 1984; Freire 1970; Goodwyn 1981; Higgins and Apple 1983; Konrad 1984; Lummis 1982; Piccone 1980; Poulantzas 1978; Przeworski 1980; Root and Branch 1975; Stame 1984; Wolfe 1984; Wolin 1981, 1982.

The quotation that heads "A Final Note" is from Grace Paley's story "Wants" (Paley 1974:8).

References

Aaron, D. 1961. *Writers on the Left.* New York: Harcourt Brace and World.

Alinsky, Saul. 1971. *Rules for Radicals.* New York: Random House.

Alkalimat, Abdul and Don Gillis. 1983. Black political protest and the mayoral victory of Harold Washington: Chicago politics, 1983. *Radical America* 17(6): 111–27.

Allen, Robert L. 1970. *Black Awakening in Capitalist America.* Garden City, N.Y.: Anchor Books/Doubleday.

Allen, Robert. 1975. *Reluctant Reformers.* Garden City, N.Y.: Doubleday Anchor.

Alperowitz, Gar and Jeff Faux. 1984. *Rebuilding America.* New York: Pantheon.

Ameringer, Oscar. 1983. *If You Don't Weaken.* Norman: University of Oklahoma Press.

Arendt, Hannah. 1958. *The Human Condition.* Chicago: University of Chicago Press.

Arendt, Hannah. 1965. *On Revolution.* New York: Viking Compass.

Aronowitz, Stanley. 1983a. *Working Class Hero.* New York: Pilgrim Press.

Aronowitz, Stanley. 1983b. Remaking the American left. Part One: Currents in American Radicalism. *Socialist Review.* 13(1):9–54.

Aronowitz, Stanley. 1983c. Socialism and beyond: Remaking the American left, Part Two. *Socialist Review* 13(3):7–44.

Aronowitz, Stanley. 1979. The labor movement and the left in the United States. *Socialist Review.* 9(2):9–62.

Aronowitz, Stanley. 1973. *False Promises: The Shaping of American Working Class Consciousness.* New York: McGraw-Hill.

Ash, Roberta. 1972. *Social Movements in America.* Chicago: Markham.

Atlas, J., P. Dreier, and J. Stephens. 1983. Progressive politics in 1984. *The Nation* 237(3):65–70.

Avorn, Jerry et al. 1968. *Up Against the Ivy Wall: A History of the Columbia Crisis.* New York: Atheneum.

Bachrach, Peter. 1982. Class struggle and democracy. Fall: *democracy* 2(4):29–42.

Bahro, Rudolf. 1982. *Socialism and Survival.* London: Heretic Books.

Bahro, Rudolf. 1978. *The Alternative in Eastern Europe.* London: Verso.

Bakke, E. W. 1940. *The Unemployed Worker.* New Haven: Yale University Press.

Baxendall, Rosalyn. 1975. Elizabeth Gurley Flynn: The early years. *Radical America* 8(6):97–115.

Beardslee, W. R. 1983. Commitment and endurance: Common themes in the life histories of civil rights workers who stayed. *American Journal of Orthopsychiatry* 53(1):34–41.

Belfrage, Cedric. 1973. *The American Inquisition. 1945–1960,* Indianapolis: Bobbs-Merrill.

Belfrage, Cedric and James Aronson. 1978. *Something to Guard.* New York: Columbia University Press.

Bell, Daniel. 1978. *The Cultural Contradictions of Capitalism.* New York: Basic Books.

Bell, Daniel. 1973. *The Coming of Post-Industrial Society.* New York: Basic Books.

Bell, Daniel. 1967. *Marxian Socialism in the United States.* Princeton: Princeton University Press.

Bell, Daniel. 1962. *The End of Ideology.* New York: Collier Books.

Bellah, R. et al. 1985. *Habits of the Heart: Individualism and Commitment in American Life.* Berkeley: University of California Press.

Bensman, Joseph and R. Lilienfeld. 1979. *Between Public and Private.* New York: Free Press.

Bentley, Eric, ed. 1971. *Thirty Years of Treason.* New York: Viking.

Berger, Bennett. 1981. *The Survival of a Counterculture.* Berkeley: University of California Press.

Berk, Sarah F. 1985. *The Gender Factory.* New York: Plenum Press.

Bernstein, Irving. 1960. *The Lean Years.* Boston: Houghton Mifflin.

Bittner, Egon. 1963. Radicalism and the organization of radical movements. *American Sociological Review* 28(6):928–40.

Bonacich, Edna. 1976. Advanced capitalism and black-white relations in the U.S.: A split labor market interpretation. *American Sociological Review* 41:34–51.

Bookchin, Murray. 1984. On 'Remaking the American Left': A comment. *Socialist Review* 14(1):113–16.

Bowles, Samuel. 1982. The post-Keynesian capital-labor stalemate. *Socialist Review* 12(5):45–74.

Bowles, Sam, D. Gordon, and Thomas Weisskopf. 1983. *Beyond the Wasteland.* Garden City, N.Y.: Anchor Press/Doubleday.

Boyer, Richard O. and Herbert M. Morais. 1970. *Labor's Untold Story.* New York: United Electrical Workers.

Boyte, Harry. 1981. Populism and the left. *democracy* 1(2):53–67.

Boyte, Harry C. 1980. *The Backyard Revolution.* Philadelphia: Temple University Press.

Boyte, Harry. 1978. Building the democratic movement: Prospects for a socialist renaissance. *Socialist Review* 8(4–5):17–41.

Boyte, Harry and Sara M. Evans. 1984. Strategies in search of America: Cultural radicalism, populism, and democratic culture. *Socialist Review* 14(3):73–102.

Brecher, Jeremy. 1972. *Strike!* San Francisco: Straight Arrow.

Brecher, J. and T. Costello. 1976. *Common Sense for Hard Times.* New York: Two Continents Publishing.

Breines, Wini. 1982. *Community and Organization in the New Left, 1962–68: The Great Refusal.* South Hadley, Mass. Bergin and Garvey.

Brock, Charles. 1962. *Americans for Democratic Action.* Washington: Public Affairs Press.

Brody, David. 1969. *Steelworkers in America: The Nonunion Era.* New York: Harper & Row.

Brody, R. A. and P. M. Sniderman. 1977. From life space to polling place: The relevance of personal concerns for voting behavior. *British Journal of Political Science* (July), 7:337–60.

Brown, Richard Maxwell. 1976. The history of vigilantism in America. In H. J. Rosenbaum and P. Sederberg, eds., *Vigilante Politics*, pp. 79–109. Philadelphia: University of Pennsylvania Press.

Buhle, Paul. 1983. Paul Novick: A radical life. *Radical America* 17(5):74–75.

Buhle, Paul. 1980. Jews and American communism: The cultural question. *Radical History Review* (Spring), 23:9–36.

Buhle, Paul, ed. 1978. The Origins of left culture in the US: 1880–1940. *Cultural Correspondence*. Nos. 6–7.

Buhle, Paul, J. Cortez, P. Lamantia, N. Peters, F. Rosemont, and P. Rosemont, eds. 1972. *Free Spirit: Annals of the Insurgent Imagination*, San Francisco: City Lights.

Burnham, Walter Dean. 1982. *The Current Crisis in American Politics*. New York: Oxford.

Cahn, William. 1980. *Lawrence 1912: The Bread and Roses Strike*. New York: Pilgrim Press.

Campbell, Angus, P. Converse, W. Miller, and D. Stokes. 1960. *The American Voter*. New York: Wiley.

Campbell, Angus, P. Converse, and W. Rodgers. 1976. *The Quality of American Life*. New York: Russell Sage.

Cantarow, Ellen. 1980. *Moving the Mountain*. Old Westbury, N.Y. Feminist Press.

Cantor, Milton. 1978. *The Divided Left*. New York: Hill and Wang.

Cantril, Albert H. and Charles Roll, Jr. 1971. *The Hopes and Fears of the American People*. New York: Universe Books.

Capra, Fritjof and Charlene Spretnak. 1984. *Green Politics*. New York: Dutton.

Carnoy, Martin, D. Shearer, and R. Rumberger. 1983. *A New Social Contract*. New York: Harper & Row.

Carnoy, Martin and Derek Shearer. 1980. *Economic Democracy*. Armonk. N.Y.: M. E. Sharpe.

Carson, Clayborne. 1981. *In Struggle*. Cambridge: Harvard University Press.

Case, John and Rosemary Taylor, eds. 1979. *Co-ops, Communes and Collectives*, New York: Pantheon.

Caute, David, 1978. *The Great Fear*. New York: Simon & Schuster.

Chaplin, Ralph. 1948. *Wobbly*. Chicago: University of Chicago Press.

Childs, John Brown. 1984. Afro-American intellectuals and the people's culture. *Theory and Society* 13(1):69–90.

Chinoy, Eli. 1955. *Automobile Workers and the American Dream*. Garden City, N.Y.: Doubleday.

Clarke, John et al., eds. 1979. *Working Class Culture*. London: Hutchinson.

Claudin, Fernando, 1975. *The Communist Movement: From Comintern to Cominform*. New York: Monthly Review Press.

Clavel, Pierre. 1986. *The Progressive City*. New Brunswick, N.J.: Rutgers University Press.

Clecak, Peter. 1983. *America's Quest for the Ideal Self*. New York: Oxford University Press.

Clecak, Peter. 1973. *Radical Paradoxes*. New York: Harper & Row.

Cochran, Bert. 1977. *Labor and Communism:, The Conflict That Shaped American Unions*. Princeton: Princeton University Press.

Cochran, Bert. 1973. *Harry Truman and the Crisis Presidency*. New York: Funk & Wagnalls.

Cockburn, Alex and Robin Blackburn, eds. 1969. *Student Power*. Middlesex, Eng.: Penguin Books.

Cohen, Jean. 1982. Between crisis management and social movements: The place of institutional reforms. *Telos* 15(2):21–40.

Cohen, Mitchell and Dennis Hale, eds. 1966. *The New Student Left*. Boston: Beacon Press.

Cole, Lester. 1981. *Hollywood Red*. Palo Alto, Calif.: Ramparts Press.

Comstock, George, S. Chaffee, N. Katzman, M. McCombs, and D. Roberts. 1978. *Television and Human Behavior*. New York: Columbia University Press.

Conlin, Joseph R. 1969. *Big Bill Haywood and the Radical Union Movement*. Syracuse: Syracuse University Press.

Converse, Philip. 1964. The nature of belief systems in mass publics. In D. Apter, ed., *Ideology and Discontent*, pp. 206–61. New York: Free Press.

Critcher, Charles. 1979. Sociology, cultural studies and the post-war working class. In J. Clarke, ed., *Working Class Culture*, pp. 13–40. London: Hutchinson.

Crossman, Richard, ed. 1952. *The God That Failed*. New York: Bantam Books.

Cruse, Harold. 1967. *The Crisis of the Negro Intellectual*. New York: William Morrow.

Davis, Mike. 1980a. Why the U.S. working class is different. *New Left Review* 123:3–44.

Davis, Mike. 1980b. The barren marriage of American labour and the Democratic Party. *New Left Review* 124:43–84.

Debs, Eugene Victor. 1948. *Writings and Speeches*. New York: Hermitage Press.

DeCaux, Len. 1970. *Labor Radical*. Boston: Beacon Press.

DeCertaux, Michel. 1980. On the oppositional practices of everyday life. *Social Text* (Fall):313–43.

Dellinger, David. 1975. *More Power Than We Know*. Garden City, N.Y.: Anchor Press/Doubleday.

Denisoff, R. Serge. 1973. *Great Day Coming*. Baltimore: Penguin Books.

Dennis, Peggy. 1977. *The Autobiography of an American Communist*. Westport, Conn.: Lawrence Hill.

Derber, Charles. 1979. *The Pursuit of Attention*. Cambridge, Mass.: Schenkman.

Destler, Chester M. 1966. *American Radicalism, 1865–1901*. Chicago: Quadrangle Books.

DeTurk, David and A. Poulin, Jr., eds. 1967. *The American Folk Scene: Dimensions of the Folk-Song Revival*. New York: Dell.

Dick, William M. 1972. *Labor and Socialism in America*. Port Washington, N.Y.: Kennikat Press.

Dickstein, Morris. 1977. *Gates of Eden*. New York: Basic Books.

Diggins, John P. 1984. *The Lost Soul of American Politics*. New York: Basic Books.

Domhoff, G. William. 1977. Why socialists should be Democrats. *Socialist Review* 7(1):25–36.

Donner, Frank. 1980. *The Age of Surveillance*. New York: Knopf.

Downs, Anthony. 1957. An economic theory of political action in a democracy. *Journal of Political Economy* 65:135–50.

Draper, Theodore. 1960. *American Communism and Soviet Russia*. New York: Viking.

Draper, Theodore. 1957. *The Roots of American Communism*. New York: Viking.

Dreyer, Edward and Walter Rosenbaum, eds. 1976. *Political Opinion and Behavior*. North Scituate, Mass.: Duxbury Press.
Dubofsky, Melvin. 1969. *We Shall Be All*. New York: Quadrangle.
Dulles, Foster Rhea. 1949. *Labor in America*. New York: Crowell.
Dunaway, David. 1981. *How Can I Keep From Singing*. New York: McGraw-Hill.
Dylan, Bob. 1985. *Lyrics. 1962–1985*. New York: Knopf.
Eagan, Eileen. 1981. *Class, Culture, and the Classroom; The Student Peace Movement of the 1930s*. Philadelphia: Temple University Press.
Eder, Klaus. 1982. A new social movement? *Telos* 15(2):5–20.
Eliot, Marc. 1979. *Death of a Rebel*. Garden City, N.Y.: Anchor Press/Doubleday.
Erikson, Erik H. 1968. *Identity Youth and Crisis*. New York: W. W. Norton.
Erikson, Erik. 1969. *Gandhi's Truth*. New York: W. W. Norton.
Erikson, Erik. 1962. *Young Man Luther*. New York: W. W. Norton.
Evans, Sara. 1979. *Personal Politics*. New York: Knopf.
Evans, Sara M. and H. C. Boyte. 1982. Schools for action: Radical uses of social space. *democracy* 2(4):55–65.
Feher, Ferenc and Agnes Heller. 1984. From red to green. *Telos* 17(1):35–44.
Finkel, P. David. 1984. *The Radical Vision of Saul Alinsky*. New York: Paulist Press.
Flacks, Dick. 1979. Socialists as socializers, notes on the purpose of organization. *Socialist Review* 9(1):102–13.
Flacks, Dick. 1977. Notes on the Hayden campaign. *Socialist Review* 7(1):59–78.
Flacks, Richard. 1971a. *Youth and Social Change*. Chicago: Rand McNally.
Flacks, Richard. 1971b. Revolt of the young intelligentsia: Revolutionary consciousness in a post-scarcity America. In R. Aya and N. Miller, *The New American Revolution*, pp. 223–63. New York: Free Press.
Flacks, Richard. 1981. Populists in search of the people. *Working Papers for a New Society* 8(1):26–37.
Flanigan, William and Nancy Zingale. 1979. *Political Behavior of the American Electorate*. 4th ed. Boston: Allyn and Bacon.
Flynn, Elizabeth Gurley. 1973. *Rebel Girl*. New York: International Publishers.
Foner, Philip S. 1965. *History of the Labor Movement in the United States. Vol. 4: The Industrial Workers of the World, 1905–1917*. New York: International Publishers.
Foner, Philip, ed. 1947. *Jack London: American Rebel*. New York:Citadel.
Forman, James. 1972. *The Making of Black Revolutionaries*. New York: Macmillan.
Freeman, Jo. 1975. *The Politics of Women's Liberation*. New York: David McKay.
Freire, Paolo. 1970. *Cultural Action for Freedom*. Cambridge, Mass.: Harvard Education Review.
Friedan, Betty. 1963. *The Feminine Mystique*. New York: W. W. Norton.
Friedland, William. 1982. *Revolutionary Theory*. Totawa, N.J.: Allanheld, Osmun.
Friedman, Milton. 1962. *Capitalism and Human Freedom*. Chicago: University of Chicago Press.
Fromm, Erich. 1941. *Escape from Freedom*. New York: Rinehart.
Fruchter, N. 1971. Games in the arena: Movement propaganda and the culture of the spectacle. *Liberation* 16(3):4–17.
Gamson, William A. 1975. *The Strategy of Social Protest*. Homewood, Ill.: Dorsey Press.
Gardner, Fred. 1970. *The Unlawful Concert: An Account of the Presidio Mutiny Case*. New York: Viking Press.

Garner, Roberta Ash. 1972. *Social Movements in America*. Chicago: Rand McNally.
Garson, Barbara. 1977. *All the Live-Long Day*. New York: Penguin.
Gaylin, Willard. 1970. *In the Service of their Country: War Resisters in Prison*. New York: Viking Press.
Gerson, Simon W. 1976. *Pete*. New York: International Publishers.
Gilbert, James. 1968. *Writers and Partisans*. New York: Wiley.
Ginger, Ray. 1962. *Eugene Debs: A Biography*. New York: Collier Books.
Gitlin, Todd. 1980. *The Whole World Is Watching*. Berkeley: University of California Press.
Gitlow, Benjamin. 1965. *The Whole of Their Lives*. Belmont, Mass.: Western Islands.
Glazer, Nathan. 1969. *The Social Basis of American Communism*. New York: Harcourt Brace.
Goffman, Erving. 1961. *Asylums*. Chicago: Aldine.
Goldberg, Harvey, ed. 1957. *American Radicals: Some Problems and Personalities*. New York: Monthly Review Press.
Goldman, Emma. 1977. *Living My Life*. New York: New American Library.
Goldman, Eric F. 1960. *The Crucial Decade—and After: America, 1945–1960*. New York: Vintage.
Goldstein, Robert Justin. 1978. *Political Repression in Modern America*. Cambridge, Mass.: Schenkman.
Golin, Steve. 1983. The Paterson pageant: Success or failure? *Socialist Review* 13(3):45–80.
Goodwyn, Lawrence. 1981. Organizing democracy: The limits of theory and practice. *democracy* 1(1):41–60.
Goodwyn, Lawrence. 1978. *The Populist Moment*. New York: Oxford University Press.
Gornick, Vivian. 1977. *The Romance of American Communism*. New York: Basic Books.
Gorz, Andre. 1981. Nine theses for a future left. *Telos* 14(2):91–97.
Gouldner, Alvin W. 1979. *The Future of Intellectuals and the Rise of the New Class*. New York: Oxford University Press.
Green, James R. 1980. *The World of the Worker*. New York: Hill and Wang.
Green, James R. 1978. *Grass-Roots Socialism: Radical Movements in the Southwest, 1895–1943*. Baton Rouge: Louisiana State University Press.
Greenstone, J. David. 1969. *Labor in American Politics*. New York: Vintage Books.
Greenway, John. 1963. *American Folksongs of Protest*. New York: A. S. Barnes.
Griffith, Robert and Athan Theoharis, eds. 1974. *The Specter*. New York: New Viewpoints/Franklin Watts.
Habermas, Jurgen. 1970. *Toward a Rational Society*. Boston: Beacon Press.
Hamilton, Richard. 1972. *Class and Politics in the United States*. New York: Wiley.
Harrington, Michael. 1972. *Socialism*. New York: Bantam Books.
Hayden, Tom. 1980. *The American Future: New Visions Beyond Old Frontiers*. Boston: South End Press.
Haywood, William. 1929. *Bill Haywood's Book*. New York: International Publishers.
Heirich, Max. 1971. *The Spiral of Conflict: Berkeley*. New York: Columbia University Press.
Herbers, John. 1983. Grass-roots groups go national. *New York Times Magazine*, September 4.

Higgins, Winton and Nixon Apple. 1983. How limited is reformism? *Theory and Society* 12(5):603–630.

Hirschmann, Albert O. 1982. *Shifting Involvements*. Princeton: Princeton University Press.

Hoffer, Eric. 1951. *The True Believer*. New York: New American Library.

Hofstadter, Richard. 1960. *The Age of Reform*. New York: Vintage Books.

Horowitz, Irving L. and William H. Friedland. 1971. *The Knowledge Factory*, Chicago: Aldine

Howard, Dick and Karl Ware. 1972. *The Unknown Dimension: European Marxism Since Lenin*. New York: Basic Books.

Howe, Irving, ed. 1984. *Alternatives, Proposals for America from the Democratic Left*. New York: Pantheon.

Howe, Irving and Lewis Coser. 1962. *The American Communist Party*. New York: Praeger.

Hunt, Alan, ed. 1977. *Class and Class Structure*. London: Lawrence and Wishart.

Isserman, Maurice. 1982a. *Which Side Were You On? The American Communist Party During the Second World War*. Middletown, Ct.: Wesleyan University Press.

Isserman, Maurice. 1982b. The half-swept house: American communism in 1956. *Socialist Review* 12(1):71–101.

IWW. 1970. *Songs of the Workers: To Fan the Flames of Discontent*. Chicago: Industrial Workers of the World.

Jacobs, Harold, ed. 1970. *Weatherman*. San Francisco: Ramparts Press.

Janeway, Elizabeth. 1981. *Powers of the Weak*. New York: Morrow.

Jara, Joan. 1984. *An Unfinished Song: The Life of Victor Jara*. New York: Ticknor and Fields.

Jenkins, Craig. 1983. Resource Mobilization Theory and the Study of Social Movements. *Annual Review of Sociology* 9:527–53.

Jennings, James. 1983. America's new urban politics: Black electoralism, black activism. *Radical America* 17(6):35–40.

Kadushin, Charles. 1974. *The American Intellectual Elite*. Boston: Little Brown.

Kann, Mark E. 1986. *Middle Class Radicalism in Santa Monica*. Philadelphia: Temple University Press.

Kann, Mark E. 1983. Radicals in power: Lessons from Santa Monica. *Socialist Review* 13(3):81–102.

Kann, Mark E. 1982. *The American Left: Failures and Fortunes*. New York: Praeger.

Kann, Kenneth. 1981. *Joe Rapaport: The Life of a Jewish Radical*. Philadelphia: Temple University Press.

Kasinsky, Renee. 1978. *Refugees from Militarism*. Totowa, N.J.: Littlefield, Adams.

Kempton, Murray. 1955. *Part of Our Time: Some Monuments and Ruins of the Thirties*. New York:Delta.

Keniston, Kenneth. 1965. *The Uncommitted*. New York: Harcourt Brace Jovanovich.

Keniston, Kenneth. 1968. *Young Radicals*. New York: Harcourt Brace Jovanovich.

Klehr, Harvey. 1984. *The Heyday of American Communism*. New York: Basic Books.

Klein, Joe. 1980. *Woody Guthrie: A Life*. New York: Knopf.

Komarovsky, Mirra. 1940. *The Unemployed Man and His Family*. New York: Dryden Press.

Konrad, George. 1984. *Anti-politics*. New York: Harcourt Brace Jovanovich.

Kornbluh, Joyce. 1964. *Rebel Voices: An IWW Anthology.* Ann Arbor: University of Michigan Press.
Kraditor, Aileen. 1981. *The Radical Persuasion: 1890–1917.* Baton Rouge: Louisiana State University Press.
Kraus, Henry. 1947. *The Many and the Few.* Los Angeles: Plantin Press.
Kroes, Rob. 1975. *Soldiers and Students.* London: Routledge and Kegan Paul.
Kuczynski, Jurgen. 1967. *The Rise of the Working Class.* New York: McGraw-Hill.
Kuttner, Robert. 1984. *The Economic Illusion: False Choices Between Prosperity and Social Justice.* Boston: Houghton Mifflin.
Lader, Lawrence. 1979. *Power on the Left.* New York: W. W. Norton.
Lakey, George. 1973. *Strategy for a Living Revolution.* San Francisco: W. H. Freeman.
Lamont, Corliss, ed. 1968. *The Trial of Elizabeth Gurley Flynn by the American Civil Liberties Union.* New York: Monthly Review Press.
Lane, Robert. 1962. *Political Ideology: Why the American Common Man Believes What He Does.* New York: Free Press.
Langer, Elinor. 1984. *Josephine Herbst.* Boston: Little Brown.
Lasch, Christopher. 1978. *The Culture of Narcissism.* New York: W. W. Norton.
Lasch, Christopher. 1969. *The Agony of the American Left.* New York: Vintage.
Lasch, Christopher. 1965. *The New Radicalism in America [1889–1963].* New York: Vintage.
Laslett, John. 1970. *Labor and the Left.* New York: Basic Books.
Laslett, John M. and S. M. Lipset, eds. 1974. *Failure of a Dream?* New York: Anchor Press.
Lens, Sidney. 1980. *Unrepentant Radical.* Boston: Beacon Press.
Lessing, Doris. 1962. *The Golden Notebook.* New York: Simon & Schuster.
Levin, Nora. 1977. *While Messiah Tarried: Jewish Socialist Movements 1871–1917.* New York: Schocken Books.
Levinson, Andrew. 1974. *The Working-Class Majority.* New York: Penguin Books.
Liebert, Robert. 1971. *Radical and Militant Youth.* New York: Praeger.
Liebman, Arthur. 1979. *Jews and the Left.* New York: John Wiley.
Lipset, S. M. 1981. *Political Man.* Expanded edition. Baltimore: John Hopkins University Press.
Lipset, S. M. 1977. Why no socialism in the United States. In S. Bialer, ed., *Sources of Contemporary Radicalism,* pp. 31–150. Boulder, Col.: Westview Press.
Lipset, Seymour M. and Philip G. Altbach. 1969. *Students in Revolt.* Boston: Houghton Mifflin.
Lipset, Seymour M. and William Schneider. 1983. *The Confidence Gap.* New York: Free Press.
Lipsitz, George. 1981. *Class and Culture in Cold War America.* New York: Praeger.
Lipsitz, Lewis. 1970. On political belief: The grievances of the poor. In P. Green and S. Levinson, eds. *Power and Community,* pp. 142–72. New York: Vintage.
Livesay, Harold. 1978. *Samuel Gompers and Organized Labor in America.* Boston: Little Brown.
Lummis, Charles Douglas. 1982. The radicalism of democracy. *democracy* 2(4): 9–16.

Lynd, Alice and Staughton Lynd. 1974. *Rank and File.* Boston: Beacon Press.
Lyons, Paul. 1982. *Philadelphia Communists. 1936–1956.* Philadelphia: Temple University Press.
Macdonald, Dwight. 1948. *Henry Wallace: The Man and the Myth.* New York: Vanguard Press.
MacPherson, C. B. 1962. *The Political Theory of Possessive Individualism.* Oxford: Clarendon Press.
Mandel, Bernard. 1963. *Samuel Gompers.* Yellow Springs, Ohio: Antioch Press.
Mann, Michael. 1973. *Consciousness and Action Among the Western Working Class.* London: Macmillan.
Mannheim, Karl. 1940. *Man and Society in an Age of Reconstruction.* New York: Harcourt, Brace and World.
Marcuse, Herbert. 1964. *One Dimensional Man.* Boston: Beacon Press.
Markowitz, Norman. 1973. *The Rise and Fall of the People's Century.* New York: Free Press.
Marris, Peter. 1974. *Loss and Change.* New York: Pantheon.
Marx, G. T. and J. Wood. 1975. Strands of theory and research in collective behavior. *Annual Review of Sociology* 1:363–428.
Marx, Karl and Frederick Engels. 1970. *The German Ideology.* New York: International Publishers.
Matles, James and James Higgins. 1974. *Them and Us; Struggles of a Rank-and-File Union,* Englewood Cliffs, N.J.: Prentice-Hall.
Matza, David. 1964. Position and behavior patterns of youth. In R. Faris, ed., *Handbook of Modern Sociology,* pp. 191–216. Chicago: Rand McNally.
McAuliffe, Mary Sperling. 1978. *Crisis on the Left: Cold War Politics and American Liberals, 1947–1954.* Amherst: University of Massachusetts Press.
McPhail, C. and R. Wohlstein. 1983. Individual and collective behavior within gatherings, demonstrations, and riots. *Annual Review of Sociology* 9:579–596.
Meeropol, Robert and Michael Meeropol. 1975. *We Are Your Sons.* Boston: Houghton Mifflin.
Michels, Robert. 1959. *Political Parties.* New York: Dover.
Milbrath, L. and M. L. Yoel. 1977. *Political Participation.* 2d ed. Chicago: Rand McNally.
Miles, Michael W. 1971. *The Radical Probe: The Logic of Student Rebellion.* New York: Atheneum.
Miller, James. 1987. *"Democracy Is in the Streets": From Port Huron to the Siege of Chicago,* New York: Simon & Schuster.
Mills, C. Wright. 1956. *The Power Elite.* New York: Oxford University Press.
Mills, C. Wright. 1948. *The New Men of Power.* New York: Harcourt Brace.
Milton, David. 1982. *The Politics of U.S. Labor.* New York: Monthly Review Press.
Montgomery, David. 1980. Interview. *Radical History Review* (Spring), 23:37–53.
Montgomery, David. 1979. *Workers' Control in America.* Cambridge: Cambridge University Press.
Morris, Aldon. 1984. *Origins of the Civil Rights Movement.* New York: Free Press.
Mortimer, Wyndham. 1972. *Organize! My Life as a Union Man.* Boston: Beacon Press.
Naison, Mark. 1983. *Communists in Harlem During the Depression.* Urbana: University of Illinois Press.
Navasky, Victor. 1980. *Naming Names.* New York: Viking Press.

Nelson, Jon S. 1977. The ideological connection. *Theory and Society* 4(3):421–48.
Nelson, S., J. Barrett, and Rob Ruck. 1981. *Steve Nelson, American Radical.* Pittsburgh: University of Pittsburgh Press.
Nie, N., S. Verba, and J. R. Petrocik. 1976. *The Changing American Voter.* Cambridge: Harvard University Press.
Niemi, R. G. and H. F. Weisberg, eds. 1976, *Controversies in American Voting Behavior.* San Francisco: W. H. Freeman.
O'Connor, F. and L. Brown. 1978. *Free, Adult, Uncensored: The Living History of the Federal Theater Project.* Washington, D.C.: New Republic Books.
O'Connor, F. V., ed. 1975. *Art for the Millions.* Boston: New York Graphic Society.
O'Connor, James. 1984. *Accumulation Crisis.* New York: Basil Blackwell.
O'Connor, James. 1973. *The Fiscal Crisis of the State.* New York: St. Martin's.
O'Neill, William. 1982. *A Better World.* New York: Simon & Schuster.
Oberschall, Anthony. 1973. *Social Conflict and Social Movements.* Englewood Cliffs, N.J.: Prentice-Hall.
Olson, Mancur. 1971. *The Logic of Collective Action.* Cambridge: Harvard University Press.
Packer, Herbert. 1962. *Ex-Communist Witnesses.* Stanford: Stanford University Press.
Painter, Nell Irvin, 1979. *The Narrative of Hosea Hudson. His Life as a Negro Communist in the South.* Cambridge: Harvard University Press.
Paley, Grace. 1974. *Enormous Changes at the Last Minute.* New York: Farrar, Straus, Giroux.
Panitch, Leo. 1981. Trade unions and the state. *New Left Review* 125:21–42.
Parrington, V. L. 1927. *Maincurrents in American Thought.* New York: Harcourt Brace.
Peck, Sidney M. 1963. *The Rank-and-File Leader.* New Haven: College and University Press.
Pells, Richard H. 1973. *Radical Visions and American Dreams: Culture and Social Thought in the Depression Years.* New York: Harper & Row.
Piccone, Paul. 1980. Why did the left collapse? *Telos* 13(4):92–96.
Pinckney, Alphonso. 1968. *The Committed.* New Haven: College and University Press.
Pitkin, Hanna. 1979. Justice: On Relating Public and Private. MS.
Pitkin, Hanna F. and Sara M. Schumer. 1982. On participation. *democracy* 2(4): 43–54.
Piven, Frances Fox and Richard Cloward. 1977. *Poor People's Movements.* New York: Pantheon.
Piven, Frances F. and Richard Cloward. 1971, *Regulating the Poor.* New York: Vintage.
Piven, Frances F. and Richard A. Cloward. 1982. *The New Class War.* New York: Pantheon.
Popkin, S. et al. 1976. What have you done for me lately? Toward an investment theory of voting). *American Political Science Review* 70:779–805.
Potter, Paul. 1971. *A Name for Ourselves.* Boston: Little Brown.
Poulantzas, Nicos. 1978. Toward a democratic socialism. *New Left Review* 109: 71–87.
Przeworski, Adam. 1980. Social democracy as a historical phenomenon. *New Left Review* 122:27–58.

Quin, Mike. 1949. *The Big Strike.* New York: International Publishers.

Raines, Howell. 1978. *My Soul Is Rested.* New York: Bantam Books.

Reinarem, Craig. 1987. *American States of Mind.* New Haven: Yale University Press.

Resek, Carl, ed. 1967. *The Progressives.* Indianapolis: Bobbs-Merrill.

Richmond, Al. 1973. *A Long View from the Left.* Boston: Houghton Mifflin.

Rieff, Philip, ed. 1970. *On Intellectuals.* Garden City, N.Y.: Anchor Books/Doubleday.

Riesman, David, N. Glazer, and R. Denney. 1950. *The Lonely Crowd:. A Study of Changing American Character.* New Haven: Yale University Press.

Robinson, JoAnn. 1981. *Abraham Went Out: A Biography of A. J. Muste.* Philadelphia: Temple University Press.

Robinson, John P. 1977. *How Americans Use Time.* New York: Praeger.

Rogin, Michael. 1970. Nonpartisanship and the group interest. In P. Green, and S. Levinson, eds. *Power and Community,* pp. 112–41. New York: Vintage.

Root and Branch, ed. 1975. *Root and Branch: The Rise of the Workers' Movements,* Greenwich, Conn.: Fawcett.

Rootes, Christopher A. 1980. Student radicalism and the capitalist state. *Theory and Society* 9(3):473–502.

Rosenstone, R. 1975. *Romantic Revolutionary: A Biography of John Reed.* New York: Knopf.

Ross, Robert J. 1978. Primary groups in social movements: A memoir and interpretation. *Journal of Voluntary Action Research* 6:139–52.

Rothstein, Richard. 1972. Representative democracy in SDS. *Liberation* 16(9): 10–19.

Rubenstein, Richard E. 1970. *Rebels in Eden.* Boston: Little Brown.

Sale, Kirkpatrick. 1973. *SDS.* New York: Random House.

Sallach, David L. 1972. Class consciousness and the everyday world in the work of Marx and Schutz. MS.

Salvatore, Nick. 1982. *Eugene V. Debs:. Citizen and Socialist.* Urbana: University of Illinois Press.

Salzman, Jack and Barry Wallenstein. 1967. *Years of Protest.* New York: Pegasus Books.

Sampson, Edward and Harold Korn, eds. 1970. *Student Activism and Protest.* San Francisco: Jossey-Bass.

Sayres, S., A. Stephanson, S. Aronowitz, and F. Jamison. 1984. *The Sixties Without Apology.* Minneapolis: University of Minnesota Press.

Schaar, John. 1970. Legitimacy in the modern state. In P. Green and S. Levinson, eds. *Power and Community,* pp. 276–327.

Schlesinger, Arthur. 1949. *The Vital Center.* Boston: Houghton Mifflin.

Schlozman, Kay and Sidney Verba. 1979. *Injury to Insult.* Cambridge: Harvard University Press.

Schumpeter, Joseph. 1942. *Capitalism, Socialism and Democracy,* New York: Harper.

Sellers, Cleveland. 1973. *The River of No Return.* New York: William Morrow.

Sennett, Richard. 1977. *The Fall of Public Man.* New York: Knopf.

Sennett, Richard. 1970. *The Uses of Disorder:. Personal Identity and City Life.* New York: Vintage Books.

Sennett, Richard and Jonathan Cobb. 1972. *The Hidden Injuries of Class.* New York: Knopf.

Shaffer, Robert. 1979. Women and the Communist Party, USA: 1930–1940. *Socialist Review* 9(3):73–118.
Sibley, Mulford, ed. 1963. *The Quiet Battle: Writings on the Theory and Practice of Non-Violent Resistance.* Boston: Beacon Press.
Sigal, Clancy. 1962. *Going Away.* Boston: Houghton Mifflin.
Sklare, Marshall and Joseph Greenblum. 1967. *Jewish Identity on the Suburban Frontier.* New York: Basic Books.
Slater, Philip, 1970, *The Pursuit of Loneliness,* Boston: Beacon Press.
Smith, David Horton et al. 1980. *Participation in Social and Political Activities.* San Francisco: Jossey-Bass.
Smith, Dorothy. 1972. The ideological practice of sociology. MS. University of British Columbia.
Sniderman, Paul M. 1981. *A Question of Loyalty.* Berkeley: University of California Press.
Stame, Federico. 1984. The crisis of the left and new social identities. *Telos* 17(2): 3–14.
Starobin, Joseph. 1972. *American Communism in Crisis, 1943–1957.* Berkeley: University of California Press.
Stave, Bruce M., ed. 1975. *Socialism and the Cities.* Port Washington, N.Y.: Kennikat Press.
Steinfels, Peter. 1979. *The Neo-Conservatives.* New York: Simon & Schuster.
Stephens. John, 1980. *The Transition from Capitalism to Socialism.* Atlantic Highlands, N.J.: Humanities Press.
Stiehm, Judith. 1972. *Nonviolent Power.* Lexington, Mass.: D. C. Heath.
Stolz, Matthew F. 1971. *Politics of the New Left.* Beverly Hills, Calif.: Glencoe Press.
Sussman, Warren. 1984. *Culture as History.* New York: Pantheon.
Swados, Harvey, ed. 1966. *The American Writer and the Great Depression.* Indianapolis: Bobbs-Merrill.
Swados, Harvey. 1957. *A Radical's America.* Boston: Little Brown.
Swanburg, W. A. 1976. *Norman Thomas: The Last Idealist.* New York: Scribner's.
Theoharis, Athan. 1978. *Spying on Americans.* Philadelphia: Temple University Press.
Tucker, Robert, ed. 1975. *The Lenin Anthology.* New York: Norton.
Useem, Michael. 1973. *Conscription, Protest, and Social Conflict.* New York: John Wiley.
Verba, S., N. Nie, and Jae-On Kim. 1978. *Participation and Political Equality, A Seven-Nation Comparison.* Cambridge: Cambridge University Press.
Veroff, J., E. Douvan, and R. A. Kulka. 1981. *The Inner American: A Self-Portrait from 1957–76.* New York: Basic Books.
Vickers, George R. 1975. *The Formation of the New Left.* Lexington, Mass.: Lexington Books.
Walker, Pat, ed. 1979. *Between Labor and Capital.* Boston: South End Press.
Wallerstein, I. and P. Starr. 1971. *The University Crisis Reader. Volumes One and Two.* New York: Random House.
Walton, Richard. 1976. *Henry Wallace, Harry Truman, and the Cold War.* New York: Viking.
Waltzer, Kenneth. 1980, The party and the polling place: American Communism and an American labor party in the 1930s. *Radical History Review* 23:104–36.
Ware, Caroline F. 1965. *Greenwich Village. 1920–1930.* New York: Harper & Row.
Waters, Mary-Alice, ed. 1970. *Rosa Luxemburg Speaks.* New York: Pathfinder Press.

Weinstein, James. 1975. *Ambiguous Legacy.* New York: New Viewpoints/Franklin Watts.

Weinstein, James. 1969. *The Decline of Socialism in America. 1912–1925.* New York: Vintage.

Wellman, David and David Matza. 1980. The ordeal of consciousness. *Theory and Society* 9:1–27.

Whalen, Jack and R. Flacks. 1980. The Isla Vista 'bank burners' ten years later: Notes on the fate of student activists. *Sociological Focus* 13(3):215–236.

Whalen, John and R. Flacks. 1984. Echoes of rebellion: The liberated generation grows up. *Journal of Military and Political Sociology* 12:61–78.

Whalen, John and R. Flacks. *Echoes of Rebellion: The New Left Grows Up.* Philadelphia: Temple University Press. Forthcoming.

Williams, William A. 1981. Radicals and regionalism. *democracy* 1(4):87–98.

Williamson, John. 1969. *Dangerous Scot.* New York: International Publishers.

Wilson, John. 1973. *Introduction to Social Movements.* New York: Free Press.

Wolfe, Alan. 1984. Toward a new politics on the left. *The Nation* 239(8):225–32.

Wolin, Sheldon S. 1982. What revolutionary action means today. *democracy* 2(4):17–28.

Wolin, Sheldon S. 1981. The new public philosophy. *democracy* 1(4):23–26.

Wright, Richard. 1977. *American Hunger.* New York: Harper & Row.

Yankelovich, Daniel. 1974. *The New Morality.* New York: McGraw-Hill.

Yorburg, Betty. 1969. *Utopia and Reality: A Collective Portrait of American Socialists.* New York: Columbia University Press.

Zalburg, Sanford. 1979. *A Spark Is Struck! Jack Hall and the ILWU in Hawaii,* Honolulu: University Press of Hawaii.

Zald, Meyer and John McCarthy, eds. 1979. *The Dynamics of Social Movements.* Cambridge, Mass.: Winthrop Publishers.

Zeitlin, Maurice. 1970. *Revolutionary Politics and the Cuban Working Class.* New York: Harper & Row.

Zinn, Howard. 1964. *SNCC: The New Abolitionists,* Boston: Beacon Press.

Zimmerman, D. H. and C. West. 1975. Sex roles, interruptions and silences in conversation. in B. Thorne and N. Henley, eds. *Language and Sex Difference and Dominance.* Rowley, Mass: Newbury House.

Index